Haile Selassie I, Emperor of Ethiopia

Haile Selassie I, Emperor of Ethiopia

Nigusie Kassaye W. Michael

LEXINGTON BOOKS
Lanham • Boulder • New York • London

Published by Lexington Books
An imprint of The Rowman & Littlefield Publishing Group, Inc.
4501 Forbes Boulevard, Suite 200, Lanham, Maryland 20706
www.rowman.com

86-90 Paul Street, London EC2A 4NE

This book is a translation of Хайле Селассие I, император Эфиопии (transliterated: Khayle Selassiye I, imperator Efiopii) published by the Peoples' Friendship University of Russia in 2019.

British Library Cataloguing in Publication Information Available

Library of Congress Cataloging-in-Publication Data

Names: Michael, Nigusie Kassaye W., author.
Title: Haile Selassie I, Emperor of Ethiopia / Nigusie Kassaye W. Michael.
Description: Lanham ; Boulder ; New York ; London : Lexington Books, [2023] |
    Includes bibliographical references and index.
Identifiers: LCCN 2023004725 (print) | LCCN 2023004726 (ebook) |
    ISBN 9781666908237 (cloth) | ISBN 9781666908244 (ebook)
Subjects: LCSH: Haile Selassie I, Emperor of Ethiopia, 1892-1975. | Ethiopia—
    History—1889-1974. | Ethiopia—Foreign relations—1889-1974. | Ethiopia—
    Politics and government—1889-1974. | Ethiopia—Kings and rulers—Biography.
Classification: LCC DT387.7 .K368 2023 (print) | LCC DT387.7 (ebook) |
    DDC 963/.054092 [B]—dc23/eng/20230210
LC record available at https://lccn.loc.gov/2023004725
LC ebook record available at https://lccn.loc.gov/2023004726

In Memory of My Mother Woizero Aregash Dera Warite

Contents

Acknowledgments

This book project has been a personal discovery, and, in the process, I have accumulated a debt of gratitude to a variety of people and institutions. I would like to thank for the help provided to me, first of all, the staff of the Peoples' Friendship University, in particular, the RUDN university scientific library staff. I would like to separately thank my scientific adviser, Professor L. V. Ponomarenko. I am eternally grateful to her for her support and inspiration. Special thanks to Professor V. A. Tsvyk, Dean of the Faculty of Humanities and Social Sciences of PFUR, Professor and Head of the Department of Ethics. He has always supported all my endeavors. With great pleasure, I would like to express my boundless gratitude to everyone who, with their advice and friendly support, played a key role in the birth of this monograph. This is, first of all, great connoisseur of African history, Professor A. M. Khazanov, who supported me with wise advice, Dr. G. V. Tsypkin, a great connoisseur of the history of Ethiopia, thanks to his advice, I began to study the history of modern Ethiopia. I remember always a great scientist and just a kind person, Professor N. N. Kosukhin, for his practical assistance at all stages of my research. I would like to express my sincere gratitude to a wonderful person and professional in her field, S. N. Evseeva, who sparing neither effort nor personal time has been helping me in my scientific works for many years. Special thanks to my friend, Professor V. N. Davydov. Thanks to him my Russian manuscript became available to readers. I would also like to thank sincerely the head of the Department of Theory and History of International Relations of Peoples' Friendship University of Russia, Professor D. A. Degterev, for his valuable advice to translate the monograph into English. Also warm thanks to Dr. Claire Amuhaya for her valued assistance. I would like to thank the State Public Historical Library of Russia, the Library of Foreign Literature, the Institute for Scientific Information on Social Sciences of the

Russian Academy of Sciences (INION), the Russian State Library (Lenin Library), the Archive of the Foreign Policy of the Russian Empire, the Archive of Foreign Policy of the Russian Federation, the Ethiopian State Archive, and the Central Library in Addis Ababa. Without their assistance, the monograph would not have seen the light of day. Dear Dr. Abdisalam Hashi Mohamed, thank you not only as an older brother but also as a mentor. Once again, I would like to say "thank you" to all those who made it possible to publish the monograph.

Introduction

"Men make their own history, but they do not make it as they please; they do not make it under self-selected circumstances, but under circumstances existing already, given and transmitted from the past," Karl Marx famously remarked.[1] In the context of this statement, Haile Selassie I comes across as an exceptionally gifted personality, in political terms.

Ethiopia, a country with a history that spans over multiple centuries, went through hard times that determined its evolution. Among those periods was the reign of Emperor Haile Selassie I (1916–1974), when the country saw the beginning of crucial transformations in domestic and foreign policy. It became clear that Ethiopia was abandoning the ideology of self-isolation and provincialism to embrace establishment and expansion of international contacts. The Ethiopian government led by Emperor Haile Selassie I was facing the challenge of overcoming the diplomatic blockade organized by Great Britain, France and Italy, whose colonial possessions in Africa bordered on the Ethiopian Empire. This is what was driving efforts of then-regent Tafari Makonnen, who advocated Ethiopia's membership in the League of Nations, as the covenant of that organization guaranteed security to its members and strove to establish diplomatic ties with the United States, in order to neutralize the pressure on the part of Great Britain and Italy, the two countries that threatened Ethiopia's sovereignty.

Chronologically, the reign of Emperor Haile Selassie I coincided with dramatic events of the world's history. First, two World Wars changed the planet's political map in a fundamental way, with the U.S. and the USSR clashing in a confrontation. Small nations often had to navigate between Washington and Moscow. Second, decolonization of Asian and African countries resulted in new states emerging on the international stage. The severity of the challenges they were facing is hard to overestimate.

1

After Eritrea, a former Italian colony, was annexed to the Ethiopian Empire, the intensity of political strife in northeastern Africa began to increase. It was a region where interests of several countries clashed. Ethiopia was embroiled into hostilities with the Republic of Somalia, with the latter's leaders proclaiming, among other goals, a Pan-Somali Greater Somalia, which they sought to create by annexing the southeastern part of the Ethiopian Empire, and then with Eritrean separatists who were backed by Arab nations.

Haile Selassie I tried to resolve some of the issues faced by his country by establishing friendly personal relations with leaders of a number of states: Ethiopia joined the Non-Alignment Movement and initiated the Organization of African Unity. The Ethiopian emperor managed, to a certain extent, to build a positive image of his country abroad. His multiple official visits to various countries in Asia, Africa, America, Europe, Australia, and Oceania clearly bear witness to that.

Beginning from the 1960s, Ethiopia emerged as an important party in inter-African relations. Addis Ababa is home to many regional organizations, including the headquarters of the United Nations Economic Commission for Africa and of the Organization of African Unity. Haile Selassie elevated his country to the rank of the political and economic center of all independent Africa.

Being aware of Ethiopia's special role on the African continent, Haile Selassie began to prepare himself for that mission back in the 1930s. "The Abyssinian emperor is fully aware that he is currently the only Negro ruler in the world and sees himself as the leader of all Negro peoples," the British Magazine *National Review* wrote in August 1935. "He eagerly repeats the phrase: 'Abyssinia is responsible for the future of all Negro peoples.'"[2]

When he became regent in 1916, Haile Selassie identified key vectors of Ethiopia's domestic and foreign policy. He was afraid that revolutionary action might lead to a dramatic social upheaval and destroy the country.

"I believe that certain western institutions, provided they are assimilated by my people, can make us stronger, strong enough to follow unaided the path of progress. But these new ideas cannot be assimilated at once. You must remember that Ethiopia is like Sleeping beauty, that time has stood still here for 2,000 years. We must take great care, therefore, not to overwhelm her [Ethiopia] with changes now that she is beginning to wake. . . . We must strive to steer a middle course between the impatience of Western reformers and the inertia of the Ethiopians who would close their eyes if the light were too strong."[3] This statement defines the style of the monarch's work—caution and slow progress.

In order to modernize the country, Haile Selassie invited overseas specialists. While they were formally styled as advisers, they de facto shaped the government's policies and played a significant role in strengthening the central authority and in building the country's positive image abroad.

When he was still regent, Haile Selassie I managed to convince his people that the country's best option to develop on the basis of knowledge and expertise residing in a well-educated elite. By the way, the first modern schools in the country were built with the regent's own funds. He dispatched young Ethiopians overseas so that they would be able to receive secular education. Those youngsters were not only from offspring of the aristocracy but also originated from the middle-class and lower orders. Afterward, Haile Selassie I used those graduates in the administration.

Emergence of an educated elite revitalized Ethiopia's social life. The government was actively involved in setting up the Ethiopian Women Welfare Association (1935), the National Patriotic Association (1935), the Ethiopia Scout Organization (1934), and the Red Cross Society (1931). They played a great role in consolidating Ethiopian society shortly before the Italian aggression.

As he was conscious that the emperor's authority based on his popularity and his subjects' ideas of the divine origin of the imperial power, of the monarch's personality as a symbol of statehood and unity of Ethiopian ethnicities, had its boundaries, Haile Selassie proclaimed a "democratic society" doctrine, with the main goal of achieving a painless transformation of traditional Ethiopian society into a modern democratic version. Paradoxically, the doctrine was largely abandoned, because by the 1970s the monarch had no more followers. Why?

Some were unhappy with an overly slow pace of transformations, especially land reform; others were dissatisfied with a government that killed socio-political initiatives.

Nevertheless, neither the conservatives nor the "progressive" elite of the 1970s had any clear idea where the country should be taken. Nobody envisioned society's political life without the emperor, and nobody admitted so much as a thought that Haile Selassie I and the Solomonic dynasty could exit the Ethiopian political stage. Therefore, the opposition elite met the 1974 February "revolution" without not only any political organization but even an idea how the country would be steered out of the crisis.

There were no political parties in Ethiopia at the time. There were, indeed, some politically minded organizations: the Ethiopian Teachers' Association, the National Literacy Society, the Ethiopian Writers' Association, the Association for the Love of the Country, and the Ethiopian Patriots Association.

When the empire's economic situation deteriorated dramatically, driven down by a global currency and energy crisis, the 1972–1973 drought that affected 9 out of 14 provinces, widespread famine that claimed the lives of hundreds of thousands of the Ethiopians, it catalyzed a broad antimonarchic movement.

In September 1974, Emperor Haile Selassie I, the founder of modern Ethiopia, fell victim to a military mutiny and a coup d'état. All vital changes in the country's domestic and foreign policy that had occurred between 1916 and 1974 are associated with his name. During his rule, the country made first steps toward modernization and democratization. He did his best to keep the monarch's power soaring above society, to see it stand above classes, religious or ethnic affiliations.

However, his attempts to turn Ethiopia into a constitutional monarchy had failed. The military regime that came to power in 1974 opted for a "Socialist" route for the country.

NOTES

1. Marx K. *The Eighteenth Brumaire of Louis Bonaparte*. Chapter 1. Translated by Saul K. Padover from the German edition of 1869.

2. Cited by Yagiya V.S. *Ethiopia in the Modern Period*. M. 1978. P.95 (hereinafter – Yagiya V.S. 1978) (in Russian).

3. Del Boca A. *The Ethiopian War 1935–1941*. Translated from Italian by P.D. Cummins. Chicago; L. 1969. P. 34 (hereinafter – Del Boca A. 1969).

Chapter 1

The Struggle for the Throne

THE BEGINNINGS: IN A WHIRLWIND
OF POLITICAL BATTLES

It is generally believed that history is made by the people and that the people are the main in driving force of history. Nevertheless, individuals always remain in the focus. In Ethiopian history, Emperor Haile Selassie I (1892–1975) was undoubtedly such an individual. He was the creator of Ethiopia's domestic and foreign policy—a policy that was pursued in the colonial period, during the Italian invasion, and the Cold War.

According to Harold Marcus, "[Haile Selassie I] governed, as had his immediate predecessors, by acting as the country's balancer of power, a method that worked well in a customary government that mediated between the ruling classes and the masses. His limited Western education directed him toward change, however, and he introduced modern institutions whose functions he never clearly understood. He found them useful, however, because they added to the imperial power and to the authority of the central government that acted in the emperor's name."[1]

Haile Selassie[2] (Tafari Makonnen from 1892 to 1931) was born on July 23, 1892, in the province of Hararghe, in the Ejersa Goro District. He received the name Haile Selassie after his coronation, but it had been given to him when he was baptized. According to Ethiopian tradition, a baptized baby is given a name used during church ceremonies—in particular, in confessions. His father, *Ras* Makonnen Wolde Michael, was an outstanding Ethiopian general and skillful politician. He was related to Emperor Menelik II, whose rule (1889–1913) was a period when Ethiopian lands were unified, and the country saw the beginnings of modernization.

In the 1890s, *Ras* Makonnen did a lot to reinforce the influence of the empire of Menelik II and to bring eastern lands under its control, as they had a strategic significance both for Ethiopia's politics and economy. Afterward, he was appointed governor of Hararghe, a province through which the nation handled trade relations with foreign powers. The province of Hararghe linked Ethiopian hinterland to the sea.[3] Furthermore, it was the seat of consulates of foreign nations: Great Britain, France, Italy, United States, Germany, and other partners.

By nature, *Ras* Makonnen was an innovator, a proponent of close ties with foreigners who were coming to Ethiopia in droves, and their flow was growing every year. Truth be told, most of them were interested only in making profit in the just unified empire of Menelik II. *Ras* Makonnen collaborated with them actively, as he seemed to regard foreigners as mediators who were able to contribute to the country's modernization and to the expansion of its influence worldwide. H. Marcus writes that Makonnen impressed the Europeans and other foreigners "with his desire to learn about the outside world."[4] Whenever possible, he tried to receive exhaustive information about events going on in Europe and in the Middle East, and to figure out its authenticity.

It was probably through communications with foreigners, especially with *Abba* Andreas Jarosseau (a trusted confidant and adviser of the *ras*), that Makonnen had deep and comprehensive knowledge of history and contemporary issues of Europe and was an expert in the mechanics of international relations. The instructions of Menelik II attest to that. For instance, in 1890, he dispatched *Ras* Makonnen[5] to Rome, to hold talks with the Italian government. After a visit to Europe, the *ras* came to the conclusion that the government's administration called for urgent modernization and that Ethiopia was in a dire need of well-developed education. In a word, Tafari Makonnen's father was a progressive political figure of his time and a general who possessed qualities of a remarkable reformer.

Tafari's mother, *Woizero* Yeshimebet,[6] came from a noble family that originated from the province of Wollo.[7] Her maternity was full of drama: Only Tafari, the last child out of her offspring, survived to adulthood. Yeshimebet died soon after Tafari's birth.[8] It was *Ras* Makonnen himself who took care of the son's upbringing, as he wanted to see Tafari grow into a well-educated man and become his heir.

Among his childhood friends, the future emperor had his cousin Imiru (1892–1981), a future *ras*, who was the closest to him. The young people's friendship was a lifelong feeling.[9] By the way, Imiru's father, *Fitawrari* Haile Selassie Abayneh, played an important role in the upbringing of the future leader. *Ras* Makonnen produced a significant impact on the formation of Tafari's personality. "Yet the rase's personality—a good mix of shrewdness, gentility, sophistication, and political acumen—provided the boy with an apt role model. From his father, the son also learned to hide his tenacity of spirit and ambition behind diffidence, and gentle grace. Makonnen taught his scion to respect learning, especially the modern education then seeping into Ethiopia. The *ras* recognized that the country had to change with the times or fall prey to imperialism. He was determined that his son would learn the new lore and become one of Ethiopia`s agents of modernization."[10]

According to Ethiopian tradition, young Tafari was homeschooled by *Aba* Samuel Wolde Kahin.[11] His education consisted in learning how to write, read, and use Ge‘ez, a liturgical language that was used in religious literature, the Amharic language and religious knowledge based mostly on the Psalms of David. This education helped Tafari develop a sagacious intellect and train his memory well.

From time to time, Menelik II dispatched the *ras* overseas, and he visited, in particular, Great Britain, where he represented the emperor at the coronation of Edward VII.[12] The *ras*'s European "mentality" revealed itself once again when he hired Dr. Joseph Vitalien, a teacher of the French language, for his son. *Abba* Samuel, who was very proficient in the language of Balzac, became one of the closest friends of young Tafari. As Haile Selassie I says in his autobiography *My Life and Ethiopia's Progress*, *Abba* Samuel "was a good man who possessed great knowledge, who applied himself to learning and to teaching, who in goodness and humility gathered knowledge like a bee from anyone, who was devoted to the love of God and of his neighbor."[13]

Abba Samuel remained Tafari's teacher and friend until his death in 1915. Communicating with the French, Tafari managed not only to learn the language but also to get acquainted with classic French literature, that is, to acquire knowledge that was considered by the Ethiopian and the world's aristocracy to be a sign of nobility and elegance.

After he had completed a three-year home education, Tafari enrolled into a missionary Capuchin school run by *Abba* Jarosseau, the same Frenchman who was also *Ras* Makonnen's adviser. When he brought his son to school, Makonnen charged the priest: "If I die, be his father. I give him to you, and God will do the rest." The *Abba* later remembered his ward "as an intelligent child, quick to learn. . . .. With his cotton clothing and unshod feet, however, he differed little from the other lads who daily struggled with Western education."[14]

Tafari Makonnen carried warmth and affection for his teachers and classmates all his life. "Our upbringing was like that of the sons of ordinary people and there was no undue softness about it as was the case with princes of that period,"[15] wrote Haile Selassie I. It is obviously an exaggeration. The Ethiopian people lived in utter poverty at the time. A peasant could hardly provide for himself and his family. A child born to a commoner did not go to school; instead, from his childhood, he learned to use his parents' simple craft in order to be able to live a longer life, which was often a heavy burden for his family. By his very origin, Tafari would not have been allowed to live, speaking today's language, according to standards of common people. From their early days, children of the upper crust were aware of their place in society. Alongside academic education, they learned to ride, shoot and hunt, which were thought to be mandatory skills for descendants of noble families at the time.[16]

The personality of the future emperor was influenced by traditional Ethiopian and Western education. The young man was brought up in two cultures that coexisted in him quite harmoniously: Ethiopian (conservative) and European (liberal and democratic). As years went by, that dualism and inconsistency would come back to haunt him. On the one hand, like most members of the Ethiopian ruling elite, he was a conservator who was unwilling to change the customary order of things. On the other, Tafari has an image of a reformer, an enlightened monarch who aspired to spread European civilization on Ethiopian soil. It is not by chance that some historians compare *Ras* Tafari's rule with the reign of Peter the Great in Russia, the Meiji era in Japan, and the Young Turks' movement in Turkey.

Tafari was an assiduous, well-disciplined, and unfailing Christian. However, not infrequently, his views and actions were far from canons of the Ethiopian church, and they may be called unorthodox.[17] The fact that all three of his early mentors were Roman Catholics was probably another factor that informed his mindset. The environment in which Tafari had grown and developed also left an imprint on the youngster's political culture. It played an important role in shaping his philosophy of international relations.

Harar, the capital of the province of Hararghe, is a small town. People of various ethnicities lived there; they spoke different languages, belonged to a wide range of religious denominations (Christianity, Islam, and others). The bulk of the population was comprised of the Oromo, Somalians, Afars, Issas, and Hararis natives of Central and Northern provinces of the empire. There were a few thousand people hailing from Asian countries (first of all, the Middle East) and from Europe. *Ras* Makonnen introduced his son to the traditions and lifestyles of all peoples of the Hararghe multiethnic society and encouraged his contacts with them.

The *ras*'s palace was simultaneously the "interior ministry," the "foreign ministry," and the "justice ministry." Young Tafari watched his father and other officials handle affairs, hold negotiations or pass sentences, collect tribute in remote corners of the province to be able to maintain the army and administrative staff. In 1903, Tafari, then 11, saw Addis Ababa, the capital city of the empire, for the first time. His father took him on to introduce the boy to the court and the emperor. Haile Selassie did not share his impressions. However, one can imagine that life in the capital city and the court atmosphere could only leave him, a provincial resident, overwhelmed and somewhat confused.

In 1905, Tafari became a full-fledged member of the ruling elite: He received the title of *dejazmach* and was appointed governor of Gara Muleta, a small district to the southwest of the capital city of Hararghe. His title and appointment were his father's initiative.[18] On that occasion, *Ras* Makonnen arranged a festivity, marking the son's formal admission to the political elite of the Ethiopian Empire. The ruler announced publicly that, as of that moment, Tafari was his heir, and he asked his officers and officials to love and respect the young protégé. The move stirred some confusion among the staff of Makonnen the Elder and caused rumors of his imminent death.

The *ras* began to initiate his son to the intricacies of the activities of a provincial administration. The young *dejazmach* had the privilege of being admitted to his father's audience at any time, which did not diminish his own responsibility for the situation in the district he was in charge of. There was not a single occasion where *Ras* Makonnen did not help his son in address-ing administrative issues. Haile Selassie I wrote: "As the love that existed between my father and myself was altogether special, I can feel it up to the present (1937.—*Author's note*). He always used to praise me for the work which I was doing and for my being obedient." Haile Selassie continues, saying: "His officers and his men used to love me respectfully because they observed with admiration the affection which my father had for me."[19] These emotional statements express well the essence of the relationship in a purely male team.

In January 1906, during a trip to Addis Ababa, *Ras* Makonnen suddenly fell sick, and, gravely ill, he was taken by his officers to Kulubi, a town not far from Harar, known for its large church dedicated to St. Gabriel. On March 20, the dying *ras* left financial papers to the British consul with a request to pass them to young heir Tafari Makonnen when the situation in the country went back to normal. Before he passed away, the dying man worried: "Oh, if only I could have lived for a few years more, until the time when he (Tafari.—*Author's note*) would be able to stand up for his own rights."[20] In order to ensure his son's safety somehow, *Ras* Makonnen wrote a letter to Emperor Menelik II, consigning Tafari to his care, and mentioning that in the next life he would ask the monarch how he had acquitted the charge.

On March 21, 1906, *Ras* Makonnen passed away. It was a hard blow to Tafari who had lost his closest relative and protector. The 13-year-old youngster had the right to inherit his father's fortune, but not the office of the governor. Nevertheless, young Tafari was hopeful that there could be exceptions to rules and that the emperor would allow him to keep the posi-tion of the governor of the province of Hararghe. A few days after his father's funeral, Tafari sent *Abba* Andreas the model of his first seal as governor, with the request that it be sent to France for engraving.[21] This is evidence that the young man was sure of his own future.

However, that move turned out to be premature, as Menelik II did not let young Tafari run the empire's most important province. Generally, governorships were bestowed on experienced diplomats who were knowledgeable in the area of relations with the three European powers that had possessions adjoining Ethiopian borders (Great Britain, France, Italy), or on seasoned administrators able to run a multiethnic province, or on a military man able to pacify some belligerent tribes, or on a savvy man of business and tax collector. Young Tafari was not ready for that mission yet. The changes in Tafari's family coincided with the conclusion of a tripartite treaty[22] entered into by Great Britain, France, and Italy in London and purported to divide Ethiopia into spheres of influence.

This far-reaching act of the members of the tripartite union caused changes in international relations and a debate among scholars. Some historians specializing in Ethiopian studies, D. R. Voblikov, wrote, for instance, "The agreement of 1906 summed up the whole period of the struggle of the colonial powers for Ethiopia. Contrary to the efforts of the imperialist powers, they failed to turn Ethiopia into their colony."[23] Yu. M. Kuzmin, notes "however, the agreement of the three powers did not turn Ethiopia into their colony. The sharp struggle of the developed states of western Europe for the predominance in northeast Africa turned out to be to some extent the anchor of salvation of this country. The 1906 treaty tied their hands to some extent and thereby reduced the threat of foreign enslavement of Ethiopia, providing it with certain foreign policy stability."[24] A. Bartnicki and J. Mantel-Niecko, wrote, for instance, that the treaty was an attempt of the three countries to settle their differences at Ethiopia's expense.[25] Harold Marcus, on the contrary, believes the treaty created favorable conditions for Ethiopia, as the country "gained considerable stability which marked the end of active British and French imperialists in the region, and eliminated, for a time, the likelihood of Italian expansion."[26]

The emperor who was concerned with the conclusion of the treaty needed a neutral ally. He sought a balance of power, as he feared the tripartite union might divide the empire. However, it is Harold Marcus who is right: The treaty, by tying the hands of the three powers, created a situation where none of them was able to act without the consent of the other two. The London treaty was concluded without consulting Menelik II. The emperor was notified of the agreement after the fact, when the treaty was finalized. The signatories assumed the Ethiopian government would automatically subscribe to their collective decision. However, on May 18, 1907, the emperor dismissed the treaty—politely but with dignity, saying: "We have received the arrangement made by the Three Powers. We thank them for their communication, and their desire to keep and maintain the independence of our Government. But let it be understood that this arrangement in no way limits what we consider our sovereign rights."[27]

The emperor decided that the unceremonious interference in the empire's internal affairs could be neutralized by resorting to assistance of a serious European partner—Germany. In 1907, at the request of Menelik II, a German delegation visited Ethiopia. A few months later, a return visit to Berlin took place.[28] The subject-matter and outcomes of the talks remained a mystery. But Menelik II began to rely on German help in addressing economic and military issues.

An external threat from the tripartite union and the emperor's deteriorating health affected the situation in the country. Centripetal forces were also strong. The latter circumstance made the monarch grieve over the untimely death of Tafari's father, who was a wise and courageous administrator. To keep the influence of the province of Hararghe as strong as ever, Menelik appointed *Dejazmach* Yilma, Makonnen's elder son, as governor. Empress Taitu, who was the aunt to Yilma's wife, had a hand in that appointment. It is precisely what Harold Marcus says: "For Menelik, Yilma was the ideal choice: his appointment would quiet his nagging wife, keep Hararge in Makonen`s family."[29]

Tafari was not aware of the emperor's decisions right until the memorial ceremony on the occasion of 40 days since Makonnen's death; the ceremony took place in Addis Ababa, at the palace of Menelik II. The emperor displayed genuine fatherly care when he offered to Tafari to stay in the capital city as a young dignitary; he also upheld his title of *dejazmach*, and appointed him governor of the district of Selale, 120 kilometers to the west of the capital city. Moreover, Tafari was invited to study at a school that had just been opened at the imperial court.

Young Tafari, who was quite satisfied with the emperor's benevolence, gave an order to his entourage to go back to Harar. During that short stay in the capital city, Tafari managed not only to establish but also to reinforce ties with remarkable personalities, outstanding political figures from whom he could borrow experience and learn the art of government.[30] Moreover, as Harold Marcus writes, "Tafari . . .wisely permitted the palace priests to rebaptize him, according to Orthodox rite, to allay suspicion that his relations with Catholics, especially with Abba Samuel, had brought him to apostasy."[31]

Tafari was a newcomer not only at the emperor's court but in the capital city. From the Ethiopian standpoint, Addis Ababa was a special city. In 1906, Ethiopia's capital, the way it does today, looked like a modern center that illustrated the country's transformation. During the reign of Menelik II, the capital city's population was about 50,000 people. There were telephone and telegraph lines in Addis Ababa, a few brick and stone buildings, a bridge, hotels, cafés, electricity, and so forth.[32]

A lot of foreigners lived in Addis Ababa, including the emperor's advisers and doctors, members of the diplomatic corps, wealthy merchants (principally from Armenia, Greece, Middle East, South-East Asia) who were in control of the country's import and export. Their agents traveled to southern and western areas of Ethiopia to make all sorts of bargains. They purchased furs and leather, grain, vegetable oils, coffee, and other commodities that were in demand worldwide. Some products were brought from towns to villages, including salt, sugar, kerosene, textiles, and so forth. It should be noted that merchants were the driving force that pushed Ethiopian society to a certain degree of modernization. Following their footsteps, the government appealed to the local population, asking them to produce goods for the external market. It was a time-tested way of reinforcing the economic pattern. Even provincial officials began to actively join trade operations.

Tafari watched the course of events at the court and in the capital city with a hawk's eye. In Addis Ababa, he mastered the rules of the big political game. Having absorbed the governing experience during the rule of Menelik II, Tafari would later transform the empirical constructs of government into a real art of statecraft.

Menelik II was skillful in upholding his authority among the Ethiopian nobility, steering his way between opposing forces. He was actively involved in activities of legislative and executive bodies, annexed new lands to the Ethiopian Empire, and was moving toward an absolute monarchy. However, absolutism in Ethiopia would gain a firm foothold only after Haile Selassie I came to power. In January 1907, an announcement was made that the emperor was gravely ill. There was a real risk of a dynastic crisis. The allies had no right to interfere in Ethiopia's internal affairs (the 1906 treaty ruled that out), but each member of the European tripartite union was concerned with the well-being of their compatriots and employees of the consulates who lived in Ethiopia and could suffer in the event of civil strife.

To protect the country from disintegration, Menelik II informed foreign powers on October 25, 1907 that he had set up a government cabinet. The emperor appointed nine ministers: of the interior, of finance, of agriculture, of the pen (the emperor's private secretary, registrar, chronicler), of public works, and a High Court justice.[33] That way, Menelik II opposed a possible interference from the outside.

In 1907, *Dejazmach* Yilma, the governor province of Hararghe, died. Tafari hoped to get that position in his native province. The young man's loyalty was beyond doubt. However, in April 1908, an experienced politician and military man, *Dejazmach* Balcha,[34] who enjoyed the emperor's trust, was appointed to that post. Once again was youth an impediment to Tafari's career growth. That said, Tafari Makonnen was destined for an equivalent position in Derassa (a district in the southern province of Sidamo). "Therefore, I had to abandon my studies and was ordered to proceed, together with the army, to my governorate of Sidamo and to take care of the business of government,"[35] he writes in his autobiography. Tafari went there with a 3,000-strong army that was largely comprised of his father's soldiers and trusted officers, including *Fitawrari* Haile Selassie Abayneh and his son Imiru.[36]

Haile Selassie, I recalled his governorship as "a time of perfect joy," as he "encountered no trouble whatever"[37] from either officials or subjects. Possibly, the matter was that Tafari did not stay long in that position. When the emperor's health deteriorated in April 1909, he had to return to the capital city, the epicenter of the struggle for the throne of Menelik II. Tafari Makonnen did not stay away from the clashes either.

TAFARI MAKONNEN AS A
CLAIMANT TO THE THRONE

During the rule of Emperor Menelik II, the Shewan nobility reinforced its power and played a significant role in the establishment of the Ethiopian Empire. However, lack of modern public institutions and a regular army subordinate to the imperial center (every general had its own armed group, and even the province of Shewa, the leading province, did not have one army), played into the hands of the nobility of northern (for instance, Tigray) and eastern provinces of the empire.

Polish historians A. Bartnicki and J. Mantel-Niecko note that, before the emperor got sick, "there were three major political factions in the country, and every one of them had its own influential representatives at court."[38] Those factions formed according to regional affiliation. Ethiopian society, which was underdeveloped economically and politically, could not influence the course of events or consolidate around progressive forces. The people supported one feudal lord or another not for their political or economic programs but based on their regional or religious affiliations (by the way, this is also a distinguishing feature of today's Ethiopian society). Moreover, alongside feudal covenants, vestiges of pre-feudal relations were also present in Ethiopia at the time. In some districts across the country, people still live amid primitive subsistence farming to date. For nomads, political strife or politics in general were of no meaning or interest.

Northern (Gonder) nobility factions led by Empress Taitu pushed claims to the throne; so did the Shewan nobility led by War Minister *Fitawrari* Habte Giyorgis and a group of the northern (Tigre, Wello) nobility led by *Ras* Mikael from the province of Wollo.

Empress Taitu, an ambitious woman who interfered in state affairs even when her husband was in good health, had gained strong positions by 1909. By that time, Menelik had had another stroke, and it became clear that he was unable to govern the country. The empress ruled in his name,[39] appointing her loyal associates to key government positions and discharging undesirable high-ranking officials. Taitu strengthened her stance significantly in the emerging conflict of interests.

All that caused resistance of the Shewan nobility who was afraid that after seizing power the empress would not only remove them from public administration but would also transfer the capital to the city of Gonder, her native town. The Shewan nobility, supported by high-ranking dignitaries of the Ethiopian church, made a stand against Taitu who had usurped power; it was their understanding that only the emperor, and not members of his family, was able to discharge or appoint state officials.

Ras Mikael of Wollo, who was married to a daughter of Menelik II, said that his own son and the emperor's grandson, *Lij* Iyasu, was the only legitimate heir to the throne. This circumstance aroused well-founded concern of the empress and of the Shewan nobility.

It is still unknown which faction of claimants to the throne Tafari had belonged to. The Polish historians said he had had close ties to the Shewan faction.[40] However, Haile Selassie I refutes that statement in his autobiography.

In 1909, the Shewan elite staged a conspiracy against the empress. Tafari refused to join coup plotters. " . . . while Empress Taitu [*sic*!], acting as plenipotentiary, was carrying out all the work of government, envious men began a conspiracy against her to deprive her of her powers and to evict her from the Palace," wrote Haile Selassie I. "When they asked me to join them in the conspiracy, I told them that I did not wish to enter into their plot; and consequently, all the conspirators began to look upon me with enmity. When Empress Taitu [*sic*!] heard about my refusal to enter into the conspiracy, she told the Emperor, and both were very pleased."[41]

Thanks to his prudent behavior, Tafari managed to win the empress's favor. Since then, she believed she had a sincere and, what is no less important, not a very strong supporter in Tafari. The young *dejazmach* did not disclose the names of the conspirators (the emperor would do away with them had he known their names). That way, Tafari earned confidence of the Shewan nobility that took the helm of state afterward.

The written proclamation prepared by Menelik II in late 1908, which was to be brought to general notice and which named *Lij* Iyasu as the emperor's heir, was never published because the empress kept it under the wraps.[42] She continued the practice of political reshuffling called "*shum-shir*" (appointments and dismissals). Tafari Makonnen, who became governor of his native province, Hararghe, was among the empress's appointees. Haile Selassie wrote: "I was biding my time . . .and thinking that I could not fail to obtain the governorship whenever it might be God's will to show me favor."[43] The Lord Almighty seemed to have heard him. It should be noted that pious Haile Selassie I always attributed his success to the Providence, to the will of God. He was perfectly aware that the Lord helps those who are able to help themselves. He painstakingly pondered over his every step, every managerial decision. Furthermore, Tafari did his best to avoid conflicts and found overt struggle burdensome. L. Mosley notes: "He knew how to wait—and he showed no sign of anger when he was thwarted. Towards pain, as towards disappointment, he had a stoic implacability."[44] A hunter's stamina indeed.

On 27 October, 1909, it suddenly became impossible for Menelik II either to move or to speak.[45] An oppressive anticipation reigned at court, among generals and nobles. Since the emperor had not proclaimed his heir, the long political strife seemed to be crowned by the empress's victory. However, a few days later, the emperor's health saw some improvement.

As he was afraid of a new attack of his ill health, on October 20, 1909, Menelik II convened a meeting of the highest dignitaries, Shewan feudal lords, and church officials to name his heir to the throne. It was *Lij* Iyasu, the son of *Ras* Mikael and the emperor's grandson, with *Ras* Tesemma[46] declared the regent[47] of the empire until the young prince came of age.

Finally, the secret that had occupied not only the minds of entire Ethiopia but those of foreigners was revealed.

On that day, the emperor's decision was announced to the people. Both the empress and the Shewans had to live with it, as insubordination to the monarch's will would mean a rebellion against God's proxy!

In early March 1910, the situation in the capital city aggravated conspicuously. Rumors spread that the empress had sent 2,000 soldiers to the province of Gonder[48] and had allocated a few tens of thousands of *talari* from the imperial treasury to build a large army and to seize power. This fact deserves special investigation, because the period between 1908 and 1911 that foreign observers perceive as the "years of chaos,"[49] was rife with political intrigues and combinations.

In the opinion of Haile Selassie I, it was *Ras* Tesemma who was spreading the rumor in order to remove Taitu from political decision-making.[50] One can agree with the emperor, because the empress kept up the fight even after the name of the heir to the throne had been announced. This time, she tried to elevate Princess Zewditu.[51]

In order to remove Taitu from political life, on March 21, 1910, a large gathering of the Shewan nobility was held in Addis Ababa, at the palace of War Minister *Fitawrari* Habte Giyorgis; they excluded the empress from public affairs. She was only allowed to take care of the sick emperor. On March 22, a declaration was made that all appointments to public offices made by the empress would be annulled. Only the appointment of *Dejazmach* Tafari remained valid.[52]

After the ambitious empress was pushed aside, *Ras* Tesemma who had been appointed regent and guardian of the heir to the throne began to play the key part in the state. As he trained the young prince for his loftiest mission, he attempted to limit the influence of the northern and eastern nobility (followers of *Ras* Mikael). Basically, the regent was holding the full scope of political and military powers in the country. His status was formally confirmed by a seal with the emblem of the Ethiopian Empire and this inscription: "*Ras Bit-woded* Tesemma, the emperor's absolute vice-regent in the Ethiopian state."[53]

The same seal was affixed to the appointment of Tafari Makonnen as governor of Hararghe. In Addis Ababa, nobody obstructed the ambitious young man. But before the young governor set off to his province, the regent introduced him to *Lij* Iyasu—they were to make an agreement in order to avoid possible conflicts between the young men in the future. The matter was that Tafari was a descendant of *Ras* Makonnen, the emperor's relative and an heir presumptive to the throne. Thus, Tafari was also a potential claimant to the throne by blood and against the emperor's will.

In the palace church, in the presence of influential representatives of the secular nobility and the clergy, Tafari made an oath that he would not be trying to ascend to the throne using artifice or warfare. Would Tafari stick to his promise? Before his departure to Harar, Tafari met with the empress. Haile Selassie I writes about the purpose of that meeting in a straightforward manner: "I felt that my conscience would reproach me if I went without saying good-bye."[54] Haile Selassie I does not mention what the conversation was about at that meeting.

The new governor arrived in Harar on May 12, 1910. He was given an enthusiastic welcome by a crowd of local residents and foreigners, Asians and Europeans; "a living mosaic of nationalities, of colors, of different features, all had become one at this moment through the same expression of joy."[55]

After a formal meeting with high-ranking officials, Tafari visited the main cathedral of the town of Harar, in order to make arrangements for a thanksgiving prayer service.

Tafari began his activities by bringing discipline to the administrative staff. His crucial goal was to alleviate brutal exploitation that had existed under previous regimes that were largely authoritarian. To achieve his aim, the young governor, without regard to the capital city, reduced land taxes and abolished forced labor. To make the administration more effective, he divided the province into 12 governorates (Chercher, Kori, Wobera, Meta, Anya, Harer zuriya, Gara Muleta, Afren kello, Jarso, Gigiga, Ogaden, Isana Gurgura).[56] The governors assumed responsibilities related to tax collection and food supplies for the army. After that, he began to study the resources available in the province and to collect data required for a future tax reform. It turned out that only 70,000 subjects[57] were able to pay a regular tax.

Simultaneously, Tafari strengthened the troops he was in charge of, by supplying them with the best weapons available at the time (in an age of change, it was not an idle precaution).

For a semi-feudal Ethiopia, reforms of the young governor could be called progressive. Tafari did not resolve upon a radical transformation of the existing socioeconomic and political pattern. He was aware that only transformation of the traditional production mode could be expected to bring the desired result. As Haile Selassie I writes, peasants were content with his reforms: "As for the peasants, since the yoke of government and taxes was lightened for them, they all set out to do their work with a calm heart."[58]

Meanwhile, *Dejazmach* Tafari did his best not to spark discontent of the regime, as he had vowed not to pose a threat to *Lij* Iyasu's power. This is the reason for Addis Ababa's tolerable attitude to the activities of the governor of Hararghe.

In 1911, *Ras* Tesemma died. The Council of Ministers of the empire announced that Iyasu, who was 16, could rule the country all by himself.

After the regent's death, the country was amid a situation where each faction was seeking to reinforce their positions, using the prince as a puppet—if they had him in their midst, they would be able to control the throne, albeit in an indirect way.

That same year, *Ras* Tafari married *Woizero* Menen Asfaw,[59] a niece of *Lij* Iyasu. This connection by marriage did not bring him close to *Lij* Iyasu, but, still, the *dejazmach* managed to enhance his stature. *Woizero* Menen belonged to one of Ethiopia's most influential and wealthiest families.

Once rid of the regent's tutelage, *Lij* Iyasu came through as a remarkable politician. But "From the beginning of his de facto reign, the prince revealed himself as undoubtedly bright, even visionary, but politically unrealistic. His dream of a ruling elite in which religious and ethnic affiliation did not matter contradicted the social situation in the empire."[60] This desire was quite natural for the father of the nation, but Iyasu himself had neither a social or an economic pillar to carry out his good intentions. Furthermore, the young monarch could not imagine how fragile and vulnerable his state was. Menelik II had managed to annex new lands and create a multiethnic empire. However, in 1909–1911, governors of provinces began to ignore Addis Ababa's authority in an ostentatious manner and to avoid taxes.

Hararghe's governor Tafari Makonnen did not side with the opposition. He paid the assigned tax in time, and he came to the capital city whenever he could in order to demonstrate his loyalty to the regime. At the same time, *Dejazmach* Tafari, a talented disciple of Menelik II, was convinced that the heir to the throne was responsible for the rise of anarchism, corruption, and for the civil unrest that was a consequence of those disorders. Tafari regarded *Lij* Iyasu's peacekeeping mission as a dangerous enterprise. The heir to the throne adamantly refused to acknowledge that his attempt to neutralize the influence of the powerful Christian church had failed.

There is no reliable information when and where Emperor Menelik II died. According to some historians, he died on December 12, 1913.[61]*Lij* Iyasu (1896–1935) became emperor of Ethiopia (he was never crowned) in late 1913, under the name of Iyasu V.

As things go, "Iyasu V" began to govern with appointment of new and dismissal of undesirable officials. Staff practices of the uncrowned monarch could not but arouse discontent of the nobility and of the provincial opposition. Frequent disturbances were put down by troops of *Ras* Mikael, the emperor's father, because Iyasu himself had not a single soldier under arms.

A policy focused on eastern provinces and his connection with Muslim communities did not add to the emperor's popular appeal.[62] England, France, and Italy's colonial administrations of the lands adjoining Ethiopia were also regarding those trends disapprovingly.

Lij Iyasu started to approach Germany and its allies—Turkey and the Austro-Hungarian Empire—which caused a vigorous reaction from London and Paris that were at war with Germany.[63] Moreover, *Lij* Iyasu was trying to act as intermediary between Turkey's agents and some representatives of Somalian clans living in the dominions of Great Britain, France and Italy, which was regarded by the European powers as blatant interference in their internal affairs.

On the eve of World War I, Germany, Austria-Hungary and Turkey reinforced their presence in the Ethiopian Empire. Engineers and advisers were invited from Germany. Austria was where machine-guns and other pieces of artillery were purchased and officers to train Ethiopian soldiers were recruited.

Germany exported to Ethiopia armaments and munitions in large batches; the young emperor needed them to put up defense from without and to suppress rebellion of the malcontent inside the country.

World War I aroused serious concern of Ethiopian authorities. The nation's troops were concentrated near the borders of Italian Eritrea—upon the pretext of bringing things to order in the northern provinces. Those maneuvers concealed yet another purpose. *Lij* Iyasu and War Minister *Fitawrari* Habte Giyorgis hoped that Rome would join the war on Germany's side, and then, having a formal excuse for invading the Italian colony, Ethiopia would liberate it and would get (back) access to the sea. Therefore, Ethiopia's War Minister Habte Giyorgis said: "Italy will go to war and her legs will be broken."[64] Contrary to expectations of strategists in Addis Ababa, Italy remained neutral. And in April 1915, it joined the war on the Entente's side. For Ethiopia, that meant three or four years of peaceful life.

Germany's superiority during the first days of the war persuaded the Ethiopian emperor of the need to strengthen ties with Berlin. However, *Lij* Iyasu's diplomatic aspirations did not strike a chord with many Ethiopian politicians, including the war minister.

Differences emerged, which were caused by attitudes to the belligerents. Lij Iyasu believed that Germany, should it win the war, might occupy Italy's possessions in northeastern Africa. Therefore, a union with Germany looked so desirable to him. The minister, on the contrary, suggested sticking to a policy of non-interference in European affairs. It should be mentioned that envoy and minister plenipotentiary Friedrich Wilhelm von Syburg, who had arrived to Ethiopia from Germany as early as in January 1913, spoke of the Kaiser's wish to guarantee the integrity of Ethiopia.[65] This promise was probably what made Iyasu V set his eyes on Berlin.

The political line of the Ethiopian leader caused manifest displeasure of the three powers, which clearly perceived the threat they would be facing should Germany build a foothold for the entire region in northeastern Africa. Therefore, Great Britain and France (with Italy joining them later) began to prepare *Lij* Iyasu's deposition.

By 1916, forces were found inside Ethiopia that would be willing to collaborate with the emperor's opponents. Those were the Shewan elite and the feudal lords of northern provinces that sided with the former. Some points from a list of their grievances against *Lij* Iyasu looked like this: He married four wives claiming: "Quran permits it to me"; he built a mosque at Jijiga with government funds and gave it the Muslims; he wore Somali Muslim clothes and the Muslim turban, held the Islamic rosary, and was seen to prostrate himself in the mosque; H. H. Ras Makonnen had built a church at Harar and had made the area adjoining the church into a dwelling for the clergy, giving the Muslims a place in exchange; then 32 years later, he (Lij Iyasu) expelled the clergy and restored it to the Muslims; he despised the descent of Menilik II, which comes direct from Menilik I, and claimed to be descended from the prophet Muhammad.[66]

On August 17, 1916, Iyasu took away the governorship of Harar from *Dejazmach* Tafari and placed under him the governorship of Kafa and Maji—The great province in southern Ethiopia, comprising the old Sidama Kingdom. By making his appointments, *Lij* Iyasu deprived Tafari Makonnen of sources of income. Most likely, that way the emperor wanted to demonstrate his power to the Shewan elite and to the Christian church. Talking to a Muslim representative, he stressed that the main objective of his policy was to build a strong state where all subjects would be equal. "though we differ in religion and tribe, I would wish all of us to be united through a nationalist sentiment . . . cooperation with the rest of your Ethiopian brothers will keep your country united and her frontiers secure,"[67] Iyasu said.

Naturally, the emperor's call to brotherhood and equality of Christians and Muslims could not but worry conservative circles of society. In a country where the Christian church and public administration had been inseparable for centuries, statements proclaiming equality of religions were perceived as unheard-of impudence or even sacrilege.

Why was the province of Hararghe chosen to pursue the emperor's policy? "Harar, Iyasu explained to Jarosseau, was the logical place to begin his new deal: he had less to fear here from the clergy or the Shewan aristocracy, and once his program showed the anticipated excellent results, he would then little by little . . . impose the same regime on the entire empire."[68] Moreover, the emperor believed that the Shewans would back him up, since it was national interests that were at stake.

Tafari understood that if that political line should win, he would be its first victim, but he did not offer any resistance, as he was afraid of *Ras* Mikael's reaction.

Only on August 13, 1916, when Tafari was dismissed from the post of governor and appointed governor to the province of Kafa, the *dejazmach* began to approach the opposition or, at times, govern its sentiments. He did his best to disguise his role in the conspiracy against his cousin Iyasu V.

Talking to a British consul, Tafari remarks: "Never have our courts been so busy. Every solder, every chief, every trader is tired of the condition of Abyssinia. Trade has diminished, prices have increased, revenue has decreased and there is no security. I view the situation with the greatest concern."[69]

Instead of leaving for his new post in Kaffa, Tafari stayed in the capital city. The opposition began to circulate rumors that the heir was creating a Muslim front and providing it with arms in order to Islamize the country. London, Paris, and Rome received news that the emperor was allegedly getting ready to invade territories under the control of European powers (England, France and Italy). The neutrality policy declared by Iyasu posed a potential threat to the Entente nations waging a war in the Middle East. The Muslim factor worries them to a certain extent until now.

On September 12, 1916, the allies (England, France and Italy) sent a note to the Foreign Ministry, complaining about Iyasus's belligerency. They demanded an immediate explanation and declared an embargo on arms imports to Ethiopia.[70] Great Britain's Minister in Ethiopia Wilfred Thesiger added four more items to those demands: First, the return to the British authorities in Somaliland of a machine-gun captured from the British by *Mohammed Abdullah Hassan,*[71] which had been sent as a ceremonial present to the Emperor in Addis Ababa; Second, he receive no further delegations from the Somali tribes; Third, that Abdullahi Sadik be removed from his post in Harar as governor of the Ogaden; and fourth, that the municipal offices at Dire Dawa be completely reorganized and, all Turks pro-Turkish Arabs removed.[72] The note of the allies remained unanswered. However, the opposition caught its underlying message.

Before Tafari had left Harar, he met with the British consul.[73] No doubt, the parties exchanged opinions on the purpose of Tafari's visit to Addis Ababa. It should be added that the *dejazmach* asked the consul to take care of his family. *Woizero* Menen, Tafari's wife, stayed in Harar, because she was expecting a child.

On September 26, 1916, when *Lij* Iyasu was in Harar, an assemblage of the Shewan nobility and clergy took place in Addis Ababa. At the meeting, the following indictment was read out: "The Christian faith, which our fathers had hitherto carefully retained by fighting for their faith with the Muslims and by shedding their blood, *Lij* Iyasu exchanged for the Muslim religion and aroused commotion in our midst; in order to exterminate us by mutual fighting he has converted to Islam and, therefore, we shall henceforth not submit to him; we shall not place a Muslim king on the throne of a Christian king; we have ample proof of his conversion to Islam."[74]

No doubt, Tafari Makonnen was the main driving force of the opposition to Iyasu. Evidence is given by the fact that on September 27, 1916 the head of the Ethiopian church read out a solemn address to the entire nation in which he announced deposition of *Lij* Iyasu and proclaimed Zewditu, the daughter of Menelik II, as empress. The same address also said that the son of *Ras* Makonnen, the great-grandson of *Negus* Sahle Selassie, Tafari Makonnen, became the heir to the throne, Zewditu's co-ruler and the country's regent with the title of *ras*.[75] The address called on everyone to be loyal and obedient to the new authorities and ended with a warning that whoever disobeyed would be excommunicated.

When *Negus* Mikael learned that his son had been deposed, he began preparations for a war. That worried greatly the opposition that had taken power in Addis Ababa: Internal strife could degenerate into a serious conflict between Shewa and the predominantly Muslim lands in the country's east and northeast.

Leading a 60,000-strong army,[76]*Negus* Mikael marched on Shewa. Meanwhile, *Lij* Iyasu was trying to find support among the Aussa, a Muslim ethnic group (in the northeast). An attempt of government troops to put up resistance to Mikael ended in complete defeat on October 17, 1916. Even War Minister Habte Giyorgis who had a relatively strong faction behind him did not seem to be able to save the situation—all the less so that the machine-guns ordered in Djibouti had not arrived in Addis Ababa. The Shewans had nothing else to do but to bide time. Therefore, Habte Giyorgis entered into negotiations with Mikael, arguing that a battle between Menelik's two old generals was something that was hard to imagine. *Negus* Mikael, who was hopeful of winning Habte Giyorgis over for *Lij* Iyasu, agreed to the talks without being aware of the war minister's plans.

After the long-awaited machine-guns had arrived, *Negus* Mikael again received a letter from Habte Giyorgis. This time, the minister called for submission to the new government, saying that *Lij* Iyasu had been irreversibly compromised. *Negus* Mikael immediately gave an order to his troops to attack Shewan units. The Battle of Segale that took place on October 27, 1916 ended in a final victory of the Shewan camp. *Negus* Mikael was taken prisoner. *Lij* Iyasu who had marched out to his rescue was too late, and with the remainder of Mikael's defeated army retreated to Wollo, in order to regroup and continue his resistance to the "usurpers."

On October 31, 1916, *Ras* Tafari Makonnen triumphantly marched into Addis Ababa, leading victorious Shewan troops. Even though *Lij* Iyasu had not been captured yet, everyone in Addis Ababa understood that the outcome of the struggle for power was a foregone conclusion. The Battle of Segale endorsed the restitution of Shewa's political hegemony.

Some historians call the deposition of Iyasu V a coup d'état. But we believe it to be a predictable, natural, and necessary outcome: The uncrowned emperor deposition saved the Ethiopian Empire from disintegration.

HIS MAJESTY THE REGENT (1916–1930)

In 1916, the victory of the Shewan nobility crowned a long struggle for the throne and began a new era of great transformation and substantial achievements. On February 11, 1917, Zewditu's coronation took place at St. George's Cathedral in Addis Ababa. On the same day, *Ras* Tafari Makonnen was crowned as heir to the imperial throne.

However, even after the province of Shewa had regained hegemony, the turf war in the Ethiopian Empire did not die down but changed over to an open phase. In early 1917, two political factions outlined in the Shewan camp, each with their own concepts of domestic and foreign policy. War Minister *Fitawrari* Habte Giyorgis, who represented the most conservative wing of the Shewan elite, was the leader of one of them. His position was undoubtedly the strongest.

Not only Empress Zewditu had no political experience,[77] but she was completely indifferent to affairs of the state. *Ras* Tafari who stayed in the background dissimulated his political ambition, but many people viewed him as a claimant to the throne. Tafari did not disprove the rumor. The "dual power" system contributed to that opinion: Formally, the empress and the regent were supposed to rule the country together. An experienced general and skillful politician, the *fitawrari* was capable of sowing discord in the tandem. Habte Giyorgis was perfectly aware that it was not the empress who was his real rival but *Ras* Tafari, a worthy claimant to state power and the chief opponent to his ideas. Many historians call the political struggle of those days, "The struggle between old Ethiopians and young Ethiopians."[78]

In September 1916, when Zewditu and Tafari were elevated to high positions, the issue of the delimitation of their authorities was also settled. The empress became the country's symbol, and the regent was appointed as head of the government, who was in charge of the matters related to domestic and foreign policy.[79] The real power and influence of War Minister Habte Giyorgis, who was the focal point for the old nobility to rally round, limited the regent's administrative resource in a substantial way, as the regent had no real social or economic support. Being aware of that limitation, Tafari, until the right moment, had preferred not to strain relations with the minister. Not by choice but by necessity, he accepted compromises, settling for a formal status.

Tafari made public statements that proposed reinforcing and centralizing state power in the country and doing away with feudal fragmentation. To make that happen, it would have been necessary to reorganize the administrative and judicial system, to develop a system of education and public outreach, to build roads, to modernize communications, to abolish slavery, and thus enhance Ethiopia's international prestige. Tafari realized that a program of transformations should be carried out step by step, in order not to arouse discontent of the Ethiopian nobility and commoners. In old Ethiopia, a revolutionary path of transformations would doom a reformer to a failure.

The war minister who had the empress's support considered the regent's proposals unacceptable. Habte Giorgis was not only the opponent of Tafari and to Europe but to modern machinery. He thought of planes as "childish toys, or an affront to the Almighty by endeavoring to extend the powers of man beyond those granted him . . . or a devilish device of the foreigner to spy out the land from abroad and so facilitate ultimate foreign conquest."[80]

The British consul in Ethiopia, wrote about Habte Giyorgis's conservatism: "If ever he visits England, he will find congenial company on the benches of the House of Lords, or this historic institution no longer be in existence, Among the heads of colleges at oxford and Cambridge."[81]

Lij Iyasu's deposition, *Ras* Mikael's capture, and neutralization of northern feudal lords did not change the situation dramatically. The period between 1916 and 1918 turned out to be favorable for the country only because the great powers embroiled in World War I had to deal with their own challenges. They less inevitably have lost its independence. By staging the coup, the Shewan nobility made a serious error in judgment. Fearing an authoritarian leader, they deliberately divided the power between people who were incapable of making compromises. As a result, the central government lost control of the provinces, and the country precipitated into chaos. All that was in line with separatist ideals of provincials. Once-powerful warlords and the aristocracy refused to comply even with moderate decrees of the central government. The treasury was depleting rapidly. The provincial nobility blatantly opposed *Ras* Tafari's attempts to reinforce the central government.

As for aid from abroad, the European partners who had supported the coup were experiencing economic troubles themselves. War undermined Ethiopia's foreign trade, which aggravated the situation in the country. The deposed *Lij* Iyasu took advantage of the economic woes and continued an armed struggle for the throne.

No less than loans and foreign investments did the regent need support of the Ethiopian church, which enjoyed a strong influence among the people. However, notwithstanding all difficulties, the regent was diligently performing his duties. "He set himself to work with undaunted courage and vigour, working from daybreak until late at night, carrying the whole burden of the state on his shoulders."[82]

Many provinces did not recognize Addis Ababa's authorities—which had never happened before. The country, as though it had re-plunged into its early days, saw slave trade flourish, lawlessness reign, domestic market virtually paralyzed, villages deserted. The nation was facing starvation.

Leonard Mosley writes, "The Council of Ministers are intriguing for their own gains. The solders are discontented, the lesser officers—summoned to Addis Ababa last September—are impoverished. The solders can only live by looting, and the peasantry are becoming desperate. They are rising out of sheer indignation against the lawlessness."[83]

Ras Tafari was disappointed with the Shewan nobility that had deprived him of real power, which he needed to put things in order in the country. If *Lij* Iyasu had been taken prisoner, the regent's hands would have been untied and he would have been able to exercise power freely, at his own discretion. But, for the time being, the former emperor was free, and rumors of his activity were coming to the capital city on a daily basis. The worried regent said to the British consul: "Until the prince is caught, I dare not move."[84]

Notwithstanding the chaos and unrest pervading the country, lack of any real help from the Council of Minister, social support and economic base, Tafari began transformations in the political and administrative areas. He strengthened his own armed group. First of all, the regent was trying to arm the service personnel of that unit with modern firearms. That formation who were personally loyal to him had more than once prevailed over opponents thanks to military advantage.

The weaponry issue remained the acutest, because an embargo on arms supplies was still in effect. The regent contacted representatives of Great Britain with a request to supply 30,000 guns. The British Minister suggested in return that "the Regent should immediately proclaim the Germans and Turks *persona non grata* and expel their legations from Ethiopia. This Tafari refused to do."[85]

The year 1918 turned out to be critical for *Ras* Tafari: With the death of Empress Taitu, the regent got rid of a strong opponent. He prepared the dissolution of the Council of Ministers and carried it out. With the dismissal of old officials, the war minister lost followers. Tafari was in no hurry to perform new appointments, as he concentrated the entire executive power in his own hands.

A new threat to the country and power came from Europe. An influenza (flu) epidemic, which had spread through Europe in 1917 and claimed hundreds of thousands of lives, reached Africa. Tafari Makonnen was one of its first victims in Ethiopia. He was taken ill with a high temperature and a remittent fever. However, a few months later, he got better. *Ras* Tafari's illness worried Europeans. "The only man who wishes his country well sighed Thesiger, the British diplomat. . . . Will he be obstinate and see the game through? . . . If he loses, the time for European intervention in Ethiopia may be near."[86] Luckily, Tafari Makonnen overcame both the disease and his overt and covert opponents.

At the same time in Europe the Great War was over, and on December 26, 1918, *Ras* Tafari choose the occasion of the Versailles Peace Conference, to send a message to British King George V on behalf of Her Imperial Majesty Empress Zewditu. The message read: "I address to you on the occasion of the forthcoming Peace Conference our heartiest congratulations on the victory of the allies. We thank God he has brought this murderous war to end and that he has granted victory to those who strove for the rights of peoples. Thanksgiving services will be held in our churches to celebrate this great event. Our people all the happier in the knowledge of the victory of the allies in that they to have suffered since the beginning of the War from the course our own political leaders have steered. This course was distasteful." And he adds: "Desirous of entering into closer relations with other nations and cementing friendship with our neighbors, we intend shortly to send to Europe a special mission which we hope will be favorably received by your majesty`s Government."[87] Greeting the king of a great power, Tafari counted on his support in the procedure of Ethiopia's admission to the League of Nations. The young reformer from Addis Ababa was facing a constant dilemma: To carry out a real foreign policy, he had to resolve a host of domestic problems. The year 1921 was marked for *Ras* Tafari by a military victory over *Lij* Iyasu whose troops were defeated. The deposed emperor was taken prisoner, and the civil war that had lasted for five years ended.

The victory allowed Habte Giyorgis to concentrate a sizable military force that the advocate of provincial feudal lords could turn against the young reformer. In the 1920s, Empress Zewditu often backed *Fitawrari* Habte Giyorgis, so the regent's reforms were constantly in jeopardy. To prevent regressive forces from action, a stamina beyond human was required, as well as a diplomatic tact (thanks to lessons of Menelik II), and certain courtly and military cunning.

Ras Tafari's burden of power was made even heavier by the external threat. Once again was the country in Italy's sphere of interests. In 1919, the Italian government demanded that London put pressure on Addis Ababa and make it grant Rome a number of concessions. That was part of the compensation that Italy demanded for its involvement in the war with Germany on the allies' side. Rome referred to the April 26, 1915 treaty on territorial matters signed by Italy and the Entente. It read: "In the event of France and Great Britain increasing their colonial territories in Africa at the expense of Germany, those two Powers agree in principle that Italy may claim some equitable compensation, particularly as regards the settlement in her favour of the questions relative to the frontiers of the Italian colonies of Eritrea, Somaliland and Libya and the neighboring colonies belonging to France and Great Britain."[88]

Italy believed the treaty would also help it reinforce its positions in northeastern Africa at Ethiopia's expense. Italy proposed to the British government taking a concerted effort in order to get economic concessions in Ethiopia.[89] Among them was a concession to build a railroad from the Eritrean border to Italian Somaliland, as the 1906 treaty specified. Going forward, it would make it easier for Italy to subdue Ethiopia. Rome's initiative, however, did not get London's validation. Albion feared the threat of Italian expansion in Egypt and Sudan and was afraid of losing control over Lake Tana and the Blue Nile. The significance of that key position was such that whoever possessed Lake Abaya had ample opportunity to influence the fate of Egypt and Sudan.

Being aware of the fact that Ethiopia was the last free country in Africa that European powers were seeking to secure a grip on, *Ras* Tafari was vehemently trying to reinforce its positions on the international stage. As soon as news came in about the foundation of the League of Nations, Tafari sent a request to that organization, asking for Ethiopia to be admitted. Furthermore, he began to look for new benchmarks and new allies, keeping "old friends" all the way.

ENTRANCE TO THE LEAGUE OF NATIONS

The internal strife of the 1920s, the period of Tafari's struggle with the empress, the war minister and the conservative nobility pushed him to pursue reforms by relying on external forces, because he could hardly count on sympathies and assistance of supporters inside the country. By strengthening and modernizing his army, the regent was simultaneously recruiting backers for reforms, by inspiring them with emoluments, titles, awards, and career opportunities. The nucleus of the "movement of young Ethiopians" was gradually emerging. In addition to *Ras* Tafari's relatives, such as Imiru, it included natives of other provinces: members of families of small landowners who had received either secular or spiritual education (*Negadras* Gebrehiwot Baykedagn, *Blattengeta* Heruy Wolde Sellase, *Lij* Takele Wolde Hawariat, and others). As V. S. Yagiya remarks, many of outstanding young Ethiopians combined political and administrative activities with literary endeavors. In their fiction or newspaper columns, they criticized outdated traditions, customs, and views that obstructed "exposure of the Ethiopians to the European civilization and denounced certain aspects of society's socio-economic and political structure."[90] The goals of young Ethiopians coincided with *Ras* Tafari's personal paradigm. They helped him concentrate foreign policy functions of the state in his hands. But it did not mean he was not taking into account opinions of the ruling elite.

He was making an emphasis on international affairs and expanded foreign relations. As they sought to derive certain benefits from the 1916 palace coup and ascension to power of the forces looking to London, Paris and Rome, European powers were favorably disposed toward Tafari.

However, Ethiopia's new leadership gave the partners to understand that independence-driven interests could not be questioned under any circumstances. When British consul, Major Dodds, asked him whose administration was preferred by Ethiopia, England's, France's or Italy's, regent Tafari said unequivocally: "We would prefer to keep our independence."[91]

In those years, there was no unanimity of opinion regarding foreign policy in the ruling circles and among the nobility. Supporters of reforms (young Ethiopians) viewed expansion of foreign relations as one of crucial means of strengthening the country's independence and giving it exposure to the European civilization, without which the country would be unable to exist. Opponents of reforms, on the contrary, believed that Ethiopia could find safety only by being isolated from the rest of the world. They were probably haunted by the sad experiences of the Italo-Ethiopian War of 1896.

Ethiopia's isolation was also in line with interests of Great Britain, France, and Italy. Therefore, those nations did their best to prevent expansion of the country's international ties, its attempts to break the traditional frame of the foreign policy triangle of London—Paris—Rome. England and Italy were carrying out an overt campaign against Ethiopia, justifying their actions, in particular, by existence of slave trade,[92] and uncontrolled arms trade in the country. They insisted that Ethiopia should be included in their dominions in any shape or form.

Ras Tafari began his first steps in international politics by showing good-will gestures to the nations that had won World War I. On that occasion, Haile Selassie wrote: "*Lij* Iyasu had not at that time permitted us to help even by supplying provisions to our neighbours; and, although we had stood apart, the victors were our neighbours; and we, therefore, decided to send envoys to them to congratulate them, adding some money for the aid of the wounded."[93] France, Great Britain, and Italy were meant. As noted, Russian historians G. V. Tsypkin and V. S. Yagiya, one of the missions of the envoys was to "explore the possibility of Ethiopia's participation in the newly founded League of Nations."[94]

Despite the goodwill gestures, the League of Nations, where Great Britain, France and Italy enjoyed a huge influence, refused to grant the request of the Ethiopian government to admit the country as a member. As we mentioned above, the formal reasons for the refusal were slavery and slave trade that still existed in the country. In reality, the English and the Italians were afraid that amid international recognition and guarantees of independence received by the country they would find it more difficult to pursue their own colonial policy.

Great Britain's policy was especially unprincipled in that period. For instance, during an official reception of the Ethiopian delegation that arrived in London in 1919 to greet the victors in World War I, King George V assured them that he respected Ethiopia's independence and was willing to offer it universal support. In reality, Great Britain's ruling circles continued their traditional policy based on the principle "England has no friends, no enemies, only interests."

Besides official London, the press and some community organizations (the Anti-Slavery and Aborigines Protection, etc.) also joined a propaganda campaign against Ethiopia, denouncing it for slavery, slave trade and uncontrolled imports of armaments, lack of a strong central power, and economic chaos.

Tafari's government did a lot to abolish slavery and put an end to slave trade. In 1918, a decree was published in Addis Ababa, which outlawed slave trade in all of its aspects. In 1922, a law was confirmed that had been passed under Menelik II and prescribed death penalty for keeping people in thralls and for slave trade. Evolution of capitalist economy in Ethiopia accelerated the decline of slavery. Slave-keeping became economically unreasonable; it was much more profitable to grant slaves freedom and to hire them back as workers. That natural but slow process started to produce results just when many Europeans came up with harsh criticism of Tafari's government. It was hard for observers from London and Rome to acknowledge that Ethiopia had seen a victory of capitalist relations over slavery.

To the accusations voiced against his government from London and Rome, Tafari replied: "Ethiopia was actively eradicating slavery and that the edict of 1918 abolishing slavery was not a gesture but a turn in the right direction." At the same time, the head of the Ethiopian government made it clear that the end of slavery would come only as a result of the country's economic development, which would allow the nation to use the intellect and forces of many free people—maybe as many as a few millions. Speaking about Ethiopian society's attitude to that issue, Tafari explained: "most of his countrymen did not perceive slavery as a social problem: the institution was historical; the slave-master relationship was normal, even mutually beneficial; and many chiefs profited from the trade."[95] To accelerate abolishment of slavery, Addis Ababa sent an instruction to all governors of provinces in 1922, ordering that slave trade be stopped at local level. The governors of Gore and Wolamo (provinces where the majority of slaves were concentrated) submitted to the decrees of the Ethiopian government.

The campaign launched by Addis Ababa could not but arouse discontent of wealthy slave owners. Minister of War *Fitawrari* Habte Giyorgis (advocate of slave trade) expressed his emotions in these words (writes Harold Marcus): "What is this? Altayework (his wife) will have to go to the river to collect water and I will have to chop wood." One graybeard of a dejazmach shook his head and lamented that "Abyssinia can no more easily do without slavery than the Europeans could go unshod."[96]

In 1923, Tafari made another attempt to join the League of Nations. "Addis Ababa was adamantly seeking membership of that organization, because it regarded it as a means of raising the influence of its state on the international stage, of reinforcing the country's security and expanding opportunities for addressing internal issues," writes Russian historian V. A. Trofimov.[97]

When a broad discussion unfolded in July 1923 with respect to Ethiopia's membership in the League of Nations, the English, in order to substantiate their negative attitude, referred multiple times to the existence of slavery in the Ethiopian Empire, to facts of uncontrolled arms imports, to absence of proper administration, and to inability of the Ethiopian leadership to prevent incursions of their subjects into border areas of the neighboring British dominions. Speaking about the attitude of the British government at the time, Italian scholar J. Baroveli wrote: "Great Britain would have no great trouble in finding legitimate motives for intervention, if only she would finally decide to battle against the disorder and misery of the country. The slavery and the trading of slaves alone would be sufficient justification."[98] According to V. Yagiya, "at that time it was no secret to anyone that England was trying to bring Ethiopia under its direct control by appointing a British official to the government, who in reality was to direct the actions of the government and administration and the country."[99] England, which needed a dam on Lake Tana to be built, could begin the construction only with Addis Ababa's permission. Therefore, as Britain had its representative in the administrative body of Tafari's government, it was able to achieve the desired result. England's selfish interests in the League of Nations were supported by Switzerland, Australia, Norway, New Zealand, and Italy.

Speaking about the reason for Rome's refusal, Antonio Salandra, Italy's representative at the League, explained Rome's fear that any League recognition of Ethiopia would lead to membership, whereupon the League's collective security would apply to the country's "independence and the integrity of its territory" under Article 10 of the charter.[100] This cynical self-exposure of Italy, which intended to make Ethiopia its colony, was quite in line with European diplomacy of the time.

The Ethiopian delegation that had arrived in Geneva in July 1923, was doing its best to dispel doubts of the League's members regarding Ethiopia's intentions. It was supported by France, sided by Belgium and other pro-French nations. Backing Ethiopia's membership, France counted on using the League of Nations to oppose the Anglo-Italian expansion in Africa.

Ethiopia's membership in the League of Nations was also discussed by the local nobility. During the debate that lasted for six days, *Ras* Tafari managed to garner support of the majority of the nobility, including representatives of the clergy who had, until recently, vehemently opposed to the country's membership in the international organization. *Ras* Tafari explained his position to the high-ranking critics, saying that accession to the League of Nations would let Ethiopia get a guarantee of preserving its sovereignty.

On August 1, 1923, *Ras* Tafari confirmed in a letter to the Council of the League of Nations that his government was prepared to accept conditions contained in Article 1 of the Covenant and to carry out all the obligations incumbent on Members. Tafari emphasized that his country valued highly the principle of collective security and international cooperation, which was acceptable for his multiethnic nation, and that collaboration with the League was producing a favorable impact on the government's activities in the name of peace and accord pursuant to the Christian doctrine.

In September 1923, an Ethiopian delegation was sent to Geneva. France's representative backed up Ethiopia's request. He reminded that Tafari's government was doing its best to comply with the Treaty of Saint-Germain-en-Laye signed in 1919; it provided for control over the trade in arms and munitions. France (unlike England and Italy) was pro-Ethiopian in the issue of slavery and slave trade. *Ras* Tafari sent to the governments of those two countries a telegram, demanding that they should explain their antagonistic policies toward Ethiopia. Nobody had any doubt that France, by supporting Ethiopia, could get certain privileges at the imperial court, and that Great Britain, on the contrary, could lose concessions for the construction of the Lake Tana dam, and Italy could lose hope for the creation of a new Roman Empire. Therefore, governments of the latter two powers gave instructions to their representatives to further Ethiopia's interests.

Thanks to insistence and huge efforts of *Ras* Tafari, on September 28, 1923, by secret ballot, Ethiopia was admitted to the League of Nations. "There was great joy at Addis Ababa," Emperor Haile Selassie writes in his autobiography. "The rejoicing was for no reason other than that We thought that the Covenant of the League would protect us from the sort of attack which Italy has now launched against us."[101] Ethiopia, the only African country, became a subject of international law. The significance of this event is hard to overestimate, because Ethiopia, like a poor relative at a dinner party, remained pretty much the most backward member of the international community in socio-political, cultural, and economic respects.

As he supposed that urban residents would be able to adapt to changes more quickly than rural populations, Tafari began his reforms from Addis Ababa. It was where the rudiments of the Western system of education were concentrated, which could, in his opinion, help in making a breakthrough toward progress of the entire society.

While regent Tafari chose not to carry out radical reforms, he firmly believed that a lot could be borrowed from the West. As Harold Marcus noted, "Tafari believed Ethiopia could learn much from Western lore and life, which fascinated him. He was an avid reader, and his study was filled with books in French on all subjects."[102] Western lifestyle and Western science captivated him and possibly, that was one of the reasons for his voyage to Western European nations in 1924.

Ras Tafari's visit to Europe was a major and unprecedented event for Ethiopia. None of Ethiopian high-ranking officials, besides *Ras* Makonnen, the regent's father, had ever been abroad. "This distinguished invitation which the European governments had extended to Us was a strange thing for all the princes and nobles and the army; they had thus great difficulty over this matter," writes Haile Selassie. "When We heard this, We gave instructions to have the princes and nobles convened in a great assembly. In the end, they all accepted the matter with pleasure, because We had convinced them that, by Our planning to go on extending our friendship with the governments of Europe, We were causing people to meet in trade and in work and getting to know each other as a sign of friendship,"[103] he continues.

Before embarking on a voyage to Europe, *Ras* Tafari promulgated a number of decrees on arms imports and on abolition of slavery. Were those just new maneuvers on the *ras's* part to invite Europe's public attention? Possibly, but even in that case, the decrees were not a "fight with windmills," but part of a program of action. As for control over arms imports, the following thing should be mentioned: The 1924 decree reinforced the positions of the government in the country, as legislation granted it the right to control those imports.

Unlike the previous decrees adopted in 1918 and in 1922, the 1924 decree on the abolition of slavery and slave trade envisaged liberation of slaves, albeit gradual and partial. The document said that if all slaves were to be freed at once, "they might become thieves, bandits and malefactors, thereby disturbing the public peace." As part of this arrangement, Ethiopia was required to phase out slavery "fifteen to twenty years" period, at the end of which it had to abolish it completely.[104]

According to the new decree, slaves were to be set free seven years after the death of their master and had the right of repatriation. Moreover, the state decided to finance education (qualification) of some former slaves and guaranteed employment to them. Slave owners and slave traders who failed to comply with the government's regulations were punished severely according to law. A special judicial body was set up for the purpose.[105]

In a report sent to the League of Nations, *Ras* Tafari said his government had taken energetic and radical measures against slave traders. Those measures were quite successful and contributed to annihilation of slave trade. The new laws, once implemented, extirpated slavery and slave trade, because slavery, as a system of relations, becomes totally obsolete without new slaves.

Even British Ambassador Claud Russell, who was prejudiced against Ethiopia, had to say that the measures seemed "reasonably conceived, and in theory calculated to deal gradually with an evil which it would admittedly be difficult to abolish out of hand." Even a notoriously anti-Ethiopian *Westminster Gazette* conceded that the new decree "marked a notable advance."[106]

French minister Louis Gaussen was enthusiastic, claiming that the new laws were guided by "great liberalism," shaped by reality, and would "have decisive results in the future." He anticipated that the regulations would transform slaves into an agricultural proletariat, thus effecting "a kind of reorganization of the whole empire."[107]

Thus, by "removing shackles" from the Ethiopian people, Tafari Makonnen turned to the European world.

He was to reinforce the ties of the two civilizations, two worlds. "I had the hope and conviction that my journey to Europe would give me three benefits," wrote Haile Selassie. "(1) to see with my own eyes European civilization and the beauty of the cities of Paris, London, Rome, Brussels,

Athens, and Cairo . . . ; (2) when returning to my country after my visit to Europe, I thought it would be possible to initiate some aspects of civilization I had observed with my own eyes, although it would be impossible to carry this out all at once and in full; (3) to find a sea-port; prior to Our journey We had received some encouragement from France and Italy as regards access to the sea."[108]

THE MISSION TO EUROPE

On April 16, 1924, the regent, accompanied by a grand retinue, which included adamant conservatives, such as *Ras* Hailu Tekle Haymanot of Goj-jam and *Ras* Seyoum Mengesha of Tigray and others, set off for Djibouti. D. R. Voblikov writes, with good reason, that *Ras* Tafari deliberately took with him leaders of the feudal opposition, old Ethiopians, as he feared that in his absence, they might seize power in the country. In addition, he wanted them to see European achievements with their own eyes and hoped to persuade them to offer support for his reforms and acquaint them with functions of the state machinery of European nations.[109] British scholar R. Pankhurst was of the same opinion.[110]

From Djibouti, the Ethiopian delegation went to Palestine, then to Egypt and from there left for Europe. They visited France, Great Britain, Italy, and a few smaller countries of Europe. Talking to European politicians, the head of the Ethiopian delegation was seeking to establish close economic, political, and cultural ties between Ethiopia and Europe. *Ras* Tafari also intended to get some nation that possessed colonies neighboring with Ethiopia to sign an agreement that would give Ethiopia a free access to the sea. Since the Ethiopian government considered other ways, including hostilities, unacceptable, the regent made an attempt to attain his goal via negotiations.

Ras Tafari put high hopes on the French government, so France was the first European country that he visited. However, the regent's intention to get a free gateway to the sea at Djibouti amounted to nothing. He got only "some hope" from the French government.[111]

When the regent was staying in Rome, on his second day there he was delivered a draft treaty prepared by Salvatore Contarini, Secretary-General of the Ministry of Foreign Affairs. The draft provided for a special zone to be provided to Ethiopia in Assab, for a period of 99 years; it would be accessed via Eritrea, and it would be possible to build a railroad there.

Territorial concessions, however, were subject to a number of economic, legal and political conditions (for instance, establishment of a joint venture with exclusively Italian staff to build port facilities, a railroad and roads to Gondar, Adwa, Mekelle and other cities), which would considerably limit sovereignty of the Ethiopian state. After he studied the draft, Ethiopia's regent said he needed to discuss it with influential officials and nobles of the empire (the draft was turned down by the Council of the Empire after Tafari had returned to Addis Ababa in September 1925).

In addition, the *ras* received from Mussolini a promise of financial aid. With all that, Tafari came back to Paris. He probably wanted to spark the interest of the French government that had learned about Rome's proposals. One way or another, the Ethiopian side did not resolve to accept the Roman draft. It is true, officials in Quai d'Orsay showed to Tafari Makonnen a (finally) prepared draft agreement on a lease of a land plot in Djibouti to Ethiopia, but they said right away that, because of the government crisis, lack of legal paperwork and specialists, the final decision of the matter had to be postponed. The regent did not lose hope, as he counted on official London.

In Great Britain, Tafari was received by King George V, who promised to return to Empress Zewditu the crown of Emperor Tewodros II that had been captured by British troops during their intervention in Ethiopia in 1867–1868. As for negotiations on granting access to the sea and on arms supplies, they did not take place. Harold Marcus writes about it: "The government continued to believe that Tafari was a native princeling who had come to Europe to confirm the grandeur of the British Empire."[112]

The regent attached a great importance to the visit to smaller European countries, such as Sweden, Belgium, and Greece. He sought closer contacts and wanted to invite economic and military advisers to Ethiopia.

European nations that did not have colonies neighboring on Ethiopia were the most desirable partners for the government, as they did not aspire to expand their influence on the continent at Ethiopia's expense. In any case, it was much safer for the government to grant concessions to firms from neutral countries. A positive outcome of the visits and talks became obvious a few years later, when Swedish and Belgian military instructors arrived in Ethiopia.

During the regent's European voyage, Soviet diplomats tried to engage in talks with him, seeking to restore diplomatic relations between the two countries suspended in 1917. Even though the Soviet government offered to "initiate restoration of normal relations," the parties failed to reach an agreement. As writes V. S. Yagiya, the reason was "interference of imperialist powers, first of all England, France and Italy, which feared that Ethiopia's ties with the Soviet Union would promote its independence."[113] G. V. Tsypkin specifies: "The regent's hesitation, scheming of West European diplomacies and the negative attitude to the move on the part of the conservative Ethiopian nobility led to a situation where restoration of inter-state relations between the two countries was postponed for nearly 20 years."[114]

One can agree with these conclusions: The three powers did all they could to keep Ethiopia in the sphere of their influence. We should add here that *Ras* Tafari was not prepared for talks with representatives of the Soviet Union. The main purpose of his visit to Europe was not to resume suspended relations but to settle the problem of the country's access to the sea.

However, he failed to do that. England, France, and Italy were aware that ceding a piece of land to Ethiopia would give it a freedom of action in addressing economic and political matters. Should France have agreed to Addis Ababa's proposals, it would have lost all its influence on Ethiopia. So far Ethiopia's foreign trade depended on France (Djibouti was Ethiopia's main link to the outer world), the latter country was the master of the situation. As for England and Italy, they were seeking complete submission of the Ethiopian Empire, and the agreement signed in 1925 is proof of their intentions.

One of the outcomes of Tafari Makonnen's voyage was the interest of the European press in Ethiopian affairs, which had spiked impressively. Furthermore, the return of the imperial crown by British king George V could also be termed as international success of the visit, in terms of prestige and preservation of traditions.

British scholar R. Pankhurst thinks the regent's visit to Europe in 1924 was no less important for Ethiopia than Peter the Great's stay abroad in the seventeenth century had been for Russia.[115] The Ethiopian delegation could not help seeing how strikingly different socioeconomic and cultural life in Europe was from that in Ethiopia. That convinced the old Ethiopians of the necessity of *Ras* Tafari's reforms.

Different attitudes were expressed in Addis Ababa toward Tafari's voyage and its outcomes. Some people believed that the purpose had been gained; others were saying that the *ras's* mission had been unsuccessful and extravagant. As for the proposals made by Italy and France, the Council of the Empire rejected them. Only the return of the crown of Emperor Tewodros II was perceived as a significant event. On July 11, 1925, the emperor's crown was shipped to Addis Ababa after a solemn ceremony.[116]

By declining Ethiopia's request to grant it access to the sea, France was probably facing a dilemma. Hence its goodwill gesture, when it supported the Ethiopia government that needed weapons to be delivered via Djibouti. In March 1925, Paris upheld *Ras* Tafari's statement at the League of Nations on the need to have the embargo on arms supplies lifted. Insisting on the principle of equality, the Ethiopian government asked that the situation in the country should be investigated, as imports of arms and munitions were for it a matter of self-defense.[117]

During a conference that took place in May 1925, England and Italy opposed Ethiopia, referring to the fact that, upon joining the League of Nations, Ethiopia had agreed to consider Africa a "prohibited zone." "France interpreted their stubbornness as a flagrant interference in the internal affairs of a member state, in Africa."[118] Since England and Italy found themselves in the minority, the League granted Ethiopia's request.

Immediately after getting back from Europe, Tafari began to modernize the army. For that, arms were bought in Switzerland and Czechoslovakia. Tafari even began to import foreign specialists and instructors to train the army and to modernize the administrative staff. "Immediately after World War I, Tafari had employed tens of low-cost White Russian émigrés as technicians, but the new men were attached to the ministries as advisers and planners," writes Harold Marcus. In 1924–1925, Tafari hired two Belgian mining engineers, a Swiss hydrologist to survey Lake Tana, two Swiss legal advisers for the Special Court and the Court of Appeals, and two French teachers.

The regent was especially interested in American specialists and American capital, so he invited the U.S. consul in Aden to visit Addis Ababa, with a view to restore diplomatic relations suspended when Washington had closed the diplomatic legation during World War I. Tafari also repaired relations with the Soviet Union, which appointed a diplomat of the old school to represent its revolutionary interest in a country ruled by a traditional regime."[119]

Tafari set a goal to build an enlightened society. In 1921 and 1922, he imported two printing presses, books started to be published in the Amharic language. In 1924–1925, the newspaper *Berhanenna Selam* (*Light and Peace*) was established, which provided urban residents with news, sermons,and so forth. Another important novelty in the country was the opening of a school in 1925—it was funded with the regent's own money and was named after Tafari Makonnen. On the day of its opening, *Ras* Tafari called on the Ethiopian nobility to follow his example: "Time for phrase-mongering is over; our people are in a dire need for enlightenment, without which it cannot defend its independence. Proof of true patriotism is the recognition of this fact. . . .Those who can help in the construction of schools must promote dissemination of education. I have built this school only for starters and as an example. I am calling on wealthy people to do the same."[120]

No one responded to *Ras* Tafari's call. Far from everyone believed that adoption of Western machinery and reliance on values of Western culture could pull the country from the abyss where it had fallen. The aristocracy was most of all concerned with amassing its own wealth, rather than with building the country's future. No wonder that Tafari's actions sometimes annoyed people, and the malcontent were preparing an assassination attempt. Luckily, the conspiracy was uncovered. In order to undermine the regent's credit, "rumors circulated that he was a Roman Catholic, that he had embezzled state funds, and that his only objective in Europe was to display himself as a 'modern' statesman, not to improve Ethiopia's international standing and certainly not to negotiate access to the sea."[121]

Despite his predictable failures at home and abroad, the *ras* was persistent in adopting new approaches and principles in foreign policy to protect the country's independence and integrity. As later events showed, he was following correct landmarks. In 1925, England and Italy made an attempt to violate Ethiopia's sovereignty.

COLONIALISTS DO NOT SLEEP!

After the country joined the League of Nations, it seemed to be immune from direct interference of foreign powers in Ethiopia's internal affairs. The reality proved to be different, however. In 1925, Great Britain and Italy made an attempt to impose concessions on Ethiopia, with Mussolini, the leader of Italy, initiating the move. In his letter of December 20, 1925 addressed to London, Mussolini writes: "I have therefore, the honor to state to your Excellency that the Royal Government [of Italy] will support the British Government with the Ethiopian Government in order to obtain from the latter the concession to construct a barrage at Lake Tana, together with the right to construct and maintain a motor road for the passage of stores, personnel, etc. from the frontier of the Sudan to the barrage. The royal Government take note, on the other hand, that the British Government will, in return, support the Italian Government in obtaining from the Abyssinian Government the concession to construct and operate a railway from the frontier of Eritrea to the frontier of Italian Somaliland."[122] Thus, the two powers, without consent of Ethiopia's government, decided to split it into spheres of influence.

Tana is the biggest lake in Ethiopia; it is situated in the northwestern part of the country, in the provinces of Gondar and Gojjam. It has about 60 mountain rivers running into it. The waters of the lake supply the main tributary of the Nile. Building a dam would make it possible to irrigate a large area, to enhance productivity of the country's agriculture, and to increase power generation in a major way. Unfortunately, an underdeveloped Ethiopia had no forces or funds to make use of its own water resources.

The issue of a dam on Lake Tana was first raised in 1902; however, the Ethiopian side postponed resolution of the issue until specialists were able to confirm that there was no danger of seeing local churches and monasteries flooded. In 1906, Great Britain had sent its specialists to the country, but when World War I began, the process was suspended.

After the end of World War I, Italy, having entered into a treaty with England, decided to obtain from the Ethiopian government a concession to build and operate a railroad from Massawa (Eritrea) via Ethiopia (to the west of Addis Ababa) to Mogadishu (Italian Somaliland). In November 1919, the Italian government addressed the British government and asked support in that matter. In exchange, Italy promised to back England whose interests were linked to concessions to build a dam on the Blue Nile and Lake Tana and to construct a road between Lake Tana and Sudan.[123]

Previously, England had disapproved Italy's stance, but in 1925, it changed its attitude, and sent a note to Mussolini's government, expressing its consent to cooperate with Italy in the division of Ethiopia into spheres of influence. However, it had a request to make to Italy: "not to construct on the sources of the Blue and White Niles and their tributaries any kind of work."[124] A few days later, the Italian side accepted the British proposal.

On July 9, 1926, diplomatic representatives of Great Britain and Italy in Addis Ababa delivered to the Ethiopian government notes, which concerned a series of concessions to be granted to the both nations. *Ras* Tafari declined the Anglo-Italian demands, reminding that nobody, apart from the Ethiopians, had the right to be in command of the country's resources. In a note addressed to Mussolini, Tafari said he would submit the matter to the consideration of the League of Nations. A message to the British government said: "We should never have suspected that the British Government would come to an agreement with another Government regarding our Lake."[125]

On July 19, 1926, the regent of Ethiopia, having had a package of the Anglo-Italian agreements with a cover letter delivered to the Secretary-General of the League, informed the latter that Ethiopia would not tolerate violation of its sovereignty in any event.[126]

Having learned about the agreement between Great Britain and Italy, France demanded explanations from its partners under the 1906 London Treaty, because they were breaching the division of spheres of influence specified in that treaty. After that, the Italian government had to make an official statement that the Anglo-Italian agreement was not infringing on Ethiopia's interests.[127]

One cannot say categorically that the countries bound by the new treaty ignored Ethiopia's interests completely. Nevertheless, France was afraid of losing its authority and influence in Ethiopia. The matter was that commissioning of the Eritrea-Italian Somaliland railroad by the Italians and of the Lake Tana-Sudan automobile highway by the British, would, according to the intention of the two partners, undermine significantly the importance of the Djibouti-Addis Ababa railroad. If the main flow of foreign trade cargo was to be rerouted to the Anglo-Italian roads, France would have lost considerable economic and political benefits.

Giving general evaluation to the Anglo-Italian agreement, Russian historian V. A. Trofimov writes that it was a "typically imperialistic deal of two powers, which agreed behind Ethiopia's back on joining their efforts to get profitable concessions, and on putting joint pressure on the government of the country (i.e., Ethiopia.—*Author's note*). *De facto*, the agreement sanctioned renewal of political expansionist activity of Italy in Ethiopia at a new historical stage."[128] We will add here that, if the plan had succeeded, England would have undermined France's influence in northeastern Africa. It was that purpose that England pursued when it favored Italy and encouraged it to acquire colonies in Somaliland and Eritrea.

After a harsh statement of the Ethiopian government and France's interference, London and Rome made haste to rectify their blunders. Conte Colli, the Italian Envoy Extraordinary and Minister Plenipotentiary, said that the Anglo-Italian agreement was of purely economic nature, based on the "respect of sovereign rights" of the Ethiopian government, that it was a new confirmation of friendly intentions of Italy and England with respect to the Ethiopian Empire, which still had the absolute right to accept that agreement or to reject it.[129]

Tafari did not accept Conte Colli's excuses. Moreover, he said Ethiopia regarded the Anglo-Italian move as an infringement on its sovereignty and drew the attention of the League of Nations to it. The Anglo-Italian agreement, the regent emphasized, was encroaching on the sphere of interests of his homeland, because it spoke about transferring Ethiopia's natural resources under the command of Western powers.[130]

The statement of the Ethiopian government also said: "Our people are desirous to do right; it is Our constant wish to lead them on the road of civilization and improvement. But what they know of their history is that among the foreigners there are few who do not desire to violate their frontiers and to impair their freedom. With God's goodness and the bravery of our soldiers we have always, whatever the circumstances, been able to remain upon our mountains proud in our independence."[131]

The statement of Ethiopia's government bolstered sweeping anti-Italian propaganda. The 1925 Anglo-Italian treaty did not only worsen relations between the two countries but also undermined trade with Eritrea, an Italian colony. As a result, London and Rome arrived at a conclusion that they would not win if they obstinately insisted on the so-called agreement. The Foreign Office of the Great Britain and Italy's Ministry of Foreign Affairs offered their apologies, pointing out that the Anglo-Italian agreement was misinterpreted by Addis Ababa.

As a result of Ethiopia's tenacious opposition backed by France's assistance, London and Rome had to give up their plan. Later, Ethiopia retracted its complaint from the League of Nations, as it believed friendly intentions of Great Britain and Italy, which unconditionally recognized Ethiopia's sovereignty and its right to be in command of its own land and resources.

Ethiopia's destiny is a patent example of a weak country that was successful in defending its interests on the international stage thanks to an adroit policy.[132] And in that, undoubtedly, a tremendous credit goes to *Ras* Tafari.

The regent's disagreement with an attempt by England and Italy to "morocco-nize" Ethiopia proved once again that he was not only a sagacious politician but also a true patriot.

In 1927, *Fitawrari* Habte Giyorgis, one of Tafari's chief opponents, died, which largely changed the balance of power in favor of the reformist wing. In that moment, the final phase of Tafari Makonnen's struggle for power began.

RE-ESTABLISHMENT OF DIPLOMATIC RELATIONS WITH THE UNITED STATES

With the death of *Fitawrari* Habte Giyorgis, the empress lost an important and strong ally, and the conservative old Ethiopian nobility was deprived of its leader. Because of that, *Ras* Tafari's positions inside the country strength-ened substantially. As he took control of the army and of the war minister's possessions, the regent became the most influential figure in the country's ruling circles.

As it was mentioned above, Tafari was pursuing a cautious and skillful policy, protecting sovereignty of the Ethiopian state. He did not want to sur-render to Europe. What made him strong? First, the regent had no doubt that sooner or later he would ascend the throne. Second, Tafari believed he was following the right path, and he preserved society's traditional living patterns. Sometime later, England and Italy, each one of them individually, launched another attack.

In 1927, England made an attempt to persuade the Ethiopian government to exchange the port of Zeila (in British Somaliland) for a concession to build a dam in the Lake Tana area. A memorandum sent to the government said England was ready to begin the construction immediately.[133] Tafari's govern-ment was deliberately backpedaling its reply.

Meanwhile, the United States displayed interest in the project of a dam in Ethiopia. *Ras* Tafari's personal representative Dr. Martin (Warqnah Ishete) was dispatched to Washington.[134] He was received by U.S. President Calvin Coolidge. Talks were held to open the U.S. embassy in Addis Ababa and to bring American capital into Ethiopia's industry—in particular, in the construction of a dam on Lake Tana.[135] U.S. monopolies hastened to snatch control over the lake from the English.

Naturally, before economic ties could be developed, diplomatic relations between the two countries had to be re-established. Since 1913, the United States had not had its mission in Ethiopia. Its interests had been represented by Great Britain's mission in Addis Ababa.[136] Since 1926, the Ethiopian side had been trying to reestablish relations with the United States, driven, first and foremost, by a concern about England and Italy's desire to bind Ethiopia with concession agreements. *Ras* Tafari preferred to grant concession rights to neutral nations, which were strong enough. Second, Ethiopia needed arms supplies, because, according to the 1906 tripartite treaty, it was deprived of the right to import weapons from Europe.

To neutralize the British-Italian union and the related embargo on arms imports, Ethiopia had to turn its attention to countries that had nothing to do with that treaty. The United States was one of those countries.

A long period had preceded establishment of ties between Ethiopia and the United States. As usual, the United States took a serious approach to the issue. To ascertain the situation in the country, U.S. representative Ralph J. Totten, Consul General detailed as inspector of the U.S. Secretary of State, arrived in Ethiopia from Aden on May 22, 1926.

Having studied the situation, Totten arrived at the conclusion that it was necessary to reestablish diplomatic relations with Ethiopia. Totten wrote: "American trade with Abyssinia is at present indirect and relatively unimportant. Formerly we supplied most of the cotton sheeting which is an important article of trade in Abyssinia, but the Japanese cotton piece goods have supplanted the American. Sewing machines, motors cars, kerosene, phonographs, toiler articles, typewriters and a few agricultural implements of American manufacture are to be seen in the stores of larger cities. . . .it seems reasonably certain that with increased production of coffee and other agricultural and natural products the purchasing power of the people will become greater. . . .The Prince Regent's trip to Europe, with his suite, and the constantly increasing number of Abyssinians who are going abroad tend to cause an interest in the simpler conveniences and necessities of modern civilization. There are at present some fifty young Abyssinians being educated in Europe and the United States who will bring back modern ideas to the country. All of these factors will combine to raise the scale of living in this country and to increase the need for imported merchandise. This is a country with an rea about equal to that of Germany and France combined, with a population larger than that of Canada; with a cool, equable climate, abundant rainfall and soil which will produce almost everything from tropical to cold climate crops; with potential and untouched mineral resources; and, which is as yet almost totally undeveloped. When it is remembered that in addition to the facts just stated the country has an intelligent, progressive and ambitious young ruler, it is impossible to be other than optimistic as to its immediate future. . . .I also recommend that our representative be sent as soon as possible after the receipt and study of this report."[137]

In the 1920s, Ethiopia was still a country isolated from European scientific and technological achievements. Hence a small-numbered intellectual community and lack of properly qualified human resources, absence of infrastructure. It is true, by 1917, the construction of the Djibouti-Addis Ababa railroad had been completed, which boosted the inflow of foreign capital to the country in a major way. The United States was hopeful that, as the Ethiopian national intellectual community expanded, forces would emerge that would play the part of intermediary. Intellectuals were to acquaint commoners with Western lifestyles and to become *Ras* Tafari's right hand, as the United States presumed him to be the future leader of the country. On December 1, 1927, with the appointment of the U.S. ambassador, resident and consul general, diplomatic relations between the two countries were reestablished.[138]

Sometime before, on November 3, 1927, J. G. White Engineering Corporation, an American company, had made an agreement with Ethiopia's government to build a dam on Lake Tana, near the sources of the Blue Nile. As relations between the United States and Ethiopia were reestablished, Great Britain, which had represented U.S. interests between 1913 and 1927, perceived a formidable rival in Africa's northeast.

A concession granted by the Ethiopian government to an American company stirred a sensation. The *New York Times* wrote: "While England, France and Italy were engaged in a quarrel between themselves, the American companion calmly entered into negotiations and plucked the largest fruit—a concession for the construction of dam on Lake Tana, which would control the origins of the Blue Nile and thereby affect British interests in Sudan."[139]

England's ruling circles immediately reacted to the Americano-Ethiopian agreement. In a special note, the British Foreign Office drew attention of Ethiopia's government to the terms of the 1902 Anglo-Ethiopian treaty that had granted England a priority in the construction of a dam on Lake Tana. A representative of the British Foreign Office said: "The Government of Great Britain and has decided that no state other than Great Britain will build dams through the Blue Nile."[140] The British press perceived in Tafari's initiative a clever move aiming to neutralize the influence of England, France, and Italy in the country.

Seeking to appease the British ruling circles, Dr. Martin on his way back to Ethiopia gave an interview to a correspondent of the newspaper *Manchester Guardian*. In it, he expressed surprise that his visit to the United States had aroused so much interest. He assured that no contract had been awarded to the American company yet, that he was holding negotiation with that company in England's interests. "All we want to do is to satisfy the desire of the British government, which intends to control the waters of Blue Nile by building a dam at its source," said Dr. Martin. "If the British government doesn't need the dam, then Ethiopian government doesn't need it."[141]

In an interview with the Egyptian newspaper *Al-Ahram*, Dr. Martin declared in a point-blank manner unwillingness of the Ethiopian government to grant a concession to England. He gave as a reason the British government's aspiration to establish control over the Blue Nile area. Moreover, emphasized Dr. Martin, if England received a concession to build a dam, it would be putting pressure on Ethiopia, trying to obtain a concession to construct a railroad via Ethiopia for Italy.[142]

Once again, Ethiopian diplomacy, following the best traditions, showcased its flexibility and tenacity. For a quarter of a century, it had done its best to repel assaults of British capital that had been seeking control over the waters of Lake Tana and Nile tributaries. Ethiopian diplomacy had first France and then the United States as temporary allies in that struggle.

The contention between England and the United States over the construction of the dam lasted from 1927 until the beginning of the Italo-Ethiopian War of 1935–1936. Correspondence between the U.S. State Department and Addison E. Southard, an American minister in Addis Ababa, can give some idea of that conflict. For instance, on April 26, 1928, Southard wrote to Washington on his talks with regent Tafari about the concession. He notified the secretary of state that the British Foreign Office had delivered a note to Tafari's government, saying that H. M.'s government had consented to the construction of a dam as a facility owned by Ethiopia. Doing so, England demanded that Sudan and Egypt be provided with enough water supply and on certain terms. In a letter of October 3, 1928 Southard said that the prince-regent (Tafari Makonnen) was in no hurry to build a dam and that Dr. Martin had left for London, supposedly for his health, but in reality, he was to conduct talks with the British government regarding the dam. In conclusion, the envoy expressed hope that the forthcoming coronation of prince-regent Tafari would make a favorable impact on the outcome of the negotiations about the concession, and assured the secretary of state that the "Tsana [*sic*!] Dam matter is always a live item in the business of this office" (i.e., the U.S. mission in Ethiopia). On October 17, Southard notified the State Department that England was intensely seeking to build the dam and that it had Italy's support. The American minister reported with regret "the very evident disinclination of His Majesty (i.e., Tafari.—*Author's note*) to displease the British," because of "the possible lack of definite intention to build such a dam."[143]

The U.S. government did not want to lose control over the source of the Blue Nile. On November 30, G. Howland Shaw, the chief of the Division of Near Eastern Affairs of the State Department, wrote to the president of J. G. White Engineering Corporation: "Mr. Southard concludes the telegram by expressing his own personal opinion to the effect that the King (i.e. Tafari.—*Author's note*) has never yet definitely made up his mind to have the Dam actually constructed. It looks to me as though the next move would have to be taken through British channels."[144]

In March 1930, the two-month talks between the Ethiopian government, representatives of the British irrigation administration in Sudan, and American J. G. White Engineering Corporation in Addis Ababa were over. As a result of the negotiations, the American company was commissioned to carry out a detailed study of the Lake Tana area. Under the agreement, the right of control over the future dam was recognized to belong to Ethiopia's government. The British government undertook to pay to Ethiopia an established amount of money for the use of the water for 50 years. A decision was made to build motorways from Addis Ababa to Lake Tana, as regent Tafari requested, instead of from Sudan, as the English had initially wanted.

The Ethiopian government approved that agreement. In October 1930, once the rainy season was over, J. G. White Engineering Corporation sent an expedition to Lake Tana in order to study the area of future works in detail. In May 1931, the expedition completed its work and returned to Addis Ababa. Its head said the Blue Nile dam construction site had been selected and two variants of a road to Addis Ababa had been designed.

Fearing that the United States and England were acting in concert, Ethiopia's government was in no hurry to build the dam until end of 1934. Further events connected to the Italian aggression made both countries abandon their intentions regarding the dam. Its construction remained in blueprints only.

Ras Tafari's attempt to strengthen the country's defense potential with U.S. assistance also failed. As it was pointed out before, the threat of external aggression did not allow the government to address only domestic matters. As it was lacking military industry and a properly qualified officer corps, it had to resort to foreign military specialists. None of the European powers whose influence was decisive in areas neighboring with Ethiopia wanted its military might to strengthen. The country had to smuggle arms, facing huge difficulties in the process. And it still did not have a gateway to the sea.

Trying to break the blockade set by England, France, and Italy, the Ethiopian government turned to the United States in 1927, asking for arms to be sold to it. Since the U.S. State Department acted in concert with the governments of England, France and Italy, the request was denied. In 1928, regent Tafari again addressed the same request to the American government. He inquired about the price of army rifles, machine rifles, machine-guns, artillery pieces, ammunition and American uniforms, and he also asked for an airplane and two tanks to be sold and for two American officers to be procured as military instructors.[145] The U.S. State Department declined that request from Ethiopia again, saying the U.S. Defense Department had no spare tanks or airplanes. Private U.S. firms also were warned that the State Department disapproved of arms exports to Ethiopia.[146]

After the failure of their 1925 agreement, England and Italy were trying to subdue Ethiopia peacefully. The politics of this conquest was linked to the activities of Italian envoy Giuliano Cora appointed in 1926.[147] Reflecting views of some circles of the Italian government, Cora gave up open and, sometimes, violent forms of pressure on Ethiopia. He believed that, in order to implement aggressive plans, and, especially, to get economic concessions, it was important to keep the country's unity, because, otherwise, there would be no guarantees for unhindered expansion of Italian capital. It is at this angle that the talks with Ethiopia about concluding the Treaty of Amity, Conciliation and Arbitration should be regarded, as well as the title of that document. The treaty was essentially a veil to conceal Italy's aggressive plans.

The talks on concluding a treaty with the Italian government began in April 1927. At that time, the Duke of Abruzzi, who was head of a top-level mission, arrived in Ethiopia. The mission also included Jacopo Gasparini, Governor of Eritrea, and Raffaello Guariglia, a high-ranking official of Italy's Foreign Ministry. They were both instructed to smooth things out between Ethiopia and Italy, and to mend the relations that had deteriorated as a result of the 1925 Anglo-Italian agreement.

The long talks between representatives of Ethiopia and Italy resulted in the signing of the Italo-Ethiopian Treaty of Amity, Conciliation, and Arbitration in Addis Ababa on August 2, 1928. Simultaneously with a treaty of amity, another agreement was concluded—on a joint construction of a motorway from the port of Assab in Eritrea to the city of Dessie and on granting to Ethiopia a free zone in the port of Assab.[148]

Article 1 of the treaty said: "There shall be everlasting friendship between the Imperial Ethiopian Government and the Royal Italian Government." "The two governments have entered into a mutual obligation not to do anything for whatever reason that might affect or damage the independence of the other and to safeguard and protect their respective interests." (Article 2), and, simultaneously, both governments "undertook to submit to a procedure of conciliation and arbitration disputes which may arise between them" (Article 5). The treaty also aimed "to develop and promote trade between the two countries"[149] (Article 3).

The signing of the document allowed Italy to establish closer contacts with Ethiopia and to set up consulates and trade missions in its territory in order to reinforce Italian influence. *Ras* Tafari, by signing the treaty, counted not so much on obtaining certain economic benefits but on alleviating Italy's enmity, and on elimination of the threat of an armed attack.

The treaty was officially registered at the League of Nations, and thus acquired an international status. So, the recognition and respect of Ethiopia's independence by Italy, which was stated in the treaty, and notification of the international community of the fact inspired hope for the treaty to play a positive role, to become the foundation for the settlement of potential contentious matters and conflict situations.

"The treaty with Italy was eminently important for the regent personally and for his confidants, as it strengthened their positions in the struggle for power," writes Russian historian V. S. Yagiya. "But it also reinforced the regent's influence among the country's establishment, because the terms of the treaty were linked to Tafari Makonnen's name,"[150] he adds.

It is a well-known fact that after the death of *Fitawrari* Habte Giyorgis, his main opponent, *Ras* Tafari was able to de facto remove the empress and her followers from public administration (especially from affairs concerning foreign policy). Thus, as V. S. Yagiya believes, he gave to understand to the Ethiopian nobility that he was not just a regent awaiting power to fall into his hand, but a fully legitimate ruler, and an active political figure who was to be reckoned with.[151]

In 1928, Tafari managed to neutralize another strong opponent, *Dejazmach* Balcha, the governor of Sidamo. The regent disarmed his troops and imprisoned the leader. After *Dejazmach* Balcha's arrest, Tafari's opponents began to side more actively with Empress Zewditu on whom they placed high hopes.

The empress who had played quite a passive role in the government emerged as the leader of the opposition. On September 5, 1928, a conspiracy broke out against Tafari at the imperial palace. Talks were conducted to put it out. To reinforce the regent's authority, a decision was made to crown him as the *negus* of Shewa. The coronation took place on October 7, 1928, at the church of Mekane Selassie in Addis Ababa, in the presence of the country's highest nobility and the diplomatic corps. The move purported to strengthen Tafari's prestige among various ethnicities of Ethiopia.

After the coronation, the regent felt himself strong enough to launch the implementation of his program on a wider scale. In 1929, he invited military instructors from Belgium—they were to build an imperial guard following European fashion. In the same year, he appointed five Ethiopian bishops, thus paving the way for independence of the Ethiopian church from the Greek Orthodox Patriarchate of Alexandria.

In April 1930, Empress Zewditu died suddenly. And on April 4, *Negus* Tafari Makonnen, the regent of the Ethiopian Empire, was declared Emperor of Ethiopia under the name of Haile Selassie I.

Thus, *Ras* Tafari's long way to the supreme power in the state was over. A few months later, a solemn coronation of the new Emperor of Ethiopia took place. The emperor would prove himself as a reformer and modernizer.

NOTES

1. Harold G. Marcus. *Haile Selassie I. The Formative Years. 1892–1936*. Berkley; Los Angeles; London, 1987. P. XI–XII (hereinafter—Harold G. Marcus. 1987).

2. Haile Selassie in Amharic means "Power of the Holy Trinity."

3. Before Eritrea was annexed to Ethiopia in 1952, the country had no access to the sea, so it used the port of Djibouti, which was in French Somaliland at the time. By 1917, the Djibouti-Addis Ababa railway had been built, and it ran across the province of Hararghe, so Hararghe was considered as a sort of corridor, or access to the sea, for the empire.

4. Harold G. Marcus. 1987. P. 2.

5. It should be mentioned that Ras Makonnen was one of the emperor's generals who played an important part in the Battle of Adwa in 1896. The Italian army suffered a defeat then.

6. Ras Makonnen's second wife.

7. My Life and Ethiopia's Progress (*The Autobiography of Emperor Haile Selassie I*), 1892–1937. Translated and annotated by Edward Ulendorff. Oxford: Oxford University Press, 1976. P. 14 (hereinafter—Autobiography (English)).

8. There is no authentic information about the death of Tafari's mother. In his autobiography, Haile Selassie I mentions her only in passing. Haile Selassie's biographers differ on her account. For instance, Richard Greenfield says she died when Tafari turned two; Peter Schwab writes that she died in labor. Her origin is also veiled in mystery. Supposedly, she was a daughter to an Oromo aristocrat. See: Schwab P. *Ethiopia & Haile Selassie*. New York: Facts on File, 1972. P. 24 (hereinafter—Schwab P. 1972).

9. The relations between Haile Selassie and Ras Imiru cooled down after the 1960 coup d'état, when conspirators appointed Imiru prime minister. Moreover, while Ras Imiru advocated administrative and land reforms in peasants' favor, Haile Selassie did not want that to happen, as he was afraid to lose support of landowners, his political base.

10. Harold G. Marcus. 1987. P. 3; Greenfield R. Ethiopia. *A New Political History*. L., 1965. P. 48 (hereinafter—Greenfield R. 1965).

11. Haile Selassie I. *My Life and Ethiopia's Progress (Amharic)*. Volume One. England Bath 1929 E.C. P. 4 (hereinafter—Haile Selassie I. 1929).

12. Mosley L. *Haile Selassie. The Conquering Lion*. L., 1964. P. 40 (hereinafter—Mosley L. 1964). Schwab P. 1972. P. 24.

13. Autobiography (English). P. 19.

14. Cit. in: Harold G. Marcus. 1987. P. 3–4.

15. Autobiography (English). P. 15.

16. Levine D. *Wax and Gold*. Chicago: University of Chicago Press, 1966. P. 156–157 (hereinafter—Levine D. 1966), Schwab P. 1972. P. 26.

17. This is probably where his famous saying comes from: "The country is our common concern; religion is a private matter."

18. At the time, a province governor simultaneously performed functions of a military leader and of all ministers (of the interior, of foreign affairs, of justice, etc.). Furthermore, he was able to confer titles and appoint lower-ranking governors of his own choice.

19. Autobiography (English). P. 21.

20. Harold G. Marcus. 1987. P. 6.

21. Ibid. P. 7.

22. Agreement between the United Kingdom, France, and Italy, Respecting Abyssinia, signed at London, December IS, 1906. https://gspi.unipr.it/sites/st26/files/allegatiparagrafo/17-02-2015/agreement_on_ethiopia_1906.pdf

23. Voblikov D.R. *Ethiopia in the Struggle for Maintaining Independence (1860-1960)*. Moscow, 1961. P. 35–36 (in Russian) (hereinafter—Voblikov D.R. 1961).

24. Kuzmin Yu. M. Anglo-Franco-Italian Agreement 1906 on the division of Ethiopia into spheres of influence. Kuibyshev, 1982; Kuzmin Yu M. Treaty on the establishment of spheres of influence in Ethiopia between Britain, France, and Italy dated December 13, 1906 International relations in XX Century. Kirov. 2009. P.28 (in Russian).

25. Bartnicki A., Mantel-Niecko J. *History of Ethiopia*. Moscow, 1976. P. 391 (in Russian, transl. from Polish) (hereinafter—History of Ethiopia. 1976).

26. Harold G. Marcus. *The Life and Times of Menelik II. Ethiopia 1844–1913.* Oxford, 1975. P. 212–213 (hereinafter—Harold G. Marcus. 1975).

27. Jones A.H.M., Monroe E. *History of Abyssinia*. Oxford, 1935. P. 153 (hereinafter—History of Abyssinia. 1935).

28. See details in Bairu Tafla. *Ethiopia and Germany: Cultural, Political and Economic Relations. 1871–1936.* Wiesbaden: Steiner, 1981. P. 111 (hereinafter—Bairu Tafla. 1981).

29. Harold G. Marcus. 1987. P. 7.

30. The life of young man from a noble family at the court of Emperor Menelik was not dissimilar to the life of a squire (lord of the manor) in medieval England, who was sent to the court of Edward I to complete education. That way, a young man not only met statesmen but was able to get acquainted with the art of politics and with political intrigue. See: Sandford Ch. 1946. P. 27.

31. Harold G. Marcus. 1987. P. 7.

32. See details in: Mosley L. 1964. P. 44–46.

33. Harold G. Marcus. 1975. P. 227–228.

34. Dejazmach Balcha 1863–1936; one of Menelik's commanders.

35. Autobiography (English). P. 28–29.

36. Ibid. P. 28.

37. Ibid. P. 29.

38. History of Ethiopia. 1976. P. 414.

39. Ibid P. 29; Haile Selassie I. 1929. P. 14.

40. History of Ethiopia. 1976. P. 417.

41. Autobiography (English). P. 29–30; Haile Selassie I. 1929. P. 14.

42. Jones A.H.M., Monroe E. History of Abyssinia. Oxford, 1935. P. 153 (hereinafter—History of Abyssinia. 1935); History of Ethiopia 1976. P. 418.

43. Autobiography (English). P. 29.

44. Mosley L. 1964. P. 52.

45. Autobiography (English). P. 31.

46. Ras Tesemma, an outstanding general and political figure, was a leader of the Shewan faction. He covered himself with glory when he had led an expedition in 1888 that reached the White Nile. Tesemma had a wide political outlook. He was vividly interested in policies of European powers, had no trouble establishing contacts

with the Europeans, and was an ardent proponent of the use of European technological achievements that he wanted to see adopted in Ethiopia.

47. Mosley L. 1964. P. 61.

48. History of Ethiopia. 1976. P. 421.

49. Mosley L. 1964. P. 61.

50. Autobiography. Amharic. P. 14.

51. The two years between 1909 and 1911 in Ethiopia seemed, to foreign observers, to bring that country to the nadir of chaos and corruption, but that was because they could envisage what was going to happen in the years to come. Mosley L. 1964. P. 56.

52. Autobiography (English). P. 34; Haile Selassie I. 1929. P. 16–19.

53. History of Ethiopia. 1976. P. 423.

54. Autobiography (English). P. 35. Autobiography (Amharic). P. 19.

55. Harold G. Marcus. 1975. P. 12.

56. Haile Selassie I. 1929. P. 21.

57. Ibid.

58. Autobiography (English). P. 41.

59. Ibid.

60. Harold G. Marcus. 1987. P. 13.

61. History of Ethiopia 1976. P. 425; Mosley L. 1964. P. 75.

62. Haile Selassie I. 1929. P. 30–31.

63. History of Ethiopia. 1976. P. 428

64. Harold G. Marcus. 1975. P. 270.

65. Bairu Tafla.1981. P. 131

66. Autobiography (English). P. 48–49

67. Harold G. Marcus. 1987. P. 15.

68. Ibid. P. 15.

69. Mosley L. 1964. P. 83.

70. Harold G. Marcus.1987. P. 17.

71. Sayyid Muhammad `Abd Allah al-Hasan—the "Mad Mullah," as he was styled by the British, was a Somali religious and patriotic leader.

72. Mosley L. 1964. P. 88.

73. Ibid.

74. Haile Selassie I. 1929. P. 30.

75. Ibid. P. 32–33.

76. History of Ethiopia. 1976. P. 433.

77. When she was only six, Zewditu was married to Araya Selassie, the son of Emperor Yohannes IV; however, that marriage was purely political. Zewditu's second husband was Gugsa Welle (1875–1930), an Ethiopian official. The empress had a few children by him; however, none of them survived to adulthood. Before ascending to power in 1916, she had lived in exile.

78. See: History of Ethiopia. 1976; Tsypkin G.V. *Ethiopia in Anticolonial Wars.* Moscow, 1988 (in Russian); Harold G. Marcus. 1987; Greenfield R. *Ethiopia. A New Political History.* L., 1965.

79. Haile Selassie I. 1929. P. 43–44.

80. Rey C. F. *Unconquered Abyssinia*. L., 1924. P. 130.

81. Greenfield R. 1965. P. 152.

82. Rey C.F. *The Real Abyssinia*. L., 1935. P. 118.

83. Mosley L. 1964. P. 114.

84. Ibid. P. 112.

85. Ibid. P. 115.

86. Ibid. P. 125.

87. Ibid. P. 126.

88. Article 13. Cit. in: Klyuchnikov Yu V., Sabanin A.V. *International Contemporary History in Treaties, Notes and Declarations. Part II*. Moscow, 1926. P. 29 (in Russian) (hereinafter—Klyuchnikov Yu V., Sabinin A.V. Part II. 1926).

89. See: Klyuchnikov Yu V., Sabanin A.V. *International Contemporary History in Treaties, Notes and Declarations. Part III*. Moscow, 1929. No. II. P. 292–293 (in Russian) (hereinafter—Klyuchnikov Yu V., Sabinin A.V. Part III. 1929).

90. Yagiya V.S. 1978. P. 39.

91. Tsypkin G.V., Yagiya V.S. *History of Ethiopia in the Early Modern and Modern Periods*. Moscow, 1989. P. 161 (hereinafter—History of Ethiopia. 1989) (in Russian).

92. Slavery was a traditional social institution in Ethiopia at the time. By holding slaves, landowners established their standing in society and their grandeur. In most cases, slaves were used as domestic labor and agricultural workers. It should be noted that slaves in Ethiopia were better off than in European dominions.

93. Haile Selassie I. 1929. P. 39–40.

94. See: History of Ethiopia. 1989.

95. Harold G. Marcus. 1987. P. 49.

96. Ibid. P. 50.

97. Trofimov V.A. *Italian Colonialism and Neocolonialism*. Moscow, 1979. P. 92 (in Russian) (hereinafter—Trofimov V.A. 1979).

98. Prof. G.C. Baravelli of the Rome University. *The Last Stronghold of Slavery. What Abyssinia Is*. Societa Edtrice Di Novisima. Roma 1935. P. 9.

99. Cit. in: Yagiya V.S. 1978. P. 57.

100. Harold G. Marcus 1987. P. 52.

101. Autobiography (English). P. 77.

102. Harold G. Marcus 1987. P. 57.

103. Haile Selassie I. 1929. P. 62.

104. Ibid. P. 59; Autobiography English. P. 81.

105. Ibid.

106. Harold G. Marcus. 1987. P. 60.

107. Ibid.

108. Haile Selassie I. 1929. P. 63.

109. Voblikov D.R. 1961. P. 42.

110. Pankhurst R. *Economic History of Ethiopia 1900–1935*. A.A., 1967. P. 271 (hereinafter—Pankhurst R. 1967).

111. Report on the visit of the Ethiopian delegation to Europe see: Autobiography (Amharic). P. 61–100.

112. Harold G. Marcus. 1987. P. 66.

113. Yagiya V.S. 1978. P. 59.

114. Tsypkin G.V. *Ethiopia in Anticolonial Wars*. M. 1988. P. 210 (in Russian) (hereinafter—Tsypkin G.V 1988).

115. Pankhurst R. Misoneism and innovation in Ethiopian history. *Ethiopian Observer*. 1964. Vol. VII. No. 4.

116. История Эфиопии. 1976. C. 443.

117. Harold G. Marcus. 1987. P. 71.

118. Ibid.

119. Ibid. P. 72.

120. Emperor Haile Selassie I. Fere Kenafer (In Amharic). Addis Ababa, 1944 (Ethiopian calendar); hereinafter—E.C.). P. 9–10 (hereinafter—Haile Selassie. 1944).

121. See: Harold G. Marcus. 1987. P. 73.

122. League of Nations. Official journal. November 1926. P. 1521–1522 (hereinafter—LNOJ); Mosley L. 1964. P. 135.

123. Haile Selassie I. 1929. P. 102.; See also: Klyuchnikov Yu.V., Sabinin A.V. Part II. 1929. P. 292–293.

124. Haile Selassie I. 1929. P. 109.

125. LNOJ. November 1926. P. 1516; Mosley L. 1964. P. 136.

126. Ras Tafari's letters sent to the League of Nations. See: Autobiography (Amharic). P. 110–117.

127. Voblikov D.R. 1961. P. 46–47.

128. Trofimov V.A. Italy's Aggression in Ethiopia and Its Consequences (in Russian). *Voprosy Instorii* (in Russian). 1976. No. 8. P. 65.

129. Cit. by: Harold G. Marcus. 1987. P. 75.

130. Full texts of Tafaris letters. Autobiography (English). P. 134–137.

131. Ras Tafari's letters sent to the League of Nations. See: Autobiography (Amharic). P. 110–117. Eng.

132. Baer G.W. 1967. P. 18.

133. Voblikov D.R. 1961. P. 51.

134. Dr. Martin (Warqnah Ishete) (October 21, 1864–October 9, 1952) was the first Ethiopian doctor to receive a diploma. He enrolled into a medical college in Lahore (British India) in 1877. After graduating from college in 1882, he worked as assistant surgeon for two years as Charles Martin, and then went to Scotland where he continued specialized education and received certificates in medicine and surgery. When he completed education in December 1891, he was appointed as doctor and surgeon to Burma. After getting back home, he was in diplomatic service. In particular, he was head of the first Ethiopian diplomatic mission to the United States in 1927; they were holding talks on the construction of a dam on the upper reaches of the River Abbay (Blue Nile). In 1934, he was appointed Ethiopia's ambassador to the United Kingdom.

135. Foreign Relations of the U.S. 1927. Vol. II. Wash., 1942. P. 600 (hereinafter—FRUS).

136. FRUS. 1927. Vol. II. P. 586.

137. FRUS. 1927. Vol. II. P. 584–587

138. FRUS. 1927. Vol. II. P. 587–595.

139. "New York Times," 13 IV 1930 cit. by Voblikov D. R. 1961. P. 52.

140. Voblikov D. R. 1961 P. 52; FRUS. 1927. P. 601.

141. "Manchester Guardian," 8 11 1927 cit. Voblikov D.R. 1961. P. 52.

142. Cit. in: Voblikov D.R. 1961. P. 52–53.

143. FRUS. 1928. Vol. II. P. 787, 789, 790, 793.

144. Ibid. P. 786–797.

145. Ibid. P. 799–802.

146. See: FRUS. 1930. Vol. II. P. 765.

147. Yagiya V.S. 1978. P. 65.

148. Documents of International Affairs. Edited by John Wheeler-Bennett and Stephen Heald. L., 1928. P. 241–242 (hereinafter—DIA 1928).

149. Haile Selassie I. 1929. P. 119–123. Autobiography (English). P. 148–149.

150. Yagiya V.S. 1978. P. 67.

151. Ibid.

Chapter 2

On the Eve of the Invasion

A REFORMER ON THE THRONE

On April 3, 1930, after Empress Zewditu's sudden death, *Negus* Tafari was proclaimed Emperor of Ethiopia under the name Haile Selassie I. A solemn coronation ceremony was deferred to November, so that the forthcoming event could be used to strengthen the new emperor's ties both with Ethiopian nobility and with foreign powers.

In order to make the coronation ceremony nationwide, invitations were sent out throughout Ethiopia to princes and nobles, as well as to all elders, abbots of monasteries, and deans of cathedrals. A letter of invitation was also written to Abbe Amda Maryam, abbot of Dabra Bizan, who remained well known and respected for his importance since ancient times, when the kings of Ethiopia consecrated it as a monastery, although today it is within the boundaries of an Italian colony (from Eritrea).[1] The "little" monarch also counted on attention on the part of dignitaries in whose friendship Ethiopia was vitally interested and whose presence at the ceremony was agreed by the court of Haile Selassie I through diplomatic channels.

The following persons were meant:

His Majesty George V, King of the United Kingdom and Emperor of India;
His Majesty Victor Emmanuel III, King of Italy;
His Majesty Hirohito, Emperor of Japan;
His Majesty Albert II, Emperor of Belgium;
His Majesty Gustav V, King of Sweden;
Her Majesty Wilhelmina, Queen of the Netherlands;
His Majesty Fuad I, King of Egypt;
Gaston Doumergue, President of France;
Herbert Hoover, President of the U.S.;

53

Paul Ludwig von Hindenburg, President of Germany;
Pavlos Kountouriotis, President of Greece;
Ignacy Mościcki, President of Poland.[2]

Regretfully, their places at the coronation ceremony were occupied by
individuals with a more modest stature: ambassadors, envoys plenipotentiary, ministers, and consuls. Arrogant and smug rulers did not deign to show
friendly concern about the fate of the young African emperor. His motives for
hospitality were sincere and clear-cut: He was seeking to reinforce his authority and to bring about Ethiopia's rapprochement with Europe, the United
States, and Japan. A lavish coronation showed that Haile Selassie's accession
to the throne was a remarkable event not only for the country but for entire
Africa. "Undoubtedly the coronation—even more than her admission to the
League of Nations seven years earlier—put Ethiopia on the map,"[3] wrote
British historian A. J. Barker.

The new monarch was striving to demonstrate to the populace and,
above all, to his rivals that the government that had established itself in
Ethiopia was enjoying considerable influence and had won international
recognition.

A question arises: Why was not a representative of the Soviet Union
invited to the solemn coronation of the Ethiopian emperor, even though Russia had always kept friendly relations with Ethiopia? The reason was absence
of diplomatic relations between the two countries. After the victory of the
October Socialist Revolution in Russia and foundation of the USSR, Ethiopia severed diplomatic relations with the Soviet Union. The toppling of the
autocratic rule in Russia, was, of course, met with hostile attitude. Therefore,
when the news about Nicholas II's execution on July 16–17, 1918 reached
Ethiopia, a special church service was arranged at the St. George Cathedral
in Addis Ababa, in the presence of the patriarch of the Ethiopian Orthodox
Church and Western diplomats.

One should not forget about incomplete information that Ethiopia had
about the events taking place in faraway Russia. G. V. Tsypkin comments:
"For the Ethiopians, information about events in Russia was brought by
White emigrants who had found a second homeland in the faraway country
of 'black fellow believers.' One can easily imagine their interpretation of
revolutionary developments in Russia. Moreover, could the Great October
Socialist Revolution be met with understanding in a country where church
was a dominating force in the nation's life? The very fact that an entire nation
would renounce religion was perceived by Ethiopian traditional society as
the workings of the Antichrist."[4] In addition, one should not forget about the
cautious attitude of the world's leading powers to Addis Ababa. If Ethiopia
had shown sympathies for the Russian revolution, it would have put on guard

the proponents of a blockade against the USSR who were already willing to deprive Ethiopia of its sovereignty.

Thus, the coronation occurred on November 4, 1930, and *Negus* Tafari became Ethiopia's emperor Haile Selassie I. At the festivities on occasion of the coronation, representatives of Great Britain, France, Italy, the United States, Japan, Belgium, Poland, Sweden, Holland, Egypt, Greece, and Turkey were present. On the same day, following the tradition of imperial succession, Haile Selassie I proclaimed his elder son, Asfaw Wossen, as the crown prince and the country's future leader.[5]

As soon as he became emperor, Haile Selassie I began to carry out domestic reforms that had been planned back when he was still regent. The reforming activities were focused on the adoption of Western institutions and technology in Ethiopia. During a conversation with French writer Henry de Monfreid, the monarch said: "I believe that certain Western institutions, provided they are assimilated by my people, can make us stronger, strong enough to follow unaided the path of progress. But these new ideas cannot assimilated at once. You must remember that Ethiopia is like a sleeping beauty that time has stood still here for 2000 years. We must take great care therefore, not to overwhelm her with changes now that she is beginning to wake. . . . We must strive to steer a middle course between the impatience of Western reformers and the inertia of Ethiopians who would close their eyes if the light were to strong."[6]

Russian scholar V. S. Yagiya describes the reforms carried out by the emperor as halfway and limited.[7] But could Haile Selassie I really go any other pathway? We believe the emperor of Ethiopia who lacked sufficient human and material resources still opted for the right way in the end, and it was a courageous move. The following transformations resulted from his policies: The country saw emergence of a well-educated elite (by 1936, there were about 200 people whose education abroad had been sponsored by the emperor); the country's first-ever NGOs were set up, such as the Ethiopian Women's Welfare Work Association, the Ethiopian National Patriotic Association, a boy-scout organization, the Red Cross Society, the Ethiopian Youth organization; the national bank was founded; schools were opened (on the eve of the Italian aggression, there were 30 state high and junior schools).[8] It is just an incomplete list of the achievements resulting from the changes initiated by the emperor.

Another effect of the reforms was development of the Amharic language and its use as the country's official, or state, language. After Emperor Haile Selassie I came to power, the Shewan dialect of the Amharic language became the literary language and was to be mandatorily studied at schools.

Ethiopia's current authorities believe and state that the Amharic language belongs to the Amhara people, an ethnic group whose power was expanded through violent means. Furthermore, they think that, alongside the advancement of that language, the country was seeing "*Amharization*." This is far from the truth. First, expeditions that were undertaken with a view to annex eastern, southeastern, southern and western lands were not led by the Amhara, contrary to widespread belief, but by the Shewans (Oromo, Amhara, Gurage, and other ethnic groups). Second, there were attempts to establish the Shewan order in those areas (such was the exigence of the time). Therefore, not only from the political and economic standpoint, but also from the standpoint of cultural relations, it was not *Amharization* that was taking place in the country, but, rather, "*Shewanization*." Finally, the Amharic language evolved into a language of interethnic communications not because the Amhara were conquerors or because it was the emperor's whim (he belonged to Ethiopia's two large ethnic groups—Amhara and Oromo), but because that written language was widely spread in the biggest provinces—Shewa, Wollo, Gojjam, and Gonder.

Speaking about Emperor Haile Selassie I's activities as a reformer, we must mention his most remarkable achievements in the political and administrative fields. On July 16, 1931, for the first time in Ethiopia's history that spans over three millennia, a constitution was adopted, which introduced changes in the country's form of government. Ethiopia (albeit formally) was proclaimed a parliamentary monarchy, with the supreme legislative, executive, and judicial power in the country vested with the emperor. One of the purposes of the constitution, J. Markakias noted, was to use it to centralize state power and to oppose those who belonged to hereditary nobility. It was for that reason that the aristocracy was opposing adoption of the constitution.[9]

To garner support of the nobility and the clergy, Haile Selassie convened in Addis Ababa a conference of all major feudal lords, military commanders, and ecclesiastical dignitaries in order to explain to them the ultimate goal for the adoption of the constitution. After that, the most influential and powerful VIPs of the Empire put their signatures under it. Among them were *Ras* Kassa Hailu (Shewa), *Ras* Hailu Tekle Haymanot (Gojjam), *Ras* Gugsa Araya (Tigray), *Ras* Mengesha Seyoum (Tigray), and others. They were joined by church luminaries: *Abuna* Qerellos, *Abuna* Yeshaq, *Abuna* Sawiros, and *Abuna* Petros.[10] The same way, Haile Selassie I managed to see the constitution recognized in the provinces and in the regions that were under a strong influence of the traditional aristocracy and clergy; he was removing all the obstacles that could prevent implementation of the new laws.

But can the 1931 Constitution be considered as a code of laws that protected the rights and interests of citizens, considering that the people did not express its will, that is, took no part in its discussion?

To answer this question, we need to quote *Bejirond* Tekle Hawariat, the primary author of the constitution: "At that time we wanted the people to adopt the laws that should have been promulgated, and these laws could be adopted only if they were discussed and adopted, first of all, by the nobility. Thus, we introduced to the parliament persons who had significant influence in the province and 'distributed' . . . them to the chambers in accordance with the degree of influence and importance in the eyes of the public. We wanted to talk to the people through these people."[11]

If one is guided by the reasons of practicability, there was certainly no need to involve the general public, with political culture and political awareness at a low level. But the constitution, as it was said above, became a means of strengthening political unity of the state and of neutralizing feudal nobility. The principal law helped the emperor's local representatives carry out the government's policy and establish absolute monarchy in Ethiopia.

The 1931 Constitution included 55 articles.[12] Articles 1 and 2 reaffirmed the unity of "all the natives of Ethiopia, subjects of the empire, [who] form together the Ethiopian Empire," and assured "the union of the territory." These provisions were aimed against all sorts of separatist trends. Article 3 said that "the imperial dignity shall remain perpetually attached to the line of His Majesty Haile Selassie I, descendant of King Sahle Selassie, whose line descends without interruption from the dynasty of Menelik I, son of King Solomon of Jerusalem, and the Queen of Ethiopia, known as the Queen of Sheba." Article 5 said, "By virtue of his imperial blood, as well as by the anointing which he has received, the person of the Emperor is sacred, his dignity is inviolable and his power indisputable. He is consequently entitled to all the honors due to him in accordance with tradition and the present Constitution. The law decrees that anyone so bold as to seek to injure His Majesty the Emperor will be punished."

One important provision of the Constitution stipulated institution of a parliament. It consisted of two chambers: the senate and the chamber of deputies. The senate included major feudal lords who distinguished themselves in imperial service, ministers, judges, and representatives of top brass. The emperor himself appointed members of the senate. Local tribal chieftains and representatives of the *Mekuanents* (the new nobility—young Ethiopians), also appointed by the emperor, sat in the chamber of deputies. The parliament did not have the right to pass any resolutions contrary to the emperor's will. According to the Constitution, a Council of Ministers was formed, which was nominated by the emperor and reported only to him. The ministers only had a consultative capacity. The legislative and executive powers were entirely concentrated in the emperor's hands. The Constitution also regulated matters of judicial procedure, civil rights, and state budget. One of the most vital articles said that none of the emperor's subjects "may be arrested, sentenced, or imprisoned except in pursuance of the law" (Article 23). The emperor was declared to be holding the country's supreme judicial power. He could grant pardons to criminals, commute penalties or reinstate (Article 16), and amend the structure of judicial procedure and of the judicature.

Adoption of the Constitution reinforced the emperor's power in a major way. The authority of Haile Selassie I and his dynasty was considered indisputable, and now it was enshrined in a legal act, which was binding upon the entire nation. Moreover, the Constitution had a role in legalizing centralization of public authority, thus strengthening the political form of government. Concentration of power in the emperor's hands was in line with the interests of the Ethiopian State at the time, which necessitated establishment of a strong central power in opposition to separatism of feudal lords. Was it even possible to entertain the thought of promoting the power of the state without a strong central power? It should be emphasized that the 1931 Constitution gave Haile Selassie I power of an extent that no Ethiopian emperor had had before him.

Alongside the Constitution, a secular criminal code was adopted in 1932. That way, Haile Selassie's government officially abandoned the former rule that stated: A criminal is to be punished according to the damage visible to the eye. A great deal of attention was paid to the establishment of a regular army. Belgian officers trained Ethiopian soldiers, and Swiss instructors were largely focused on drilling the emperor's personal troops. To train the national officer corps, the country's first military college was opened in Genett near Addis Ababa in 1935; it was called the Genett Military School. Five Swedish officers were instructors there.[13] In order to ensure control over arms and ammunition supplies and to centralize them, Ethiopia's government entered into an agreement with Britain, France, and Italy in 1930. Those countries undertook to authorize exports of military equipment and munitions through official channels only. If they should have found the political situation in the empire unstable, they had the right to deny shipments and transit of arms through their dominions.

However, the agreement on which reinforcement of the Ethiopian army and of the country's unity depended so much was not always strictly followed. For instance, the Italians, in contravention of the obligations they had undertaken, often supplied arms to individual feudal lords who were seeking to liberate themselves from the ubiquitous control of the center. France and Britain prevented full supply of the Ethiopian army with required arms and munitions. It was one of the reasons for Ethiopia's poor preparedness for repulsing the Italian invasion in 1935.

Furthermore, the treasury lacked funds to pay for arms supplies. The government increased the amount of the customs duties it was collecting, after it had sold the monopoly on salt imports, production and domestic trade to the French, and introduced various taxes. For instance, in February 1934, a regulation was adopted according to which every person aged 18 or more, who was capable to work, was to pay 1 Ethiopian dollar or 1 Maria Theresa thaler to the treasury, with the exception of those who were employed and were paid in money—they were to pay 20% of their annual income. Even foreigners who worked in Ethiopia were to pay those taxes. As a result of the reform, in a matter of one year, according to incomplete data, the treasury received 2.4 million Ethiopian dollars.[14]

In order to boost tax revenue incoming to the central treasury, the government passed a resolution on land survey, on abolishment of many charges and duties from peasants and, finally, on the establishment, alongside the dime, of a single land tax for the entire country, in the amount of 30 Ethiopian dollars per one *gasha*.[15]

It goes without saying that the national bank and the national currency play a huge role in accelerating economic development and in the improvement of the financial situation in any country. On August 29, 1931, the Bank of Abyssinia was officially liquidated (the Ethiopian side paid a compensation to the National Bank of Egypt), and the Bank of Ethiopia was set up; 60% of its capital belonged to the state. On May 1, 1932, the Bank of Ethiopia issued a new currency into circulation—the Ethiopian dollar. However, the novelty did not bring about the desired result. "The new notes were mainly used by merchants and traders . . . on the eve of war they circulate only in Addis Ababa, Gonder and Harar,"[16] wrote British scholar R. Pankhurst. G. V. Tsypkin and V. S. Yagiya write that the Italian aggression prevented circulation of the Ethiopian currency.[17]

Walking the path of reform, the government continued the policy of complete annihilation of slavery. On July 15, 1931, an additional law was passed, according to which slaves were to be liberated immediately after the death of their owner.[18] In 1932, a special anti-slavery directorate was opened in Addis Ababa, and it had offices across the country. However, slavery de facto existed until the Italian aggression of 1936. Assessing the problem of the abolishment of slavery, Haile Selassie believed it would be eliminated in 15 or 20 years. According to him, over 250,000 people became free between 1924 and 1935.[19]

The emperor was aware of the difficulties faced by the government which was trying to abolish slavery: lack of funds and opposition of conservators, as well as lack of local human resources in the provinces.

After Emperor Haile Selassie's coronation, the Ethiopia's educational system began to take shape. At that time, the Ministry of Education and Fine Arts was established. "The Emperor give orders that solders should learn to read and write and that priests should instruct the youth. Ernest Work, an American advisor at Ethiopia's Education Ministry, draw up a plan. It included six years of primary, six years of secondary and four years of university education, as well as special attention to teacher training and agriculture. The lack of the proper number of teachers was the main reason for the failure of the program development school and university education system proposed by the emperor in the country."[20] Despite the difficulties, general and professional education establishments were set up within a short period of time, and they were not concentrated in the capital city alone but were located in other cities as well. Alongside expansion of secular education, training at missionary schools was also on the rise. Clergymen of the Ethiopian church undertook to teach their parishioners how to read and write.

The measures undertaken by the government in order to develop transportation, to build roads, radio stations, telegraph, and phone lines promoted political and territorial consolidation of the empire. The sources show that the emperor was proud of his achievements. When Haile Selassie was asked in 1936 about the country's achievements during his reign so far, he noted, above all "construction of schools, hospitals, roads, the financial reforms, the buyout of the Bank of Abyssinia and establishment of a state bank, fight against slavery and building schools for liberated slaves."[21]

In terms of Ethiopia's socioeconomic and political standing, the reforms brought about shifts toward centralization of public authority, on the one hand, and consolidation of the class domination of feudal lords, on the other.

In the 1930s, as before, a very influential and powerful opposition represented by the traditional nobility was standing in the way of reforms. During those years, not only persons who were interested in strengthening regionalism but also those who did not want to see Haile Selassie on the throne were opposing central authorities.

To the largest extent, regionalism was prevalent among residents of the country's northern regions, especially of the province of Tigray. To weaken the authority of traditional rulers in that province, the emperor divided it into two parts, putting descendants of Emperor Yohannes IV, *Ras* Mengesha Seyoum and *Ras* Gugsa Araya, at the top in them. Dynastic marriages were a frequent occurrence. For instance, Haile Selassie arranged the marriage of Crown Prince Asfaw Wossen with the daughter of *Ras* Seyoum, and he married his daughter Zenebework to *Dejazmach* Haile Selassie Gugsa (the son of *Ras* Gugsa).[22]

Among the persons who did not want to see Haile Selassie on the throne was *Ras* Hailu Tekle Haymanot, the ruler of Gojjam. In 1932, after an attempt to reinstall *Lij* Iyasu on the throne (he was under arrest at the town of Fitche), the *ras* was condemned to death. But the emperor commuted the sentence of death and arranged that he should stay, with his property confiscated, in confinement at a specified place. In the opinion of Haile Selassie I, the Italians were involved in *Ras* Hailu's conspiracy. He wrote: "In 1909 (=1916), when *Lij* Iyasu was deposed, the Italians had manifested their opposition to him. . . . But now they pretended to be friendly towards him and aided his escape from Fitche (a town to the north of Addis Ababa.—*Author's note*); this proves that they were devising plans to take Ethiopia by provoking us to fight each other, while they themselves would not have a single soldier killed in battle."[23]

In 1933, the ruler of the Kingdom of Jimma was arrested for slave trade and ties with the Italians, and the autonomy, albeit limited, of the kingdom was finished. *Ras* Desta Damtew, a Shewan by birth and the future husband of Tenagnework, the emperor's elder daughter, became the new governor; he was killed by Fascist aggressors during the years of resistance.

By 1935, Haile Selassie had appointed governors in some other provinces across the country. Representatives of the central government, vested with a wide scope of powers, were dispatched to some regions as assistants to local authorities. As many noble and influential feudal lords were removed from power or saw their power limited through full or partial confiscation of their property, a tougher control was established in some regions and a number of reforms were carried out. Ethiopia was moving toward political centralization. First steps toward absolutism were made.

Even the Italians noted those developments as they were unfolding active preparations for the invasion into Ethiopia in the early 1930s. Back in 1932, Raffaele Guariglia, a high-ranking official at Italy's Ministry of Foreign Affairs, said, "Ethiopia was no longer a weak, decentralized state, but rather, under Haile Selassie, an armed and unified nation . . . it represents a new and potent danger to Italy's east African possessions. To counter this threat Italy must take a strong military and political stand on the Ethiopian frontier."[24] This statement gives evidence that Ethiopia had accomplished renovations in a matter of a few years. In addition to the reforms completed in the 1930s, the threat of a Fascist aggression also consolidated the population, boosted patriotism and nationalism.

The promulgation of the Constitution, no doubt, reinforced the country's stature on the international stage. The Ethiopian leaders could now say with good reason that Ethiopia was a modern state keeping a certain domestic order. It was what Tekle Hawariat, one of the authors of the Constitution, meant, when he noted the following: "We had particular interest in letting foreign governments know that we had a constitution and that the government of Ethiopia is constitutional. This was mainly done to answer our accusers of arbitrariness, existence of feudalism, undefined rulers, and all in all chaotic rule. In this we had been successful, and we had a good ground to fight against the Italian accusations in the League of Nations."[25]

Haile Selassie successfully pursued external ties. Between 1930 and 1935, as he was overcoming political isolation created by Great Britain, France and Italy, the Ethiopian monarch was stepping up the search for new partners on the international stage. Japan became such a partner. The role of Japan and of the United States, as a guarantor of Ethiopia's independence, was insignificant. However, those countries managed to enlarge mutual contacts with Ethiopia. Japan did that, above all, through trade. As a result, the Land of the Rising Sun was able to put considerable competitive pressure on West European and American products in Ethiopia's market. In 1932–1934, Japanese goods accounted for 60% of Ethiopian imports. In the second half of 1934, Japan imported 8.6 million francs worth of goods into Ethiopia, and the imports of six other countries, put together, Great Britain, France, Germany, Italy, the United States and Egypt, amounted to just 6 million francs.[26]

Ethiopian-Japanese relations became especially strong after a visit to Japan in 1932 of *Blattengeta* Heruy Wolde Selassie, Ethiopia's Foreign Minister. At the time, Tokyo ratified the Treaty of Friendship signed by the two countries in 1930. In 1934, a Japanese-Ethiopian treaty was concluded in Tokyo, which allowed emigration of the Japanese to Ethiopia to work at cotton plantations. Penetration of Japanese goods, which was accompanied by the substitution of the products originating from the United States and West European countries, was taking place amid a global economic crisis, so it inevitably worried ruling circles of European countries, especially Italy. The newspaper *Il Popolo* wrote on February 13, 1935 that "Japanese policy in Ethiopia poses an extraordinary threat for Europe" and that "European countries need to understand the necessity of preventing the onslaught of Japanese imperialism as soon as possible."[27]

The British press also expressed concern about the Japanese rapid encroaches in Ethiopia. "Giving to Japan concessions creates a danger for Great Britain, France and Italy. Instead of quarreling between themselves, they should seek out common interests and avoid weakening their position at the expense of each other,"[28] wrote the newspaper *The Morning Post.*

The Europeans, perceiving a formidable rival in Japan, did their best to hinder bilateral contacts of Tokyo and Addis Ababa. Even the plans for the marriage of a nephew of Emperor Haile Selassie I and a Japanese princess were disrupted.[29] Massive pressure on Japan by European powers drove it to offer support to Italian fascism. The move reflected the similarity of the socio-political nature of power in Italy and Japan at the time.

In the first half of the 1930s, a positive political line toward the Soviet Union appeared to take shape in Ethiopia. Despite obstacles from the imperialist powers of the West, on October 24, 1931, the two countries managed to conclude a trade agreement. In addition, Soyuzneftexport signed an agreement in Djibouti for the supply of petroleum products to Ethiopia through the National Society of Trade and Industry.[30]

In December 1934, that society contacted the USSR People's Commissariat for Foreign Trade and proposed working out joint measures to boost trade relations. On January 4, 1935, Heruy Wolde Selassie, Ethiopia's Minister of Foreign Affairs, holding talks with Maksim Litvinov, the USSR People's Commissar of Foreign Affairs, asked him to accelerate a reply to this inquiry of the country's business circles and to enter into contacts in order to restore normal diplomatic relations with the Soviet Union. In his reply of February 16, 1935, Litvinov said, notably, that the Soviet government also wished to establish normal relations with Ethiopia, which could be most conveniently done if the proposal made by the Ethiopian side could be formalized by diplomatic representatives of the USSR and Ethiopia in Paris, and that the Soviet ambassador had been given relevant instructions.[31]

Despite mutually beneficial trade deals and the resumed dialogue of the two countries, they failed to restore diplomatic relations that had been severed in 1920. The war with Italy was at fault.[32]

Diplomatic activity of Haile Selassie I was crowned by the signing, on December 26, 1934 in Paris, of the Polish-Ethiopian Treaty of Friendship, Commerce, and Settlement. The treaty was signed by *Bejirond* Tekle Hawariat, Ethiopia's ambassador to France (he would later become the country's envoy to the League of Nations), and by Alfred Chłapowski, the Polish ambassador to Paris.

The treaty consisted of four articles, which emphasized that friendly and peaceful relations would be kept between the two countries and that both parties intended to exchange diplomatic and trade missions. The principle of the most-favored nation treatment was guaranteed in trade, customs, and emigration policy. However, as the Italo-Ethiopian relations were aggravating, the act did not take effect but remained a mere statement of intent.

At the same time, Ethiopia enlarged trade and friendly relations with Czechoslovakia, Greece, Switzerland, Sweden, and other nations. Addis Ababa took advantage of any international pretext to reinforce its political positions worldwide. Crown Prince Asfa Wossen also began to be involved in diplomatic activity. After the coronation, he went on return visits to the European capitals from where representatives had come to the ceremony. A year later, the heir to the Swedish throne was received in the Ethiopian capital city, and that visit promoted Ethiopian-Swedish ties, especially in trade; advice of specialists dispatched by the Scandinavian power for government service in Ethiopia was equally important.[33]

Faced with the imminent Italian threat, Ethiopian diplomacy was successful in looking for and finding ways of putting an end to the country's international isolation. The emperor of Ethiopia initiated some major foreign policy steps. After the monarch-cum-reformer came to power, countries that had closed down their missions, for instance, the United States, restored diplomatic relations with Ethiopia, as did European nations and Japan.

The Ethiopian government did not give up attempts to acquire a gateway to the sea. With that purpose, in 1931, the Ethiopian leadership offered to Italy a portion of lands in Ogaden (a southeastern area of the empire) in exchange for territories in one of the neighboring Italian dominions. In 1934, the same proposal was made to Great Britain. For a small enclave in British Somaliland with the port of Zeila, the British would have received vast lands in Ethiopia, which were adjacent to that colony. However, both Rome and London turned down the proposals. That inflexibility produced a very pernicious effect on the hostilities waged in 1935–1936.

As it had no military industry of its own, Ethiopia had to purchase weapons abroad. Belgium and Sweden were its major partners in the arms market; Czechoslovakia and a few private firms also helped Ethiopia replenish its arsenal, albeit on a somewhat smaller scale. Major European arms manufacturers were unwilling to have a hand in strengthening Ethiopia's military power, the main guarantor of its sovereignty.

THE 1934–1935 ETHIOPIAN-ITALIAN CRISIS AND THE LEAGUE OF NATIONS

The 1930s turned out to be unfavorable for Ethiopia. The 1929–1933 global economic crisis aggravated the country's economic situation. As Fascist Benito Mussolini came to power in Italy in 1922, and Nazi Adolf Hitler in Germany in 1933, it became clear that independence of the countries that those regimes disfavored would be jeopardized.

In the early 1930s, Italy's ruling circles began to carry out the plan that had been developed back in the late nineteenth century: Unification of Eritrea and Italian Somaliland with simultaneous annexation of Ethiopian territory. Once that plan was implemented, it would build a single colonial dominion in northeastern Africa.

As noted by Russian historian V. A. Trofimov, preparations for the invasion in Ethiopia were the biggest military move of Mussolini's Fascist regime. His opinion is supported by a memo submitted to Italy's Ministry of Foreign Affairs by its employee Dino Grandi. In particular, it put forward an idea of the necessity of taking possession of Ethiopia. "If we want to create a genuine Italian empire, we can only try to do so in Ethiopia,"[34] it said. In the summer of the same year, Emilio De Bono, Italy's Minister of Colonial Affairs, instructed the commander of Italian troops in Eritrea to begin drafting a Memorandum on Offensive Actions against Ethiopia. In late November, he sent to War Minister Pietro Gazzera, Air Force Minister Italo Balbo, and Eritrea Governor Riccardo Astuto his proposals regarding a possible plan of Italy's hostilities in Ethiopia.

G. V. Tsypkin writes, "The rate of preparing colonial expansion accelerated even more when Mussolini filled the post of war minister and the posts of Air Force and Navy ministers in July 1933, which signified the intention of the Fascist dictator to take into his hands the general command in the preparation of a war against Ethiopia."[35]

In order to make a new invasion successful, Italy was trying to avoid past mistakes (the defeat in the Battle of Adwa is meant.—*Author's note*). Using the 1928 treaty as a cover, Italy opened its consulates in Ethiopia, about 40 all in all, which collected information, were engaged in intelligence work and subversive activities.[36] Swedish General Eric Virgin, an advisor to Emperor Haile Selassie, stated: "During recent years Italy had installed in Abyssinia a crowd of consuls and agents *commerciaux* in places where there was not a single Italian or any good reason for their presence. These people who had many agents working under them carried on intensive pro-Italian propaganda, distributed arms and bribes and tried to stir up feeling in the different districts against the central government, while at the same time striving with all their might to provoke dissensions among the local authorities—dissensions which gave the Italian government a pretext for interference and for attacks on Abyssinia in the Fascist press."[37]

Simultaneously, public opinion in Italy was manipulated: Anti-Ethiopian hysteria was stirred up in the spirit of vulgar chauvinism; the readership's attention was specifically drawn to ostensibly aggressive intentions of Addis Ababa with respect to Eritrea and Italian Somaliland. Alessandro Triulzi writes, "These reports (from Italian military and diplomatic sources.—*Author's note*) were dictated by the need to justify the Italian military build-up in Eritrea."[38]

Thus, when a fierce clash occurred on December 5, 1934 between Ethiopian and Italian troops in the oasis of Wal Wal,[39] which was later captured by the Italians, it was not a surprise either for Italian nationals or for the public opinion worldwide. The events in Wal Wal unleashed Italo-Ethiopian diplomatic warfare. After a ceasefire in Wal Wal, the parties exchanged a few protest notes from December 6 to 10.

On December 11, 1934, the Italian mission in Addis Ababa handed a note worded as an ultimatum to the Ethiopian minister of foreign affairs. As official Rome laid the responsibility for the incident on the Ethiopian side, it also set forth a series of claims that were definitely unacceptable for Ethiopia. They de facto meant annexation of the territory of a sovereign state:

1. Wal Wal and Warder must be part of Italian Somaliland;
2. Italy does not reprobate actions of Captain Roberto Cimmaruta, who had commanded the Italian unit;
3. The Ethiopian side must acknowledge its fault and admit its guilt;
4. The Ethiopian side must offer apologies and pay reparations.

Italy put forward the following demands:

1. *Dejazmach* Gebre Mariam (governor of the province of Hararghe) must personally, on behalf of the government of Ethiopia, offer apologies to the commander of the Italian armed units, and Ethiopian soldiers must do honors to the Italian flag;
2. The government of Ethiopia is obliged to pay to the Italian mission in Addis Ababa a monetary compensation in the amount of 200,000 Maria Theresa thalers;
3. Individuals who are found to be guilty of crimes must be arrested and punished immediately after they had done honors to the Italian flag.[40]

By presenting this provocative ultimatum, Italy probably thought its terms would be complied with. For Addis Ababa, the note of Rome would mean the actual recognition of the Fascist regime's right to part of Ethiopian territory.

Haile Selassie turned to Great Britain for help. But the Foreign Office had a peculiar reaction to the appeal of the Ethiopian monarch. On December 8, 1934, John Simon, Foreign Secretary of Great Britain, recommended the following to Sidney Barton,[41] the British Minister in Addis Ababa: ". . . the British government's eagerness to avoid complications with Italy."[42]

On the eve of the Italian aggression, Haile Selassie, just like in the 1920s, faced certain problems. The Ethiopian nobility and military commanders got excited and spoke in favor of an immediate march against Italy. Dignitaries recommended to the emperor to teach those "Eyeties," that is, to repeat the 1896 military triumph of Menelik II. The capital city's public opinion voiced reproaches aimed at the monarch and his foreign advisors. American Everett Colson, Swedish General Eric Virgin and his Swiss colleague Jacques Auberson bore the brunt of that criticism.[43]

Wise Haile Selassie was well aware that Italy was not the same country whose army had been defeated by Menelik II in 1896 in the Battle of Adwa. A new war could bring the empire to catastrophe. In the local Wal Wal conflict, Italy showed obvious military superiority.

Menelik II had won the 1896 war not only because his troops were more numerous than the enemy's, but also thanks to aid from France and Russia. Haile Selassie did not have that support. France was gradually losing interest in northeastern Africa. Soviet Russia had not resumed ties with Haile Selassie's empire yet. The emperor proposed to Rome a compromise option for the conflict settlement on the basis of Article 5 of the 1928 treaty. But the Italian side refused.

On December 14, 1934, the Ethiopian leadership sent to Geneva, attention of Joseph Avenol, Secretary-General of the League of Nations, a wire in which it advised him of the attack of Italian troops on an Ethiopian unit that was accompanying the British-Ethiopian commission, of the occupation of Ethiopian lands and of Italy's unwillingness to settle the conflict peacefully.[44]

The Italians, in turn, continued to accuse Ethiopia of belligerence, arbitrarily interpreting provisions of the 1908 Italo-Ethiopian border agreement. Rome unilaterally proclaimed the Wal Wal oasis and adjacent areas to be a region under Italy's protectorate as part of Italian Somaliland. It looked as though Ethiopia had encroached on Italy's sacred rights and lands.

Ethiopia's Foreign Ministry insisted on discussing the conflict situation at the Council of the League of Nations. On January 3, 1935, the Geneva phase of the Italo-Ethiopian conflict began. Resolution of that international issue depended to a large extent on the positions of Great Britain and France. But what did they come up with, those guarantors of peace, those advocates of justice?

French Foreign Minister Pierre Laval said: "I shall defend the interests of France and Premier Mussolini will defend the interests of Italy, and because we have the same understanding of the grave difficulties at this time, we shall defend together the interests of peace."[45] As a result, on January 7, 1935, the so-called Rome Pact, otherwise referred to as the Laval-Mussolini Treaty, was signed. According to the treaty, France ceded to Italy part of its colony in Africa and a 7% stake in the Djibouti-Addis Ababa railway in exchange for Italy's friendship and preservation of Austria's independence.[46]

The Rome accord could not help affecting the work of a new session of the Council of the League of Nations that had opened on January 11, 1935. Paris was sticking to "neutrality" with respect to Italian policy in northeastern Africa. London's sympathies were also with Rome. A January 12, 1935 wire to Sidney Barton from his boss, British Foreign Secretary John Simon, said: "If the Emperor wanted to reach a settlement, he, rather than Mussolini, should make the concessions, including one which would tacitly admit Ethiopia's guilt."[47] Ethiopia was expressly given to understand that it should not harbor any delusions and count on the assistance of European partners and the League of Nations!

Europe's leading powers were condoning the aggressor. In order to put a varnish of legality on its actions, Italy agreed to hold negotiations with Ethiopia. The emperor, who had turned down John Simon's proposals at first, agreed to meet the author of the discord halfway.

The governments agreed to settle the dispute in accordance with Article 5 of the 1928 Italo-Ethiopian treaty. The Council of the League of Nations officially confirmed that in the event of new Italo-Ethiopian conflicts, the matter would be discussed at a new session of the Council. This formal approach of the League of Nations was upsetting for Ethiopia. Italy was de facto given a mandate to raise its troops and redeploy military equipment to pursue tactical mission in Africa. At the same time, the entire world refused to sell arms for self-defense to Ethiopia.

Haile Selassie had nothing to do but to appeal to Avenol, Secretary-General of the League of Nations, again. A memo of March 17, 1935 said that Italy's military preparations were visible in border regions and that it was obvious Italy was not going to resolve the issue by peaceful means. "The Independence of Ethiopia—member of the League of Nations—in danger," the document stressed. Ethiopia was ready to settle its relations with Italy by way of arbitration.[48]

As he was striving to involve Great Britain into the settlement of the critical situation, in May 1935, the emperor offered to London the coveted concession to build a dam in the Lake Tana region. Simultaneously, British officials were to be appointed advisors to serve on administrations of some provinces, and British troops would be allowed to enter Addis Ababa to protect the diplomatic mission. Mussolini, well aware that, once it had received the long-awaited concessions, Great Britain would get in the way of Italian aggression, promised to respect British interests in Ethiopia. It was enough for Great Britain to back out from the talks with Addis Ababa.

As he had very limited diplomatic resources, Haile Selassie asked the United States "consider means of enforcing the Paris Pact (the Kellogg–Briand Pact, or the General Treaty for Renunciation of War as an Instrument of National Policy, which was signed on August 27 in Paris.—*Author's note*)," thinking the parties would be able to settle the matter through the mediation of the League of Nations.[49] However, the United States refused, which was to be expected.

Hopeful to convince the United States and Great Britain to side with him, Haile Selassie signed with a representative of Rickett, a British American corporation, a concession contract whereby the company secured oil and mineral rights in Africa. According to the contract, Rickett received the right to mine in Ethiopia's eastern areas adjacent to Eritrea and Italian Somaliland, to produce oil and extract other minerals. The concession was signed for 75 years.[50]

However, foreign policy agencies of the United States and Great Britain were unshakeable: Rickett was forced to give up lucrative terms of business. The British government, referring to the 1906 treaty, said that "the emperor should refrain from granting the concession prior until consultations of Britain, France and Italy."[51] As a result, the Rickett concession was annulled.

Meanwhile, the situation near Ethiopian borders was aggravating: Italian troops unceremoniously violated the empire's frontiers. In Italy itself, mobilization was underway, the armies were replenished with recruits born in 1913 and 1914. In April 1935, Ethiopia's government appealed to the Secretary-General of the League of Nations again, in connection with Italy's ongoing military preparations in northeastern Africa. The Ethiopian government suggested discussing the settlement of the Italo-Ethiopian conflict at the forthcoming 85th session of the Council of the League of Nations. However, under the pressure from John Simon and Pierre Laval, representatives of Great Britain and France, the League Council declined Ethiopia's request.

Italy agreed to convene an arbitration commission, subject, however, to a condition that the discussion will be confined to the armed clash in Wal Wal. The Ethiopian side was forced to accept Italy's proposal—first, in order to suspend its war preparations, and, second, in order to call on the Council of the League of Nations to study matters related to the bilateral relations of the two countries.

After a discussion in Geneva, which lasted from May 22 to 25, the League Council passed a resolution on the settlement procedure of the Italo-Ethiopian conflict. However, the talks were postponed until the adoption of a resolution by the arbitration commission. The nations in conflict were invited to reach an agreement no later than on August 25.

The designation of an exact date for the completion of the bilateral negotiations was an achievement of Ethiopian diplomacy. To a large extent, it was aided by a constructive and effective stance of the Soviet Union. As early as in April 1935, Maksim Litvinov, head of the USSR delegation in Geneva, said that "the world is indivisible and matters of security in Europe should not be considered separately, we must not tolerate a threat to peace in other parts of the world either."[52] In accordance with that narrative, said the Soviet minister, the USSR would staunchly speak at the international forum in favor of sovereign rights of weak nations, such as Ethiopia.

Italy's intensive preparations for the invasion of Ethiopia worried some rational thinkers in Great Britain's political class. Symptoms of that concern were manifested in the so-called "newspaper war," which lasted for a few months. In June 1935, Anthony Eden, Great Britain's representative in Geneva, visited Mussolini in Rome and tried to reach an agreement with him on the settlement of the conflict with Ethiopia. Eden promised that the British government would help Italy get a concession for the construction of a railway via Ethiopia (from the port of Massawa in Eritrea to Mogadishu in Somaliland), a 100 km strip along the railway, and the right to annex the area of Ogaden to Italian Somaliland. In return, Ethiopia would get a gateway to sea via the port of Zeila in British Somaliland. However, contrary to expectations of the Ethiopian government, on June 25, 1935, the arbitration commission of the Council of the League of Nations suspended its work without issuing any recommendations. The emperor insistently tried to let international public opinion know that his country was only after peaceful goals. In an interview with the French newspaper *Le Petit Journal*, Haile Selassie I said on July 28 that Ethiopia wanted to live in peace with its "neighbors." It was not engaged in mobilization, even partial, and was not concentrating its troops on the borders, as it trusted the authority of the League of Nations. In the same interview, the emperor stressed that his country was carrying out wide-scale domestic reforms and noted that especially great attention was being devoted to abolition of slavery in all its manifestations.[53]

Mussolini was of the opposite opinion. In an interview for *L'Écho de Paris*, the *Duce* went on a rant: "The League of Nations seems to imagine that it can impede life and the course of history. Must the world and civilization be at a standstill because the Covenant of the League of Nations? If so, let it perish."[54]

On July 31, 1935, meetings of the extraordinary session of the Council of the League of Nations began, focused on the Italo-Ethiopian conflict. On August 3, 1935, the Council passed two resolutions, one concerning the competence of the arbitration commission (which was limited to the Wal Wal incident), and the other designating the date of another meeting to discuss the full scope of Italo-Ethiopian relations—September 4.

Once again, the League of Nations, unprincipled and plagued by red tape, showed its helplessness when a real conflict settlement was called for.

On August 1, 1935, a so-called Neutrality Act was passed in the United States. According to its provisions, the U.S. president was authorized to announce the state of war between two or more foreign nations.[55] The act allowed imposition of embargo on the export of arms, ammunition, or implements of war to all belligerent countries, irrespective of whether they were an aggressor or a victim of aggression. Transportation of arms, ammunition, and implements of war for belligerent nations by American vessels was prohibited.

On August 16, Paris hosted a conference of Great Britain, France, and Italy. At the conference, the first two powers promised they would be insisting on establishment of economic and financial control of the League of Nations in Ethiopia. They proposed including Italians as advisors to the League of Nations. Great Britain reaffirmed its promise to give Ethiopia a gateway to sea through the port of Zeila in British Somaliland.[56]

Mussolini declined those constructive proposals. The British cabinet also showcased its "integrity": On August 22, when the Italo-Ethiopian conflict was discussed, a resolution was passed to impose embargo on arms exports both to Italy and to Ethiopia.[57] It is easy to imagine whose national interests were damaged more.

Why did the dominating public opinion put the victim of aggression on a level with the aggressor? No doubt, Europe was condoning the aggressor out of solidarity. The Neutrality Act passed by the U.S. Congress, the British cabinet's decision to impose embargo on arms exports, France's fear of the

German Nazis, its willingness to attend to Italy's wishes ultimately contributed to Italy's African gamble.

The Euro-Atlantic dovish rhetoric was not worth a lot. Rome's militaristic pressure deprived Ethiopia of all hope for a peaceful outcome. Expectations of the results of the session of the Council of the League of Nations, which began on September 4, 1935, turned out to be a pipe dream. A day before that, the arbitration commission that included representatives of Italy and Ethiopia (Ethiopia was represented by French jurisconsult Albert de Geouffre de La Pradelle and his American counterpart Pitman Potter) and was chaired by Greek diplomat Nikolaos Politis, had passed its resolution. Based on a false assumption that Wal Wal was a disputed territory, the commission made a paradoxical conclusion that served the purposes of the Italian aggressor: Neither the government of Ethiopia nor the government of Italy were responsible for the Wal Wal events. No way could this verdict be called a decision worthy of Solomon.[58]

The resolution of the arbitration commission was quite in line with the plans of the Mussolini government. Possibly, it was what made Italy seek Ethiopia's expulsion from the League of Nations and undertake steps to achieve that end. Italy submitted to the Council an extensive memorandum on the situation in Ethiopia and on Italy's relations with that country. The memo stated that Italy had always sought good relations with Ethiopia. Simultaneously, a message was put across that Ethiopia did not have a moral right to be a member of the League of Nations, because it was pursuing an aggressive foreign policy and was making Italy undertake appropriate measures to protect its dominions in Africa.[59]

In response, the Ethiopian delegation reiterated once again that military buildup was indeed taking place, but only on Italy's part. And that was precisely the reason why Ethiopia was asking the League Council to nominate a special committee to work out measures to prevent a war.

Out of all members of the League of Nations, only the stance of Maksim Litvinov, head of the Soviet delegation, was objective. He demanded that most drastic and resolute sanctions be imposed on Italy. "We are undoubtedly faced with a threat of war," he said. "It is a threat of aggression that the representative of Italy himself does not deny, but, moreover, that he confirms. Can we overlook this threat and forget about the implementation of Articles 10, 11 and 15 of the Covenant of the League of Nations? Would its violation by the entire Council not mean a total negation and abolition of the pact?"[60]

However, the Council of the League of Nations (not without input by Great Britain and France) postponed resolution of the issue of preservation of Ethiopia's sovereignty indefinitely. On September 6, 1935, a Committee of Five was set up, which included representatives of Great Britain, France, Poland, Spain, and Turkey. The committee was instructed to consider all the matters related to the Italo-Ethiopian conflict, and to work out a draft of the settlement. Even though a relevant committee was set up (Ethiopian leadership was probably skeptical about that body), the Ethiopian delegation did not give up fighting at the Geneva forum. In his statement at a session of the General Assembly of the League of Nations on September 11, 1935, Ethiopia's representative Tekle Hawariat[61] called for help, addressing the world's nations. "The people of Ethiopia is calling on all people of goodwill not to allow an atrocious injustice as a result of which blood of their brothers in Africa would be shed to be committed," he said. He emphasized that "Ethiopia will welcome any proposals that will raise its economic level, if they come from the League of Nations and are implemented in the spirit of its present Covenant."[62]

Speaking about the Soviet Union's attitude to the Italo-Ethiopian conflict, Maksim Litvinov, head of the Soviet delegation, said that "the Soviet government's negative attitude to the colonial system, the policy of spheres of influence, mandates and everything that has to do with imperialist goals is based on principles. The Soviet delegation is only concerned about protecting the Covenant of the League as an instrument of peace."[63]

Thus, in this important moment for Ethiopia, the USSR, even though it did not have diplomatic relations with the faraway African nation, was speaking up for it. Only the Soviet Union articulated clearly and precisely its position toward aggression and the colonial system, with the remaining members of the League de facto abstaining from providing any assistance to Ethiopia.

On September 18, 1935, the Committee of Five (Britain, France, Poland, Spain and Turkey) submitted to the League of Nations and to the representatives of Italy and Ethiopia its recommendations how to preserve Ethiopia's independence subject to international control over it, "not only for the improvement of the life of the Ethiopian people and the development of the country's resources (this is how the members of the committee interpreted their position), but also for providing the Ethiopian empire with the opportunity to maintain peaceful relations with its neighbors." Simultaneously, proposals were made to cede Ogaden and Danakil, as well as part of French and British Somaliland, to Italy. In addition, some concessions in Ethiopia were promised to the Italian government.[64]

The committee seemed to have satisfied Italy's colonial appetites. However, further developments showed something quite different: On September 22, 1935, Baron Pompeo Aloisi, the Italian representative in Geneva, notified Salvador de Madariaga, Chairman of the Committee of Five, that his government would not accept the proposals for the conflict settlement. The Ethiopian delegation signaled its consent to accept the committee's proposals as the basis for the discussion related to the final settlement of the conflict.

Haile Selassie tried to get a war loan from Great Britain and other members of the League of Nations (secured by guaranteed income from trade monopolies and stocks of the Djibouti-Addis Ababa railway). "I make this request, in the interest of peace," wrote the emperor to the league of the nation. "If Ethiopia can use this loan, as well as its own funds, Italy will think before attacking a state, well-armed and supported by the world community."[65]

However, none of the Western powers acceded to the request. The only thing that the League of Nations did was to set up another formal group, a Committee of Thirteen, with the same tasks at hand.

Diplomatic delays allowed Italy to make its war preparations without any haste. Basically, neither the League of Nations nor the great European powers could offer anything to Ethiopia anymore, except for occupation. So, the nation was to face the enemy alone.

On October 3, 1935, the aggression, of which Ethiopian authorities had warned the international community on multiple occasions, began. Italian troops commanded by Generals Emilio De Bono and Rodolfo Graziani invaded Ethiopia by two converging columns from the north and south.

Addis Ababa immediately appealed to the Secretary-General of the League of Nations, asking him to advise the League Council and member nations about Rome's act of aggression.

The League of Nations was confronted with a serious challenge. Faced with an overt and unprovoked aggression, it was to prove the practical significance of its authority as an international organization for peacekeeping, of the letter and spirit of the Covenant that guaranteed inviolability of borders to all members. The effectiveness of humanity's first peacekeeping institution was at stake. Small nations that had suffered a lot from wars and lawlessness put high hopes on the League of Nations. Thanks to the Covenant of the League of Nations, the precedent of peace enforcement was to become common international practice in the second half of 1935; however, it did not happen.

On October 5, 1935, at Ethiopia's request, an extraordinary session of the Council of the League of Nations began. Tekle Hawariat was the first to take the floor. Based on Article 16 of the Covenant, which stipulated those sanctions against an aggressor should be imposed by all members of the League, he recommended taking that rule for guidance.[66] On October 5, the League Council set up a Committee of Six, which consisted of representatives of France, Great Britain, Denmark, Chile, Romania, and Portugal. The committee was instructed to work out relevant military solutions against Italy. On the following day, the Committee of Six published a report stating that Italy had violated the Covenant of the League of Nations. On October 7, 1935, the League Council pronounced Italy the aggressor. Formally, Italy was acknowledged to be in conflict with all member nations of the League. Members of the League, in accordance with Article 16 of the Covenant, were to impose

economic sanctions on Italy and to take action in other spheres, even apply
military measures against it. On October 10, the Assembly voted a resolution
on the imposition of anti-Italian economic sanctions. A Coordination Committee was set up, which was to designate the date for the enforcement of the
sanctions (out of 54 members of the League of Nations, 50 voted for the sanctions; only Italy was against the collective decision, with Austria, Hungary and
Albania abstaining).

The Coordination Committee set up a Committee of Eighteen, or the Big
Committee, which recommended to League members on October 19, 1935:
(1) to impose embargo on arms exports to Italy; (2) to refrain from extending
loans and credits to Italy; (3) to cease import of Italian goods; 4) to impose
embargo on some exports to Italy; (5) to aid one another in the enforcement
of the sanctions.[67]

The Big Committee designated November 18 as the date on which the
sanctions imposed on Italy were to take effect, and it was the 46th day of the
war. The international community raised its voice, trying to protect civilization's biggest value—peace. Most member nations of the League of Nations
(39) resorted to measures of financial boycott against Italy, and 10 agreed to
take the same measures. Austria, Hungary, and Albania refused to impose
sanctions on the aggressor.

Formally speaking, the League of Nations defined its position with respect
to the aggressor. De facto, however, the sanctions were applied discrimi-
nately. They did not concern the most important types of strategic commodities for Italy—for instance, oil and other kinds of fuels and lubricants. As it
was condemning the aggressor, the League did not offer any assistance to
Ethiopia that was suffering from the aggression.

Winston Churchill was very critical and preferred to call a spade a spade.
"I was never in favor of isolated action by Great Britain, but having gone so
far it was a grievous deed to recoil. Moreover, Mussolini would never have
dared to come to grips with a resolute British Government. Nearly the whole
of the world was against him, and he would have had to risk his regime upon
a single-handed war with Britain, in which a fleet action in the Mediterranean
would be the early and decisive test. How could Italy have fought this war?
Apart from a limited advantage in modern light cruisers, her navy was but
a fourth the size of the British. Her numerous conscript army, which was
vaunted in millions, could not come into action. Her air power was in quantity
and quality far below even our modest establishments. She would instantly
have been blockaded. The Italian armies in Abyssinia would have famished
for supplies and ammunition. Germany could as yet give no effective help. If
ever there was an opportunity of striking a decisive blow in a generous cause
with the minimum of risk, it was here and now. The fact that the nerve of the
British Government was not equal to the occasion can be excused only by

their sincere love of peace. Actually, it played a part in leading to an infinitely more terrible war."[68]

Alas, in history, there are no givens, and Churchill's logic was not the same as the opinion of the British elites that were making London's foreign policy at the time. Even Mussolini was astonished at that logic. At a Stresa conference on April 11, 1935, the *Duce* confessed "he had been 'especially disposed' to talk about Ethiopia at the time and had been annoyed at the British for avoiding the subject. He had hoped for an opening which would allow him to bargain with Great Britain over Ethiopia. What he got must have looked even better to him when he stopped to think about it. The British had apparently decided to let him his way in Ethiopia without raising a word of objection."[69] A few years later, Fulvio Suvich, Under-Secretary of the Italian Ministry of Foreign Affairs, confirmed that "the Ethiopian war was made by a gentlemen's agreement with England."[70]

British journalist G. Ward Price cites one curious fact in this connection. Ahead of the invasion to Ethiopia, Mussolini asked British Prime Minister James Ramsay MacDonald about Great Britain's attitude toward that move on Rome's part. MacDonald remarked in a flowery style: "England is a lady. A lady's taste is for vigorous action by the male, but she likes things done discreetly—not in public. So be tactful, and we shall have no objection."[71]

Based on the resolution of the League of Nations, the United States banned arms exports both to Italy and Ethiopia on October 5.[72] Members of the League of Nations were immediately reminded that "the U.S. have already taken certain measures in accordance with our own legislation and policy that these measures include far-reaching actions in limiting trade and financial ties with the belligerent countries and that we wish to pursue our course."[73]

Official Paris showcased its adherence to principles: The administration of French Somaliland kept the weapons and ammunition purchased by the government of Ethiopia abroad until the end of the war, giving as a reason its unwillingness to jeopardize the railway, as it could be bombarded by Italian aircraft. Germany, which had previously agreed to extend a loan of 11 million German marks to the Ethiopian government,[74] canceled its decision. The formal obstruction to the aggression and indifference to the fate of the African empire only aggravated the already hard situation of the defensive side.

The Soviet Union, the only consistent advocate of interests of the Ethiopian people in the League of Nations, resolutely condemned the aggressor and defended Ethiopia's sovereignty. Soviet diplomacy submitted a proposal to the coordination committee to ban oil exports to the country that had committed the aggression. "Oil" sanctions could put up the strongest obstacle to the escalation of the conflict by Italy. It is a known fact that back in mid-October 1935 the military had warned Mussolini that in case of oil embargo hostilities in Ethiopia would have to be suspended.[75]

The Soviet Union's proposal submitted on December 6, 1935 was backed by 10 countries, including Romania, Iraq and Holland, which accounted for 74.5% of Italian oil imports.[76] However, the "oil blockade" of the aggressor failed to bring the "desired" result.

On December 8, 1935, negotiations of British Foreign Secretary Samuel Hoare with France's Prime Minister Pierre Laval began in Paris. The world clearly saw their outcome—the Hoare-Laval Pact, or a project of peaceful settlement. According to the plan, Emperor Haile Selassie I was to "cede" to Italy the entire Ogaden area, the eastern part of the province of Tigray, and the area of Danakil. In return, Ethiopia was to get from Italy a narrow strip of Southern Eritrea with a gateway to sea in Assab. The emperor was insistently recommended to hire Italian advisors and to grant exclusive economic privileges to Italy. The central part of Ethiopia was to be placed under the control of advisors of the League of Nations who would be representatives of Great Britain, France, and Italy.[77] Every clause of the plan reeked of self-interest and egocentricity. Addis Ababa's national interests were not included into the plan even for the sake of protocol formalities.

The Hoare-Laval plan meant de facto annexation of a considerable part of Ethiopia's territory by Italy. The Ethiopian government officially declined the plan, as it rightly believed that the Paris proposals purported to make Addis Ababa give away about one-half of its land to the conqueror. Going forward, it could only expect full annexation. Emperor Haile Selassie I said on that occasion: "We desire to state, with all the solemnity and firmness which the situation demands today, that our willingness to facilitate any pacific solution to this conflict has not changed, but the act by us of accepting even in principle the Franco-British proposals would be not only a cowardice towards our people, but a betrayal of the League of Nations and of all the States which have shown that they could have confidence up to now in the system of collective security. These proposals are in the negation and abandonment of the principles upon which the League of Nations is founded."[78]

The secret Hoare-Laval Plan was not disclosed, but its contents were leaked to the press. The League of Nations had to make a comment on the Hoare-Laval agreement. The issue of oil sanctions was deferred indefinitely. "The adjournment put an end to any effective action against Italy," wrote A. J. Barker.[79] The thinly veiled imperialistic solidarity of the Europeans left no chance for the besieged in Africa.

By January 1936, the Ethiopian issue in international politics had begun to recede into the background. The Council of the League of Nations referred the matter of the oil sanctions to various committees. Using today's vernacular, Western powers were unwilling to keep the pressing matters on the agenda.

They were now focused on events in Germany. The only thing that the League of Nations suggested was a truce. The proposal came from France.

However, Italo-Ethiopian talks never took place. The following circumstances prevented them: (1) Great Britain's refusal to assume the role of mediator between Italy and Ethiopia; (2) Hitler's declaration about remilitarization of the Rhineland made at the Reichstag on March 7, 1936, which turned out to be a priceless trump card for Italy in the League of Nations. Thus, politically, the Ethiopian issue was a winning point for Italy. The outcome of the conflict in Ethiopia was now fully dependent on the hostilities and the goodwill of the winners.

Few people doubted that Rome would win in the reckless game of the war. To oppose an enemy by deploying an army that was significantly inferior in terms of technology and weapons and with untrained troops was to fight a losing battle. Ethiopian troops began to suffer defeats indeed. Not content with tactical gains, the Italian Fascists treacherously violated international conventions on the use of poisonous substances[80]—barbaric weapons of mass destruction.

Gas attacks were used not only against Ethiopian military units but also against all living things. "Any living creature who was touched by that drizzle of mustard gas falling from the aircraft or who drank poisoned water or who ate contaminated food was going through horrible suffering. They ran to die in a hut or in the thick of the woods." Tens of thousands of Ethiopian civilians, including old people, women and children, died of poisonous gas during the years of the Fascist aggression. "It is difficult to find words to describe the ghastly sight of the people who see their skin come off and their bodies covered with blisters," recalls Soviet cameraman Boris Tseitlin who visited one hospital. "The suffering of those people is hard to put in words."[81]

Ethiopia's government protested on multiple occasions against violations of the international convention by Italy and appealed to the countries that had signed those conventions (the 1907 Hague Conventions forbidding the use of poison or poisoned weapons and prohibiting bombardment of civilians, and the 1925 Geneva Protocol banning the use of gas). None of the nations that had signed those conventions responded to Ethiopia's appeal.

Aware that he could not rely on European humanism and international solidarity, Haile Selassie I decided to fight a decisive battle. The choice of Maychew (an area in the south of the province of Tigray) as the battleground, determined the course of the campaign. It was Fyodor Konovalov, a former colonel of the Russian imperial army and a military advisor to Emperor Haile Selassie I, who helped the emperor plan out the operation.[82]

On March 31, at 5:00 a.m., Ethiopian troops advanced and began the Battle of Maychew. The Ethiopians had only moral superiority on their side: They were fighting for their homeland. Naturally, the Ethiopian army, weak in every respect, could not offer proper resistance to the aggressor. After a fierce combat, the Ethiopian troops were beaten. Ethiopia suffered a defeat in an encounter with a well-trained and well-armed enemy that also outnumbered the African nation's army. Ethiopia could be said fighting not only against Italy. The aggressor was in certain ways backed by quite a few League member nations. Some were helping by their non-interference, others by their ineffective economic sanctions, and there were those who were providing overt assistance to the invader.

After the defeat of the Ethiopian army in the Battle of Maychew, the enemy began to advance toward Addis Ababa. By that time, the fate of the southern front had also been sealed. The Ethiopian army started to retreat hinterland, opening access to the cities of Harar and Dire Dawa for the enemy.

Amid those developments, Takele Wolde Hawariat, the Mayor of Addis Ababa, and his followers, Fikre Mariam Abba Techan and Heruy Wolde Selassie, suggested abandoning the capital city, gaining a foothold in Gore (southwestern Ethiopia) and continuing resistance by guerilla action.

They hoped that seasonal rain showers would impede the advance of the Italians. A nearly three-month lull in the hostilities (while the rain season would last) would allow the Ethiopian troops to regroup and deal a blow to the enemy. "If the Italians were held and supplies could be arranged through the Sudan and Kenya, the empire might still be saved,"[83] said the mayor of Addis Ababa.

Unfortunately, none of the countries that had diplomatic relations with Ethiopia came to help. British minister Sidney Barton said expressly that he was unable to give assurances that his country would back sanctions against Italy in a situation where part of the country was occupied. And all that despite the fact that Sudan and Kenya were dominions of Great Britain.[84] The emperor's followers insisted that he should make a trip (along with some members of his government) to Europe, in a bid to defend the country's interests in the League of Nations.

However, Haile Selassie preferred to stay in the country. He changed his mind only after the Council of the Crown by a majority of votes (21 out of 24) acknowledged that his departure for Europe would be advisable.[85] The emperor wrote about it later in his autobiography: "When we received news that our presence in the capital is pushing the Italians to destroy both the city and its civilians from aircraft (as happened on the northern front—*Author's note*), we decided to leave the country, proceeding from the considerations that this could save the lives of civilians from barbarism."[86]

On May 2, Haile Selassie, his family and a few prominent dignitaries left the country and went to Great Britain that had granted political asylum to them.

Before the departure, the emperor instituted an interim government of Ethiopia to be led by Bitwaddad Walda Tsadeq and gave him an order to move to Gore.[87] Furthermore, Haile Selassie I appointed *Ras* Imiru to command troops in the west, *Ras* Desta to lead the army in the south, and *Dejazmach* Hailu Kebede to be in charge of the northern front. When saying his good-byes, the emperor said: "I place my reliance on the League of Nations. I will come before it and will seek help. . . . Do fight. I will continue my struggle in Europe. Even though it might take us years, we will win, because justice is on our side."[88]

On May 5, 1936, after a bloody seven-month war, Italian troops occupied Addis Ababa. Ethiopia was annexed to other Italian possessions in Africa. In a diplomatic note of May 18, 1936 sent to Secretary-General Joseph Avenol, Haile Selassie requested that Mussolini's decision be qualified as illegal. The League of Nations disregarded that request as well. The emperor's departure and the entry of the Italians into Addis Ababa did not mean that the Ethiopian state had ceased to exist. The interim government was trying to establish liaison with armed units loyal to their homeland and with the areas that had not been occupied by the enemy, and to raise public resistance against invaders among residents of the areas uncontrolled by Rome.

IN EXILE (1936–1941)

On May 5, 1936, Italian troops entered Addis Ababa. Marshal Pietro Badoglio, commander of the Italian troops, demanded in his address to the population that they lay down arms, and proclaimed hypocritically that "under the protection of the victorious Italian flag, the Ethiopian people will find freedom, justice and prosperity."[89] On May 9, 1936, speaking from a balcony of a Venetian palace, in front of which a big crowd gathered, Mussolini declared the conquest of Ethiopia. On the same day, a decree on Ethiopia's annexation to Italian possessions in Africa was promulgated. Marshal Graziani was appointed the Vice King and Governor-General of Ethiopia. Italy's King Victor Emmanuel II received the title of Emperor of Ethiopia. Now Italian eastern Africa was comprised of six provinces: Eritrea with the capital in Asmara; Somaliland with the capital in Mogadishu; Amhara with the capital in Gonder; Harrar with the capital in Harar; Galla-Sidamo with the capital in Jimma; Shewa with the capital in Addis Ababa.[90]

Vice King Graziani hoped that his recourse to terror would put an end to the Ethiopian resistance movement very quickly, of which he hastened to assure Mussolini. However, the Ethiopian people had a different opinion on the matter. Despite reprisals, the resistance guerrilla movement that had spread across many areas of the country from the summer of 1936 was growing day by day. The invaders were unable to sow the seeds of quarrel among Ethiopia's numerous ethnicities. The resistance movement was gaining momentum in all provinces.

On May 22, Ethiopia's emperor and government in exile arrived in Londonincognito, in keeping with the request of the government of Great Britain. Notwithstanding, a crowd of many thousands of people was lining up along London streets all the way down from the Waterloo railway station, and they shouted: "Haile Selassie, Haile Selassie!"[91]

Official London did not meet the Ethiopian leader. Only on the following day, Great Britain's Foreign Secretary Anthony Eden paid a visit of courtesy to Ethiopia's diplomatic mission where the emperor was temporarily staying.

To please the British establishment, Eden had to keep distance. Prime Minister Stanley Baldwin and King Edward VIII were afraid that if asylum was officially granted to the emperor and if the government with him at the helm were recognized, it might push Mussolini to seek rapprochement with Hitler.

Mussolini, in turn, said: "My politics never involved any prejudice to interests of the British Empire." He insisted that Italy did not have any aggressive intentions with respect to Egypt, Sudan, and Palestine. "Believe me, the victory in eastern Africa brings Italy into the ranks of 'satisfied' countries. England and France must understand the importance of this fact,"[92] noted the *Duce*.

Haile Selassie was fully aware that in the situation at hand he could not count on understanding, let alone help, on the part of Great Britain and France, which were making concessions to Mussolini to have him on their side. The emperor relied exclusively on the Assembly of the League of Nations.

On June 26, 1936, Haile Selassie, as the head of the Ethiopian delegation, arrived in an inhospitable Geneva. Contrary to all rules of diplomatic protocol, the emperor was not allowed even to stay at his own villa in Vevey. For the short duration of the Assembly, the Ethiopian delegation had to settle for Geneva's Carlton Park Hotel.

Belgium's Prime Minister Paul van Zeeland was elected the new chairman of the Assembly of the League of Nations. For the Ethiopian delegation, it was an unpleasant fact. The matter was that Belgium had colonial interests in Africa and had sympathies for Italy; enough evidence is given by the public reading, inside the Assembly walls, of a letter from Gian Galeazzo Ciano, Italy's Foreign Minister, in which he justified the invasion of Italian troops into Ethiopia.

The emperor of Ethiopia spoke at the 16th session of the Assembly of the League of Nations on June 30, 1936. In his highly dramatic speech, he said:

I, Haile Selassie I, Emperor of Ethiopia, am here today to claim that justice which is due to my people, and the assistance promised to it eight months ago, when fifty nations asserted that aggression had been committed in violation of international treaties.

There is no precedent for a Head of State himself speaking in this assembly. But there is also no precedent for a people being victim of such injustice and being at present threatened by abandonment to its aggressor. Also, there has never before been an example of any Government proceeding to the systematic extermination of a nation by barbarous means, in violation of the most solemn promises made by the nations of the earth that there should not be used against innocent human beings the terrible poison of harmful gases. It is to defend a people struggling for its age-old independence that the head of the Ethiopian Empire has come to Geneva to fulfil this supreme duty, after having himself fought at the head of his armies.

It is my duty to inform the Governments assembled in Geneva, responsible as they are for the lives of millions of men, women and children, of the deadly peril which threatens them, by describing to them the fate which has been suffered by Ethiopia. It is not only upon warriors that the Italian Government has made war. It has above all attacked populations far removed from hostilities, in order to terrorize and exterminate them.

. . . The Ethiopian Government never expected other Governments to shed their soldiers' blood to defend the Covenant (of the League of Nations.— *Author's note*) when their own immediately personal interests were not at stake. . . . Ethiopian warriors asked only for means to defend themselves. On many occasions I have asked for financial assistance for the purchase of arms. That assistance has been constantly refused me. What, then, in practice, is the meaning of Article 16 of the Covenant and of collective security? . . . I assert that the problem submitted to the Assembly today is a much wider one. It is not merely a question of the settlement of Italian aggression. It is collective security: it is the very existence of the League of Nations. . . . It is the principle of the equality of States on the one hand, or otherwise the obligation laid upon small Powers to accept the bonds of vassalship. . . .

Should it happen that a strong Government finds it may with impunity destroy a weak people, then the hour strikes for that weak people to appeal to the League of Nations to give its judgment in all freedom? God and history will remember your judgment. . .

I renew my protest against the violations of treaties of which the Ethiopian people has been the victim. . . . I ask the fifty-two nations, who have given the Ethiopian people a promise to help them in their resistance to the aggressor, what are they willing to do for Ethiopia?. . .

And the great Powers who have promised the guarantee of collective security to small States. . . . I ask what measures do you intend to take? . . . What reply shall I have to take back to my people?[93]

The League of Nations was silent and did nothing. The great powers did not react to the emperor's appeal in any way. In an official letter to the Secretary-General of the League of Nations, Haile Selassie advised him that the

Ethiopian government was functioning in the city of Gore (in the country's southwest), where 135,000 troops loyal to the emperor remained.[94]

The Ethiopian delegation proposed two resolutions to be adopted by the League of Nations: (1) on a categorical refusal to recognize the violent annexation; (2) on extension of financial aid to Ethiopia in the form of a loan of 10 million pounds sterling guaranteed by member nations of the League of Nations.[95]

Despite the force of Haile Selassie's arguments and support of the international community, of delegates of the USSR and some other nations, the Assembly did not agree with Ethiopia's proposals; moreover, it resolved to lift the sanctions imposed on Italy, and to do so on July 15, 1936. The speech of the emperor of Ethiopia delivered at the League of Nations was widely covered and commented on in the media across the globe and in anti-Fascist circles. However, that was surely not enough.

As the Italian government was not denounced by Great Britain and France in the League or by the United States outside the League, it started to seek expulsion of Ethiopia from the League of Nations.

Even though he had suffered a diplomatic mishap in Geneva in June and July 1936, Emperor Haile Selassie did not lose hope to come out as the winner in the end. When he came back to London, he began to get ready for a new session of the League of Nations, which was scheduled for September 1936.

Avenol, Secretary-General of the League of Nations, was deeply concerned with the accreditation of the Ethiopian delegation for a new session, that is, its participation in it. The Italian Ministry of Foreign Affairs strongly objected against the presence of Ethiopia's representatives at the sessions. To discuss the fate of the Ethiopian delegation and to coordinate further interaction with Italy, the Secretary-General of the League went to Rome. During a private audience with Mussolini, Avenol promised that he would see Ethiopia expelled from the League. When he came back to Geneva, he instructed a few officials to prepare a plan of expulsion: Those were Luis Agustín Podestá Costa, Legal Advisor, Massimo Pilotti, Under Secretary-General, and Jules Basdevant, Legal Adviser, of Frances Ministry of Foreign Affairs, and Professor of International Law at the Paris Diderot University. Instead of implementing the Covenant of the League, the leadership of the organization prepared a plan called the Mussolini-Avenol-Pilotti Plan to expel Ethiopia from the League. As we can see, not only God but diplomats also favored big battalions.

France and Switzerland worked in sync: The Emperor of Ethiopia again was not allowed to use his villa in Vevey. Staying at the Carlton Park Hotel was also out of the question because it already provided lodgings to Italian experts who were taking part in the conference via radio and telecommunications.

Paris prohibited to Dr. Gaston Jèze, professor of law at the University of Paris, legal counsel for the Ethiopian delegation at the League of Nations to offer consultations to Haile Selassie on matters of international relations. However, the Paris and Geneva demarche became public knowledge. Under public pressure, the French who were accused of bias, went back on their disgraceful decision.

However, at the session of the Assembly of the League of Nations, a question arose about powers and authorities of Ethiopia's delegates. Unwilling to assume responsibility, the mandate commission decided to refer the matter to The Hague International Tribunal. According to regulations, the tribunal could pronounce its decision only after the end of the session, so the Ethiopian delegation was allowed to attend the session and discuss only matters related to Ethiopia. On the one hand, it was a gross violation of the Covenant of the League of Nations and de facto meant Ethiopia's expulsion from the organization. On the other, it caused a big moral damage to the authority of Emperor Haile Selassie I, because in the 1920s, it was he who had convinced his people that the League of Nations was the guarantor of Ethiopia's independence.

Perfidious behavior of the secretary-general of the League of Nations bore its fruit on October 24, 1936. Germany was the first to recognize Italy's colonial rights to Ethiopia. The German mission in Addis Ababa was converted into a consulate. In November 1936, Albania, Austria and Hungary, in December 1936, Switzerland's Federal Council, and on June 28, 1937, Japan also sided with Italy.[96]

In March 1936, the United States closed down its consulate in Addis Ababa and recalled the envoy. The State Department rejected outright the request of Emperor Haile Selassie and Dr. Martin (Warqnah Ishete), Ethiopia's ambassador in London, to be granted entry visas to the United States, which deprived them of the opportunity to take part in the negotiations about a loan required to provide help to Ethiopian patriots. The White House did not want to complicate relations with Americans of Italian descent, fully aware of the close ties they had with their ancestral land. The demand of Italian Americans that the United States should abstain from policies hostile to Italy's political and economic interests was not an empty phrase, which, notably, famous American historian Joseph Harris said.[97] The scholar noted that when the war in eastern Africa began, many Americans of Italian descent started to organize mass rallies and fund-raising. Large capitals were concentrated in their hands, and they were holding a significant place in the political and social spheres. The Italian community, which was very well organized, had a huge influence on the White House. For instance, then-New York Mayor Fiorello H. La Guardia was in direct contact with the U.S. president. It should also be taken into account that American bankers (including those of Italian descent) were not interested in providing funds to the Ethiopian government.

After his unsuccessful visit to Geneva, the emperor had to come back to London. According to J. H. Spencer, if Anthony Eden had not been Great Britain's Foreign Secretary, Haile Selassie would not have been granted political asylum in Great Britain.[98] After his return to Great Britain, Haile Selassie was assigned residence in Bath. The house where he stayed with his family became the headquarters of the Ethiopian government in exile.

The first years in Bath were darkened by the empress's disease. In addition, the family's financial situation was deteriorating year by year, because all accounts of the Ethiopian state were frozen. The emperor and his family had to live in poverty. "It must be realized," said the Emperor about this time, "that we have absolutely no income. We must live on what little capital we have. When one has a small capital and no income—when it is all out-going and no in-coming there is bound to be anxiety."[99]

Official London denied political status to the emperor, members of his family and of the Ethiopian government in exile, because the British government stuck to the principle of consolidating peace and liberating Italy from German tutelage. After Anthony Eden's retirement, Prime Minister Chamberlain and Lord Halifax, the new Foreign Secretary, entered into open negotiations with the Italian government. On April 16, 1938, Prime Minister Chamberlain concluded the so-called "gentlemen's agreement" with Mussolini, one clause of which obliged Great Britain to get the League of Nations to adopt a resolution on granting League member nations the right to independently decide whether they would recognize Ethiopia as an Italian colony.[100] Italy, in turn, undertook to respect British interests in the Lake Tana area and in cooperation with Great Britain to maintain the status quo in the Mediterranean and in the Red Sea. That Anglo-Italian agreement gave a sort of an indulgence to Rome, which justified the invaders' actions in Ethiopia.

At the May session of the Council of the League of Nations, Lord Halifax raised the question of recognizing Ethiopia as an Italian colony, abiding by the "gentlemen's agreement." He acknowledged that the system of sanctions was not working, that some League member nations were accustomed to the fact that Ethiopia had been de facto transferred to Italian governance, while other countries were not. Lord Halifax suggested that the League of Nations should allow all countries to address that issue of their own accord.[101] Haile Selassie who was present, even though he was sick at the moment, delivered a speech in which he asked the British government to remove from the agenda the suggestion to recognize the annexation of Ethiopia by Italy, because the fighting Ethiopia people was in control of the larger part of the country.[102] "Italy in Ethiopia controls only those cities and villages where there are garrisons, and there are many Ethiopian provinces where they have little or no control. . . . I ask that Ethiopia be allowed to remain among you (League members author) as the living image of violated right. But should our appeal remain unanswered, our war against Italy will go on, whatever happens, until justice triumphs."[103]

Soviet representative Maksim Litvinov spoke in favor of the emperor of Ethiopia again. He said that if Ethiopia was to be recognized as a colony it would be equal to a stab in the back to the nation the peoples of which "cause amazement and admiration across the world by the courage of their sons who continue to fight against the aggression with unabated energy, persistence and indefatigability."[104] The Soviet delegation was supported by delegates of China, Bolivia, and New Zealand. However, a majority of votes approved Lord Halifax's resolution. Quite soon, Great Britain and France, on which not only the emperor relied but many European diplomats, recognized the annexation of Ethiopia by Italy. It was a serious defeat of Haile Selassie's diplomacy.

Ethiopia's delegation was no longer regarded as a full-fledged participant of the events taking place at the League of Nations. Great Britain and France, having settled their relations with Italy, publicly confirmed their treacherous policy with respect to Ethiopia. Churchill, the head of the British government, noted later: "Mussolini succeeded in his bluff (bluff about Great Italy?— *Author's note*), and from this fact one observer drew far-reaching conclusions for himself." That observer was Adolf Hitler.[105] Great Britain, France and the United States, which could have prevented the war by stopping Mussolini, de facto gave a free hand to the Fascist aggressors in Europe, in Northern Africa, and in the Far East. This short-sighted and mercenary policy, in our view, was what caused World War II.

"Benito Mussolini's Italian conquest of Ethiopia was destined to become the most important single factor in the destruction of the League of Nations and the failure of collective security against aggression," writes Thomas M. Coffey. "His bluffing, bullying conduct of foreign relations exposed the flabbiness and cynicism of the western European and American democracies and demonstrated to his junior colleague, Adolf Hitler an idea *modus operandi* for the manipulation and intimidation of those countries for the next three years. The conquest of Ethiopia, was not, of course, the primary cause of World War II, but more than any other single event, it opened the route toward the cataclysm."[106]

The annexation of Ethiopia by Italy showed quite vividly the inability of the League of Nations with its Covenant to keep peace between nations pursuing opposing interests. The lessons taught by World War II were what humanity needed to get rid of a romantic delusion about inviolability of the pillars of international law and the right of peoples to self-determination.

However, Italy's situation in the so-called Eastern Africa was getting more and more unstable every year. The larger part of the territory was under control of the Ethiopian patriots, which complicated the situation of the Italian invaders. Neither torture nor shootings nor arson attacks nor deportations of old people, women, and children to Italian Somaliland could destroy the people's will to resist.

An assassination attempt against Vice King Graziani was the culmination of the struggle. On February 19, 1937, a self-made bomb exploded in Addis Ababa. It happened at a moment when a big crowd gathered in front of the emperor's palace. Those were Ethiopian feudal lords who collaborated with the Fascists and city beggars who were to receive coins distributed by the vice king seeking popularity. As a result of the explosion, a few superior officers from Graziani's retinue were wounded, including General Aurelio Liotta, Commander-in-Chief of the Italian air force in Ethiopia. Graziani ordered[107] reprisals against the population of Addis Ababa. Soldiers were shooting at everyone who was found in the streets. Unarmed people were also killed in their dwellings. The invaders set houses on fire and shot those who were trying to get out. Addis Ababa was surrounded by troops, and all communications were cut off.

The violence that had begun on February 19 continued for a few days. According to some data, about 30,000 people were killed in the capital on those days. Residents of nearby villages were also victims of the reprisals. The Ethiopian intellectual community, small as it was, was annihilated. In May 1937, Graziani ordered shooting the monks of the famous Ethiopian monastery of Debra Libanos, located in the east of the capital city. Clergymen, monks, deacons, and hermits died.

The Resistance movement was especially wide in the province of Shewa, homeland of Emperors Menelik II and Haile Selassie I. The retaliations weakened the guerrilla movement in Shewa, but reenergized skirmishes in other provinces: Wollo, Tigray, Begemder and Semien, Gojjam, Sidamo, Welega, and Bale. Graziani's policy, which was aimed at "total annihilation of the people," failed. In late 1937, the Italian government recalled Graziani from the position of the vice king of Ethiopia, and appointed Duke Amadeo d'Aosta in his place.

In 1938, in a telegram addressed to all Christian churches, Emperor Haile Selassie I gave a detailed description of the havoc wreaked by the Italians: (1) destruction of churches, cathedrals, and the clergy; (2) killings of priests of the Ethiopian Church and Muslim sheikhs after the assassination attempt against Graziani; (3) refusal of the Italian authorities to allow burial of the Ethiopians killed between February 19 and 23 according to Christian rituals. The Italian authorities did not allow relatives to take away the remains of the dead and cremated them instead; (4) destruction of St. George Cathedral in Addis Ababa, of one of the oldest monasteries in Debre Libanos, and of many other churches; (5) public execution in Addis Ababa of Abuna Petros, who refused to collaborate with the Italians; (6) dispatch to Rome of a fourth-century historic monument—Obelisk of Axum.[108]

It is noteworthy that not a single nation denounced the slaughter of February 19, 1937. Moreover, Europe did not seem to notice that the Italian aggressors had used chemical weapons against Ethiopian defenders in 1936.

To lead the patriotic campaign, a Committee of Unity and Collaboration was set up in 1938. It was in permanent contact with Emperor Haile Selassie I. The organization coordinated the Resistance movement and the guerrilla campaign in all areas across the Ethiopian Empire.

The new vice king of Italy's eastern Africa, who still used reprisals against the patriots, was generally pursuing a policy of appeasement with respect to local populations. Ethiopian feudal lords were appointed to petty administrative offices, and advisory bodies were established from representatives of local nobility collaborating with the Italians; some imprisoned patriots were released from jail and concentration camps. The Italians called on patriots to lay down arms in exchange for security assurances, arranged visits to Italy for Ethiopian dignitaries who had entered their service. To enlist sympathies of the Christian clergy, the new vice king permitted that a patriarch be elected. The Ethiopian Church was declared an independent religious organization; however, the move was not approved by the Ethiopian clergy.

Duke d'Aosta's "soft" measures did not rid Ethiopia of the guerrilla movement. Gian Galeazzo Ciano, Italy's Foreign Minister, wrote in his diary on March 14, 1939: "Duke d'Aosta is optimistic about the situation in the Ethiopian Empire. I must, however, add that among many people who have arrived from there, he is the only optimist."[109]

Ciano's statement is justified. The people perceived the Italians' actions as genocide, so even after the Great Slaughter the guerrilla movement continued to spread. One evidence is the uprisings in Gojjam (in the country's west), in Wollo and Begemder (in the north), and in Welega (in the south-west).

By the end of 1938, sound coordination had been established between separate guerrilla groups, as well as a close liaison between the Resistance movement in the country and emigration centers. The Italians felt more or less secure only in their garrisons and in large cities.

Because of the resistance of the population, the Italian invaders were unable to carry out their plans of economic exploitation. As early as in October 1936, enormous outlays on military operations and occupation had led Italy to bankruptcy, and the Italian lira devalued.

To find a way out of that situation, the Roman dictator made multiple attempts to force Ethiopia's emperor to give up power and become king of Shewa, and then abdicate in favor of his elder son, Prince Asfaw Wossen. Mussolini acted through intermediaries from France, Vatican, and Switzerland. Cardinal Pacelli, Vatican's Secretary of State (later Pope Pius XII), met with the emperor and offered him one million pounds for the abdication, but the emperor declined the offer vehemently.[110] Having been disappointed in the League and the great powers, in the spring of 1938, Emperor Haile Selassie began to get ready for his return to Ethiopia in order to take over the leadership of the Resistance. He held secret negotiations with Count Carl Gustaf von Rosen,[111] and asked him to arrange his arrival in the city of Gore, where the headquarters of the interim government was located. When the British Foreign Office learned about Haile Selassie's plans, its officials persuaded him to refrain from returning, because the Italians could kill the Ethiopian monarch during that dangerous journey.

London's ostensible humanity was dictated by self-serving intentions. While it opposed Italy's aggression in the League of Nations, Great Britain, however, signed the Mediterranean Agreement of 1937–1938, in order to keep Mussolini away from Hitler. The emperor and his family were allowed to remain in Albion as refugees. That said, London was engaged in negotiations with Italy regarding the Ethiopian leader's abdication. If Italy were to enter the war on Hitler's side, Haile Selassie would go back to Ethiopia as an ally of Great Britain and would lead hostilities against Italy.

In 1939, Great Britain and France came to a final conclusion that Italy would indeed become Germany's ally. Soon after, the Foreign Office began to carry out its "Ethiopian plan." The government of Great Britain started to publicly offer help to the Emperor of Ethiopia. In the summer of 1939, Haile Selassie's special representative Lorenzo Taezaz and people from his escort—French Colonel Paul Robert Monnier and a few anti-Fascists he had recruited—crossed the Ethiopian border and met the patriots in the province of Gojjam in the country's west. They wanted to get detailed information about the operations of the Resistance forces.[112]

On June 10, 1940, the *Duce*, speaking from the balcony of the same Venetian palace where he had announced formation of Italy's eastern Africa and collapse of the Ethiopian Empire to his fellow citizens a few years back, declared that Italy had entered the war on Germany's side. As it feared for its dominions in Africa, in the Near and Far East, Great Britain started to assist the Ethiopian patriots. To effectively control those activities, London needed someone who would enjoy unconditional authority among people of the occupied territories and would guarantee stability in Ethiopia. There was no one better suited for that mission than Emperor Haile Selassie I.

Naturally, the emperor of Ethiopia was well aware of the motives that drove Great Britain to side with him. He understood that the Queen of the Seas probably had not given up her intention to annex the provinces of Welega and Gojjam to the Anglo-Egyptian Sudan. Great Britain was revising its policy, in order to get a foothold in Ethiopia.

This assumption can be supported by a May 16, 1941 message from Herschel Johnson, the Minister-Counselor of the U.S. Embassy in London, who referred to a statement made by a responsible official of the British Foreign

Office about Great Britain's true intentions with respect to the Ethiopian Empire. "The Foreign Office . . . desires to use the Emperor as an instrument of authority in a part of Ethiopia and has accordingly given his government a measure of recognition but is making clear to the Emperor that he must act only by and with British consent," Johnson wrote to Wallace Murray, Director of the Office of Near Eastern and African Affairs, U.S. State Department. "The British Government is far from being prepared to admit the Emperor's government to the status of an ally or to state when it might again recognize Ethiopia as a fully independent state."[113]

Nevertheless, the ruling circles of Great Britain and France realized how important for them a union with the emperor was, as he was the supreme legitimate representative of Ethiopia. Anthony Eden and Winston Churchill publicly declared . . . "The upshot of the meeting was no treaty but agreement to recognize Haile Selassie as leader of a war of liberation, to be given full freedom of movement, and to be kept in touch with every development which concerned Ethiopia. The Ethiopian refugees were to be armed and trained and known as Patriot Army. The rebellion was to be encouraged with arms and money and coordinated by a trained British staff."[114] Not all politicians shared their view; there were people on the banks of the Thames who wanted to make Ethiopia a British protectorate—those were, for instance, high-ranking military men and colonial officials of the Anglo-Egyptian Sudan.

On June 10, 1940, after Italy had declared war on Great Britain and France, Winston Churchill and Anthony Eden publicly acknowledged the illegitimacy of Ethiopia's annexation by Italy. They did not wait to see navigation in the Mediterranean to be closed, and on June 24, they decided to dispatch Haile Selassie to the Middle East.

THE VOYAGE OF "MR. STRONG"

In 1940, Haile Selassie (just like in 1936) incognito set off on his journey from the Paddington station, and, via France and Malta, he went to Egypt. He traveled under the nom de guerre of Mr. Strong. In the Middle East, there were only four people who knew about that secret traveler: Sir Miles Lampson (future Lord Killearn), Great Britain's ambassador to Egypt; General (later Earl) Archibald Wavell, Commander-in-Chief, Middle East; Brigadier Iltyd Clayton, head of the Middle East Intelligence Centre; Mr. (later Sir) Edwin Chapman-Andrews, a former British consul in Harar, an expert in Ethiopian affairs and the emperor's friend (he later became his political advisor). Haile Selassie, with his son Prince Makonnen and other members of his circle, arrived in Alexandria on June 25, 1940. He was met by Chapman-Andrews.[115]

A lot of Italy's subjects were stationed in Alexandria, so the emperor's presence was kept in strict confidence. In the morning of June 26, 1940, after a short stay in Luxor, the emperor and his retinue flew to Sudan, and Governor-General Stewart Symes received a telegram notifying the emperor's intention of going to Khartoum.[116] Sudanese authorities were annoyed by the news of the arrival of the emperor of Ethiopia in Khartoum, so they sent a telegram, signed by Symes, that the emperor would be staying in Wadi Halfa (a small village on the border of Sudan and Egypt). They were afraid that Italy might attack Sudan from Eritrea and Ethiopia, so they altered the emperor's traveling route. The emperor stayed in Wadi Halfa, a Khartoum suburb, for a week. During that time, the Sudanese administration was arguing with Middle East Command that insisted that Haile Selassie must be allowed to pass to Khartoum. Ultimately, Sudanese authorities had to obey the order of Middle East Command. On July 3, 1940, the emperor arrived in Khartoum. Sudanese authorities placed a solitary villa under enhanced security on a Niles bank at his disposal. For the sake of secrecy, the residence did not even have a phone. But the emperor learned that the British were doing nothing to form Ethiopian units, that Kenyan colonial authorities were using Ethiopian refugees in construction works, regarding them as Italian subjects, that Ethiopian emigrants not only were not allowed to complete military training to take part in hostilities with the Italians, they were restricted in everything. The emperor had every reason to despair.[117] He could not demand anything from the authorities of the Anglo-Egyptian Sudan.

Given an extremely difficult situation, Haile Selassie sent a proposal to Anthony Eden, Great Britain's Secretary of State for War, who was in Cairo at the time, that a long-term official treaty on friendship and union be concluded between Ethiopia and Great Britain. Surprisingly, the head of the British War Office heard him. After three-day consultations in Cairo, the secretary of state for war recognized Haile Selassie I as the leader of the Ethiopian Liberation Army. In his new capacity, he had an unrestricted freedom of movement, an opportunity to be informed about the developments going on in Ethiopia and to build an army of Ethiopian patriots in emigration. Middle East Command was obliged to provide material and moral support to Haile Selassie. To keep up contacts with the emperor, to offer military training to Ethiopian emigrants and to develop plans, Middle East Command of the British armed forces appointed a middleman—Major (later Major General) Orde Wingate, an officer of the Royal Artillery.[118]

Haile Selassie could not rule out that the British would be using him as a puppet; his response to Wingate's speech during their first meeting in October 1940 gives evidence of his misgivings. Wingate said, in particular: "I bring you most respectful greetings, sire" . . . "and my warm personal admiration." . . . "In 1935, fifty-two nations let you and your country down. That act of aggression led to this war . . . I came as your advisor to you and the forces that will take you back to your country and your throne. We offer you freedom and an equal among the nations. But it will be no sort of place if you have no share in your own liberation. You will take the leading part in what is to come." The Emperor reflected upon Wingate and his words. "What part can I play?" . . . "Nothing is being done. They have even prevented my escaped troops from coming here from Kenya, I sit here and time passes. I am being used as a pawn."[119]

After Wingate's arrival, full-scale training of the Ethiopian patriotic army began in Khartoum. Ethiopian refugees were transferred from Kenya to Sudan where they were receiving military training in the hands of British sergeants and officers. Major Wingate was not only a training officer for future soldiers, he became a close aide and advisor to the emperor.

One incident that took place in December 1940 is noteworthy. Colonel Brocklehurst arrived in Cairo one day; he was an envoy of Kenyan and Rhodesian (now those lands are in Zambia and Zimbabwe) white settlers who wanted to establish an East African Federation under British colonial control after the war. They wanted fertile lands of Ethiopia's south to be part of the federation. The colonel arrived in order to hold consultations with General Wavell, Commander-in-Chief, Middle East, on organizing an uprising of the "Galla" (*Oromo Author's note*) people, both against Italian invaders and against Emperor Haile Selassie I.[120]

When he learned about the purpose of the colonel's mission, Wingate immediately came to the emperor and advised him to act without delay. "The theory of the Brocklehurst Mission means dividing Ethiopia against herself and . . . . You must get into touch with London and tell them that you suspect the motives of behind this move and smell a colonial plot."[121]

Haile Selassie sent a telegram to Prime Minister Churchill, declaring his strong protest, and a few days later, he received assurances from General Wavell that he would not allow Brocklehurst to enter Ethiopian territory.[122]

Haile Selassie was aware how costly restoration of Ethiopia's sovereignty would be. By sending a wire to the head of the government of Great Britain, he still wanted to avoid a conflict with colonial authorities of the Anglo-Egyptian Sudan, even though he knew about the plans, which were in the works, to establish the rule of the British administration in the territory of so-called Italy's eastern Africa. The wise and patient monarch did not harbor ambition or pride.

In January 1941, British-Ethiopian troops began their advance into Italy's eastern Africa. On January 20, 1941, at 6:40 a.m., Emperor Haile Selassie I and an 800-strong battalion he was leading crossed the Ethiopian border. Haile Selassie raised Ethiopia's national flag at Omedla in the province of Gojjam (in the country's west). On the same day, British troops under command of General William Platt advanced through Kassala (a city in the east of

Sudan) to Eritrea, and General Alan Cunningham crossed over from Kenya. In March 1941, Belgian units joined them from south-west.

Meanwhile, Middle-East Command of the British armed forces (with headquarters in Cairo) designed a plan of establishing control over the areas retaken from Italian invaders. For the Ethiopian leadership, it was a complete surprise. Indeed, during the five-year Italian occupation, Ethiopia did not lose its sovereignty, and its government had been functional all along. Great Britain considered Ethiopia enemy territory only because the European nation had to recognize legitimacy of its occupation by Italy once.

In February 1941, in order to hold official negotiations with Emperor Haile Selassie I, Maurice S. Lush, a representative of Middle-East Command, arrived in the province of Gojjam. His mission was to announce British plans. Those plans were not approved. On March 20, 1941, Philip Mitchell (a former governor of Uganda) met with Anthony Eden, Great Britain's Secretary of State for War, and General (later Field Marshal) John Dill, Chief of the General Staff, in Cairo. When the matter was discussed, Eden rejected a plan of establishing a protectorate.

Lord Rennell of Rodd wrote: "Rejection of any idea of protectorate, or provision of a strong western administration in the country (Ethiopia *authors note*) not only would such a policy be contrary to H.M.G.s general line, and wholly unacceptable to the Emperor, but the military commitment involved was beyond British resources at a time when General Wavell needed every man and weapon in the Middle East for other purposes and proposed to withdraw all the British troops as soon as the Italians had been liquidated."[123] Russian (Soviet) scholar V. S. Yagiya had a different opinion: "The British abandoned their plan to establish a protectorate in Ethiopia because, first, Great Britain did not have enough troops to carry out that idea, and, second, because London was afraid lest it might provoke indignation (and, ultimately, an uprising) of the entire Ethiopian people and also feared a negative reaction of the democratic community worldwide and, especially, of nationalistic forces in colonial nations of Asia and Africa."[124]

Lord Rennell of Rodd and V. S. Yagiya were possibly right. But one should also take into account the key reasons that made British authorities give up an idea of direct invasion of Ethiopia. As likely as not, it was an economic factor, and, to a lesser degree, political considerations. Indeed, ahead of World War II, British economy was undergoing a deep crisis. The country was unable (and it was not to its advantage) to conquer and control new colonies, such as Ethiopia. Governing postwar Ethiopia would mean investing huge funds into the infrastructure, in public administration, and, finally, in the social sector. British capital was incapable of outlays of that extent. As for the opinion of the democratic community, it was of no importance. It is a well-known fact that protests of the European public in the 1930s did not save Ethiopia or Czechoslovakia or Poland or other countries from the Fascist and Nazi aggression. Therefore, it is hard to support the opinion that annexation of Ethiopia by Great Britain could spark a massive public outcry. And it would be problematic to expect any action on the part of the nations that were under Great Britain's colonial influence.

Disguising direct annexation, official London wished to be if not the only but at least the most influential power in the political, economic, and even cultural life of the Ethiopian Empire. Great Britain was putting up a front of being in negotiations with the Ethiopian leadership. Here is their outcome:

1. Emperor Haile Selassie I was recognized as being entitled to issue pronouncements, called "Awaj," the Amharic equivalent of "proclamations," and the British occupying authority would only issue "Public Notices" (interim laws).
2. Ethiopian Courts would deal with cases arising among Ethiopians, and death sentences were to be approved by the emperor. The Authorities would however, have to insist on war crimes being tried by British Military Courts, as well as cases in which foreigners were involved.
3. The emperor would appoint officials following consultations with the British occupation authorities.[125]

It was a temporary retreat of the Ethiopian administration. As long as Italian invaders were still in the country and the national administrative apparatus was unable to function (and even its future place in liberated Ethiopia was debatable), it would be unwise to aggravate the already complicated relations with British authorities.

By the moment when the agreement between Emperor Haile Selassie and Maurice Lush was signed, the situation across the fronts in northeastern Africa had changed in favor of the allies. The South-African units under command of General Cunningham, having liberated British Somaliland and Ethiopia's south, approached Addis Ababa. Units of General Platt were pressing the enemy in Eritrea. Ethiopian units under the emperor's command fully liberated the province of Gojjam, and, on April 5, 1941, took its principal city, Debre Markos. A road to Addis Ababa was opened. However, further advance of Ethiopian troops was suspended. Wingate received a strict order from Khartoum to check further advance of the emperor and to keep him in Gojjam.

Some Western historians explain this decision of British command by a desire to prevent bloodshed between Ethiopian population and the Italians stationed in the capital. Soviet (Russian) authors are of another opinion, and they believe that the main reason for the delay of the emperor's return to the capital was the willingness of British authorities to get ahead of him. They wanted to buy time in order to set up bodies of British military administration. On April 6, the South-African units led by General Cunningham made the Italian garrison in Addis Ababa surrender. The war was approaching its end, but Ethiopia's ruling elite still did not have permission to enter the capital city.

In all the places from whence Italian invaders had been driven out, bodies of British military administration were vigorously established. Brigadier Maurice Lush became head of the administration (i.e., military governor) and commander of the British troops. The head of Middle-East Command (through the head of the political section) was in charge of general control in the administration. To exercise control everywhere, occupation authorities divided the country into nine provinces: Gonder, Tigray, Gojjam, Wollo, Shewa, Welega, Sidamo, Jimma, and Harrar. In order to involve local chiefs in cooperation, a special mission was sent to every district. The emperor of Ethiopia protested against those arbitrary decisions.[126]

British authorities allowed the emperor to come back to the capital only sometime later. For that event, Haile Selassie I picked May 5, 1941. On that day, the emperor, accompanied by Ethiopian troops raised by Orde Wingate in Khartoum in 1940 and by a 7,000-strong unit of Ethiopian patriots under command of *Ras* Abebe Aregai, entered Addis Ababa. Until the 1974 revolution, that day was celebrated in Ethiopia as the Liberation Day on which the country became free from the yoke of Fascist Italy.

In Addis Ababa, the emperor made a historic speech, in which he said: "This day is a day on which a fresh chapter of the history of the New Ethiopia begins. . . . Do not return evil for evil. Do not indulge in the atrocities which the enemy has been practicing in his usual way, even up to the last moment. Take care not to spoil the good name of Ethiopia by acts which are worthy of the enemy. We shall see that our enemies are disarmed and sent the same way they came."[127]

NOTES

1. Haile Selassie I. 1929. P. 142–143.

2. Ibid. P. 142.

3. Barker A.J. *The Civilizing Mission: The Italian-Ethiopian War 1935–1936.* L., 1968. P. 46 (hereinafter—Barker A.J. 1968).

4. Tsypkin G.V. *Ethiopia in Anticolonial Wars.* Moscow, 1988. P. 209 (hereinafter—Tsypkin G.V. 1988) (in Russian).

5. Haile Selassie I. 1929. P. 145. See details in: Archives of Merse Hazen Wolde Kirkos. Doc. No. 29 02.08 EMML (Amharic). 1923 (Ethiopian Calendar).

6. Cit. in: Del Boca A. *The Ethiopian War 1935–1941.* Chicago; London, 1969. P. 34.

7. See: Yagiya V.S. 1978. P. 72–73.

8. See, for instance, Chernetsev R.B. in: Ryszard Kapuściński's book *Emperor* (Moscow, 1992. P. 124) (in Russian).

9. Markakis J. *Ethiopia: Anatomy of Traditional Policy.* Oxford, 1974. P. 271 (hereinafter—Markakis J. 1974).

10. Mahteme Selassie Wolde Maskal. *Zekra nagar.* Addis Ababa, 1942 (Ethiopian Calendar). P. 789–807 (in Amharic) (hereinafter—Mahteme Selassie Wolde Maskal 1942).

11. Cit. in: Clapham Ch. *Haile Selassie's Government.* L., 1970. P. 141.

12. See the text of the 1931 Constitution in: Mahteme Selassie Wolde Maskal. 1942. P. 777–808; James C.N. Paul, Christopher Clapham. *Ethiopian Constitutional Development: A Source Book.* Addis Ababa, 1972. Vol. 1. P. 326–336 (hereinafter—Ethiopian Constitutional Development).

13. See: Perham M. *The Government of Ethiopia.* L., 1948. P. 165 (hereinafter—Perham M. 1948).

14. Mahteme Selassie Wolde Maskal. 1942. P. 204–205.

15. One *gasha* was equivalent to 25 hectares. Despite the resolution, payment of taxes in kind was practiced until 1975.

16. See: Pankhurst R. *Economic History of Ethiopia 1800–1935.* Addis Ababa. 1968. P. 492 (hereinafter—Pankhurst R. 1968).

17. Tsypkin G.V., Yagiya V.S. 1989. P. 147.

18. According to the 1924 law, slaves were to remain in possession of the deceased owner's heirs for 7 years.

19. Autobiography (English). P. 81.

20. See: Pankhurst R. 1968. P. 682.

21. Yagiya V.S. 1978. P. 91.

22. Later, Haile Selassie Gugsa collaborated with the Italians.

23. Autobiography (English). P. 206.

24. George W. Baer. *The coming of the Italian—Ethiopian War.* Cambridge, Massachusetts 1967. P. 23.

25. Cit. in: Markakis J. 1974. P. 271.

26. See: Yagiya V.S. 1978. P. 93.

27. cit. by Voblikov D.R. 1961. P. 62.

28. Ibid. The Morning Post 6 XI 1933 cit. by Voblikov D.R. 1961. P. 62.

29. Barker A.J. *The Civilizing Mission: A History of the Italo-Ethiopian War of 1935–1936.* New York. 1968. P. 10 (hereinafter—George W. Baer. 1968).

30. Gertik I. *Across the Red Sea.* M. 1933. P. 84–85.

31. Documents of the USSR Foreign Policy. Moscow, 1973. Vol. XVIII. P. 108–109 (in Russian).

32. During the war, in the spring of 1936, Ethiopian-Soviet negotiations on establishment of diplomatic relations took place again—in Moscow and in Paris.

33. The agreement signed in Addis Ababa on August 1, 1935 was never ratified. Details about Ethiopian-Swedish relations see in: Hallidin V. Norberg. *Swedes in Haile Selassie's Ethiopia 1924–1952.* Uppsala, 1977.

34. Trofimov V.A. 1979. P. 147.

35. Tsypkin G.V. 1988. P. 214.

36. Ibid. P. 222.

37. Cit. in: Greenfield R. 1965. P. 194.

38. Triulzi A. Italian Colonialism and Ethiopia. _Journal of African History._ 1982. Vol. 23. No. 2. P. 239.

39. On November 23, 1934, a special British-Ethiopian commission set up to put an end to border conflicts arrived at the Wal Wal oasis, which is located hinterland, 100 km from the then-Ethiopian border with Italian Somaliland. The commission was guarded by a 600-strong unit of Ethiopian troops led by _Fitawrari_ Shiferaw. As soon as it arrived at Wal Wal, the commission suddenly saw an Italian armed unit that had about 250 people in it. After the Italians refused to withdraw from Ethiopian territory, an armed clash between the Italians and the Ethiopian servicemen accompanying the commission occurred. Historians call the conflict "the Wal Wal incident."

40. See: Thomas M Coffey. _Lion by the Tail: The Story of the Italian-Ethiopian War._ N.Y., 1974. P. 14–15 (hereinafter—Thomas M Coffey. 1974); Greenfield R. 1965. P. 191.

41. Sidney Barton was a career diplomat who had served in Shanghai and in 1932 was appointed Great Britain's minister in Ethiopia. By some accounts, he was an unofficial advisor of Emperor Haile Selassie. See: Coffey M. Thomas. 1974. P. 10.

42. Thomas M. Coffey. 1974. P. 16.

43. See: Greenfield R. 1965. P. 192; see also: Marcus H.G. 1987. P. 170.

44. Thomas M Coffey. 1974. P. 19.

45. Cit. in: Thomas M Coffey. 1974. P. 24.

46. Ibid. P. 30.

47. Ibid. P. 37.

48. League of Nations Official Journal. L., May 1935. P. 572 (hereinafter—LNOJ).

49. Foreign Relations of the United States. Washington, 1935. Vol. 1. P. 727 (hereinafter—FRUS)

50. See details in: Nesterova T.P. The Rickett Concession in Ethiopia (April–September 1935). International Relations in the Balkans and the Middle East. Sverdlovsk, 1988. P. 62–73 (in Russian).

51. Peace and War. United States Foreign Policy 1931–1941. Washington, 1943. P. 261 (hereinafter—PWUSFP).

52. Cit. in: Right M.V. The Soviet Union and the Struggle of Ethiopia's Peoples against Italian Aggression. Main Issues of African Studies. Ethnography. History. Philology. Moscow, 1973. P. 218–225 (in Russian). See also: History of Ethiopia. 1976. P. 475.

53. History of Ethiopia. 1976. P. 477.

54. Ibid.

55. PWUSFP. P. 271.

56. LNOJ. November 1935. P. 1133–1134.

57. Voblikov D. R. 1961. P. 71.

58. LNOJ. November 1935. P. 1352–1355.

59. Documents of International Affairs. Edited by John Wheeler-Bennet and Stephen Heald. L., 1935. Vol. II. P. 60–84 (hereinafter—DIA 1935).

60. Litvinov M.M. *Fighting for Peace*. Moscow, 1938. P. 84 (in Russian) (Litvinov M.M. 1938).

61. Tekle Hawariyat was a diplomat and military commander. He graduated from the Corps of Pages in St. Petersburg and lived in Russia for 12 years. During the Italo-Ethiopian War, he represented Ethiopia in the League of Nations.

62. Cit. in: Voblikov D.R. 1961. P. 75; History of Ethiopia. 1976. P. 482.

63. Cit. in: Litvinov M.M. 1938. P. 92–93.

64. LNOJ. November 1935. P. 1621–1624.

65. Steer G. Caesar in Abyssinia. Boston, 1937. P. 125. Cit. in: Voblikov D.R. 1961. P. 77.

66. LNOJ. Special supplement. Geneva, 1935. P. 112–113.

67. History of Diplomacy. Moscow, 1965. Vol. III. P. 620 (in Russian).

68. Winston S. Churchill. *The Second World War. The Gathering Storm. Book one From War to War 1919-1939*. Boston, New York. 1961 Vol. I. P. 158–159. (Hereinafter—Winston S. Churchill. 1961).

69. Thomas M. Thomas. 1974. P. 62.

70. Ibid.

71. Cit. in: Price G. Extra Special Correspondents. L., 1957. P. 242.

72. For details on the US position, see Brice Harris, Jr. *The United States and the Italo-Ethiopian Crises*. Stanford, CA: Stanford University Press, 1964.

73. Cit. in: Voblikov D.R. 1961. P. 89.

74. See: Robertson E.M. Mussolini as Empire-Builder. *Europe and Africa 1932–1936*. 1977. No. 4. P. 118.

75. Harris B. *The United States and the Italo-Ethiopian Crisis*. Stanford, 1964. P. 71.

76. History of Diplomacy. Moscow, 1965. Vol. III. P. 621.

77. For the text of the Hoare-Laval Plan see: DIA. 1935. P. 360; Haile Selassie I 1929. P. 209–210.

78. Cit. in: Barker A.J. 1968. P. 203–204.

79. Ibid. P. 204.

80. See: Articles of the Convention respecting the Laws and Customs of War on Land (1907). https://www.icrc.org/rus/resources/documents/misc/hague-convention-iv-181007.htm (accessed 20 July 2022).

81. Cit. in: Tsypkin G.V. 1988. P. 241.

82. See: Tsypkin G.V., Yagiya V.S. 1979. P. 178; Greenfield R. 1965. P. 216.

83. Greenfield R. Op. cit. P. 221.

84. See: Yagiya V.S. 1978. P. 112.

85. Mosley L. 1964. P. 230–231.

86. Haile Selassie I 1929. P. 243–244.

87. Haile Selassie I 1929. P. 143–144. Some historians assert it was *Ras* Imiru who was head of the government. See, for instance: Yagiya V.S. 1978. P. 113; History of Ethiopia. 1976. P. 511, etc. *Ras* Imiru became regent on July 20, 1936.

88. See: Yagiya V.S. 1978. P. 112.

89. DIA. P. 463. (462) Voblikov D.R. 1961. P. 101.

90. Documents on Italian war crimes submitted to the United Nations War Crimes Commission by the Imperial Ethiopian Government. Vol. I: Italian Telegrams and Circulars. Addis Abeba, 1949. P. 31.

91. John H. Spencer. *Ethiopia at Bay. A Personal Account of the Haile Selassie Year.* Michigan, 1984. P. 71 (hereinafter—John H. Spencer 1984).

92. Cit. in: Voblikov D.R. 1961. P. 101.

93. Autobiography (Amharic). P. 253–264.

94. Voblikov D.R. 1961. P. 128.

95. Emperor Haile Selassie I. *Autobiography.* Addis Ababa, 1934 (Ethiopian Calendar). Part II. P. 21–22 (in Amharic) (hereinafter—Autobiography. 1934).

96. See: Autobiography. 1934. P. 46–47; Voblikov D.R. 1961. P. 129–130.

97. Harris Joseph E. *African-American Reactions to War in Ethiopia, 1936–1941.* Baton Rouge: Louisiana State University Press, 1944. P. 93–103.

98. John H. Spencer 1984. P. 71. The author agrees that Anthony Eden played a positive role with respect to Ethiopia in those years. As Great Britain's representative in the League of Nations, it was he who had proposed sanctions against Italy.

99. Leonard Mosley Haile Selassie. *The Conquering Lion.* L. 1964 P. 243; Autobiography (Amharic). Part II. 1934. P. 73; See details in Keith Bowers. *Imperial Exile. Emperor Haile Selassie in Britain 1936-40.* Addis Ababa. 2016. P. 94–96.

100. Voblikov D.R. 1961. P. 131.

101. Ibid.

102. Ibid.

103. Leonard Mosley. 1964. P. 247.

104. Cit. in: Autobiography. 1934. P. 144–145; Voblikov D.R. 1961. P. 132.

105. Winston S. Churchill. 1961. P. 159.

106. Thomas M Coffey. 1974. P. XI.

107. History of Ethiopia. 1976. P. 527; According to Ian Campbell, the massacre, which was conducted over three days, was authorized at the highest levels of the Fascist Party in Rome, and organized by the head of the Party in Addis Ababa, *Guido Cortese.* Ian Campbell. The Addis Ababa Massacre: Italy's National Shame. https://oxford.universitypressscholarship.com/view/10.1093/oso/9780190674724.001.0001/oso-9780190674724-chapter-006 (accessed 24 July 2022). According to Yagya V.S. Guido Cortese was also among the wounded. Yagya V.S. 1978. P. 129.

108. Autobiography. 1934. P. 53–71. See also: Documents on Italian War Crimes Submitted to the United Nations War Crimes Commission by the Imperial Ethiopian Government. Vol. I: Italian Telegrams and Circulars. Published by Command of His Imperial Majesty. Addis Ababa: Ministry of Justice, 1949.

109. Cit. in: History of Ethiopia. 1976. P. 514.

110. Autobiography. 1934. P. 81–94.

111. Von Rosen was a Swedish subject, later employed as the chief instructor for the Imperial Ethiopian Air Force. His contribution during the years of the war with the Fascists was considerable. Shocked by barbaric attacks of the Fascists, he volunteered for frontline duty, where he carried wounded Ethiopian soldiers to safety in the most difficult situations, under never-ceasing fire from the enemy aircraft. He was the

only pilot who ventured to make flights, often without local maps, in order to rescue the wounded and victims of gas attacks. He also received mustard gas burns. After the fall of Addis Ababa and the emperor's departure, he continued his humanitarian mission outside of the occupied territories.

112. Autobiography. 1934. P. 178.

113. FRUS. 1941. Vol. III. P. 350.

114. Leonard Mosley. 1964. P. 255; Autobiography. 1934. P. 285.

115. Leonard Mosley. Ibid. P. 251.

116. Ibid.

117. Ibid. P. 253.

118. Orde Charles Wingate (1903–1944) was a British major general. With an excellent track record in guerrilla war, in the 1930s he contributed to establishment and training of irregular Jewish groups that carried out operations against Arabs in Palestine, and in 1941, he organized Sudanese and Ethiopian guerrilla forces to offer resistance to Italian invaders and restore Ethiopia's sovereignty. He created and led the Chindits, a guerrilla group in Burma that fought behind Japanese lines. He died in a plane crash soon after the beginning of a second, a more large-scale, jungle penetration operation of the Chindits. After his tragic death, in memory of this outstanding commander the General Wingate School was established in Addis Ababa on May 5, 1946.

119. Cit. in: Mosley L. *Gideon Goes to War*. New York. 1955. P. 103.

120. Mosley L. 1964. P. 260.

121. Ibid. P. 261.

122. Autobiography. 1934. P. 252–254.

123. Lord Rennell of Rodd. *British Military Administration of Occupied Territories in Africa during the Years 1941–1947*. L., 1948. P. 63 (hereinafter—Rodd R. 1948).

124. Yagiya V.S. *Ethiopia in 1941–1954*. Moscow, 1969. P. 28 (hereinafter—Yagiya V.S. 1969).

125. Rodd R. 1948. P. 64.

126. Perham M. *The Government of Ethiopia*. L., 1969. P. 345.

127. Autobiography. 1934. P. 315–316.

Chapter 3

For Sovereign Ethiopia

BRITISH OCCUPATION AUTHORITIES

With the emperor back in the capital city, the country seemed to get back its political independence. In reality, to restore its sovereignty turned out to be an extremely complicated thing that took a long time to accomplish. Great Britain's ruling circles were regarding Ethiopia as a war trophy.

Speaking in the House of Commons in February 1941, Anthony Eden said that "Her Majesty's government will welcome the revival of the independent Ethiopian state and will recognize the claims of Emperor Haile Selassie I to the throne; that Great Britain has no territorial claims . . . that at this stage of the military campaign of the armed forces of Her Majesty in some regions of Ethiopia a military administration will be established, that it carries out its activities in consultation with the Emperor (Haile Se-lassie I.—*Author's note*) and will be eliminated (suspended) as soon as the situation in the country returns to normal."[1] A misleading harangue that sounds very much like a children's counting-out rhyme: "Don't say 'yes,' and don't say 'no'!"

In practice, British military authorities did not want to abandon their laurels and treated Ethiopia as "occupied enemy territory." The country was under control of the British military administration. Ethiopia was considered to be part of Italy liberated by British troops, so everywhere, once Italian invaders were driven out, British military administrative bodies were put in place. They were headed by Philip Mitchell, Chief Political Officer for the Commander in Chief, East Africa.

In the opinion of British military authorities, Haile Selassie I had no right to claim power (!) before a peace treaty was signed between Great Britain and Italy. Until then, the king of Italy remained formally the lawful ruler of Ethiopia.

According to occupation laws, the country was to be ruled by a vice king. Since the Duke d'Aosta had been recalled from Addis Ababa to Rome, his powers were transferred to Philip Mitchell. For some time, he had been governor of Uganda and knew how to communicate with local tribal chieftains. Mitchell thought of Haile Selassie I as a chief that could be bribed or removed or deceived.

Mitchell divided Ethiopia into nine districts: Gondar, Tigrai, Gojjam, Wollo, Showa, Wollega, Sidamo, Gimma, and Harrar.[2] Against Haile Selassie's will, a mission led by a British officer was sent to each district. General Maurice Lush, Mitchell's deputy, was head of the Ethiopian administration. He went out of his way to win sympathies of the local Ethiopian nobility. The struggle for sovereignty was unfolding amid a dismal background of devastation.

According to estimates of the Ethiopian government, the damage caused by Italy amounted to 132.5 million pounds sterling. Human casualties equaled 750,000 people, (i.e., 10% of the population), and there were many more wounded and injured. Houses, roads, and bridges had been destroyed.[3] As a result of the use of chemical weapons, many localities were no longer fit for living.

Serious impediments arose because of lack of local governance. In 1936, the Italians had canceled the Ethiopian administrative system established in the 1920s and replaced it with a colonial administration.

Reconstruction of the ruined economy required huge funds and qualified workforce. Public coffers were empty, and virtually none of the Ethiopian specialists who had been educated at home and abroad were living anymore (many of them had died during the terror of February 1937).

The Ethiopian government had to put up with the moves of the British military authorities that taking full control of the territory and had to consult them on its own actions aimed at the country's revival.

In 1941, Emperor Haile Selassie I agreed to Ogaden (the eastern part of Ethiopia's territory in the province of Harar) staying under governance of the British administration of Italian Somaliland. Furthermore, British authorities were in full control of the country's finances; they collected duties and funds that covered spending of the Sudan administration and the military administration. They were also in control of the Ethiopian part of the Addis Ababa-Djibouti railway. Ethiopian foreign trade was carried out through the British company Middle East Supply Centre.

Unwilling to put up with that situation, the emperor began to reinforce the central administration. On May 11, 1941, Haile Selassie I formed his government and appointed the governor of the province of Shewa (central part of Ethiopia). The British military authorities were not advised of the fact, contrary to the March 1941 gentlemen's agreement.

The move displeased Philip Mitchell, Chief Political Officer for Great Britain's Middle East Command. To find out the circumstances, he dispatched his envoy, General Maurice Lush, to Addis Ababa (previously, Lush had served in Sudan, and, according L. Mosley, did not like the Habesha people). Lush was to perform a special mission and meet the emperor. He was received by the emperor's aide, Wolde Giorgis. Lush reminded that "His Majesty (Haile Selassie I.—*Author's note*) cannot fully reassume his status and powers as Emperor until a peace treaty has been signed with Italy. Until that happens the King of Italy remains the legal ruler of Ethiopia," and demanded that the decree appointing ministers be annulled.[4] Finally, the two parties reached an agreement that the appointed ministers would perform duties of advisors for the headquarters of the British military administration.

On May 23, 1941, Philip Mitchell himself arrived in Addis Ababa. In the course of negotiations, Haile Selassie I showed a draft of the future treaty between the two countries, Great Britain and Ethiopia, to the head of the military administration. The document contained the following provisions:

1. a regular army was to be created in Ethiopia very shortly;
2. financial activities were to be streamlined;
3. civil administration was to be restored;
4. financial and legal advisors from Great Britain were to be sent to Ethiopia.[5]

The treaty also raised the issue of the size of the compensation for England's participation in the liberation war against Italian Fascism. Mitchell promised to the emperor to communicate these proposals to the government of Great Britain.

Since the members of Haile Selassie's government appointed on May 11 were still considered ministers, legality of the emperor's decrees and their implementation did not raise objections. By making some concessions to England, he remained the principal figure in Ethiopian politics. As he invested his ministers with powers and authorities, the emperor proved to the people, dissatisfied with the military administration, that he was protecting public interest. He thus garnered sympathies of "patriotic nationalists" who believed that the emperor and his retinue were unworthy to rule the country, because during the hostilities they had lived in Europe, far away from the war.

London was not happy with the decree of May 11, 1941. At a meeting of the war cabinet on June 9, Mitchell received an instruction to begin negotiations on concluding an official agreement between the two countries, once he was back to Addis Ababa. In late June, a meeting was held between Haile Selassie I and Philip Mitchell. During that encounter, the British side brought so-called covenants up for discussion. They stipulated that the emperor would be obliged to follow advice of the British government; to get London's preliminary approval of all matters related to taxes and expenditure; to recognize the right of the commander-in-chief of the British troops to establish war control in any part of the country, if necessary; to get consent of the British government to any movement of Ethiopian military units and to hostilities, if he should wish to wage them of his own accord; to retain jurisdiction of British courts with respect to foreigners residing in Ethiopia.[6]

The Ethiopian side refused to accept Mitchell's proposals, because it would mean voluntary transfer of sovereignty into the hands of the military administration.

Moreover, the British side was persistently demanding territorial concessions according to the borders instituted by the Italians. Eritrea was to get from Ethiopia the province of Tigray, and Italian Somaliland was to receive the province of Harrar and the district of Ogaden. The Ethiopian side did not agree to those concessions.

Another subject that gave rise to heated debate was evacuation of Italian prisoners-of-war and civilians. The Ethiopian side insisted that Italian citizens who wished to live and work in the country (and there were quite a lot of such people) should not be evacuated. Ethiopia was badly in need of qualified specialists (electricians, mechanical engineers, builders, telegraph operators, etc.). British occupation authorities probably regarded those citizens as competitors.

By September 1941, the political situation in the Ethiopian Empire aggravated. Both the nobility and the populace expressed discontent with the British military administration. Large rallies were organized in Addis Ababa. Population demanded that military administration be abolished, that British troops be pulled out, and that an agreement for the settlement of Anglo-Ethiopian relations be concluded.

In October 1941, those relations reached an impasse, and the negotiations were suspended. Philip Mitchell, head of the military administration, went to London for consultations with the leadership of the government of Great Britain on looking for ways out of the crisis and the prospects of making a treaty.

As a result of the consultations, a special committee chaired by Lord John Anderson was set up under the War Office; it was to work out a new course of Great Britain's policy. London discussions to amend the draft agreement and war convention between the Ethiopian Empire and Great Britain lasted for nearly two months.

A break in the bilateral negotiations was not on the emperor's agenda. The Ethiopian nobility, dissatisfied with their situation, uncontrollable crowds, often armed, were a threat for the government of Haile Selassie I. In that situation, a clash of the population with troops of Great Britain could ignite very easily.

According to Waterfield, "Some races (the highest military leaders of Ethiopia), who fought against the Italians, even began, under the leadership of fugitive Italian officers (after the decision to deport them, they began to flee the concentration camps), to prepare their squads in case of a patriotic war against the British troops."[7]

In early November, without notifying representatives of the military administration, Haile Selassie I sent a wire to British Prime Minister Churchill, in which he asked for an explanation why the signing of the agreement was delayed. Churchill replied that "the delay was due entirely to the desire of the British Government to ensure that nothing remained in the agreement which could be interpreted as interfering with your sovereign rights or the independence Ethiopia."[8]

Having received these assurances from London, Haile Selassie I addressed the nation over the radio. In his speech, he referred to the reply of the British prime minister and said that there were no grounds to distrust the English. "If there are any anxious people who feel that the British now wish to restrict our independence, let them realize their error."[9] By making his speech, the emperor was pursuing two goals:

1. to comfort the Ethiopian people, especially radical patriot chiefs who could launch massive actions against the English;
2. to deal a psychological blow to the so-called group of "Cromerites" who openly advocated establishing control over Ethiopia according to the Sudanese model. They proclaimed being solicitous about the material values created by the Italians (industrial enterprises, means of communications, etc.), which, in their opinion, would become unusable in Ethiopian hands. The group was led by Maurice Lush, Deputy Chief Political Officer for Ethiopia.

On December 12, 1941, Mitchell returned to Addis Ababa with new drafts of the agreement prepared by Lord John Anderson's committee and approved by the government of Great Britain.

This time, negotiations pertaining to the conclusion of an Anglo-Ethiopian agreement were going faster, once a few amendments on which the Ethiopian side insisted were made, especially those related to territorial concessions. On January 31, 1942, the ceremonial signing of the Anglo-Ethiopian agreement and military convention took place at the imperial palace in Addis Ababa. On behalf of the Ethiopian Empire, the agreement was signed by Emperor Haile Selassie I, and on behalf of the British government, by Major General Philip Mitchell, Chief Political Officer for Great Britain's Commander in Chief, East Africa.[10]

In the recitals of the agreement that came down to history as the 1942 Anglo-Ethiopian agreement, the British government recognized Ethiopia as an independent and free state, and Emperor Haile Selassie I as its lawful ruler. Article I proclaimed restoration of diplomatic relations between the two countries through the appointment (accreditation) of ambassadors' plenipotentiary. A special clause said that a representative of Great Britain would have the upper hand compared with any other foreign minister accredited to His Imperial Majesty (i.e., Haile Selassie I).

At the request of His Majesty (Haile Selassie I), the government of Great Britain was to dispatch (facilitate dispatching) to Ethiopia British subjects as advisors to the emperor and his administration, and also police commissioners, officers and inspectors, and judges. As for the authorities, entitlements, emoluments and duties of the advisors, that matter was to be covered in a separate treaty between the two parties.

His Imperial Majesty also undertook not to appoint additional advisors without first consulting the government of Great Britain. Great Britain undertook to provide financial aid to Ethiopia in the amount of 1.5 million pounds sterling during the first year and 1 million pounds sterling during the second year of the treaty; if the agreement were to remain valid, a sum of 500,000 pounds sterling was to be provided during the third term, and 250,000 pounds sterling during the fourth term of the accord.[11]

The emperor was to consult the government of Great Britain on all matters related to currency circulation in the Ethiopian Empire. The East African shilling became the country's monetary unit.

Civil administration and the justice system were passed under the control of the Ethiopian government (art. III). Prisoners-of-war were to be handed over to British authorities, and the latter were to evacuate them from Ethiopia, if possible (art. VII). The British government promised to do its best in order to bring home the Ethiopians held prisoners by the Italians[12] and to render assistance in repatriation of the pieces of art that belonged to His Imperial Majesty, the Ethiopian State, private individuals, and local religious communities (art. VII).

Only British aircraft enjoyed free passage over Ethiopian territory, and airplanes of other countries were able to fly to Ethiopia only subject to consent of British authorities (art. XI).

As for the military convention, the parties agreed that the British government would send a military mission to Ethiopia in order to establish and train a regular Ethiopian army and would also cover all related expenses (art. II). Eastern territories remained under British military jurisdiction.

Thus, the 1942 agreement guaranteed that financial and military aid to Ethiopia would be provided by the government of Great Britain. The country was able to begin revival of its public administration that had been destroyed during the years of the Italian aggression and occupation. It needed not only reestablishment (restoration) of former institutions and ways of life, but transformation of the government and, most importantly, continuation of the reforms that had been begun before the Italian aggression, in order to reinforce a centralized state.

On January 29, 1943, instead of formerly existing seven ministries, eleven were set up: of war, foreign affairs, finance, justice, the interior, transport and public works, education and fine arts, post, telephone and telegraph, trade and industry, agriculture and ministry of the pen. Ministries were divided into departments headed by directors. Ministers and other high-ranking officials inside ministries were appointed by the emperor.

Ministers and deputy ministers reported to the emperor, instead of parliament, which also resumed work. Members of the parliament could not be appointed to ministerial offices.[13] The division of power, Ethiopian style, had its historical roots and motives that will be elucidated below.

In September 1943, a Council of Ministers was set up. It was led by prime minister. The main mission of the Council of Ministers was to make the emperor's orders and instructions known by ministers and to coordinate activities of ministries. Special assignments were given to the Ministry of the Interior, which controlled and directed local administrative bodies.

Since former borders of many provinces disappeared during the war and occupation, Ethiopian leadership instituted a new territorial division of the country. Twelve provinces were established: Arsi, Begemder and Semien, Gamu-Gofa, Gojjam, Illubabor, Kaffa, Sidamo, Tigray, Welega, Wollo, Hararghe, and Shewa. The provinces, in turn, were divided into 64 sub-provinces, which consisted of 321 districts and 1221 sub-districts.[14] After the 1974 revolution, the country's leadership gave up the reforms carried out by the government of Haile Selassie and returned to dividing the country into ethnic units, which gave rise to an interethnic conflict.

Borders of the provinces did not depend on their ethnic differences, so the novelty consolidated various ethnicities of Ethiopia into a single national community. Provinces were headed by governor-generals appointed by the emperor and reporting to the interior minister. In order to limit authorities of governor-generals, representatives of various ministries were delegated to provincial administrations, and those outsiders obeyed only the orders coming from the center.

Officials were appointed to high positions in provincial administrations only with the emperor's consent. Governor-generals were not allowed to have their own troops. Police were subordinated to the Interior Ministry.

Governor-generals were prohibited from entering into negotiations and signing agreements and treaties with foreign powers. The measure precluded some provincial feudal lords who were disloyal to the central government to enter into collusion with foreign powers (what they had done during the years of the war with Italy).

Governor-generals were also prohibited from levying any other taxes and duties on the population of the territories under their controls, except for those imposed by the State. A representative of the Finance Ministry supervised tax collection, and taxes were collected by specially appointed collectors.

Financial activities of governor-generals were supervised by an official appointed by the emperor. Thus, heads of provinces were deprived of any political, financial and administrative independence or military power, and were unable to affect activities of the central machinery of the state or oppose the center.

To neutralize the feudal nobility that was traditionally in opposition, Emperor Haile Selassie I appointed representatives of regional elites to some governorships, but deputies of governor-general's were proponents of reforms and innovations and were loyal to the central government. His personal experience of a provincial official and a monarch contributed a lot to the reinforcement of statehood.

After the agreement and the military convention had been signed on January 31, 1942, British troops began to leave Ethiopian territory. An exception was made for the areas that were to be controlled by the British military administration: The Reserved Area, Ogaden, the Ethiopian part of the Addis Ababa-Djibouti railway, and the cantonments (garrisons) in Addis Ababa, Dire Dawa, and Harrar. After the signing on December 28, 1942 of an agreement on the accession of French Somaliland to the anti-Hitler coalition, Great Britain pulled out its troops from the northern part of the Reserved Area and from Hararghe; the city of Dire Dawa became the headquarters of the British troops.

The developments in French Somaliland allowed Haile Selassie I to demand that British troops be pulled out from Ethiopia's occupied territory. To exercise control over those lands, the Ethiopian army and police were undergoing successful training even before any agreements were reached with London.

In 1943, a British military mission led by Major General Stephen Butler arrived in Ethiopia. Members of the mission began to train the troops (infantry, a mountain artillery regiment, an armored regiment). All servicemen were now receiving a fixed emolument. A soldier of the guards received 11 Maria Theresa thalers every month, and the rank-and-file of other units were getting 10 thalers each. By these measures, Haile Selassie's government was building a regular professional army.[15]

An Imperial Guard (the emperor's personal security detachment) and a territorial army organized from individuals who were carrying arms, in particular, former patriots, were created. In early February 1942, a decree was signed to organize police with high commissioner at the helm. He was to follow instructions and orders of the interior minister. To help the high commissioner do his job, the Main Department of Public Security was set up; it handled financial matters.

In addition to the office of high commissioner,[16] British officers were holding all major positions in the Ethiopian police. They were teaching at the police school, and at a college for police officers opened in 1946. No doubt, the police force played a huge role in normalizing the domestic situation and in reinforcing the powers of the governors accredited by the central administration.

Training national workforce was a major vector of activities of the government of Haile Selassie I: The emperor made the Ministry of Education and Fine Arts responsible for the revival of educational institutions and for the development of education in the country.

As it was said above, during the years of the Italian occupation, a large part of national workforce had perished.[17] In the 1940s and the 1950s, Ethiopia was in dire need of teachers. The government invited educators from Great Britain, Egypt, India, Sweden, Canada, and other countries.

In 1942, Great Britain's consulate opened an education center for Ethiopian children in Addis Ababa; in 1944, British educators were instrumental in organizing a Center for Teachers' Training. Ethiopian young people were also sent to study abroad.

Quite soon, the policy of national workforce training bore fruit. In the early 1940s, Ethiopian schools employed only 410 teachers, and by 1948, their number went up to 1,088 people.[18]

Creating an independent state was a process that affected the church as well;[19] in other words, this institution also underwent a radical reform.

In 1942, the government of Haile Selassie I adopted a Regulation for the Administration of the Church. Its purpose was to limit jurisdiction of the church, to introduce centralization in church governance, to make financial affairs of the church transparent, and to set up a central church treasury. According to the regulation, taxes were to be collected from all church lands. The funds collected for the central treasury were used to pay salaries to teachers of theological schools, retirement benefits to the clergy, to rebuild and repair churches, to educate, to do charity work, and so on. The top clergy were appointed by a church Council, subject to the emperor's approval.

Secular matters were no longer included in the church jurisdiction, and church courts could not render judicial verdicts on them; the clergy could only divorce spouses if they had been married in church.

To train a well-educated clergy, a college of theology was opened in 1944. The government was now paying for the training of students in departments of theology abroad.

The government of Haile Selassie I also considered the relationship between the Ethiopian Orthodox Church and the Coptic Orthodox Church of Alexandria. Over centuries and on multiple occasions, the Ethiopian Orthodox Church had raised the question of splitting from the Church of Alexandria, that is, the issue of autocephaly; however, the patriarchate had always refused even to discuss the matter.[20] For the emperor, the issue of autocephaly of the Ethiopian Orthodox Church became one of the most essential vectors of foreign policy. For a wise monarch, no other thing is as important as giving spiritual guidance to the nation.

First negotiations took place in 1942, after *Abuna* Qerellos IV, leader of the Ethiopian Orthodox Church, came back to the country. Together with *Abuna* Qerellos, a delegation of the Patriarch of Alexandria arrived in Addis Ababa; it tried to revive the influence of the Coptic Church and to restore its reputation. The problem was that Alexandria had not given pecuniary or spiritual support to the struggling Ethiopian people. It had not protested against the massacre of the clergy in the monastery of Debre Libanos by the Fascist invaders in 1937. Graziani, then-ruler of Italian East Africa, was the butcher who ordered the killing of the monks. Ethiopian Patriarch Qerellos had to leave the country, even though he had recognized new authorities. The believers regarded his action not as humility but rather as cowardice.

The patriarch expressed his disapproval only when Duke d'Aosta, who replaced Graziani, declared independence of the Ethiopian Church and appointed *Abuna* Abraham, an Ethiopian, as the new archbishop. The Ethiopian side insisted on the increase of the number of Ethiopian bishops, so that an Ethiopian would finally become the nation's spiritual leader. Alexandria ignored the requests of the Ethiopian emperor, explaining sluggishness in addressing them by the grief caused by the death of Pope John XIX of Alexandria.

When the monarch made the will of the clerical hierarchy public (that a citizen of Ethiopia should govern the Ethiopian Orthodox Church), Macarius III, the new Patriarch of the Coptic Church, sent a delegation to Addis Ababa. It was the Ethiopian side that formed the agenda for the meeting. The hosts insisted, first, that the right of ordaining Ethiopian clerics as bishops should be granted to the *abuna* (an Ethiopian by birth); second, that the Ethiopian Orthodox Church should take part in the election of the patriarch of Alexandria; third, that delegates of the Ethiopian Church should sit in the Coptic Synod as equals. Seeking a compromise in settling clerical divisive issues, the Ethiopian side was aware that Alexandria would not give up its lucrative possessions in the East African parish voluntarily; as he rationally juxtaposed momentary achievements and long-term benefits, the emperor of Ethiopia declared: "The Ethiopian Orthodox Church has no desire to secede from the Alexandrian Patriarchal throne."[21] The caution stemmed from the concern lest tough talks and unilateral severance of relations might irritate believers and ordinary clergymen, pit spiritual and temporal authorities in the country against each other.

Negotiations of the church delegation came to nothing. Disregarding the opinion of the Coptic Synod, Ethiopia's government was implementing the Regulation for the Administration of the Church.

Taking diplomatic measures in an effort to advocate equal rights of the Ethiopian Orthodox Church, Haile Selassie I did not forget about the Reserved Area occupied by British authorities and about a gateway to sea. The latter foreign policy mission was closely connected to the destinies of kindred peoples of Eritrea and Italian Somaliland. The British yoke was no better than the Italian slipknot.

Formally, the 1942 agreement and military convention guaranteed the Ethiopian Empire's sovereignty. But in reality, the government of Emperor Haile Selassie I was not enjoying all freedoms of a sovereign country and could not choose the ways of the nation's development independently. British presence was felt everywhere. That feeling of foreign presence and ubiquitous control was aptly rendered by Russian classic writer A. I. Goncharov in his immortal *The Frigate Pallada*: ". . . poetic picture that catches the eye of the traveler. What picture do you see? Not one of overwhelming beauty with the attributes of strength, not with the spark of demonic fire in the eyes, not with a sword, not with a crown, but simply with a black frock-coat, a round hat, a white vest, and a parasol in hand. . . .

This creature rules in the world over minds and passions. It is everywhere. I saw it in England, on the street, at the counters of stores, in the palaces of justice, at the stock exchange. . . . I went up the mountain; there, under the porticoes, through garlands of vines, I spied the same figure; with cold and severe gaze he observed how the dark-skinned natives, covered with sweat, gathered the precious juice of their soil, how the barrels rolled to the shore and were sent to the far corners of the earth, for which the overlords gave to the workers the right to eat the bread of their own soil."[22]

London was holding the Ethiopian Empire on the microscope stage. But the government of Emperor Haile Selassie I was aware that without diplomatic, economic, and cultural relations with other countries the extremely painful issue could not be resolved. After the signing of the 1942 agreement, Ethiopian political circles were making an effort to have the agreement annulled, as it de facto was putting a fence between Ethiopia and the rest of the world, as though the nation was a quarantined patient in a leprosarium. The Ethiopian government wanted to build a road to the sea across annexed territories, to create a national currency because the East-African shilling did not reflect sovereignty of the Ethiopian Empire as a legal tender either economically or politically. Despite impressive achievements in education, the empire was unable to train enough workforce: Great Britain could not provide the sufficient number of specialists for Ethiopian renaissance.

To make a crucial step like amending the 1942 agreement and obtaining territorial concessions, public opinion and backing of great powers were required. Ethiopia's leadership believed back then that the United States was the only power that could provide any real assistance. By signing the Declaration by United Nations dated January 1, 1942, Addis Ababa became a permanent attendee of UN conferences. In May 1943, the Ethiopian delegation attended a conference of the Interim Commission on Food and Agriculture held in Hot Springs, Virginia. Yilma Deressa, Ethiopia's Deputy Finance Minister, who was representing Ethiopia, met with a representative of the Department of the Treasury and then with U.S. President F. D. Roosevelt. During those meetings, the African ambassador advised American partners of potentially attractive projects in law, financial management, and security.

American financial aid was a separate item of the agenda. A loan of 1.5 million ounces of silver was provided to issue the national currency—the Ethiopian dollar.

This time, the United States displayed good sense and forward thinking, and diplomatic efforts of the government of Haile Selassie I were crowned with success: A financial specialist and a legal advisor were sent to Ethiopia.

As John Spencer (an advisor to the Ethiopian government on international matters) noted, "several factors caused the United States to adopt a reciprocally favorable attitude towards Ethiopia. Foremost was the consideration that Ethiopia had become the first of the states opposing Axis aggression to be freed from its domination. The United States was anxious to embark upon a program of rehabilitation there to serve us encouragement to the peoples of countries still under enemy occupation."[20] Of course, J. Spencer's conclusion is convincing, since in those years Ethiopia was one of the few free countries that were ready to support the Allies in the fight against the Axis countries. As known during the war, Ethiopia was the only African nation that continued to supply foodstuffs to allied troops and Middle Eastern countries. It could be upgraded on insignificant investments. U.S. political interests were founded, first, on the idea that Washington was able to rehabilitate economy of one particular underdeveloped country. Second, U.S. support to the Ethiopian Empire raised the prestige of the "most democratic nation" among African American employees of the Pentagon. Third, the United States intended to use Ethiopia as a foothold for taking British and French possessions in the Middle East.

On April 21, 1943, the Ethiopian Empire established diplomatic relations with the Soviet Union. Thus, Haile Selassie I not only expanded the limits of the empire's external ties but received recognition of another great power. In 1942–1944, Ethiopia opened its consulates in Jerusalem, Aden, and Nairobi.

On January 31, 1944, the 1942 Anglo-Ethiopian agreement, which had limited Ethiopia's sovereignty, expired. However, as it feared lest the northern province of Tigre could be annexed to Eritrea, the eastern territory of Ogaden to Somaliland, the southern provinces of Sidamo and Gamu-Gofa to Kenya, and the southwestern provinces of Illubabor and Welega to Sudan, the Ethiopian government still did not dare to unleash confrontation with London.[24] Therefore, Haile Selassie I suggested that a new treaty be concluded. The British side was in no hurry to give a reply.

As far back as in 1943, Robert Howe, the British minister in Addis Ababa, having reminded to London of the expiration of the 1942 agreement, had made a curious proposal. In a letter addressed to Anthony Eden, Howe openly said that after the war London should seek ways of exercising British influence in Ethiopia—for instance, by establishing a system of "advisors." In the interests of Great Britain, he suggested "adjusting" borders of Sudan, Eritrea, and former Italian Somaliland. Consequently, Haile Selassie's concern that some territorial losses could be sustained was not completely unfounded.

To conclude a bilateral treaty, a committee for Ethiopia was set up in Cairo. It was led by Lord Moyne. According to preliminary considerations, Addis Ababa was offered the south of Eritrea in lieu of the Christian part of the province of Tigray, which was to be annexed to Great Tigray under protectorate of Great Britain. Moreover, Ethiopia was to recognize the United Lands of Somaliland (including Ogaden), and transfer of a few wells to Kenya, and of the waterhead of the Baro River to Sudan. Moyne suggested that Great Britain should tighten its grip of Ethiopia to the utmost. This function was entrusted to the Anglo-American Council.[25] Washington could not be satisfied with this modest role, in view of its strengthened foothold in the region. Moreover, the American government included Ethiopia in its lend-lease program; to make required arrangements, a technical mission headed by Perry Fellows was sent to Addis Ababa on May 16, 1944. Haile Selassie I snatched at this opportunity.

On May 25, 1944, London received a notice from Addis Ababa that the 1942 agreement would be terminated in three months. This statement of the Ethiopian leadership caught the English unawares, and on September 26, 1944, a British delegation led by Lord De La Warr arrived in Addis Ababa. The high-ranking diplomat proposed small and insignificant amendments to the 1942 agreement.

From the first minutes, the negotiations were tough. Before the very eyes of the English, the Ethiopians, from humble and flexible, turned into uncompromising negotiators. For instance, the British side offered to Ethiopia 3 million pounds sterling, which would be paid by the London-based Treasury, but distribution of the funds was to be supervised by a joint Anglo-Ethiopian committee. The Ethiopian side insisted on a loan of 10 million pounds sterling. The Ethiopian side was not heard.

The British delegation refused to discuss the Reserved Area and Ogaden. Since Ogaden was part of personal possessions of Haile Selassie I, Ethiopia could hardly be expected to go softer on the matter during the negotiations.

On November 4, 1944, the Ethiopian delegation issued a memorandum. It said: "If Ethiopia, the first to inter the war against the Axis, should be treated as enemy territory, what the future of those other countries still under Axis occupation? Must they, like Ethiopia, suddenly become enemy territories to be parceled out at a peace settlement? The memorandum noted that Britain had insisted that the Ogaden, and the Reserved area were for prosecution of war in the Pacific; but Prime Minister Churchill himself had conceded that the burden of the war in the Pacific was primarily an American one. . . . If the United States should agree on the military necessity of such territorial arrangements for the prosecution of the war against Japan, Ethiopia as a contribution to the war effort, would gladly agree to transfer the administration of the Ogaden for the British military administration for the duration of the new agreement or until the end of the war, whichever comes first."[26]

It was not by chance that the United States and the war in the Pacific against Japan were not mentioned. Everything signaled that it would no longer be London but Washington that would be deciding the destinies of smaller nations; moreover, U.S. Ambassador John K. Caldwell was involved in the negotiations and gave advice to the Ethiopian government on multiple occasions.

Having read the memorandum, the head of the British delegation threatened to suspend the negotiations, which would mean that the 1942 agreement would be automatically extended. The government of Ethiopia had to agree to see the Reserved Area and Ogaden governed by the British military administration.

Meanwhile, Ethiopia remained the lawful owner of the mineral reserves and lands of the Reserved Area. The British side allowed raising Ethiopia's national flag side by side to its own banner. This precedent only emphasized the interim nature of the British presence in the territory of the Ethiopian Empire. By that time, the Somali Youth League (the foster child of British military authorities) had begun its activities, insisting on creation of Great Somaliland by uniting British, Italian, French reserved areas and, naturally, Ogaden.

The signing of the agreement on December 19, 1944 by Ethiopia put an end to the British monopoly in foreign policy. London transferred the Djibouti-Addis Ababa railway under control of the government of Haile Selassie I; from now on, British troops could not move about the country's territory without the Ethiopian government's consent; Ethiopia now could invite advisors from any country; the British diplomatic representative no longer had precedence over all ministers accredited in Ethiopia; organization, training, and deployment of the British military mission, its strength and movements about Ethiopia's territory were controlled jointly with Ethiopia's war minister; the British side was no longer the sole user of the Ethiopian Empire's airspace.[27]

The agreement was signed, on behalf of the British side, by delegation head De La Warr, and, on behalf of the Ethiopian side, by Prime Minister Makonnen Endelkachew. The Ethiopian leader emphasized by that move that Lord De La Warr was not his equal.

The Ethiopian leadership insisted on the pullout of British troops from the Reserved Area and Ogaden, and also on getting a gateway to sea by means of territorial concessions. The issue was Tafari Makonnen's concern even during his regency and one of the main goals of his visit to Europe. Its importance became especially evident when France refused to export arms via Djibouti. It was from the sea that invaders came.

The beginning of 1945 was marked by a major foreign policy success. On February 4, Haile Selassie I suddenly received an invitation from U.S. President F. D. Roosevelt, who was returning from the Yalta Conference. According to Caldwell, head of the U.S. diplomatic corps in Ethiopia, the Emperor, when "learned that he was to meet with the president was so pleased that for the first time . . . [he] discussed such an important matter of official business in English instead of through an interpreter."[28] The result of the Surprise Factor?

The meeting with the head of the leading nation of the free world raised the prestige of the leader of a backward African country devastated by the war in the eyes of the international community. Haile Selassie I could communicate his requests to his powerful counterpart.

Neither Washington nor Addis Ababa advised London of the meeting they were contemplating to have in Egypt. Until a plane of the U.S. Air Force with the Ethiopian leader on board took off, the diplomatic representative of Great Britain in Addis Ababa was unaware of the forthcoming negotiations. Harold Marcus wrote in connection with that secret voyage: on 12 February 1945 "Howe (*Great Britain's minister*), after learning that the emperor had departed on a USAAF DC-3, telegraphed Churchill, arranged transport from Aden and trailed off after the Lion of Judah (*Haile Selassie I.—Author's note*), and his small troop of officials and advisers."[29]

This insistent and jealous escorting of the emperor by a high-ranking British diplomat shows how important Ethiopia was for London. To lose sight of Ethiopia would mean for the British to weaken their influence on the Arabian Peninsula, in the north and northeast of Africa. It would mean losing dominions in Africa, which actually happened a few years later.

The meeting of Haile Selassie I with U.S. President F. D. Roosevelt took place on February 13, 1945 on board the USS *Quincy* moored in the Great Bitter Lake in the Suez Canal area. Even though the U.S. president had initiated the dialog, the emperor was the one who talked most of the time during that hour. He identified essential objectives for the Ethiopian State, and at the end of the meeting handed to the U.S. president a six-point memorandum.

The authors of the document (the emperor was one of them) insisted on complete control over the Addis Ababa-Djibouti railway. In accordance with article II of the concession treaty concluded between Ethiopia and France in 1908, the Addis Ababa- Djibouti railway was to be transferred to Ethiopia in the event of hostilities. However, when the war began in 1936, France did not keep true to its commitments. This is why the Ethiopian side insisted on canceling the formal treaty and demanded that the transport artery, including French Somaliland, should be under full control of Addis Ababa. That said, Ethiopia needed a contractor to operate the railway and asked assistance of the United States.

The second point of the memorandum concerned issues associated with a gateway to sea; Ethiopia did not have access to the ports of Djibouti (France's zone) and Aden (Great Britain's zone), so financial transactions were carried out only in the sterling area, which was in no way conducive to the development of trade or the national banking system, and goods imported into Ethiopia were much more expensive than their real cost.

Eritrea (a colony of Italy) deserves a special mention. The matter was that Eritrea and its residents were an integral part of the Ethiopian Empire. Ethnic, racial, cultural, economic, and geographic connections gave Ethiopia basis to claim annexation. Furthermore, the memorandum stressed that the cession would recognize "the existing historical, racial, cultural, economic and geographic ties which bind Eritrea integrally to Ethiopia and redress in part the injustices visited upon Ethiopia by the Fascist regime. As a result, 'the President made no commitments, promises or assurances in response to the Emperor's requests for help' made in connection with the five memoranda."[30]

Ethiopia was the first country liberated from the Fascists, so it had legal and moral rights to sit on international commissions dealing with war crimes and reparations and to be appropriately compensated for the losses. Ethiopia hoped to get international aid in order to equip its own 40,000-strong army. It needed U.S. investments to discover oil wells, to develop civil aviation and other sectors of economy, which would enable it to keep up stability.

After the meeting, the emperor presented the U.S. president with a confection by a palace jeweler of a four-inch globe with the continents incised on it, along, with the location of their meeting, fashioned out of the slightly reddish gold from the Adola (the southwest of Ethiopia, in the province of Wollega) mines "At the parting Roosevelt stated that he was making the gift of four command cars to Ethiopia's leader."[31]

The semi-secret meeting had another achievement that cannot be converted into monetary equivalent. First, discussing matters of interest for his country, Haile Selassie I himself, as the best-informed expert, proposed ways for their resolution. Second, the meeting helped him escape surveillance by British diplomacy. Third, the government of the Ethiopian monarch realized its own self-reliance. Ethiopia has risen from her knees. Curiously, an hour before he was to get back home, Ethiopia's emperor received an invitation from Prime Minister Churchill to meet him in Cairo. The emperor agreed to see the prime minister at his VIP quarters of an American airbase in Payne Field, a few miles outside Cairo. For Churchill the proposal was unacceptable. The meeting was to take place at the British embassy. When asked by an aide to Churchill what points he wished to discuss, the emperor responded curtly: "None."[32] The meeting was pro forma, and Great Britain could do nothing about it. London could no longer dictate its agenda, and it needed to learn the art of dialog.

Haile Selassie's meetings with the leaders of the two countries in Egypt gave evidence of declining influence of Great Britain. The world had entered a period of a global competition between the United States and the Union of Soviet Socialist Republics. Both giants were opposing political colonialism in Africa, but their approaches, means and strategies of involvement in the destines of the peoples of the continent were different.

Haile Selassie arrived at the conclusion that in a real word a weak nation must pursue a multi-vector policy. Having garnered U.S. support, the monarch did not wait to be helped. It could be a long wait, and he had but extremely little time to address momentous tasks of historical significance, so he turned his attention to potential allies, or, more specifically, donors, in Europe.

Sweden, just like the United States, came out of World War II with its infrastructure and industrial power unscathed. Sweden's nationals had been employed by the government of Haile Selassie I and by various public institutions of the empire prior to the war.[33]

Back in early 1944, the head of Ethiopia's diplomatic mission in Moscow had presented to a Swedish counterpart a memorandum that stated Ethiopia's need to have more doctors, nurses, engineers, experts in administration, agronomists, and chemists. Stockholm was not long in answering and extended a loan of 7.5 million kronor to Ethiopia in 1945–1946 to cover tickets and wages of Swedish experts, as well as purchases of required equipment. By July 1946, Swedish presence was very noticeable in all walks of life of the African country, including the military area. Swedes were training servicemen of the imperial guard and of Ethiopia's air force.

In an effort to defend sovereignty, Haile Selassie I established friendly ties with the USSR. As a power fighting against imperialism and colonial domination, the Soviet Union was an important antagonist of Great Britain.

Even though the regime of Haile Selassie I never favored communism, Ethiopia's leader understood the significance of friendship with the Soviet Union. Russia was the only country that had sent its doctors to Ethiopia after the war with Italy on 1896. Russian military specialists had played a large role in expanding the country's borders to the south, southeast and southwest. Finally, the emperor could not forget Soviet Union's backing during diplomatic battles in Geneva at the League of Nations in the mid-1930s.

Celebrating a year of establishment of the Soviet-Ethiopian diplomatic relations, the official government newspaper *The Ethiopian Herald* reported on June 8, 1944: "A sense of trust and understanding has always existed between Russian and Ethiopians. Russians are known as a noble people, as sincere friends. . . . Our country remembers that, despite the absence of official relations between Ethiopia and the USSR, the latter, without hesitation, defended the interests Ethiopia in the League of Nations."[34]

THE 1947 PARIS PEACE CONFERENCE

Foreign policy of the government of Haile Selassie I in 1945–1947 was addressing three interrelated challenges: (1) settlement of the issue of Eritrea and former Italian Somaliland; (2) liberation of Ogaden and the Reserved Area; (3) expansion of foreign policy contacts.

After the emperor's meetings with the top officials of the United States and Great Britain in Egypt, the government began to get ready for the San Francisco conference. The Ethiopian delegation was led by Prime Minister *Makonnen* Endalkachew, a prominent politician and the author of over 20 books.

In San Francisco, the delegation was in for another disappointment. As wrote J. Spencer, the UN Charter, just like the Covenant of the League of Nations, was only a smokescreen that strong countries could use as a cover in order to commit any unlawful act at any time and under any pretext, and go unpunished.[35] The UN, under the Charter, is a voluntary association of independent sovereign States. Its existence depends on the capability and desire of its members to collaborate with one another in order to defend peace. Thus, the UN had no clear-cut and refined mechanism of protecting smaller countries from aggression—for instance, protecting of Ethiopia from the Arab League or pressure of the Common Market led by England. The fate of the world and small countries was still decided by great powers. And Ethiopia and others of her ilk were invited to put their signatures to the charter of a new international organization.

In the summer of 1945, the negotiations on the disposition of former Italian colonies, which had begun at the Potsdam Conference in 1945, were to be continued in London, at a meeting of foreign ministers of the four great powers. Ethiopia stated its desire to take part in the meeting, but received a flat refusal; it was invited to submit a memorandum.

The memorandum was sent immediately, but hardly any of the great powers displayed any interest in Addis Ababa's urgent needs. The peace conference in San Francisco did not resolve Ethiopia's issues either. Therefore, the government of Haile Selassie I had to get involved into a complicated diplomatic fight. Under the 1944 treaty, in the territories occupied by British troops Ethiopia had the right to land, subsoil, and economic activities, and could use all resources, except water.

American company Sinclair Oil was the pioneer in the exploration, development, and operation of Ethiopian natural gas and oil fields.[36] It is true though that the deal was more political rather than economic: Presence of Americans in that part of Ethiopia was regarded as a guarantee of support on the part of the United States.

The beginning was promising. In 1945, Sinclair sent its representative from New York to Ethiopia. The British administration that ruled in Ogaden permitted . . . transportation of Sinclair's equipment, drilling machines and personnel via British Somaliland, bypassing Ogaden. This irrational route made the expedition replace Ethiopian license plates and prepay a 1.5% tax on all imported equipment and trucks. Geologists were required to open a bank account (as a guarantee that the equipment imported into Ogaden would go to its destination point); moreover, every three months, the expedition was to renew a drilling and exploration permit.[37]

Thus, British military authorities ignored the 1944 treaty, prejudicing the Ethiopian side's right. Military authorities in Ogaden put up obstacles, preventing Sinclair's operations. They incited local residents to attack the company's employees. The Americans suffered especially hard from the hands of the so-called Somali Youth Club, an organization set up in 1943. In 1945, it had about 5,000 members. In 1947, as the international environment had changed, the Club was transformed into the Somali Youth League, a political organization that sought to unite all Somali residents (including Ethiopians), to teach all Somalians, to develop the written Somali language, to control situations that could prejudice interests of peoples of Somaliland.[38]

The Somali Youth League had an office in Jijiga, in Ethiopian territory. The league that was controlled by British authorities did not recognize the authority of Emperor Haile Selassie I, and considered Ogaden as part of Great Somaliland. Therefore, it was determined to prevent Sinclair's operations.

According to article VII of the 1944 treaty, the British military administration was to govern the Reserved Area and Ogaden with consent of the Ethiopian government, which wanted to "contribute to the war effort in World War II."[39] Simultaneously, it was mentioned that this measure must not prejudice Ethiopia's sovereignty and interests. De facto, London emissaries became rulers of those territories.

Even though British military authorities assured the Ethiopian side that they were ready to offer to Sinclair the same favorable terms as though Ogaden was under Ethiopian control, in reality they were pursuing anti-Ethiopian policy. As a result of attacks of members of the Somali Youth League (with tacit consent of British authorities), on May 14, 1948, the American company had to suspend its exploration of oil and natural gas in Ogaden. The U.S. government showed no interest in the incident and did not require that British authorities protect American citizens and the company's interests.

Haile Selassie I, having granted a concession to Sinclair Oil, never saw any reciprocity on the U.S. part. Washington did not back the African leader either in the diplomatic or in the political field.

Even though the Ethiopian leader was opposing British presence in Ogaden, nevertheless, he would not attempt to exacerbate the situation and did not denounce the 1944 treaty unilaterally. The emperor was unwilling to lose potential support of Great Britain, which had been declared in 1948 at a hearing on the disposition of the former Italian colonies of Eritrea and Somaliland.

Since two years after World War II Great Britain was in no hurry to return illegally occupied territories to Ethiopia and refused to implement articles of the 1944 agreement, the government of Haile Selassie I entered into negotiations with London.

In September 1947, Aklilu Habte-Wold, Ethiopia's Minister of Foreign Affairs, handed over to the British side a draft treaty on friendship and trade. One article of the treaty would restore Ethiopia's jurisdiction over occupied territories. The British government haughtily ignored the proposal to sign a peace treaty and would not pull its troops out of Ogaden. Addis Ababa decided not to denounce the treaty and handed the matter over to the International Court of Justice.

Another important foreign policy issue for Emperor Haile Selassie I was a gateway to sea. That long-cherished idea could become reality if former Italian colonies Eritrea and Italian Somaliland were to be annexed to Ethiopia. According to art. X of the truce signed by Rome on September 3, 1943, a military administration to govern the former Italian colonies was to be set up. Eritrea and Italian Somaliland were governed by the British military, and later, control of the African territories was transferred to the Foreign Office.[40]

The Berlin Conference (from July 17 to August 24, 1945), having established a Council of Foreign Ministers (CFM) that had representatives of foreign policy agencies of the USSR, the United States, Great Britain, France and China, created an effective mechanism for postwar peace settlement. The Moscow Conference (December 16–27, 1945) approved terms of a peace treaty with Italy worked out by foreign ministers of the USSR, the United States, Great Britain, and France.[41]

The first session of the CFM that was held in London from September 11 to October 20, 1945 worked out a draft peace treaty with Italy. To read the document and to sign the peace treaty, a conference of nations of the anti-Hitler coalition was convened,[42] which included countries that had won World War II. Invitation to the conference was sent to Austria, Belgium, Belarus, Brazil, Canada, Czechoslovakia, Greece, India, the Netherlands, New Zealand, Norway, Poland, Ukraine, South Africa, Yugoslavia, and Ethiopia. The latter was mostly concerned with the question of the former Italian colonies—Eritrea and Somaliland.

Small allied states that had suffered from the aggression of the Axis countries, just like Ethiopia, were to attend the Paris Peace Conference as observers. At a London meeting, the CFM decided that matters related to the world patterns after World War II were personal responsibility of the four powers. In those circumstances, Haile Selassie I did not have a strong chance to get a coveted gateway to sea.

At the London session of the CFM, when a discussion began about the disposition of the former Italian colonies, the great powers were unable to reach a compromise. Thus, U.S. State Secretary James F. Byrnes proposed a collective trusteeship system led by an international civilian body appointed by the UN Trusteeship Council. According to Byrnes' plan, Eritrea and Libya would become independent in a decade (no deadline was given for Somaliland). Ethiopia would receive the port of Assab.[43] However, nothing was said about how that port could be accessed.

Vyacheslav Molotov, Soviet Minister of Foreign Affairs, rejected Byrnes' proposal. He insisted on applying an individual trusteeship system and required that the Soviet Union be entitled to govern Tripolitania[44] (a province in Libya). France was pro-Italian. By taking that approach, it wanted, on the one hand, to neutralize Great Britain, its former ally and present-day rival, which had managed to establish domination in Northeast Africa, including in Ethiopia. On the other hand, giving independence to the Italian colonies would result in a demand of independence for French colonies in Africa. Therefore, Minister of Foreign Affairs Georges Bidault proposed that those territories be returned to Italy under an individual trusteeship system, without specifying the date when independence could be granted. The French proposal contravened trusteeship articles of the UN Charter, because art. 86 says that only a UN member may be a trustee, but Italy was not a member of the UN at the time.[45]

Great Britain's plan was the most acceptable for Emperor Haile Selassie I. With respect to Eritrea, Foreign Secretary Ernest Bevin proposed to include its western provinces in the Anglo-Egyptian Sudan, and to transfer the eastern part, including the port of Assab, to Ethiopia, because Eritrea was an artificially created subject. It could not exist independently, if not within the framework of a protectorate system.[46]

It should be mentioned that Great Britain's plan to divide Eritrea had originated back in 1942, when negotiations began between Ethiopia and Great Britain. According to that plan, in return for a gateway to sea, the Ethiopian side was to abandon Ogaden and the Reserved Area in favor of Great Britain, which was going to create Great Somaliland by uniting Italian, British Somaliland, and Ogaden within a mandated territory of Great Britain.

As they failed to reach an agreement, great powers arrived at the conclusion that the Italian colonies were subject to the UN Charter provision on trust territories. They referred the matter to deputy foreign ministers for a detailed study on the basis of a plan proposed by the United States. Italy received an invitation to the London meeting of the CFM, and Ethiopia was recommended to submit its suggestions in the form of a memorandum.[47]

In its memorandum, the Ethiopian side listed its historical, geopolitical, economic, ethnic, and cultural motivations in support of its claims to the territories of Eritrea and Italian Somaliland. "Ethiopia demands justice for the people of Eritrea and Somaliland, who were cut off from their homeland and were subjected to terrible oppression; justice for oneself, so as not to be subjected to more aggression from those territories that Italy has selected; justice for his people, who must no longer be condemned for being denied access to the sea by Italy, and who must no longer suffer losses by being the victim of aggression",[48] the memorandum said.[49]

The Ethiopian leadership's call to restore historical justice in the region made no impression on representatives of the great powers. At a new meeting of the CFM, which took place on July 3, 1946, the attendees were mainly concerned with European issues: the future of Germany, Austria, Trieste, the Dodecanese, and the legal foundations of the presence of Soviet troops in Eastern Europe. Moreover, the Ethiopian issue became more complicated when Italy, supported by France, did not intend to cede African lands, and Egypt, believing that this was the country from which Italy unjustly seized Eritrea, began to claim this territory.

At the Paris session, U.S. representatives spoke in favor of a collective trusteeship system, and France favored return of the territories to Italy. The Soviet Union, fearing isolation, supported the U.S. idea on a joint trusteeship: Each Allied power would receive control over one colony. Ethiopia, a UN member, was even denied the right to attend meetings of the CFM.

Great Britain suggested that Eritrea should be divided between Ethiopia and Sudan, and that a united independent state should be established in Libya; in addition, by uniting British, Italian Somaliland and Ogaden, a new state, Great Somaliland, should be formed. The United States, after a little demur, agreed to the London plan.

During the Paris meeting, the parties managed to overcome certain differences; however, they were unable to work out a single formula for the resolution of the issue of the Italian colonies. A half-way decision in the nature of a compromise was worked out: "It was finally agreed that the ultimate disposition of the colonies should be made by the four principal Allied powers in light of the wishes and welfare of the inhabitants and world peace and security, taking into account the views of other interested governments."[50]

This resolution of the CFM did not discourage the Ethiopian monarch. Haile Selassie I did not give up further attempts to settle territorial issues. At the Paris Peace Conference (July 29 to October 15, 1946), the most important thing for Ethiopia were draft articles 33–38 and Annex XI. Article 38 recognized October 3, 1935 as the date of the start of the Italian occupation. It was from that date that Italy was to pay reparations. Article 23 prescribed the following:

1. Italy was to abandon all rights and titles to the Italian territorial dominions in Africa, namely to Libya, Eritrea and Italian Somaliland.
2. Until the ultimate disposition, those territories would remain under their current administration.
3. The disposition of those dominions would be finally determined jointly by the governments of the Soviet Union, the United Kingdom, the United States and France within a year after the treaty took effect, by the way specified in the joint declaration dated February 10, 1947, which was adopted by the above-mentioned governments and cited in Annex XI to the draft treaty, which says that:
   1. The governments of the four power agree, by a jointly adopted resolution, to determine, within one year after the peace treaty with Italy of February 10, 1947 takes effect, the ultimate disposition of Italy's territorial dominions in Africa.
   2. The four powers will determine the ultimate disposition of the territories in question and will adequately rectify their borders, taking into account wishes and welfare of the inhabitants, as well as interests of peace and security, and also viewpoints of other interested governments.

3. If the four powers fail to agree on the disposition of any of those territories within one year after the peace treaty with Italy takes effect, the matter will be referred to the UN General Assembly for the latter to make recommendations on the issue, and the four powers will have to adopt those recommendations and take appropriate measures for their implementation.

4. Deputy foreign ministers will continue to consider the disposition of the former Italian colonies with a purpose of submitting their recommendations on the matter to the CFMs. Furthermore, they will send a commission of investigation to each of the former colonies, in order to provide required data on the matter to deputy foreign ministers and to determine the views of the local population.[51]

Neither recommendations of the conference nor provisions of the peace treaty with Italy could not satisfy the Ethiopian side. Therefore, in his statement, Aklilu Habte-Wold, head of the Ethiopian delegation, tried to convince the attendees, citing historical, geographic, economic, ethnic, and strategic reasons to substantiate Ethiopia's claims to the territories of Eritrea and Somaliland.

As it was waging diplomatic warfare for a gateway to sea through the territory of Eritrea and Somaliland, the Ethiopian government was focused mainly on Eritrea, of which a memorandum addressed to participants of the Paris Peace Conference gives evidence.

Ethiopia insisted on its right to take part in deciding the disposition of Somaliland. As for Eritrea, the memorandum said, it was "only the question of returning under Ethiopia's sovereignty that territory that has economic and cultural ties exclusively with Ethiopia, which includes access to the sea . . . which was twice used as a staging ground for the invasion of Ethiopian territory." Based on that, Aklilu Habte-Wold made a proposal to amend[52] article XVII, suggesting that "the status of Eritrea was fully restored under the sovereignty of Ethiopian Empire."[53] Italy also thought that many provisions of the peace treaty were unfair and even "punitive." In his statement, the representative of Rome said that the resolutions of the Peace Conference were not consistent with interests of Italy and interests of the international community.

France unscrupulously opposed Ethiopia on territorial matters. Belgium and Brazil were pro-Italian. The Soviet Union, strange as it might seem, also supported Italy, for ideological reasons. Looking ahead, Moscow thought that it would see its Italian allies, socialists and communists, win the forthcoming election. Egypt was against both Ethiopia and Italy, because it was keen on getting Eritrea. Such was the geopolitical "solitaire."

It is true, though, that Ethiopia at the Paris Peace Conference was backed by representatives of Greece, India, Canada, Yugoslavia, and Great Britain.[54] Greece and India had a large diaspora that controlled trade in Ethiopia. Yugoslavia supported Ethiopia, first, because Italy had been its enemy for a long time. Second, during the war, Ethiopian patriots captured by the Italians and exiled to Italy, had escaped, joined the Yugoslavian Resistance led by Josip Broz Tito, and waged a guerrilla war in Italy. Abdissa Aga[55] was among those who had fought for Yugoslavia's freedom. At Marshal Tito's request, the emperor promoted Aga to lieutenant-colonel.[56] Canada supported Ethiopia because of long-standing friendship and interests of cooperation between the two countries. Great Britain was still hopeful of getting Ogaden. The United States abstained from active involvement in the discussions on the Ethiopian issue.

The conference resulted in peace treaties signed with Italy, Bulgaria, Hungary, Romania, and Finland. The Ethiopian side signed the part that concerned Italy. Provisions of article XXIII were left unchanged.

The Paris peace treaty altered the borders between Italy and Yugoslavia. Yugoslavia received the Istrian Peninsula and part of the Julian March, the city of Fiume, the province of Zara with adjacent territories, the city of Pula with neighboring islands. Trieste was declared a "free territory." Greece received the Dodecanese. The Franco-Italian border was altered in France's favor. In addition, the treaty defined the amount of the reparations to be paid by Italy: $5 million to Albania, $25 million to Ethiopia, $105 million to Greece, and $125 million to Yugoslavia.[57]

$25 million is meager compensation for human casualties and material losses, for pillaged sacred archives, for valueless pieces of art, religious and historical artifacts taken out of the country.

The Paris Peace Conference had little effect as a tool of protecting interests of small states. The only thing that distinguished the UN from the League of Nations was the replacement of the countries that had the right to dictate the destinies of the rest of the world. The previously neutral United States began to pursue a tough policy, and had no scruples when pushing its close allies, such as Great Britain and France, from their spheres of influence.

Since France was in full control of Ethiopia's foreign trade, which was carried out through the port of Djibouti, prices of goods skyrocketed. J. Spencer (the emperor's advisor on legal and international issues) speaks about that quite eloquently: "By 1947, the charges had become so outrageous that I found it less expansive to fly my 11-cubic-foot refrigerator from Aden direct to Addis Ababa than to bring it by rail from Djibouti."[58] The socioeconomic situation in Ethiopia was shaping up quite dramatically.

LACK OF FINALITY IN THE MATTER
OF THE GATEWAY TO SEA

The peace treaty with Italy was signed on February 10, 1947 and took effect on September 15, 1949. Ethiopia ratified it on November 6, 1947. The period of one year mentioned in clause 3 of the joint declaration of the Great Powers on the disposition of former Italian colonies began on September 15, 1947.

On October 3, 1947, deputy foreign ministers started to review the disposition of former Italian colonies according to clause IV of Annex XI to the peace treaty. It was decided that representatives of the four powers would launch an investigation in Libya, Somaliland, and Eritrea. The council of deputy foreign ministers set up a commission,[59] which was to collect information on political, economic, and social conditions of the local population. The commission held its first meeting in London on October 21, 1947; on November 12, it established its headquarters in Asmara, and its activities lasted until January 3, 1948.

During their stay in Eritrea, members of the commission made a few trips to "problem" territories. They studied resources and welfare of Eritrea, held consultations with leaders of political parties, organizations, community leaders, and representatives of the British administration.[60] Addis Ababa, in turn, established contacts with political movements that wished Eritrea's merger with Ethiopia.

As far back as in 1941, Hager Fikir Maheber (Association for the Love of the Motherland led by *Abuna* Zena Markos, Archbishop of Eritrea) had declared that the purpose of the organization was to join the compatriots. In 1947, the Unionist Party was set up, which had Christians and Muslims of Eritrea as its members. Gebre Meskel Woldu arose as its main activist both in Eritrea and Ethiopia. In September 1945, he led a rally in front of the British embassy in Addis Ababa. The rally protested against policies of the British administration. A year later, Colonel Negga Haile Selassie was appointed a liaison officer in Asmara. The Ethiopian Empire unfolded its active presence in Eritrea's political life. Britain denied the government of Ethiopia the right to open its consulate there.

The movement of oppositionists, or separatists, who called for Eritrea's independence, was led by *Ras* Tessema Asberom and his son Abraha Tessema, and also by Woldeab Woldemariam. A few months before the commission of investigation's visit, the Liberal Progressive Party was created, which was approved by London; the party would agree either to declaration of independence or to governance under British trusteeship. The Muslim League of Eritrea led by Ibrahim Sultan Ali, who had been the most active member of the Unionist Party[61] prior to 1948, became the most adamant fighter for independence and, simultaneously, enemy of any cooperation with Christian

Ethiopia. The league backed by Sudan and Italy declared independence of Eritrea.

No wonder that in that situation ethnopolitical and sectarian conflicts originated and were artificially fueled by colonialists. In August 1946, Sudanese separatists killed 40 Christians. In September 1947, they tried to assassinate Woldeab Woldemariam, a leader of the Liberal Progressive Party, and also Hassan Ali from the Muslim League. British authorities accused the Unionist Party and followers of the Ethiopian emperor of the crime.

During the commission's visit to Italian Somaliland, disorders broke out there. As a result of clashes between Somalians and Italians in Mogadishu, 14 Somalians and 51 Italians were killed. Thus, the Somalians demonstrated their displeasure to Italy.[62]

The commission, alongside investigations in Eritrea and Somaliland, appealed to the opinion of the so-called interested states from among the signatories of the peace treaty with Italy, including India and Pakistan. A proposal was made that governments of those countries should submit their viewpoints on the matter to deputy foreign ministers. Thus, there were 19 nations all in all that were trying to influence the fate of the divided peoples. The Ethiopian Empire was the key player, so the government of Haile Selassie submitted a memorandum, in which Eritrea and Italian Somaliland were treated as lost territories. In the opinion of Ethiopian authorities, in historical, ethnic, cultural, religious, economic and geographic respect, those regions were an integral part of Ethiopia.[63] Since those territories had been used as a stepping stone for numerous invasions of the Italians into Ethiopia, their political and strategic significance for Ethiopia could not be put into question.

There was one meaningful detail: As they were under the authority of foreign nations, local chieftains still were paying tributes to the Ethiopian Empire, even though invaders were ruling in littoral lands. After Egypt's defeat (it was to Egypt that Turkey had passed the right to rule those territories) in the 1875–1876 war, Ethiopia, Great Britain and Egypt signed a trilateral agreement in 1884, which recognized Ethiopia's right to the northern part of Ethiopia (now part of Eritrea) and the free port of Massawa.

The Ethiopian government thought that the optimal solution would be a reunion of the population of Eritrea and Somaliland with their historical homeland. "With the return of Eritrea and Somalia, not only would the situation improve, but economic progress would even accelerate. . . . Ethiopia was not only the best suited to govern Eritrea and Somalia, whose populations had the same composition, but Ethiopia is fully prepared to take responsibility related to the management of these territories," said the memorandum.[64]

If Addis Ababa's well-grounded interest were disregarded, the African Horn, a potentially explosive region, could become an area of permanent wars that would suck not only regional but global centers of power into a funnel of instability.

If those territories became independent, they could degenerate into an arena of political and economic struggle of several groups, including the Western bloc (the United States, Great Britain, France, etc.), the Soviet coalition (the USSR and its allies), and the Arab East (the Islamic world), which would destroy the Ethiopian Empire, where antagonisms between various ethnicities were verging on the brink of an armed conflict.

Italy's return would immediately unleash another war with Ethiopia, because, even despite ratification of the peace treaty, most Ethiopians believed Rome to be an enemy; on the other hand, this development would inevitably undermine the authority of Emperor Haile Selassie I, who had a lot of difficulty to redeem himself in the eyes of his subjects after the European exile in 1936–1941.

Egypt was also among claimants to the former Italian colonies. However, after Great Britain decided to grant independence to the Anglo-Egyptian Sudan, Cairo's interest in those lands weakened noticeably. As a result, that removed tension in Ethiopian-Egyptian relations, which thawed appreciably. The two countries that shared the waters of the sacred Niles resumed negotiations between the Ethiopian Church, which was seeking autonomy, and Alexandria. The Egyptian government took diligent efforts to build a constructive dialog. Ultimately, an agreement was reached with Patriarch (Pope) Joseph II of Alexandria on ordination of five Ethiopians as bishops, and also that after the death of the current archbishop of the Ethiopian Church, *Abuna* Qerellos IV, an Ethiopian would be elected and would be entitled to be ordained as bishop. The Ethiopian Church, in turn, recognized the supreme power of the Patriarch of Alexandria.[65]

The autonomous status of the Ethiopian Church promoted the imperial power and centralization of the state.[66] Archbishop Basilios concentrated in his hands the entire church, administrative and spiritual authority in Ethiopia, which allowed Emperor Haile Selassie I to avoid possible interference of foreign nations in Ethiopia's domestic affairs through the Coptic Church. Those were not hypothetical concerns by far, of which foreign policy activity of members of the government of "new Italy" gives evidence. Rome's politicians hypocritically declared their "progressive intentions" in assisting colonial peoples in getting independence. Italy, governed by "humane considerations," wanted to turn former colonies into its protectorate.

Not being a UN member, Rome launched initiatives of that kind relying on the support of the Soviet Union and its partners, with neutrality of the Franco-Latin-American union. The prediction largely came true. For instance, in a report of four deputy foreign ministers made to the CFM on September 1, 1948, France proposed: "with the exception of the territories situated between the Gulf of Zula and French Somaliland, Eritrea should be placed under the trusteeship of Italy" and that the territories situated between the Gulf of Zula and French Somaliland should be assigned to Ethiopia in full sovereignty. The Soviet Union recommended placing the former Italian colony of Eritrea "under the trusteeship of Italy for a definite acceptable term." No timeline was specified. The opinion of the United Kingdom was more constructive: "Ethiopia should be appointed to be administering Authority in years,"—after which "the General Assembly of the United Nations would decide whether, and if so under what conditions, Ethiopian administration should continue indefinitely."[67] Great Britain recommended appointment of an Advisory Council authorized to suspend any legislative act of the Ethiopian administration, and of a special UN Commission for Eritrea. The commission was to be completely different from the Trusteeship Council or Trusteeship Committee under the General Assembly.

The United States version differed from the others by its ethnopolitical nuances: It proposed that the "southern section of Eritrea (including the Danakil coast and the districts of Akale Guzai and Serae" be ceded to Ethiopia and, that Foreign Ministers to recommend to the General Assembly of the United Nations that the question of the disposition of "the reminder of Eritrea predominantly, Moslem portion including Asmara and Massawa, be postponed for one year."[68]

The only aspect in which the four powers had similar views was the idea of bringing Italy back to Italian Somaliland. Here, in Somaliland, the Italians could get a chance to show what their understanding of protectorate was.

France suggested that Libya's fate should be decided by the UN. The United States and Great Britain sided with that standpoint, but wanted Great Britain to rule in Cyrenaica. The USSR recommended to transfer Libya under Italy's protectorate. Finally, by the deadline specified in Annex XI to the peace treaty with Italy, the CFMs had not arrived to any agreement. The rift between the Great Four became wider than in 1945, when the CFM first convened in London.

The only power that advocated transfer of Eritrea to Italy was the Soviet Union, which proposed new formulas every time. As Ernest Bevin, representative of Great Britain, put it, "the Soviets proposal was not so generous to the Italian people."[69] In the opinion of Soviet representative A. A. Gromyko, the main obstacle to working out a resolution was Great Britain's intention to strengthen its domination in the Mediterranean Sea and the Red Sea. The policies of the United States, Great Britain and France, A. A. Gromyko said, were aimed at pursuance of military and political interests in those territories, so that they could be used as strategic bases against the USSR and people's democracies.[70]

Despite the hard line of the Soviet Union, Addis Ababa was willing to keep friendly relations with it. As a result of that level-headed policy of the Ethiopian leadership, the Soviet Union and other socialist countries provided aid to the freedom-loving nation. In 1947, in response to the Ethiopian monarch's request, a Soviet hospital named after *Dejazmach* Balcha, Ethiopia's national hero who had distinguished himself in battles against Italian aggressors, was opened in Addis Ababa. The hospital, in addition to its direct purpose, improved the political situation in Eastern Africa in a major way. J. Spencer, admitted that the opening of the hospital could be one reason for which the United States began to support Ethiopia in its demand of having a gateway to sea: The United States feared that the Soviet Union could step up its influence in Ethiopia.[71]

After restoration of diplomatic relations with Czechoslovakia in 1948, a trade mission from that country visited Addis Ababa. As a result of that visit from Prague, the two parties agreed on the construction of Ethiopia's first munition factory. The construction that began in 1950 was carried out by Czechoslovak specialists. Equipment was also supplied by Czechoslovakia.[72]

In 1948, Ethiopia established diplomatic and trade relations with the Polish People's Republic, and in 1948, an Indian goodwill mission arrived in Ethiopia. Emperor Haile Selassie I passed through it a special message to the Indian government, in which he expressed willingness to enter into diplomatic relations with Delhi.[73] As a result, India evolved into Ethiopia's major exporter, ahead of the United States and Great Britain.[74]

After that, diplomatic contacts with Lebanon, Iraq and Iran were to follow, which built positive attitude to the foreign and domestic policy of the government of Emperor Haile Selassie I in Muslim countries.

THE BIG FOUR AGAINST RETURN
OF ERITREA TO ETHIOPIA

On September 15, 1948, representatives of Great Britain, the United States, the USSR, and France addressed the UN Secretary General. The official note of the great powers said: "On the instructions of the Governments of the United States, France, United Kingdom of Great Britain and Northern Ireland and the Union of Soviet Socialist Republics, we have the honor to inform you that, in application of article 23 and paragraph 3 of Annex XI the treaty of peace with Italy, the question of the disposal of the former Italian colonies is referred to the General Assembly in order that, in conformity with its rules of procedure, the General Assembly may examine this question during the session which is to open on September 21."[75]

The disposition of the former Italian colonies was referred to the First Committee (policy and security committee). It is no secret that this variant was more favorable for Italy, which was not a UN member at the time. With that board of international arbitrators, Rome counted on support of Latin American partners whose votes were decisive in consideration of certain issues of postwar settlement.

The session of the General Assembly regarded the issue of the former Italian colonies as being of secondary importance and decided to consider it during the second part of the third session of the General Assembly. Not only the objective historical process but political factors contributed to the decision:

First, pro-Italian nations wanted to defer consideration of the issue of her former colonies; second, the December 1948 presidential election in the United States overshadowed the urgency of the issue of the former Italian colonies, and Washington's self-effacement from the negotiation process at the General Assembly may bring so controversial debate to a deadlock.

In view of the complexity of the situation, Aklilu Habte-Wold, head of the Ethiopian delegation, suggested that the territorial issue should be referred to a special committee of the General Assembly. But the proposal of the diplomat from Addis Ababa was not upheld by a majority (i.e., two-thirds of votes). Meanwhile, the commission whose authority he alluded to had visited those territories and was aware of the real situation there.

The representative of Great Britain pointed out to the difficulties that London was facing when governing those challenging territories, noting, and with good reason, that delays might damage the prestige of the UN, because the fallout of the annexation of African lands had been discussed by the international community for a few months, but the UN was keeping silent. Socialist countries led by the Soviet Union also wanted to see "prompt decision" of that obvious divisive issue. However, Ethiopia's proposal was not supported by a majority again.

In that respect, the Paris session of the UN General Assembly was fruitless. The matter that concerned Ethiopia's vital interests remained unsettled not only because the four powers that had assumed responsibility for the fate of the postwar world were unable to agree between themselves but also because Italy had a strong international influence. Its diplomats managed to win over even France and the Soviet Union.

The meetings and consultations that Aklilu, Ethiopia's Minister of Foreign Affairs, had with influential U.S. politicians, Secretary of State George Marshall and Senator Tom Connally, did not accelerate resolution of the Eritrea and Somaliland issues.[76]

The UN resumed discussions of the disposition of the former Italian colonies only in April 1949, at the so-called second part of the third session of the General Assembly, which was held in New York. The discussion was

launched by the U.S. representative. The diplomat suggested that three territories—Cyrenaica, Fezzan, and Tripolitania—should be governed by Great
Britain until a full-fledged state was created.

Washington suggested that the eastern part of Eritrea be attached to Ethiopia, and the western section, where the majority of the population was Muslim, to Sudan. Somaliland, since it was lacking statehood, the United States
wanted to see governed by Italy, but subject to the UN consent. London
backed the United States position. The Soviet Union proposed a compromise,
that is, a collective trusteeship system for the three colonies. France sided
with Moscow.

Italy was represented by Count Carlo Sforza. A career diplomat, he was
minister of foreign affairs in 1920, under Prime Minister Giovanni Giolitti;
then, six months before Mussolini came to power, he became Italy's ambassador to France. In 1922, when Fascism triumphed in Italy, Sforza led the
opposition to the aggressive regime. When a new Italian republic led by
Alcide De Gasperi, leader of the Christian Democracy Party, was formed in
1947, Sforza became Foreign Minister and remained in the office until 1951.

In his statement, the seasoned politician not only rejected Ethiopia's claims
to Eritrea and Italian Somaliland, but he also threw in doubt their ability to
exist independently.

The count began his controversial speech with a haughty statement: "The
new Republic of Italy is not responsible for those acts of the fascist administration." He also expressed Rome's willingness to give Addis Ababa any
security guarantees, to promote development of the disputed territories and to
prepare them for independence as soon as possible. Between 1869 and 1903
various parts of Eritrea were occupied by Italy. None of these parts were
seized from Ethiopia.[77] One phrase sounded extremely ambiguously, coming
from him: "The annexation of Eritrea to Ethiopia would be an unbearable
burden for the latter."[78]

Aklilu Habte-Wold, Minister of Foreign Affairs of Ethiopia and head of
the Ethiopian delegation, declared once again fairness of Ethiopia's claims to
the territories it had lost as a result of colonial invasion. Aklilu made it clear
for the General Assembly that Fascism was not something out of a faraway
past for Rome. Moreover, taking into account the fact that figures like pro-
Fascist politician Enrico Cerulli[79] were in the government of new Italy, the
high-ranking diplomat from Addis Ababa said: "If our appeal is not heeded
and Italy returns to Eritrea and Somali, Ethiopia will be forced to take the
necessary measures to defend against possible aggression for the fourth
time."[80] Furthermore, Aklilu rejected the proposal made by the United States
and Great Britain that Eritrea should be divided into two parts and that Italy
should return to Somaliland. In his wire dated April 16, 1949, Haile Selassie
I approved the speech delivered by the head of the Ethiopian delegation to

the UN[81] The emperor's wire was more than pertinent, because during discussions at the General Assembly one could hear cynical arguments in favor of colonialists as skillful and competent managers from Rome, who were able to transform economically under-developed colonies. "Various arguments were also put forward in support of the transfer of a part of Eritrea to Ethiopia with references to 'justice,' 'compensation for damage caused by aggression,' 'the need to provide Ethiopia with access to the sea,'" and so on.

After a series of debates, the international organization recommended to conduct a poll among local populations in Eritrea. For that, Great Britain suggested setting up a subcommittee, which would screen groups for that poll. On April 11, 1949, that mechanism was created. It was a Committee of Eleven, that is, representatives of eleven nations served on it. The committee's working group submitted information on political parties in Eritrea.

Having considered the report of the Committee of Eleven, the First Committee recommended to hear Eritrea's leading political organizations. Representatives of the Muslim League, the New Eritrea Party, and the Italo-Eritrean association were against a union with Ethiopia and demanded independence, with the Unionist Party reaffirming its pro-Ethiopian stance.[82]

The debate on the former Italian colonies in Africa ended in the First Committee on May 13, 1949.[83] The representative of the Soviet Union suggested granting independence to the three colonies after a decade of collective protectorate. The British delegate recommended granting independence to Libya in a decade and passing Cyrenaica under Great Britain's protectorate, merging the Western Province of Eritrea with Sudan, and annexing the remainder to Ethiopia.[84]

Since the parties were unable to reach an agreement on Eritrea, the General Assembly rejected all draft resolutions and postponed disposition of the former Italian colonies until the fourth session.

This tough diplomatic fight revealed weak spots of the new international organization. As it was striving to work out compromises, the General Assembly, as it is customary in international law, was creating working bodies in the form of committees, subcommittees and multilateral commissions, which could not be objective arbitrators by definition, because of the difference of specific national and coalition interests of their members. A new Subcommittee of Fifteen, which consisted of the Big Four, and also of Australia, Brazil, Chile, Denmark, Egypt, Ethiopia, India, Iraq, Mexico, Poland and South Africa, was no different, as de facto at the very first meeting it turned out it had representatives of three groups in its midst: pro-Italian, advocates of the Anglo-American plan, and proponents of the pro-Soviet line.

Italy, having become a member of NATO, had to side with the United States and Great Britain. As for Ethiopia, Aklilu Habte-Wold, Minister of Foreign Affairs, said about the situation at the moment: "For countries as

lonely and seeking justice as Ethiopia, there is nothing to do but wait with
the hope that the UN will make a historic and just decision."[85] On May 10,
1949, when the Subcommittee of Fifteen held its first meeting, the so-called
Bevin-Sforza Plan emerged. The plan was based on discussions which had
taken place between the British and Italian Foreign ministers (negotiations
between the two ministers began on May 6, 1949). According to the plan,
Eritrea would be partitioned and the eastern areas and the eastern areas
would be incorporated in Ethiopia, the western province being added to the
Anglo-Egyptian Sudan.[86] After an exchange of opinions, the Subcommittee
of Fifteen approved in principle the Bevin-Sforza formula as the basis for a
resolution, and submitted it to the First Committee.

According to the Bevin-Sforza Plan, Libya was to be divided into three
parts: Cyrenaica (Great Britain), Fezzan (France) and Tripolitania (Italy),
for a period of ten years, and after that, a united and independent Libyan
state was to be established. Italy would get back to Somaliland as a governing authority. After the expiration of a 10-year period, Somaliland would
be granted independence. The eastern part of Eritrea, including the cities of
Asmara, Massawa and Assab, would be merged with Ethiopia, which was
to guarantee that the rights of the Italians who lived in that part of Eritrea
would be respected. The cities of Asmara and Massawa would be granted
the right of autonomy. The western territory of Eritrea would be joined to
Sudan.[87]

Aklilu, Ethiopia's Minister of Foreign Affairs, requested[88] the emperor's
recommendations. All the more so that an envoy of Great Britain who had
visited Addis Ababa recommended to the emperor of Ethiopia to have his
representative in the UN collaborate with the British delegation.

The United States tried to get the Ethiopian minister interested: The Americans were persuading him to give backing to Israel's membership in the UN,
and in return, he was promised Washington's influential support. Aklilu
Habte-Wold, well aware what repercussions that step could have (displeasure
of the Arab East and Islamic world), refrained from any moves.

The emperor was clearly aware that at the moment the UN was unable to
propose a settlement plan that would meet Ethiopia's interests, and in his mis-
sive of May 12, 1949 he gave an instruction to Aklilu Habte-Wold to support
only that part of the Bevin-Sforza Plan that concerned Eritrea. With respect
to Somaliland and Tripolitania, Ethiopia's minister of foreign affairs was to
act at his own discretion.

When the draft resolution was put to vote on May 17, 1949, the plan
of merging Eritrea, with the exception of its western part, with Ethiopia
was adopted by a two-third majority vote. Draft resolutions on Somaliland
and Tripolitania were not passed. As a result, as British Foreign Secretary
Ernest Bevin put it, the project "died and his funeral took place."[89] Thus, the

representative of Ethiopia voted against the resolution concerning Somalia and abstained from the part concerning Tripolitania.

The reasons for the failure of the Bevin-Sforza Plan were discussed in the political circles of Addis Ababa. Some believed that the Ethiopian issue was not resolved only because Aklilu Habte Wold and his formal boss, the Minister of Pen, Wolde Giorgis, opposed the British plan. Others assumed that the Ethiopian envoy was incompetent. "If Ethiopia had a good ad-vocal, the issue of Eritrea and Somalia would have been resolved long ago," they said.[90]

In our view, Ethiopia's envoy had a realistic thinking and anticipated complications that Ethiopia would face with the approval of the Bevin-Sforza Plan. A vote for Italy's return to Somaliland would mean renouncing the principle of protecting the empire's national interest. Finally, this position was in conflict with the UN Charter provision on trusteeship. According to the Charter, only UN members were entitled to trusteeship. And, besides, if Aklilu had voted for a resolution on Libya, Ethiopia's relations with Muslim nations would be extremely jeopardized.

Aklilu Habte-Wold tried to convince his counterparts that a resolution on Eritrea must be adopted separately, rather than in association with that on Somaliland and Tripolitania. France, backed by Latin American countries, and the Soviet Union with its partners opposed that. As a result, the matter was postponed until the next, fourth, session. The UN General Assembly referred that critical issue to the First Committee.[91]

The United States and Great Britain insisted on transfer of Somaliland to Italy, on trusteeship over Libya and on division of Eritrea between Ethiopia and Sudan. France spoke for transfer of part of Eritrea to Ethiopia. Ethiopia's representative reaffirmed Addis Ababa's willingness to see both Eritrea and Somaliland merged with Ethiopia. He also reiterated his country's desire to agree to the proposals that Great Britain and the United States had made with respect to Eritrea.

The Italian representative made a surprising statement: "Italy demands the immediate granting of independence to Libya and Eritrea and the transfer of Somalia to under her tutelage." he said.[92] Latin American countries backed Italy. The USSR and its allies insisted on independence of Eritrea. Delegates of South Africa and Israel were against division of Eritrea, saying that the Eritreans did not want to see their nation divided.

Discussions in the First Committee lasted from September 30 to October 11, 1949. The parties managed to find common ground on many contentious issues. A provision on the country's independence was included in a draft resolution on Libya.

Opinion was divided on Eritrea. The Soviet Union suggested that it should be granted independence five years later (before that, it was to stay under the UN's trusteeship). Ethiopia would get a gateway to sea through the port of

Assab. But how that port could be accessed, the authors of the Soviet draft did not say.

The draft resolution proposed by the United States provided for a reunion of Eritrea with Ethiopia, except for the Western Province that was to be annexed to Sudan. Municipal charters for the cities of Asmara and Massawa were a debatable issue. What would become of Asmara and Massawa? Would they be free cities? Or cities with a special status?

The Soviet Union suggested that Somaliland should be declared an independent state in five years. The United States insisted on trusteeship for Somaliland by Italy. Pakistan thought that Eritrea's independence should be proclaimed in three years, and Somaliland's in at least ten years.

On October 11, 1949, the First Committee established a subcommittee of 21 members to work out a draft resolution. It was largely dominated by the Franco-Latin-American group. Aklilu Habte-Wold called that body "Italy's committee," because most of its members sided with Rome. The Ethiopian envoy insisted that "the issue of Eritrea should be discussed first. If Ethiopia is not fully confident in the return of Eritrea, then the threat of Italian aggression from the transferred Somalia is inevitable."[93] The Ethiopian diplomat was not heard.

The Franco-Latin-American proposal on Libya's independence was adopted by a majority of votes. A contradiction arose there: Italy, not a member of the UN, was elected member of the Advisory Council, which had preparation of a constitution for independent Libya among its functions. The authority of "Roman Law" seemed to have spread to international lawmaking!

The proposal on transfer of Somaliland to Italy was also passed by a majority of votes. Aklilu Habte-Wold called on the high assembly to be governed by article 79 of the UN Charter, which said: "The terms of trusteeship for each territory to be placed under the trusteeship system, including any alteration or amendment, shall be agreed upon by the states directly concerned." Aklilu recommended to refer the debatable issue and interpretations of articles 12, 37, 79 of the UN Charter to the International Court of Justice. However, under pressure from Latin American countries, Ethiopia's reasonable proposals were rejected.[94]

Establishment of a UN Commission for Eritrea was a surprising decision for the Ethiopian delegation in the UN. The United States proposal on merging Eritrea with Ethiopia within the framework of a federation was rejected.

Aklilu Habte-Wold regarded the decision to launch a new investigation in Eritrea as an implicit attempt to introduce Italian rule. "If a new investigation is needed to consider Ethiopia's claims, then a new commission must be created to check the situation in Somalia. Do the people of Somalia agree to

Italy's return?"[95] Ethiopia found understanding only in Norway and Liberia, which were in the minority.

The UN General Assembly discussed the complicated regional issue on November 19, 1949. Resolution of the General Assembly 289 (IV) of November 21, 1949 said:

> With respect to Libya: . . . That Libya . . . shall be constituted an independent and sovereign State . . . not later than 1 January 1952.
>   . . . With respect to Italian Somaliland: .. independence shall become effective at the end of ten years from the date of the approval of a Trusteeship Agreement by the General Assembly. . . . during [that] period . . . , Italian Somaliland shall be placed under the International Trusteeship System with Italy as the Administering Authority.
>   . . . With respect to Eritrea: That a Commission consisting of representatives of . . . Burma, Guatemala, Norway, Pakistan and the Union of South Africa, shall be established to ascertain more fully the wishes and the best means of promoting the welfare of the inhabitants of Eritrea, to examine the question of the disposal of Eritrea and to prepare a report for the General Assembly, together with such proposal or proposals as it may deem appropriate for the solution of the problem of Eritrea.[96]

Aklilu Habte-Wold spoke with bitterness about the fourth session, describing it as "negotiating the terms of the deal, accompanied by mutual concessions" (between Italy and members of the General Assembly.—*Author's note*). In his opinion, "the victim of aggression had to wait in sub-committee . . . until the demands of the aggressor to return to Somaliland had first been satisfied. . . . This was not the first time, that Ethiopia had suffered at the hands of an organization piously dedicated to collective security and self–determination of peoples."[97]

Emperor Haile Selassie I also denounced the resolution of the fourth session of the General Assembly. In a wire addressed to members of the General Assembly, he writes that when his country became a member of a new body, the United Nations, he and his people hoped and believed that truth would triumph; that he and his people were concerned about the UN decision to bring Italy back to Somaliland.

Ethiopia's leadership understood clearly that the United States was the main ideologist and mastermind of actions of the UN General Assembly; that Latin American countries that orchestrated rejection of Ethiopia's demand to a large extent were only so many extras that were allowed to appear in crowd scenes, provided they played up to the Washington, the main character on the stage.

Loss of foreign policy illusions helped the government of Haile Selassie I review vectors of international cooperation. On some matters, especially those that concerned colonialism, Addis Ababa was beginning to side with the Soviet Union and its partners. Ethiopia was strengthening relations with Scandinavian nations, was expanding ties with India and Middle-Eastern countries. At the same time, the country's leadership was quite tolerant with regard to the American stance in Africa.

A FEDERATED EMPIRE

According to Resolution 289 (IV), the General Assembly elected a UN commissioner for Libya on December 10, 1950. On December 8 and 9, the Trusteeship Council had met for a special session in Lake Success in order to discuss the duties assigned to it by Resolution 289 (IV). Atlantic solidarity reminded of itself: Italy was invited to take part in the session, Ethiopia was disregarded.

Official Addis Ababa referring to article 79 of the UN Charter decided to take part in the session of the Council, as a state "directly concerned" to withhold approval of the agreement which would emerge from the council. The key issue on the Council's agenda was the border issue between Somaliland and Ethiopia. While border delimitation of the neighboring territories had been carried out under the 1908 treaty between Ethiopia and Italy, demarcation was not completed. This procedural procrastination and controversies in the selection of the measure (the nautical mile [1853 m] of the Italians or the common British mile [1609 m] of the Ethiopians) aroused a tumultuous debate.

Ethiopia's inflexibility was not subjective but, rather, legitimate, with Addis Ababa's opponents guided by the "principle of expediency," that is, the right of the strong. For instance, the U.S. representative recognized the UN to be competent in the settlement of the border between the two states (Ethiopia and Somaliland), even though the second part of Ethiopia's peace treaty with Italy specified that the border settlement was not within the General Assembly's purview. Dag Hammarskjöld, the UN Secretary General, expressly backed by the United States, said that "the UN had the right to interfere in the border settlement between Ethiopia and Somaliland. The Ethiopians asserted that no third party or state could dictate to any state what its boundaries should be. For the secretary general to do so would be to violate article 2 paragraph 7 of the Charter, by invading the domain of domestic jurisdiction which, in this case, had to be the two limitrophe states." In this case, those were Ethiopia and Somaliland (meaning "Great Britain"). This time, solidarity with Ethiopia was displayed by South Africa and Peru and a group of the USSR's allied nations.

The extremely imperfect 1948 agreement between Ethiopia and Great Britain was also a matter of discussion. It said that Great Britain would pull out its troops only up to the administrative line set by Fascist Italy after it had occupied Ethiopia's territories. It meant that Ethiopia was de facto stripped of its territories, with its own consent. Addis Ababa strongly insisted on a temporary nature of the 1948 agreement, as it only meant withdrawal of the troops from the territories that Ethiopia had temporarily transferred to the allies (of Great Britain) to wage war against the Axis countries. Moreover, the agreement, which was null and void from the standpoint of international law, did not say anything about delimitation of the border between Ethiopia and Somaliland.

After a series of debates, the United States and Great Britain had to make concessions, faced with Ethiopia's principled and consistent stance formulated by Emperor Haile Selassie I. Demarcation of the territories between Ethiopia and Somaliland began with the crossing of the three border: between British Somaliland, Italian Somaliland, and the Ethiopian Empire; the coordinates were 8°N, 48°E. This starting point was specified in the 1908 Italo-Ethiopian treaty. Great Britain adopted that marker as the ultimate line for the withdrawal of its troops from Ethiopia's territory.

On April 1, 1950, Somaliland was transferred under administration of the Italian government. Under the trusteeship treaty, Italy undertook, within a decade, to create conditions in the mandate territories for Somaliland to be granted independence. General Guglielmo Nasi (the very Fascist who had organized carnage in Addis Ababa and its suburbs in 1937, as the governor of Hararghe under Marshal Graziani) was appointed governor of Somaliland. Despite Ethiopia's protest and appeal of Somaliland's representatives to the UN General Assembly to prevent Italy's return to Somaliland, the UN, with energy that could be better spent elsewhere, began implementation of Resolution 289 (IV) of November 21, 1949.[98]

Legal inadequacy of that act was evident even to people who were uninitiated in jurisprudence. In a memorandum addressed to the United Nations, the delegation of Somaliland was calling for the renunciation of that destructive decision: "According to the peace treaty, Italy renounced its rights and claims to its former African colonies. . . . The Somalis do not want to be ruled by Italy . . . a) during fifty years of Italian rule, the Somalis were deprived of education and enlightenment; b) trade and industry were monopolized by Italians; the Somalis were not allowed there; c) Somalis were not allowed to form political organizations; there was no freedom of speech and freedom of action; d) Somalis were treated like slaves; e) Italy is a poor country; she cannot properly finance her country, and even less—our country—Somalia."[99]

In the situation with Eritrea, fairness was taken off the table in international law as well. Representatives of two countries in the commission for Eritrea—Pakistan and Guatemala—were adamant opponents of Ethiopia's government. Pakistan thought the Ethiopian Empire was oppressing Muslims, so its representative in the UN, Mr. Muhammad Zafarullah Khan,[100] objected against Eritrea's merger with Ethiopia. Guatemala supported Italy, or, to be more exact, its claims to the former Italian colonies in Africa.

After a series of preliminary sessions in New York and Cairo, the UN Commission for Eritrea convened its first meeting in Asmara and called on Eritrea's populations, asking them to express their opinion on the future, orally or in writing. Governments of Ethiopia, Great Britain, France, Italy, and Egypt were involved in this quasi-referendum as advisors.

From January to June, evidence from representatives of various political parties, leaders of religious organizations, and private individuals was heard. A working group conducted polls among populations in different parts of Eritrea. The ethnic and religious makeup of the population, its geographic distribution, linguistic groups, lifestyles, economic situation, similarities and differences between ethnic groups, and preparedness of Eritrea's population for self-government have been carefully analyzed.

The commission visited 37 inhabited localities across Eritrea and held 64 meetings. In every community, it held two sessions for each of proponents of independence and for advocates of a merger with Ethiopia. Consultations with local populations showed that in three areas of Eritrea, where Christian population was in a vast majority, the idea of immediate merger with Ethiopia prevailed. A large part of the Muslim population also agreed to be joined to Ethiopia. The Muslim League, which opposed the centralistic approach of Haile Selassie I, managed to win majority only in remote areas of the Western Province.

On April 9, 1950, the commission held consultations with Ethiopia's government, visited the cities of Gonder, Debre Zeyit (today's Bishoftu) and Addis Ababa, various public institutions. The government of Haile Selassie I requested that the entire Eritrea should be included into Ethiopia.[101] Trying to accommodate the wishes of the population in the Western Province, Addis Ababa was ready to consider a compromise option of the set-up and governance.

The Ethiopian side reminded the international body the background of the issue, in particular, that 3,000 or 4,000 years before the Hamites and the Semites who had immigrated into Ethiopia settled in Tigray (a northern province of Ethiopia), and Eritrea was part of Tigray at the time. Rulers of that region were vassals who were dependent on their sovereign, Ethiopia. Consequently, historical ties had existed over centuries between Eritreans and Ethiopians, based on ethnic and social similarities, with their languages, customs, art, and religions being identical. Moreover, 75% of Eritrea's population was in favor of an immediate voluntary merger with Ethiopia.[102]

Eritrea's economic dependence on Ethiopia was also an argument for the merger. For instance, Eritrea's imports were twice as big as exports; Eritrea was unable to keep up its trade balance, and the ports of Massawa and Assab were capable of generating income only thanks to Ethiopian transit trade. Ethiopia was the main source of Eritrea's imports. 90% of Eritrean cattle-farmers depended on the pastures located in Ethiopia. To cut a long story short, objective factors gave to the imperial diplomats the reason to state that Italy is trying to restore control over the territory of Eritrea, "by applying a formula that at the same time contradicts the obvious economic facts, with the wishes of the population, with the political possibilities and considerations of state security of Ethiopia. Ethiopia will no longer passively tolerate such a threat to its existence under the clear guise of the so-called Italian independence of Eritrea." Even religious bias had to back down when faced with eloquent facts. Answering to the speculations of Mian Ziauddin, Pakistan's representative on the commission, who alleged the country lacked religious tolerance, Ethiopia's government said that one-quarter of Ethiopia's population was Muslim, as were one-third of high-ranking government officials, 17% of students in the country's elementary schools and 22% of Ethiopian university students whose studies abroad were sponsored by the government. As far as the Italian minority is concerned (the topic was developed by the representative of Guatemala) the Ethiopian Government drew attention to the presence of thousands of Italians in Ethiopia, who have themselves sought permission to stay rather than return to Italy.[103]

Finally, the commission concluded that Ethiopia's needs were so closely intertwined with Eritrea's past and future that when elaborating a plan conducive to Eritrea's welfare, Ethiopia's interests should also be taken into account. The Egyptian government supported the desire of the Eritrean people to ensure the country's unity and gave up claims to that territory.[104]

France said that constructive decisions on Eritrea's disputable jurisdiction must be approved both by the Ethiopian and Italian governments, in order to pave the way for their cooperation in the future. Official Paris believed that "such collaboration would be the most certain pledge of the maintenance of security and development of prosperity in that part of the world."[105]

In the letter dated April 17, 1950, addressed to the Chairman of the Commission Count Sforza, the Italian Minister of Foreign Affairs, stated that "Italy's government no longer seeking trusteeship over Eritrea. At the same time, a note submitted by the Italian government pointed out that the country was supportive of the idea of directing Eritrea towards independence, as the Italian government believes that its independence will not harm Ethiopia's interests."[106]

London, consistent in its arguments, reiterated that "the establishment of an independent Eritrean state does not represent a practical solution to the issue, since from an economic point of view, Eritrea is not and has never been a viable territory, and that it has neither national, nor religious, nor racial, nor geographic, nor language unity, which are mandatory elements for the creation of an independent state." Furthermore, Great Britain's government was against appointment of an Italian administration in Eritrea. Trusteeship for a definite or indefinite period would, in the opinion of the Foreign Office, be a pointless and meaningless thing to do: Eritrea's population would not agree in the near future to be ruled by the power to which trusteeship would be assigned. Through its representative in the UN, London said it would not agree to assume responsibility for trusteeship over entire Eritrea or any part thereof.[107]

Given the commission's opinion, the UN General Assembly proposed the following solutions to the problem: (a) Eritrea to be constituted a self-governing unit of a federation of which the other member shall be Ethiopia, under the sovereignty of the Ethiopian crown; (b) Each member shall possess local legislative and executive autonomy, but full authority shall be vested in the federal government with regard to such matters as defense, external affairs, taxation, finance, inter-state commerce and communications; (c) A customs union between the two members shall be obligatory; (d) A common citizenship shall prevail throughout the federation. No discrimination shall be practiced as regards religious, personal, civic, or property rights and equal rights and privileges shall be guaranteed in the constitution for all minorities; (e) The federation shall be established following a transitional period not exceeding three years.[108]

The Burmese delegation detailed proposals in 15 clauses on the elements of the future federal government, where the Ethiopian emperor was offered the title of constitutional monarch, because the federation would consist of a federal government of Eritrea and Ethiopia.

It is true that the Burmese[109] variant of the solution was speculative and did not take into account the political experience of the Ethiopian Empire. A simplified mechanism of transition from absolute to constitutional monarchy was to be created. Ethiopian statehood, with its history spanning over a millennium and with a well-developed political culture, was destined to go through trials and tribulations once again.

The stance taken by Norway's delegation looked more realistic than that of others, as it said that such a merger of the parties would be best achievable through their complete and immediate reunion.

Norwegian diplomats did not believe that establishment of relations between Ethiopia and Eritrea on the basis of a federal status would be the best constitutional solution. In the opinion of the Scandinavian experts, artificial equality of the parties would cause conflicts and public disturbances, and, ultimately, would jeopardize peace in East Africa. Diplomats from Oslo recommended to merge Eritrea with Ethiopia, provided, however that the opposition of the Western Province was to remain under the authority of the

British administration for a limited period of time (to prevent it from mounting obstacles to the merger).[110]

The latter wish did not hold water either, because it amounted to matching the unmatchable—political and administrative resources.

Diplomatic solos, when attempts were made to adapt them into something coherent within UN walls, produced discordance. During discussion of the report of the UN commission for Eritrea, Great Britain ruled out a solution based on granting independence and introduction of a protectorate. The United States and its allies advocated a union of the Ethiopian Empire and Eritrea on the basis of a federation. Italy and its Latin American followers asserted Eritrea's right to independence. Ethiopia suggested that Eritrea should be absorbed into the empire. It was backed by Norway in that endeavor.[111]

At the fifth session (November 8 to 25, 1950), controversy aggravated again. A draft resolution recommended building a federation of Eritrea and Ethiopia. Representatives of the Soviet bloc, Pakistan, and some Latin American countries voted against that scenario.

As we can see, things did not simmer down. In terms of theory of international relations, participants of the discussions made curious adjustments to their viewpoints. The Soviet Union, for instance, recommended immediately granting independence to Eritrea, pulling out British occupation troops within three months after a resolution to that effect was passed by the General Assembly and ceding to Ethiopia part of Eritrea's territory that would be sufficient to ensure for Ethiopia a gateway to sea via the port of Assab.[112]

The representatives of India, Guatemala, Honduras, and Haiti considered that nothing could be decided upon until a United Nations Commission had made an investigation on the spot. Outright independence was advocated by Argentina and Israel, a proposal which was endorsed by the representative of Saudi Arabia, who declared that he was now prepared to support a solution based on the principle of self-determination, inasmuch as most of the arguments advanced in favor of partitioning the territory were untenable. Independence, with due provision being made for the Ethiopian claims, was also recommended by Lebanon, Yugoslavia, China, and Venezuela.[113]

The viewpoint of the USSR was supported by the representatives of Czechoslovakia, Poland, the Byelorussian SSR, and the Ukrainian SSR. A United Nations Trusteeship was suggested by the representative of South Africa. Strong objection to a plebiscite or the appointment of a new Commission of Investigation was registered by the representative of Ethiopia, who insisted that the work had already been done by the Four Power Commission of Investigation. He asked that the territory be reintegrated within the framework of Ethiopia, a proposal in which the representative of Greece concurred. The representative of the United Kingdom reiterated the position adopted by his delegation during the third session of the Assembly, and the

representative of Italy advocated complete independence. The representative
of Pakistan insisted that overruling consideration must be given to the wishes
of the local populations of the region.[114]

On December 2, 1950, the joint draft was promoted to the status of official
document.

The General Assembly passed Resolution No. 390-A (V) at the 316th
plenary session. Clause 1 stated that "Eritrea shall constitute an autonomous unit federated with Ethiopia under the sovereignty of the Ethiopian
Crown."[115]

Addis Ababa's envoy supported the idea of federation, but, in our view, by
doing so, he yielded to despair. We believe that Great Britain's proposal on
merging the eastern part of Eritrea to Ethiopia or the Soviet Union's suggestion that Ethiopia should be granted a gateway to sea via the port of Assab
were more acceptable options for Ethiopia.

Why was this essentially marginal issue the focus of attention of the international community for five long years after the end of World War II? Was
the purpose to divert humanity from more urgent problems? Or to redistrib-
ute footholds between rival political systems? Possibly. Without ruling out
strategic intentions of the world's leading actors, we should mention that
every party involved in this new arbitration addressed their tactical goals in
their own way. The United States wanted to secure its long baseline radar in
Asmara, using the help of the Ethiopian government that was in control of
Eritrea and the western coast of the Red Sea. Great Britain, with its economy
no longer permitting to keep troops and an administrative apparatus in Northeastern Africa, was trying to save face when dropping out of the game. The
Soviet Union, waving the flag of anticolonial struggle, was reinforcing its
foothold in Africa.

It is a well-known fact that for Ethiopia and its peoples the Eritrea issue,
this five-year diplomatic drama artificially created by the great powers, had
adverse effects.

Before 1946, no political discord had existed among Eritrea's populations.
On the contrary, a popular movement emerged, as the people were waging
a war on Italian aggressors and the nation's self-awareness was evolving.
Growing stronger, that sentiment was naturally driving the willingness to
join the neighbors who considered the Eritreans their brothers. No insur-
mountable differences or religious controversies existed. Urban dwellers,
countryside residents, Muslims and Christians alike, all lived in perfect harmony, irrespective of their beliefs or tribal customs. However, as resolution
of the Eritrean issue was delayed, it complicated the relations of that region's
natives with the Ethiopian Empire.

Resolution No. 390-A (V) did not guarantee peace and security in East
Africa, as Resolution No. 289/ IV had demanded, because after a plan of

Eritrea's autonomy popped up, a Muslim opposition emerged that was ready to begin hostilities against the federal center.

For the creation of a federated state, a transition period was set until September 15, 1952. During that period, the Eritrean government was to be formed, and Eritrea's Constitution was to be drafted and put into effect. For that purpose, the office of the UN Commissioner in Eritrea was established, to be appointed by the General Assembly (art. 10). On December 2, 1950, Eduardo Anze Matienzo (Bolivia's representative in the UN, an adamant antagonist of the Ethiopian Empire and Italy's "advocate" at meetings of the General Assembly) became that commissioner. Knowing the commissioner's track record, one can easily imagine whose interests he had at heart, Rome's or Addis Ababa's. Meeting the commissioner for the first time, the Emperor of Ethiopia noted to the "Italian insider man" that Ethiopia understood that a federation did not mean "not the unification of two independent states, but a form of transferring the powers for internal self-government to the authorities of Eritrea."[116]

Thus, Haile Selassie I delicately and unequivocally gave the commissioner to understand that neither Ethiopia's government nor the UN commissioner had any right to amend the resolution that was advisory in nature.

In defiance to the monarch's reasonable remark, Matienzo decided to work out a constitution for Eritrea, which, in his view, "would give the government of this territory broad powers." And, at his own initiative, Matienzo sent a series of tricky questions to political parties of Eritrea: (1) Should there be one or two Assemblies in Eritrea? (2) How should the deputies be elected (by direct or indirect voting)? (3) What is more preferable, to appoint or to elect the head of Eritrea's government (the Chief Executive)? (4) What is the role of the emperor of Ethiopia in the appointment or election of the head of Eritrea's government? (5) What should be the official languages in Eritrea? (6) Should Eritrea have a special flag?[117]

The poll, as it should have been expected, only polarized public sentiment. The Unionist Party and pro-Ethiopian political organizations that sided with it favored creation of a single National Chamber for the Assembly of Eritrea. They recommended to pick Tigrinya as the official language in Eritrea, with Amharic to be the language of interethnic communication at the federal level. The head of Eritrea's government, they said, was to be appointed by the emperor, and the flag of the Ethiopian Empire should become the flag of Eritrea and of the federated State.

Eritrea's Democratic Front (independence bloc) demanded that two Assemblies be set up, and also advocated different official flags for Eritrea and for the federation. That faction considered Eritrea and Ethiopia to be two independent and equal states, and opposed the right of the emperor of Ethiopia to appoint the head of Eritrea's government; they suggested that Tigrinya, Arabic, and Italian should be the official languages.

After the Ethiopian leader interfered, the Constitution of Eritrea's autonomy (Matienzo's version) was somewhat amended. In the final version, the text of that basic law, consisting of 99 articles, was approved by Eritrea's administration and Ethiopia's government. The Constitution had the following articles that were of vital importance for the Ethiopian Empire:

- art. 3: "Eritrea shall constitute an autonomous unit federated with Ethiopia under the sovereignty of the Ethiopian Crown";
- art. 10: "There shall be a representative in Eritrea of His Imperial Majesty, the Emperor of Ethiopia, Sovereign of the Federation";
- art. 12: "The Representative of the Emperor, having noted that the Chief Executive has been elected by the Assembly, shall formally invest him in office in the name of the Emperor, Sovereign of the Federation";
- art. 14, 58: "the representative of the Emperor . . . may transmit a request to the Chief Executive . . . for reconsideration of the draft legislation by the Assembly . . . ."[118]

According to art. 9 of UN Resolution 390-A (V), the administering power, that is, Great Britain, was responsible for the creation of the Eritrean parliament (Assembly) and government. Therefore, in April and May 1952, elections of deputies were held. With the exception of the cities of Asmara and Massawa, the elections were held by indirect voting. In other words, the deputies were elected by local elders or influential people. As a result, the two rival parties (the Unionists and the Democratic Front) received an equal number of seats.

On August 11, 1952, Ethiopia's Emperor Haile Selassie I, in the presence of the UN commissioner and General Duncan Cumming, Chief Administrator of the British military administration in Eritrea, ratified the Eritrean Constitution, and on September 11, 1952, he ratified the federal act, which said, specifically:

- Eritrea's territory is united and is merged with the Ethiopian Empire, including the islands;
  - the state is still called the "State of the Ethiopian Empire";
  - the flag of the Ethiopian Empire shall remain the national flag;
  - all international treaties, conventions, and international commitments of the Ethiopian Empire shall be fully valid and operative in the said territory (Eritrea);
  - the 1931 Constitution of Ethiopia shall be effective in Eritrea; all citizens of Eritrea shall have the same rights, privileges, and protection as all the other Ethiopian subjects;

- ◦ the Federal Act and the 1931 Constitution, federal laws, international treaties and commitments of the Ethiopian Empire, which are effective in Eritrea's territory, shall hereby become effective in the other territories of the Ethiopian Empire;
- ◦ all residents of Eritrea, with the exception of the persons who have a foreign citizenship, are declared to be subjects of the Ethiopian Empire and citizens of Ethiopia.[119]

On October 4, 1952, for the first time in Ethiopia's history, the Emperor of the country crossed the border and addressed the people of Eritrea: "Today, for the first time since the time of Emperor Yohanes IV, I am on the land of Eritrea—your Emperor and your Supreme ruler . . . the emperor of Ethiopia and Eritrea . . . Today the page of sadness which separated the fraternal peoples for many centuries is closing."[120]

Afterward, Haile Selassie I went to Massawa (a port on the Red Sea), in order to celebrate Ethiopia's return to the sea. So, he completed the mission of getting a gateway to sea set as far back as in 1924, when he was still the regent of the Ethiopian Empire.

In view of the ratification of the Federal Act by Ethiopia's emperor on September 11, 1952 and his proclamation issued on September 15, 1952, which declared the end of the authorities of the administering power, the resolution of the General Assembly dated December 2, 1950 was thus implemented and the mission of the UN commissioner ended.

By ratification of the Eritrean Constitution and the Federal Act Emperor Haile Selassie I recognized and legitimized existence of the territory of Eritrea. Ethiopia had to merge in a federation with a territory that it used to possess once without reservations.

However, as it was ratifying the Constitution and the Federal Act, the government of Haile Selassie I failed to take into account that at any moment Eritrea was able to assert its right to self-determination and cessation, to demand that the federation be disbanded, thus jeopardizing the existence of Ethiopia itself. Norway's representative in the UN, a member of the commission for the investigation of the situation in Eritrea in 1949, said with good reason: "To impose obligations on Ethiopia to organize its relation with Eritrea on the basis of a federative status, without any knowledge as to whether this would be the best constitutional solution, could easily lead to future conflict and unrest, and in the end endanger the peace of East Africa."[121] And he was right. Sometime later, underground nationalistic organizations began their subversive activities against the federal government.

NOTES

1. Autobiography. 1934. P. 284–285.

2. Rodd R. 1948. P 71.

3. See: Autobiography. 1934. P. 325; *New Times and Ethiopia News.* September 4, 1942; September 28, 1946.

4. Mosley L. 1964. P. 275.

5. Autobiography. 1934. P. 333.

6. Rodd R. 1948. P. 75–76.

7. Waterfield G. *Morning Will Come.* L., 1944. P. 65.

8. Autobiography. 1934. P. 337.

9. Emperor Haile Selassie I. *Fre Kenafer* (Selected speeches). Addis Ababa. 1944 (Amharic) P. 188. (hereinafter—Haile Selassie 1944).

10. Agreement and military convention between the United Kingdom and Ethiopia. Addis Ababa, January 31, 1942 (Ethiopia No. 1, Cmd. 6334, London, 1942). P. 2 (hereinafter—Agreement. 1942). See also Rodd R. 1948. P. 539–558.

11. Rodd R. 1948. P. 90.

12. Among prisoners-of-war was *Ras* Imiru, his cousin and childhood friend, one of resistance leaders during the years of the occupation, and the emperor's daughter, Princess Romanework. She was died in Turin.

13. *Nagarit Gazeta.* January 29, 943.

14. *New Times and Ethiopia News.* June 22, 1944.

15. John H. Spencer 1984. P. 148.

16. A Major Jacobs was the first High Commissioner of the Ethiopian police; in December 1942, he was replaced by Lieutenant Colonel Bullock, and then by Brigadier P.N. Banks. In September 1956, Brigadier General Tsiege Dibu, an Ethiopian, was appointed High Commissioner of the police; he was killed during an attempted coup d'état in 1961.

17. According to Pankhurst, 75% of the Ethiopians who had been educated before the Fascist occupation died. See: Pankhurst S. *Ethiopia. A Cultural History.* P. 458.

18. Haile Selassie. 1944. P. 409–410.

19. Even though the Orthodox Church in Ethiopia was formally subordinate to the emperor, in practice the ecclesiastic nobility had the plenitude of power. If the clergy had not been well-disposed to the emperor, the days of his reign would have been numbered.

20. According to canonical law, the patriarch of Alexandria appointed a priest hailing from Egyptian Copts as archbishop of the Ethiopian Orthodox Church. The Ethiopian Church was subordinate to the Coptic Church of Alexandria.

21. *New Times and Ethiopia News.* July 15, 1944.

22. Goncharov I.A. *The Frigate Pallada.* Translated by Klaus Goetze. New York: St. Martin's Press, 1987. P. 11–12.

23. John H. Spencer. *Ethiopia at Bay. A Personal Account of the Haile Selassie Year.* Michigan, 1984. P. 103 (hereinafter—John H. Spencer. 1984).

24. Ibid. P. 143.

25. Ibid. P. 144–145.

26. Ibid. P. 150–151.

27. Agreement Between His Majesty in Respect of the U.K. and His Imperial Majesty the Emperor of Ethiopia. Addis Abeba; London, 1945; December 19, 1944 (Ethiopia. No. 1 Cmd. 6584).

28. Harold G. Marcus. *Ethiopia, Great Britain and the U.S. 1941–1974. The Politics of the Empire.* Berkley: University California Press, 1983. P. 48 (hereinafter—Harold G. Marcus. 1983).

29. Harold G. Marcus. 1983. P. 49.

30. FRUS. 1945. Vol. VIII. P. 5–7. Harold G. Marcus 1983. P. 52.

31. John H. Spencer. 1984. P. 160.

32. Ibid. P. 161.

33. See more details in: Hallidin N.V. Sweeds in Haile Selassie's Ethiopia. 1924–1952. Uppsala, 1977.

34. *The Ethiopian Herald. June 8.1944.*

35. John H. Spencer. 1984. P. 163.

36. Voblikov D.R. 1961. P. 152.

37. John H. Spencer. 1984. P. 191.

38. For details see Sylvia Pankhurst E. *Ex-Italian Somaliland.* L. 1951. P. 175–184.

39. Ibid. P. 192.

40. United Nations. Report of the United Nations Commission for Eritrea. General Assembly. Official records. Fifth session. Supplement No. 8 (A/1285). Lake Success, New York, 1950. P. 1 (hereinafter—Supplement No. 8).

41. Ibid; FRUS: Diplomatic Papers. 1945. General: Political and Economic Matters, Volume II. P. 816–817.

42. Ethiopia joined the anti-Hitler coalition after Italy and Germany declared war in 1941.

43. Sulzberger C.L. Soviet Seeks Hold in North Africa by a Trusteeship. *International Affairs.* September 19, 1945. P. 12; Zewde Retta. *The Affair of Eritrea in the Era of Emperor Haile Selassie I. 1941–1963.* Addis Ababa. 2000. P. 26 (hereinafter—Zewde Retta. 2000).

44. Molotov V.M. Press Conference. Soviet News. 10 September 1945. London. Soviet Embassy. No. 1259. P. 2.

45. See: Durdenevsky V.N., Krylov S.B. *The United Nations: A Collection of Documents Covering UN Establishment and Activities.* Moscow, 1956. P. 54–55 (in Russian).

46. See: John H. Spencer. 1984. P. 211; Pankhurst. 1953. P. 132.

47. Yugoslavia, a victim of Italian aggression, was invited to take part in the discussion of territorial matters.

48. Memoranda Presented by the Imperial Ethiopian Government to the Council of Foreign Ministers in London, September, 1945. Ethiopia. Ministry of Foreign Affairs. St. Clements Press, Limited, 1946.

49. In 1941, the military leadership of Great Britain allowed Emperor Haile Selassie I to call on the peoples of Somaliland and Eritrea to rebel against Fascist

invaders, and to join their homeland, Ethiopia. That way, British authorities formally recognized Ethiopia's sovereignty over those territories.

50. Paris Conference of Foreign Ministers. Department of State Bulletin. Vol. XV. No. 369. July 1946. P. 169.

51. See: Supplement No. 8 (A/1285). P. 1; Council of Foreign Ministers. Draft Peace Treaty with Italy. July 18, 1946. Art. 17.

52. The only amendment that was adopted concerned article 33–38, where October 3, 1935 was recognized as the date of the beginning of the aggression against Ethiopia. It was from that day that Italy was to pay reparations.

53. John H. Spencer. 1984. P. 180.

54. Ibid. P. 181.

55. Capitain Abdisa Aga In the Italian deserts. The story of a Hero—Patriot of the Italo—Ethiopian War. Addis Ababa 1960 (Ethiopian calendar in Amharic).

56. John H. Spencer recalls that many children in Yugoslavia born in the early twentieth century were named Menelik, in honor of the Ethiopian emperor's victory over the Italians in the Battle of Adwa in 1896.

57. John H. Spencer. 1984. P. 183.

58. Ibid. P. 190.

59. After the commission was set up, Ethiopia was involved in complicated and long negotiations with members of the Council of Deputy Foreign Ministers (1947–1949) and debates in the UN General Assembly (1948–1952).

60. Supplement No. 8. P. 9–17.

61. See: Tekeste Negash. *Eritrea and Ethiopia: The Federal Experience.* Uppsala. 1997. P. 39 (hereinafter—Tekeste N. 1997).

62. John H. Spencer. 1984. P. 198.

63. Supplement No. 8. P. 24.

64. United Nations Documents A/C 1.W.8. P. 127.

65. On the negotiations, see: Archives of Mersie Hazen Wolde Kirkos. 02.08 doc. No. 29. EMML. 1923 (Ethiopian calendar); 02.17 doc. No. 40. M. 1938; 04.10 doc. No. 84. EMML. 1938 (Ethiopian calendar); 14.05 doc. No. 217. EMML. 1943 (Ethiopian calendar); 05.02 doc. No. 86 EMML. 1948; 05.02 doc. No. 86. EMML 1949 (Ethiopian calendar); 04.05 doc. No. 73. EMML. 1950 (Ethiopian calendar); 05.03 doc. No. 87 EMML 1958; 04.05 doc. No. 73. EMML. 1958; 07.06 doc. 113. EMML 1958.

66. In 1951, after Qerellos's death, *Abuna* Basilios became archbishop. In 1959, the Ethiopian Church obtained consent of the Coptic Synod to autocephaly. *Abuna* Basilios was elected Patriarch of Ethiopia.

67. Department of the State. Disposition of the Former Italian Colonies. United States' Position in the Council of Foreign Ministers on the Question. Press Release. No. 733. 14 September 1948.

68. Ibid.

69. UN DOC. A/C. 1/SK. 249. P. 8.

70. UN DOC. A/C. 1/SK. 240. P. 2–4.

71. John H. Spencer. 1984. P. 193.

72. *New Times and Ethiopia News.* January 15, 1949.

73. *New Times and Ethiopia News.* October 30, 1948.

74. Diplomatic relations with India were established in early 1950, after India became a republic on January 26.

75. See: Document A/645 (Official records of the first part of the third session of the General Assembly, plenary sessions, supplements to brief reports on the meetings). P. 149–150; see also: United Nations. Department of Public Information. Shaping a People's Destiny: The Story of Eritrea and the United Nations. 1953. No. 4.

76. John H. Spencer. 1984. P. 201.

77. Supplement No. 8. P. 74–76.

78. Zewde Retta. 2000. P. 112.

79. Enrico Cerulli was Deputy Governor in Italian East Africa for three years. He was on the list of war criminals.

80. Zewde Retta. 2000. P. 127.

81. Ibid. P. 128.

82. DOC A/C. 1/SR 247. P. 3–7; DOC A/C. 1/SR 251. P. 2–3; DOC A/C. 1/ SR 253. P. 7–9.

83. See: Official records of the second part of the third session of the General Assembly. First committee, brief reports of meetings. P. 394.

84. See details of the vote in official records. P. 393–394, 593–596, 608 (in English); Official records. P. 608 (in English).

85. Zewde Retta. 2000. P. 117.

86. Report on the disposal of the former Italian colonies in accordance with the terms of the Treaty of peace with Italy of 1947. 10 April 1953. London. P. 7.

87. For more details see: Zewde Reta. 2000. P. 151–152.

88. Aklilu had concerns about the autonomous status of the cities of Asmara and Massawa, because in the last adopted formula Italy was named as a party that could be involved in the development of legislation. In addition, any backing of the plan to return Somaliland would mean giving up claims to those territories. And any backing of a plan of Libya's division would mean loss of support by the Muslim world.

89. Zewde Retta. 2000. P. 180.

90. Ibid. P. 181–182.

91. Resolution 287 (III) of May 18, 1949.

92. United Nations. Annual report of the Secretary-General on the work of the organization from July 1, 1949 to July 30, 1950. General Assembly. Official records. Fifth session. Supplement No. 1 (A). New York, 1950. P. 28 (hereinafter—Supplement No. 1 (A)).

93. John H. Spencer.1984. P. 215.

94. Ibid. P. 215–216.

95. Ibid. P. 217.

96. Supplement No. 8. P. 3. (In Russian); Question of the disposal of the former Italian colonies. https://digitallibrary.un.org/record/666748?ln=ru (accessed 25 July 2022).

97. See: John H. Spencer. 1984. P. 217–218; Zewde Retta. 2000. P. 262–268.

98. See the text in: United Nations. General Assembly. Official records. Clause 21 of the agenda; supplement. Fifth Session. New York, 1950. P. 74. (In Russian)

99. Ibid. P. 75.

100. Pakistan maliciously tossed up other negative "facts" to fuel public opinion: on the pressure exerted on Eritrean population by the local Coptic Church, on pro-government terrorists (Shifta), and so on.

101. See more details about the statements made by Ethiopia's government: Document A/AC. 34/SR 43; A/AC. 34/SR 44; A/AC. 34/SR 187; A/1285. P. 66–71.

102. See. Resume of Memorandum on Ethiopia's Claim to the Return of Eritrea and Italian Somaliland Sent to the Five Foreign Ministers Council in London on August 24, 1945. from the collection of the State Public Historical Library of Russia No. 3650. 1963.

103. Report of the United Nations Commission for Eritrea. General Assembly official Records: Fifth Session. Supplement No.. 8 (A/1285) P. 22. (Hereinafter—Supplement No.. 8 (A/1285).

104. Supplement No. 8 (A/1285.). P. 22.

105. Ibid. P. 22.

106. Ibid. P. 22.

107. Ibid. P. 23.

108. Ibid. P. 25–26.

109. Burma's representatives worked on the draft in cooperation with diplomats of the Union of South Africa (later transformed into South Africa).

110. Supplement No. 8 (A/1285). P. 28.

111. John H. Spencer. Hearing before the subcommittee on African Affairs of the committee of foreign relations. U.S. Senate, 94th conf. Wash., 1976. P. 26.

112. The Yearbook of the United Nations. 1948-49 Part 1: The United Nations. Section 3: Political and security questions. Chapter D: The question of the disposal of the former Italian colonies. P. 270.

113. Ibid.

114. Ibid.

115. See details on the vote: United Nations. General Assembly. Official records. Par. 21 of the agenda. Supplement. Fifth session. New York, 1952. P. 115–117; Text of the resolution. Final report for Eritrea. General Assembly. Official records. Seventh session. Supplement No. 15. New York, 1952. No. 15/A/2188. P. 87–89.

116. Haile Selassie I. 1944. P. 485; Zewde Retta. 2000. P. 333.

117. United Nations Final Report of The United Nations Commissioner in Eritrea General Assembly Official Records: Seventh Session Supplement no. 15 (a/2188). New York, 1952. P. 14-16 (hereinafter—Supplement no. 15 (a/2188).

118. Full text of the constitution. Supplement no. 15 (a/2188. P. 79–89; Source Book. P. 376–379.

119. Source Book. P. 375.

120. Zewde Retta. 2000. P. 371.

121. General Assembly Official Records. Supplement No. 8 (A/1285). P. 31 (in Russian).

Chapter 4

In Search for Allies. 1952–1970

MILITARY AND POLITICAL COOPERATION
WITH THE UNITED STATES

In the postwar years, Haile Selassie I, in pursuit of his idea of a gateway to sea, was trying to rely on the resources and influence of the United States. The emperor could propose to Washington a close military and economic cooperation in the area of the African Horn.

However, Ethiopia, from the standpoint of the American State Department, was of no interest to the United States as either a potential economic partner (a backward agricultural country) or as a military ally that would be able to protect the superpower's interests in a region with so many issues.

Washington, indeed, entertained some of the emperor's geopolitical aspirations—for instance, the annexation of Eritrea to the Ethiopian Crown. Pragmatic politicians from the banks of the Potomac had their reasons to act that way.

If Haile Selassie I was falling short of the title of "strategic partner," he suited Washington quite well as a "tactic ally." In that connection, the U.S. National Security Council recommended to the White House: "It is in the interests of United States security to prevent any potentially hostile power from obtaining a hold in the Middle East, the Mediterranean area, or in Africa. . . . A decision to grant any of the Italian Colonies immediate independence would result in the creation of weak states which would be exposed to Soviet aggression or infiltration."[1]

Loyalty in exchange for territory—this is how the Ethiopian American relations could be characterized in those years. It was a territory that provided access to the sea for Addis Ababa, or, to be more specific, to the Ocean, exchanged for water crossroads of global trade, world civilization. Pragmatic

George Marshall, the U.S. State Secretary, backed Addis Ababa's claims to Eritrea, having in mind that the United States would have no obstacles in operating a radio station in Eritrea and military installations in Asmara and Massawa. When the Ethiopian side wanted to formalize this idea of the U.S. State Secretary in the form of agreement, Washington backed out of an international treaty, fearing a reaction from official London, its strategic partner, which de facto had been the owner of Eritrea since 1941, and from Rome that had claims to that territory.

Despite a statement of a high-ranking U.S. official that it was necessary to support Ethiopia, before the beginning of a military intervention in Korea, Washington refused to provide meaningful military, economic, and diplomatic aid to the Ethiopian Empire.

The war in Korea convinced Washington that emergence of a weak state in the Middle East was not in the United States best interests. "Eritrea is neither socially, politically, administratively, nor economically, qualified for independence, nor will it be for some time. An independent regime would be unable to maintain law and order against the internal ravages of bunion with Ethiopia—which would not be unlikely—by the people of the central plateau. If attacked from outside, it would be unable to maintain its territorial integrity without external aid"[2] says a report of the Division of Research for the Near East and Africa at the U.S. State Department.

It was the Ethiopian leadership that initiated deepening of relations between the United States and Ethiopia. On August 12, 1950, a secretary of the Ethiopian emperor handed to the U.S. ambassador in Ethiopia a memorandum, in which Haile Selassie I proposed assistance to the United States, a friendly nation, in its warfare in Korea on behalf of the UN.

The memorandum says that "Ethiopia has respected her international obligations and has been and continues to be a firm believer in collective security. The stand Ethiopia took in 1935 and 36 against Fascist invasion is proof of this. He (the emperor of Ethiopia.—*Author's note*) still believes in justice of UN and collective security and does not swerve from this belief. His Imperial Majesty is guiding the international affairs of Ethiopia along these lines. . . . Ethiopia will always be found at side of . . . her friends, US and UK and she is hopeful of receiving assistance from these governments in order to carry out her desires in this respect . . . "[3] Haile Selassie I was aware of the aid provided by the United States to other countries, and he could not conceal his surprise, as he could not fathom why Ethiopia was not receiving similar support from the United States in order to implement its plan for the development of its economy. For instance, Italy, which only yesterday, having violated its commitment to the League of Nations and principles of collective security, unleashed an aggressive war against Ethiopia, today was receiving considerable military and economic aid from the United States. But Ethiopia, which was adhering to the same principles in the past and in the present, had been a victim of aggression, did not receive any aid for the revival of its army and economy in the wake of the war. Italy was allowed to come back to the Somaliland, despite Ethiopia's protest in the UN; its tanks and aircraft were in the neighboring territory, posing a threat to Ethiopia. The government of His Majesty (Haile Selassie I) met with a refusal when it wanted to purchase tanks and aircraft in the United States.

Many statements, propagandistic in nature, and comments from abroad, the memorandum said, suggested that Ethiopia was an open field for the infiltration of world Communism. His Imperial Majesty considers that suppression of Communism depends upon successful carrying out of his program of economic development however, Ethiopia's needs for economic assistance have been relatively ignored by US. . . . Ethiopia does not wish to delay her assistance to the democratic governments and wishes to be at their side in order to share their fortunes or misfortunes and His Imperial Majesty would wish to make the following inquiries:

(a) To what extent would US be able to assist in equipping and arming a unit of approximately 1,000 officers and men and to transport them to and supply them at the fighting front?

(b) To what extent is US prepared to assist in further equipping and strengthening the Ethiopian Armed Forces in order that Ethiopia may be able to increase her usefulness in the common defense of democratic institutions and her friends and allies?

(c) What practical steps may be taken by Ethiopia to obtain US financial assistance to enable her to develop more rapidly her economic resources for her own needs and the needs of the world in peace and in war?

His Imperial Majesty would be grateful to the American Ambassador if he would convey this message to US Government and obtain its reply."[4]

The United States was in no hurry to meet the Ethiopian emperor halfway; it was only seeking to appease him for a while. The imperial message was echoed by George R. Merrell, the U.S. ambassador in Ethiopia, who had received through Albert H. Garretson (a U.S. citizen, a legal advisor to the Ethiopian Ministry of Foreign Affairs) a message that the emperor was concerned by lack of American military aid and, at the same time, by the presence of Italian aircraft and other munitions in the Somaliland. Merrell wrote to the State Department: "It is therefore suggested as best present means of satisfying Emperor who is good friend of US . . . that an outstandingly well-known and high-ranking American general be sent here . . . : 1) to explain to the Emperor, what we conceive Ethiopia's role to be in general matter of defense of non-Communist world; 2) if feasible, to assure him that US would not permit Ethiopia to be aggressed against; 3) to discuss possibility of sending military mission to Ethiopia similar to those sent number other countries, and; 4) to dissuade him from military expense beyond economy of country."[5]

Nevertheless, Washington was in no hurry to reply to the proposals of its ambassador. The United States did not perceive anything of value in Ethiopia, except for the emperor's goodwill and his desire to stay in the democratic camp. Even after the annexation of Eritrea, when Ethiopia's strategic significance on the global stage increased beyond all doubt, when there were more and more countries that wanted to expand their sphere of influence as far as the Western coast of the Red Sea, Washington did not find it expedient to supply the Ethiopian army.

In the early 1950s, Ethiopia's government sent a request for military aid to the State Department—in particular, asked to be provided with some aircraft for the imperial air force. However, the State Department declined that request of the Ethiopian government, saying that provision of military aid was the prerogative of the Department of Defense.

Then Haile Selassie I decided to go down a different route. He supported the UN and the United States in the Korean War. In July 1950, the Ethiopian government donated 100,000 birr, or Ethiopian dollars (U.S. $40,000), to supply the UN forces with medications, and in November of the same year, Ethiopia offered to send a military contingent of 1,069 officers and soldiers to be used in Korea.[6]

Nevertheless, the U.S. State Department regarded the offer of the Ethiopian leadership as a political gesture that was only of propagandistic value. The matter was that a contingent of troops from an independent African nation among UN troops would help to offset the Soviet claim that the Korean War "is white imperialist aggression against the colored races of the world," and would contribute to the doctrine of "collective security."[7]

For its services (sending troops to Korea), the Ethiopian side was hoping to get U.S. military and economic support. But it did not happen. Haile Selassie did not get what he had expected. Instead of military aid, Washington decided to send to Ethiopia a representative of the military agency who would pursue multiple goals: (1) to secure U.S. positions, using Ethiopia's role in the protection of non-Communist nations; (2) to provide technical assistance to the U.S. ambassador in drafting a treaty between the U.S. and Ethiopia; (3) to persuade Haile Selassie I to give up "unnecessary" military spending (this is how the United States labeled the Ethiopian leadership's plan to strengthen national defense); (4) to convince the emperor that he would not need to raise the issue of military aid anytime soon.

To complete the mission, General Charles L. Bolte, Deputy Chief of Staff for Plans, U.S. Army, was designated. Before leaving for Ethiopia, General Bolte received an instruction, according to which he was to do the following, to: (1) explain to the emperor why the United States cannot provide Ethiopia with equipment; (2) encourage the emperor to avoid large disbursements for military purposes of funds needed for economic development; (3) assure the emperor, if the question is raised, that the United States takes seriously its obligations under the UN Charter to support the United Nations in effective collective measures for the suppression of acts of aggression ; and (4) explain, if the question is raised, why the United States would be unable to send a military mission to Ethiopia.[8]

General Bolte arrived in Addis Ababa on June 12, 1951. The meeting with Emperor Haile Selassie I, where the general handed to him a letter from the U.S. president took place on June 13, 1951. During the conversation, Haile Selassie I made it clear that military aid was a top priority matter for Ethiopia and insisted on practical steps toward getting it.

When he came back to Washington, DC, General Bolte came up with a few suggestions that were in the nature of recommendations: (a) a training program in Ethiopia for the training of replacements for the Ethiopian contingent in Korea. This program would necessarily include the use of American equipment; (b) an assurance to Ethiopia of U.S. protection of our Radio Station at Asmara; (c) U.S. assistance for the development of the ports of Massawa and Assab; (d) modest assistance for Ethiopia's armed forces in the form of reimbursable aid.[9]

In Bolte's opinion, Ethiopia needed a small army to ensure its domestic security; sending an American military mission would not be of any use in the military respect and would not be justified politically; military aid would pent up Ethiopia's demands of more military equipment and munitions. It was inadmissible for a country of so small importance.[10]

Even though Ethiopian troops took part in the Korean war as a U.S. ally, and the Ethiopian leader reiterated his adherence to Western democracy and declared his loyalty to the principles of collective security on multiple occasions, Ethiopia still was not regarded an ally of the "free world."

Even the changed political situation in the Middle East, radicalization of Gamal Abdel Nasser's regime in Egypt, the growing influence of the Soviet Union in the area of the Mediterranean and Red Seas, and the beginning of a wave of liberation movements in Africa (so often backed by the USSR) did not drive Washington to start treating Ethiopia as its ally and the backbone of freedom in the Western coast of the Red Sea.

Washington was not counting Ethiopia among countries that could play the part of defender of "freedom" and Western values. One proof was the "defensive wall" to protect the free world, of which Turkey, Iraq, Iran, and Pakistan were just a few ramparts. The second encirclement of that wall was conceived to include countries of the Arab East led by British Egypt.

Thus, Emperor Haile Selassie I, who wanted his country to become part of the Western world, did not get either military or economic support or recognition, because the United States believed that Ethiopia occupied an insignificant place in its geopolitical plans. It is true, a few agreements were signed between the United States and Ethiopia in 1951–1952: On February 27, 1951, an agreement on construction of highways in Ethiopia; on June 12–13, 1952, an agreement on mutual defense assistance; on May 15, 1952, an agreement on technical cooperation and a cooperative agricultural education program. But these agreements and what ensued out of them could not meet Addis Ababa's urgent needs. The Ethiopian side expected to receive a cost estimate of $25 million for military items for Ethiopia,[11] but Washington provided only purely symbolic help.

From 1950 to 1974, American investments accounted for a pittance of what the Ethiopian government requested. Only a handful of projects and plans were implemented with U.S. assistance: a vocational school to train specialists in agriculture (agronomists) built in Jimma (in the country's south), a college in Alemaya (in the east), a center for the crop improvement in Kobo-Alamata (in the north), a center for locust control, a center for animal disease control, a medical center in Gonder (in the northwest), a center for training nurses in Asmara, water treatment facilities in Addis Ababa, and so forth.[12]

The United States focused its economic assistance largely in agriculture and healthcare, because, first, Ethiopia was still an agricultural country, and, second, only developing this sector of economy, expanding production of export goods, it was possible to accelerate development of other industries, for instance, consumer and processing industries.

Nevertheless, Washington did not give up a military base in Eritrea. In October 1952, the two countries began negotiations toward formal recognition of the status of the American troops based in Ethiopia. A project of the negotiations prepared by U.S. representatives gave America an exclusive right to the military base in exchange for limited military aid. Washington regarded the facilities in Eritrea not as a military base but only as a means of communications. It was noted that the draft of the agreement was formal in nature and was conceived to legitimize the proposal of the Ethiopian government published back in 1948.*

However, according to Art. I of the draft agreement, it would be wrong to say that the base was not a facility of military importance. Addis Ababa wanted compensation in the form of the presence of a permanent military

---

* In 1948, Ethiopia's Ministry of Foreign Affairs said to George Marshall, U.S. State Secretary, that in the event of a merger of Eritrea with Ethiopia, the United States would be able to still use the military base in Asmara.

mission for training and provision of the Ethiopian army with military equipment, but Washington did not agree to that.

Washington made it clear that Ethiopia was to pay for the supplied equipment and weapons, while Addis Ababa counted on being offered a most-favored nation regime, similar to the one granted to Turkey and Greece, which were beneficiaries of the U.S. military aid program.

Meanwhile, the government of Haile Selassie I continued to be insistent in requesting military and economic aid from the United States. In order to find final settlement of the relations between the United States and Ethiopia, and also of the military aid issue, the emperor dispatched another delegation led by Aklilu Habte-Wold, Minister of Foreign Affairs. The Ethiopian delegation stayed in the United States for over a month, and discussed in that period the following matters with the State Secretary and high-ranking officials of the U.S. Defense Department: (1) military aid; (2) sending a U.S. military mission for training Ethiopian armed forces; (3) the U.S. rights to the military bases located in Eritrea's territory. After a series of negotiations, on May 22, 1953, the parties signed an agreement on mutual defense assistance[13] and on military aid, and an agreement concerning the utilization of Kagnew Station, named after the Ethiopian contingent that took part in the hostilities in Korea, and other installations in Eritrea, for 25 years.[14] Washington agreed to train, provide with equipment and armaments three divisions of 6,000 people. With limited military aid, the United States received an unlimited right to the military bases.[15]

In contents and nature, these documents look very similar to the 1944 agreement between Great Britain and Ethiopia. Then as now, Ethiopia and the United States were not on equal footing in their relationship. Americans were allowed to build fortifications, harbors, wharves and roads, to conduct topographic, hydrographic and geodesic investigations of military nature, aerial surveys, and so forth. U.S. aircraft were given the right to fly over Ethiopia and to use its airfields. The Pentagon had the right to carry out military maneuvers in Ethiopia's territory without involving the imperial armed forces. Ethiopia's government undertook to buy from private individuals land plots needed for the U.S. military base. The treaty did not stipulate that after its expiration the Pentagon's communications were to be transferred under the jurisdiction of the Ethiopian Empire.

No doubt, the United States won from the signing of the agreement, and it began right from the start to expand the Radio Marina (lit.: "Radio Navy") station built by the Italians. Using that radio station, the United States was able to transmit and receive radio signals from Europe, the Middle East, Southeast Asia, Japan, and the United States. That fact could not but stir displeasure of the Soviet Union, which could consider the radio station and U.S. military bases as a foothold for attacking its territory and territories of the states friendly to it.

The United States deliberately did not include a clause in the agreement specifying how the parties would be acting in the event of a threat to Ethiopia's security on the part of the USSR or Arab nations.

International jurists and political scientists had different views on this bilateral instrument. According to J. Spencer, this agreement was "a payment for the service rendered by the United States to Ethiopia during the years of the consideration of the Eritreas problem in the UN."[16] Other experts called it "an immoral accord which placed Ethiopia under the effective control of American imperialism and of the Zionist world."[17] Yet some others believe that, having signed the agreement with Ethiopia, Washington assumed responsibility for the fate of democracy and Western values amid disintegration of the colonial system of Western Europe. "Washington had to assume the primary responsibility for the defense of capitalist system, which, it accomplished by establishing a worldwide system of bases, by raising huge forces, and by arming client states, which were incorporated into the imperialist network," writes Harry Magdoff.[18]

One can agree with the conclusion made by John Spencer: In international relations, especially when there is cooperation of two unequal actors, the strongest always benefits. In this particular situation, one reason why the United States was backing Haile Selassie I in his project of annexing Eritrea was the desire to get an exclusive right to the operation of military installations in Eritrea. In other words the agreement was payment for the service rendered by the United States to Ethiopia during the years when the Eritrean issue was deliberated in the UN.

As for the moral aspect of the matter mentioned by Petros Desta, he probably fails to fully understand that Haile Selassie I wanted to reinforce his country's defense capacity amid a rising threat of Pan-Arabism. To achieve his goal, he needed to find an ally (protector, sponsor). In that period, the United States was the only possible ally.

One cannot agree with Harry Magdoff's statement either. Washington never considered Ethiopia a backbone of global capitalism or an ally in defending Western democracy from the Communist threat. Therefore, neither the U.S. government nor American businesses were seeking to sponsor Ethiopia's economy, in order to transform its ways of life, political or economic structure, as it was customary in many countries of Asia and the Middle East.

Having signed the agreement, Ethiopia automatically became subject to the standards of the "Nixon Doctrine."[19] It meant protection of United States' regional and local interests was put into the care of local authorities. That said, an agreement on mutual defense assistance did not oblige the United States to protect Ethiopia in case of war, military threat, or intervention.

Why did Haile Selassie I fail to use the well-tried policy of inter-imperialist controversies, for instance, by refocusing his political line toward the Soviet

Union? In our view, the main reason was the presence of British troops in Ethiopia's territory and the authorities ruling in the Italian Somaliland. Welcoming the Soviet Union would mean facing a direct threat on the part of Western nations that insisted on the monarch's extreme loyalty. With all his political savvy, Haile Selassie I still believed in the effectiveness of the UN Charter, collective security, Western democracy. This is why in his speeches before reporters and in dialogs with foreign political figures, one statement was omnipresent: "Ethiopia is an ally of democratic society."[20] One important achievement in the emperor's foreign policy activities was his official visit to the United States and European countries in 1954.

On October 14, 1953, the U.S. embassy in Addis Ababa received a telegram that U.S. President Eisenhower had approved an official visit of Emperor Haile Selassie I to the United States in April–May 1954. On October 19, the U.S. ambassador personally delivered a wire with the invitation to the imperial palace.[21]

The purpose of the emperor's trip was to get economic, political, and military aid. The program of the visit of Haile Selassie I was next on the agenda. He was expected in Washington on May 26, 1954. On the same evening, he was to attend a dinner given in honor of the high guest by U.S. President Dwight Eisenhower. On May 27, U.S. State Secretary Allen Dulles, in turn, was giving dinner in the emperor's honor. On May 28, the emperor was giving dinner in honor of the U.S. president at Ethiopia's embassy. On May 29, the monarch was slated to visit Princeton and New York. The mission was to be over on June 3. It was to be followed by an unofficial trip to Canada and Mexico, and then by a diplomatic tour in Europe.[22]

During the meeting with President Eisenhower, the emperor discussed Ethiopia's urgent issues, such as expansion of investments of American capital, development of the port infrastructure, getting a few ships for the coast guard, development of Ethiopian airlines.[23]

The president empathized with the requests of the monarch of a "friendly nation." He instructed relevant agencies to work out variants of cooperation. However, official figures in Washington, DC, while sympathizing with Ethiopia, being aware of its goals and aspirations, failed to convince American capital that investments in the economy of the African partner would pay back. The only thing that the emperor had success with during his visit was getting a tumultuous applause when he addressed the Congress, but that political dividend could not be converted into something more tangible.[24]

However, the zero result did not discourage the emperor. He doubled his effort, trying to promote national interests, this time in Europe.

Back in 1947, the Ethiopian government had sent to London the text of a treaty that was to bring the Ogaden under Addis Ababa's jurisdiction. The British Crown reacted to the document only in 1950, and proposed its own version of the treaty, which precluded return of disputed territories to Ethiopia. Haile Selassie I, with his characteristic dignity, rejected the British version of the settlement of the territorial issue. Having made a pause in the dialog, Great Britain proposed a new draft agreement in 1954. The Ethiopian side accepted the Foreign Office's new proposal, because the text acknowledged existence of the issue of occupied territories.

Why did the British side display complaisance? Because the UN's resolution on granting independence to the Somaliland upon expiration of the Italian protectorate ruled out creation of Greater Somalia. Presence of coalition troops in those territories, "under the pretext of their strategic importance for waging war against Axis countries," fourteen years after the end of World War II, looked preposterous. All the more so that Britain had pulled out its military mission from Ethiopia in 1951.

Annexation of those territories to the British Somaliland would mean a gross violation of the UN Charter. With notorious diplomatic foot-dragging that the British foreign policy agency was thriving on, the process of negotiations, spurred by objective circumstances and insistence of the Ethiopian leader, was approaching its logical conclusion. The agreement on the withdrawal of Great Britain's troops from the Reserved Area and its transfer under the jurisdiction of the Ethiopian Empire was signed in London on November 29, 1954. Under the agreement, effective on February 28, 1955, the authority of the government of His Imperial Majesty Haile Selassie I was to cover the Reserved Area and the Ogaden.[25] Great Britain was beginning to evacuate its troops. Given local specifics, pastoralist tribes of the British Somaliland were allowed to migrate with their herds to pastures in Ethiopia and back, and Ethiopian cattle farmers were permitted to do the same in the British Somaliland. The agreement was to stay valid for 15 years.

The 1954 agreement was an unqualified success of the diplomatic tour of Haile Selassie I. It meant reaching an important landmark in the emperor's 14-year struggle for getting back the annexed lands. The withdrawal of the British troops reduced England's influence in northeastern Africa to a minimum.

In addition to London, the emperor visited Bonn, West Berlin, Brussels, Amsterdam, Copenhagen, and Stockholm. These visits were not pursuing any business-related purposes and were more of educatory nature.

As Cairo got out of control of Western powers, the Ethiopian Empire remained the only country in Africa that was friendly to America and kept its military bases on its own territory. Based on the political situation in the Middle East, the Pentagon revised its relations with Addis Ababa. It was provided with minimal American military aid in the amount of $5 million every year (to meet the needs of Ethiopia's Air Force and Navy).[26]

Furthermore, a favorable foreign policy environment also had a positive impact on Ethiopia's economy. A growing demand for food boosted exports. Revenues from coffee export alone amounted to $122 million as of 1953.[27] American partners understood that the Ethiopian Empire was able to buy military equipment and armaments.

The paltry military aid provided by Washington could not satisfy Addis Ababa, because, with the annexation of Eritrea and the withdrawal of Great Britain, which, at least partially, was protecting Haile Selassie's regime from Pan-Arabism, and with the rise to power of radically minded regional leaders like Gamal Abdel Nasser who was ready to export revolution, Ethiopia had to strengthen its defense capacity.

Washington had its own reasons. The United States did not perceive the threat of global Communism's penetration into the African Horn controlled by allies: Great Britain, France, and Italy. Consequently, Ethiopia was an apt beneficiary of the Point Four Program, which was conceived as a program of aid to postcolonial nations of Asia and Africa.

The Point Four Program[28] included training of local human resources, technical assistance for the development of agriculture, healthcare and education. The United States believed the program would promote transformation of primitive pre-industrial underdog economies into industrial and well-developed ones. As a result, democratic institutions were believed to emerge in the countries that would accept the donor's help. Practice showed differently. Given special features of their socioeconomic patterns, many nations were unable to borrow the West's living standards and political culture. Moreover, some third-world countries preferred military buildup to economic development.

Having appraised the situation, Emperor Haile Selassie I decided to play on U.S. fears and that way to get expanded aid and use it, among other things, for the building of the Ethiopian army and providing it with weaponry. The emperor did not manage to convince Washington of the importance of reinforcing the Ethiopian army, a loyal ally of the NATO. Therefore, the United States did not supply him with military aid in required quantities.

Nevertheless, Haile Selassie I continued to remain a loyal friend of the United States, if not an ally, and he was a true and stalwart partisan of Western democracy. One evidence of that, in addition to the laws and orders promulgated by the emperor, was the 1955 Constitution granted by the emperor to his subjects on the occasion of the 25th anniversary of his coronation.

The 1955 Constitution addressed the task faced by the Ethiopian leader since the beginning of his rule (creation of a centralized state with the emperor's absolute power, rather than creation of a constitutional monarchy, as some historians believe).

According to Art. 2, imperial dignity was to remain perpetually attached
to the line of Haile Selassie I. Art. 26 points out that the sovereignty of the
Empire is vested in the emperor as the Head of the State. The emperor exercises the supreme authority over all the affairs of the Empire.

*art. 27:*The emperor determines the organization, powers and duties of all ministries.
art. 28:The emperor appoints mayors.
*art. 30:The emperor exercises the supreme direction of the foreign relations of
  the Empire. He alone has the right to ratify, on behalf of Ethiopia, treaties and
  other international agreements.*
*art. 33:The emperor has the right to convene the annual sessions of the delibera-
  tive Chambers and to convoke extraordinary sessions thereof. He has the right
  to postpone the opening of and to suspend, and to extend any session of Parliament, to dissolve the Chambers or either of them.*
*art. 66:The emperor has the right to appoint and dismiss the Prime Minister and
  all other ministers.*
art. 68:Each minister shall be individually responsible to the emperor.
art. 127:An elected and appointed bishop shall be approved by the emperor.
art. 37:Equality of citizens in the eyes of the law.
art. 40:Freedom of religion if not used with political purposed.
art. 41:Freedom of speech and of the press.
*art. 45:*Freedom of assemblies.[29]

Speaking about the Revised Constitution, the emperor said «Nearly a quarter of a century ago (1931 Nigusie Kassaye). We were pleased to grant to Our
beloved people the first Constitution in the history of this three-thousand-
year-old Empire. Today, on the Jubilee Anniversary of Our Coronation, We
are pleased to proclaim a Revised Constitution consolidating the progress
achieved, and preparing the way for future advances. On that day, 24 years
ago, We laid the basis of the modern Government of Ethiopia.[30] All regions
of the Empire are now closely knit together under a single unified direction
capable of guiding them all along parallel lines of progress and integrating
all into a common national endeavor. In addition, all vestiges of "feudalistic"
and other classes of personal privileges have been wiped out, so that all Our
beloved subjects may live together as equals and brothers in the same family.
Ethiopia, under Our guidance, must consolidate this progress. She must do
more. She must advance yet further. To assure the progressive welfare of Our
beloved people is Our sole goal of life. There can be no justification for any
government, whatever be its form, except that of ensuring and promoting the
welfare of its subjects.[31]

Haile Selassie I thus tried to adapt some elements of Western democracy to
Ethiopian realities. The vast majority of the Ethiopian people never enjoyed

those rights. The Constitution was largely addressed to the outside world, for it to perceive Haile Selassie's regime as progressive and democratic. But that very outside world was still hostile to Addis Ababa.

Relations with Great Britain were complicated by the unwillingness of British authorities to pull out their troops from the Reserved Area and Haud, according to the 1954 agreement signed in London. In order to bridge the gap, representatives of the two countries met in January 1955 in Harer. Those meetings did not bring any results, because the British side wanted territorial concessions in favor of the British Somaliland, which the Ethiopian side refused.

In April 1956, Great Britain's government sent to Addis Ababa a delegation led by Dodd Parker, who was personally acquainted with the Ethiopian emperor. The English veiled their geopolitical interests by referring to a threat from the Soviet Union and the Communist bloc, which allegedly were destabilizing the situation in the Middle East, were engaged in subversive activities, arming Arab nations. Moreover, the Arab nationalism inspired by Egypt's ruling circles and funded by Saudi Arabia was directed against Ethiopia. Britain, which for nearly 100 years had collaborated with the Arab elite that still enjoyed influence, for instance, among *fellahs* in Egypt, and with the Iranian elite that was in control of the oil money and enjoyed a huge influence in Iraq and Pakistan, was ready to help the Ethiopian Empire. "In return the Ethiopian government should cede the Haud and the Reserved Area to the British Somaliland Protectorate."[32] Parker spoke about the influence of the British Empire in the Muslim world, without turning an eyelash at the fact that just a few years before, after the nationalization of the Suez Canal, nationalization of the Anglo-Iranian Oil Company had taken place in Iran, and so on.

Aklilu Habte-Wold, Ethiopia's Minister of Foreign Affairs, said to the English without paying much respect to diplomatic subtleties: "Ethiopia could never agree to dismember itself in order to expand the British Empire. Contrary to British assertions Ethiopia's relations with Egypt were good as were those with the Soviet Union."[33]

Parker's mission failed. At the same time, representatives of Great Britain came on frequent visits to the British Somaliland. During one such visit on May 29, 1956, Lord Alexander Lloyd, Under-Secretary of State for the Colonies, indicated that "union of the British and former Italian Somaliland's would be favorably viewed by the British government. Three years later, Alan Lennox-Boyd, Secretary of State for the Colonies at the time, put forward an idea of creating Greater Somalia consisting of the British and Italian Somaliland, including Ogaden with the Haud and the Reserved Area."[34] That naturally worried Ethiopia's leadership, because confrontation with London was becoming imminent.

The proposal made by Dodd Parker and the statement of his boss, Lennox-Boyd, were unacceptable for Ethiopia not only because of the threat of territorial annexation but also because the country was running the risk of losing face on the international stage, and, in particular, in the Middle East. If territorial exchange between two countries—Ethiopia and Great Britain—could be explained to the international community, how can one justify abandonment of national territory and people? The government of Haile Selassie I could be slammed both domestically and abroad, especially by the Arab world, where his actions could be regarded as complicity in the expansion of the territory of Great Britain.

In the settlement of the arising controversies between the two countries, the United States, to which Haile Selassie I leaned, was neutral. This standing of the United States caused concern of Ethiopia's leadership. By 1955, difficulties had emerged in the relations between the two countries.

As it was mentioned above, the Ethiopian side believed the United States was not giving its assistance within required scope (especially in the military sector). The United States viewed the issue differently: Washington believed that Ethiopia was receiving exactly the aid it deserved.

In September 1955, Egyptian authorities signed a contract on arms supplies with Czechoslovakia. In December of the same year, Washington, proceeding from its own interests, offered to Egypt financial aid in the amount of $40 million. Egypt was to use the funds to build the Aswan Dam. This move of Washington's was a surprise blow for Addis Ababa. The United States did not even notify the Ethiopian leader of its decision, even though he considered himself if not an associate but still a friend of the West; moreover, it is in Ethiopian territory that the Nile takes its source.

Haile Selassie I desired to be explained how come that America was providing a large amount of money to the anti-West revolutionary regime in Cairo, while pro-West conservative Ethiopia was suffering from lack of capitals for development?[35] After meeting with the emperor, U.S. Ambassador Joseph Simonson reported to the State Department the situation in Addis Ababa; he tried to convince Washington how important Addis Ababa's loyalty to the United States was in light of the competition with the Soviet Union, given its ever-increasing influence on the peoples of Asia and Africa.

Washington did not react to the message of its envoy. Only Cairo's subsequent action made the United States revoke its proposal for the construction of the dam. The change of heart was caused by the recognition by Egypt of the People's Republic of China, conclusion of an arms supply agreement with Czechoslovakia, and nationalization of the Suez Canal, which dealt a blow to the financial standing and prestige of Great Britain and France, U.S. NATO allies.

As Great Britain was looking for ways out of the crisis and was trying to improve relations with Egypt, it prepared a conference on the Suez Canal, which took place in London in August and September 1956. Ethiopia was among the nations invited to take part in it.

The conference, in which 18 nations participated, set up an international board for operating, maintaining and developing the Suez Canal, where Egypt was offered membership. Because Cairo refused to take part in the conference, it was decided to send a delegation to let Nasser know of the board's decision. The delegation included Aklilu Habte-Wold, the Ethiopian Minister of Foreign Affairs. The mission failed.

Among the members of the delegation, Ethiopia was the most interested party, because most of its export and import was going through the Suez Canal. Other members of the mission were the prime minister of Australia (as chairman), representatives of the foreign ministries of Sweden and Iran, and a U.S. Undersecretary of State.

Involvement of the Ethiopian minister of foreign affairs complicated the already complex relations between the two countries. In retaliation, Nasser prohibited Ethiopian airplanes from crossing Egyptian air space. Since that time, relations between Egypt and Ethiopia began to deteriorate. In 1957, a Cairo-based radio station started to broadcast an anti-Ethiopian program. It frequently invited professors from Al-Azhar University who called on the people of the Somaliland and the Ogaden to win independence, to join the League of Arab States, and to fight for the cessation of Eritrea from Ethiopia. On the whole, Pan-Arabism found an enemy in Ethiopia, and that enemy was to be destroyed.

The United States and Western Europe did not come to the rescue of the Ethiopian Empire. Ethiopian trade suffered most from the closing (blockade) of the Suez Canal in 1956, because Ethiopian export and import had to be carried out via South Africa. Moreover, by that time, the market of Ethiopia's main product, coffee, had been saturated because of overproduction in Latin America and some African countries.

Thus, in 1956, Ethiopia was to face the Suez crisis alone. On March 11, 1957, U.S. Vice President Richard Nixon arrived in Addis Ababa on an official visit. Ethiopia thought that this visit of a high-ranking White House representative was related to the previously signed treaties on mutual defense assistance.

The United States had other objectives: It needed more land to expand its military base. The move would require additional spending by Ethiopia, as it was necessary to make up for the losses of local residents.

In short, Nixon's mission did not improve Ethiopia's situation. Following the footsteps of the vice president, James Richards, a special envoy of the U.S. president, arrived in Addis Ababa in April 1957. He wanted to introduce the so-called Eisenhower Doctrine "Eisenhower Doctrine "protect-ing the Middle East from the infiltration of Communism."[36] The mission also planned to discuss military and economic aid to the countries covered by the Eisenhower Plan.

Negotiations in Addis Ababa stymied. To the suggestion of the Ethiopian minister of foreign affairs that the issue of military aid should be addressed without delay, the American side replied in the negative, because, in its opinion, global Communism was not threatening the Ethiopian Empire. Afterward, J. Spencer, who had taken part in the negotiations between the Ethiopian minister of foreign affairs and Richards as an interpreter, wrote: "Talks on a joint communique proved to be especially difficult. The ambas-sador was insistent that Ethiopia follow the line adopted in the other countries visited, stressing the danger of communism. Why then Aklilu asked, should Ethiopia do so when the ambassador had just said that Ethiopia was not men-aced by communism."[37]

Events in Sudan, when Egypt invaded northern territories of that country, and Egypt's more active efforts in Lebanon worried the government of Haile Selassie I. On July 14, 1958, a revolution occurred in Iraq. The United States failed to protect its friends from "Socialist radicals."

All that convinced Haile Selassie I that he was not on the list of U.S. friends. When negotiations with Italy on the settlement of the border issue between the Italian Somaliland and the Ethiopian territory of the Ogaden began in 1955, the Ethiopian side suggested that the border issue should be settled on the basis of the 1908 agreement signed by Emperor Menelik II and Italy. The Italian side, which represented the interests of the Somaliland, rejected Ethiopia's proposals. It was decided to refer the issue to a session of the UN General Assembly. It is a known fact that Ethiopia had put off this question in the early 1950s, because the Eritrean issue was higher on the agenda. In addition, the Ethiopian leadership, which had not recognized Italy's return to the Somaliland, did not think it necessary to negotiate with the Italians. Proposing UN mediation as a resolution, the Ethiopian leadership insisted on arbitration. Because of differences between the parties and the United States refusal to back Ethiopia, border issues remained unsettled. This matter caused conflicts between the Ethiopian Empire and the Somali Republic.

In 1960, the Somaliland was to get independence, as Italy's protectorate expired. In March 1958, the United States, allegedly fearing penetration of the Soviet Union, began negotiations with Great Britain, France, and Italy. The Ethiopian Empire, which was the most interested party, was not even invited to take part in the discussion.

Since the Reserved Area and Haud could be included in Greater Somalia if a decision was made to create such a state, Ethiopia's minister of foreign affairs regarded this step on the part of the United States as a plan that would be implemented at his country's expense, that is, his country would lose territory, and he said he would put this matter before the UN. Spencer writes: "The British ambassador was horrified when Aklilu raised this possibility, since it would open the door to Soviet participation in the financing."[38]

In the late 1950s, as the process of the abolishment of the federation began, initiated by the Eritrean Parliament, Ethiopia's international situation, especially its relations with the Arab-Muslim world, started to become increasingly more complicated. Tension remained between Ethiopia and Egypt. Alongside anti-Ethiopian broadcasts from Cairo that continued, the Arab East began to launch open attacks. Weapons were delivered to Eritrean fighters from Syria and South Yemen across the Red Sea. Government troops did not have means to spy on smugglers, to seize and destroy those weapons.

The Communist bloc was not friendly to Haile Selassie's regime either, even though it never turned against it openly. The Ethiopian leader needed to make a diplomatic breakthrough. It could, if not improve, at least mitigate, the attitude of the Arab world (in particular, Egypt) to Ethiopia, and could help get the relations with the Soviet bloc on the right track (the United States stopped reacting to the emperor's requests). Haile Selassie decided to make official visits to Egypt and the Soviet Union.

Worried by the forthcoming visit of Emperor Haile Selassie I to Moscow, a U.S. representative in Addis Ababa sent a wire to Washington, DC, saying: "West would now have to take strong measures to nullify the opening to the socialist bloc . . . Washington ought quickly to support Addis Ababa on the Somali problem, strengthen naval and air programs, help to develop educational institutions, and facilitate Ethiopian acquisition of loans and grants from Western-influenced banking consortia, international organizations, and multinational corporations; assist Ethiopia in obtaining loans and grants from Western banks and international organizations, transnational corporations."[39]

Washington did not accept the proposals of its envoy, all the more so that the collapse of colonialism and emergence of new states in Asia and Africa made the United States review its foreign policy, and the Ethiopian Empire was pushed into the background.

The demise of colonialism affected foreign policy activities of Haile Selassie I. The Ethiopian Empire was to establish relations with nascent states and find ways of coexistence with them.

"THE THIRD WORLD"

Before the late 1950s, the Ethiopian Empire had kept political, economic, and cultural ties with West European countries: Great Britain, France, Italy, which were in control of Sudan, Kenya, the Somaliland, Djibouti, and the

Middle East. Surrounded on all sides by colonial powers that frequently were antagonistic to one another, the Ethiopian Empire used those antagonisms between them in its foreign policy for its own survival.

Even though those powers infringed on its independence from time to time (for instance, in 1896, and from 1936 to 1941 Ethiopia had to fight, including with arms at hand, against Italy), their proximity pushed the empire's rulers to begin the country's modernization. In addition, it provided protection of Ethiopia from incursions of nomads from the south and the west, and thwarted aggressive plans of some nations of the Arab and Muslim world (in particular, Egypt and Turkey), which was the empire's main potential opponent.

Demise of colonialism as a result of Europe's transition to a better developed economy and more intensive production method, costly maintenance of multitudes of administrators and armies defending security of overseas territories, permanent pressure on the part of the United States and the Soviet Union, both of which needed to reinforce and expand their spheres of influence after World War II—all that led to granting independence to colonial territories and to transferring their administration to the local elite which was ill-prepared for peaceful coexistence with neighbors.

Thus, as a result of emergence of independent states in the Middle East and in Africa, the Ethiopian Empire found itself vulnerable, as it was facing ideological attacks (for instance, the radio in Cairo was broadcasting calls in support of Eritrean insurgents) and, afterward, direct interference into its domestic affairs, to say nothing of material aid to the fighters for Eritrea's independence and proponents of creating Greater Somalia by severing the Ogaden from Ethiopia.

Haile Selassie I was aware that the country's resources were insufficient to eliminate external threats that the army was inferior to the opponent's armed forces and that means of propaganda that could have international impact were insignificant. The United States, on whose support the emperor counted, did not provide aid to Ethiopia. Then the monarch established friendly relations with nations of the Muslim East and Africa that had won independence in the 1950s and the 1960s. Thus, the "Third World," represented by countries of the Middle East, Asia and Africa, emerged as a key vector of Ethiopia's foreign policy activity.

At the initiative of India, Indonesia, Burma, Pakistan and Sri Lanka, an Afro-Asian conference was to be convened in the city Bandung (Java Island, Indonesia) and was to be held from April 18 to 24, 1955. Australia, Israel, North Korea, Republic of Korea, New Zealand, the USSR, Taiwan, and South Africa were not invited by the organizers. Emperor Haile Selassie I decided to take part in the forum, even though he was aware that the effects of his step could have negative repercussions for his relations with the United States and West European nations.

Delegates of 29 African and Asian countries took part in the conference. They represented interests of 1.5 billion people: Afghanistan, Burma,
Cambodia (Kampuchea), Ceylon (Sri Lanka), China, Vietnam (Democratic
Republic of Vietnam), Egypt, Ethiopia, Gold Coast (Ghana), India, Indonesia, Iran, Iraq, Japan, Jordan, Laos, Lebanon, Liberia, Libya, Nepal, Pakistan,
the Philippines, Saudi Arabia, Siam (Thailand), South Vietnam, Syria, Sudan,
Turkey, and Yemen.[40]

On the back of seven stress-filled days of "creating a new world," a common Front of Asian and African Peoples consolidated on the basis of an
anti-imperialist and anticolonial platform emerged. The ideology of the new
international movement made Haile Selassie I review his foreign policy line
and find his country's place among nations of the third world. The emperor
sympathized with key provisions of the final document adopted in Bandung,
which included the five principles of peaceful coexistence of the Panchsheel
Treaty, an Indian-Chinese agreement concluded in 1954.[41]

According to the Bandung document, the ten principles of peaceful coexistence in international relations were: 1. Respect for fundamental human rights
and for the purposes and principles of the Charter of the United Nations. 2.
Respect for the sovereignty and territorial integrity of all nations. 3. Recognition of the equality of all races and of the equality of all nations large and
small. 4. Abstention from intervention or interference in the internal affairs
of another country. 5. Respect for the right of each nation to defend itself,
singly or collectively, in conformity with the Charter of the United Nations.
6. Abstention from the use of arrangements of collective defense to serve
any particular interests of the big powers and abstention by any country from
exerting pressures on other countries. 7. Refraining from acts or threats of
aggression. 8. Settlement of all international disputes by peaceful means. 9.
Promotion of mutual interests and cooperation. 10. Respect for justice and
international obligations.[42]

"Fighter against world Communism, an ally of the West, adherent of
democracy and collective security" Haile Selassie I agreed to the creation
of a de facto anti-American international organization, the Non-Aligned
Movement, where leaders of Communist China, the Democratic Republic of
Vietnam, and Egypt were the key figures. If prior to the first half of the 1950s
the Ethiopian Empire enjoyed influence among African and Asian peoples
fighting for independence, after the Bandung Conference, Egypt emerged as
the indisputable leader of the third world in Africa and in the Middle East.

After the nationalization of the Suez Canal and a few courageous steps
aimed against dictatorship of the leading powers of the West (Great Britain
and France), Nasser's influence among radically minded African leaders
surged, and in 1957, he initiated the Afro-Asian People's Solidarity Organization (AAPSO), which included as members, besides Afro-Asian states,

Central Asian republics of the Soviet Union. This organization supported creation of Greater Somalia by detaching territories of Ethiopia and Kenya, and also by full annexation merger of the French Somaliland.

Nasser had a rival who also could claim the title of leader in Africa. It was another radical politician, Kwame Nkrumah, the leader of the Gold Coast (Ghana), who created in 1958 a new organization—All-African Peoples' Conference (AAPC). Its purpose was to fight colonialism and neocolonialism, to search for ways of Africa's economic and social development. This organization declared non-recognition of state borders inherited from the colonial past.

Consolidation of African countries was a controversial process. In April 1958, Nkrumah convened a conference of independent African states. Those included Ghana, Liberia, Libya, Morocco, Egypt, Sudan, Tunisia, and the Ethiopian Empire. Delegates of the conference spoke against tests of nuclear weapons in Africa, condemned colonialism and neocolonialism, discussed issues related to Algeria's independence.

The leadership of the Ethiopian Empire, who was interested in good relations with countries of the third world, had to support the National Liberation Front (Algeria), which was fighting against France that was pro-Ethiopian on the international stage and was not supportive of the idea of creating Greater Somalia.

In those years, Africa's best minds were looking for ways of achieving full independence (economic, political, military, and cultural) of the continent from European domination. Opinions of leaders of African countries differed: Some believed that Africa would be able to achieve the desired outcome if it immediately began to unite all nations of the continent; others thought that the most effective solution would be creation of an economic union on the basis of the relations established by colonizers. These differences structured the African administrative elite, as radical (Kwame Nkrumah, Sekou Toure, Gamal A. Nasser), moderate (Leopold Sedar Senghor), and conservative (Félix Houphouet-Boigny) politicians emerged in its midst.

In 1958, Prime Minister Nkrumah convoked a Conference of Independent African States in Accra (capital city of Ghana). It was attended by representatives of Ghana, Liberia, Libya, United Arab Republic (UAR), Morocco, Sudan, Tunisia, and Ethiopia. Among the multiple issues discussed at the conference, the most urgent ones in that historical moment were: Working out a common foreign policy of African nations; measures to protect independence, sovereignty, and territorial integrity of the continent; ways and means of expanding economic cooperation between African nations based on technical, scientific, and information exchanges; cultural exchange between African countries.[43] The participants pledged to remain faithful to the UN Charter and the principles of the Bandung Conference.

The conference ruled that every year April 15 would be celebrated as the African Freedom Day, and also resolved to set up a Coordination Committee and Secretariat of the African Advisory Group under the UN. The resolution concerned all African peoples. It called for their unity.

It was clear that leaders of nations were the real driving force that had the authority and means for the attainment of that goal. In other words, the fate of the unity was to a certain extent in their hands. The idea of unity was promoted among the educated elite that had an adequate vision of its real meaning, unlike the majority of the population that perceived African unity as an abstract notion.

The idea of African unity looked utopian, because in reality none of the African leaders wanted to give up an ounce of their power for the sake of common goal. Therefore, federalism was never achieved in Africa. Private interests and nationalism stood up against common interests that African leaders were so fond of talking about.

In early 1960, first inter-state political groups emerged in Africa. In 1961, representatives of Cameroon, Central-African Republic, Chad, Congo (Brazzaville), Gabon, Ivory Coast (since 1985, Republic of Côte d'Ivoire), Malagasy Republic, Mauritania, Niger, Senegal, Republic of Upper Volta (since 1984, Burkina Faso) and other countries met in Abidjan (its second meeting was held at Brazzaville, the city from which the Group derived its name), in order to discuss the situation in Algeria, the Congo crisis, and the admission of Mauritania to the UN.[44] These countries had nothing in common, except for a common colonial past and the fact that French had become their official language. They were supposed to be speaking about the mediatory role of the former French colonies in the conflict between Algeria and France. But since many of those nations strongly depended on Paris, none of the delegates had the courage to criticize the cruel foreign policy of General Charles de Gaulle, aimed, in particular, against Algeria's National Liberation Front, and advocating nuclear tests in the Sahara Desert. At the Brazzaville conference, a communique was passed. In it, the parties emphasized aspiration for a more intensive cooperation in economy and culture, and also for working out a common standing in foreign policy, creation of a permanent secretariat and a common defense system.

It should be noted than relations between the above-mentioned countries had not always been based on full mutual understanding and trust: Leopold Sedar Senghor, the leader of Senegal, and Félix Houphouet-Boigny, the leader of Ivory Coast, were overt rivals, and Ahmed Sekou Touré, the leader of Guinea, and Houphouet-Boigny were open enemies.[45] Nevertheless, the Brazzaville Group proved to be quite harmonious and numerous. It united leaders of 12 African nations with a political line characterized by conservatism and moderation.

The radical Casablanca Group began its activities in January 1961, after a conference held in Morocco. That conference was attended by delegations of Egypt, Ghana, Guinea, Mali, Morocco, Ceylon, Libya, Tunisia, Nigeria, Liberia, and the interim government of the Republic of Algeria (Togo declined the invitation).[46] On the back of the conference, the African Charter was adopted, and it was resolved to create a military command of African States and an African Common Market. Furthermore, permanent bodies were set up, including economic, cultural, and political committees, supreme command and headquarters in Bamako (Mali). This association of countries opposed Mauritania's independence because of Moroccan interests in Western Sahara. The Casablanca Group backed Patrice Lumumba's government in Congo. Libya moved later to another group, known as the Brazzaville Group.

The Monrovia Group took shape after a conference held in Monrovia (Liberia) in May 1961. That forum was attended by representatives of 19 African countries. The group included nearly all the members of the Brazzaville Group, Libya, and most of the former British colonies.[47] The Monrovia Group met again in January 1962 in Lagos (Nigeria), in order to create a permanent secretariat and a standing commission of finance ministers, so that these bodies would be able to launch the mechanism of approval of the Charter of The African and Malagasy Union (AMU).

Other independent African nations joined the Monrovia Group. Their leaders believed that Africa's international policy was not adequately represented by the Casablanca Group and the Brazzaville Group. It included Nigeria, Ivory Coast, Senegal, Sierra Leone, and Liberia. The group had Ethiopia, Sudan, and Somalia as sympathizers.

The two groups were sticking to different viewpoints in the matters concerning the role of the state in national economy, and also in relations with former colonizers. They also had different reactions to the presence of Communist regimes (the USSR, East European countries, China) in Africa. The Casablanca Group suggested establishing state control over all production means, arguing that political freedom was possible only amid complete economic independence. It meant it was necessary to expand the public sector in national economy by nationalizing enterprises owned by foreigners. State-controlled enterprises in Ghana were first established in the early 1960s.

Nkrumah strongly believed that the Socialist approach would help accelerate transformation of a backward traditional economy into a well-developed and industrial one. Mali and Guinea introduced state monopoly in domestic and foreign trade. Egypt also carried out nationalization of many enterprises. It was a response to former metropolitan countries that, in the opinion of the Casablanca Group, were trying to exercise control via various economic and diplomatic gimmicks and mechanisms, which was "unfair and illegitimate."

Members of the group called on the Africans to take a tough common standing with respect to neocolonial methods of Africa's exploitation.

In Addis Ababa, there was understanding that if two opposing groups, the Casablanca Group and the Monrovia Group, failed to reach a compromise, their confrontation would degenerate into a Pan-African conflict, as a result of which the Ethiopian Empire would inevitably suffer, as its territory was close to the hostile Middle East. Resolution of controversies and rapprochement of young African nations were among the principal goals of Ethiopian diplomacy in the early 1960s. Many Africans believed that the difference in the views of the two group would not disappear anytime soon and that African unity was unattainable. But in May 1963, an event occurred that reconciled the two rival groups of African leaders: The Organization of African Unity (OAU) was set up.

There is still a popular belief that the nations which had adhered to different viewpoints joined the OAU out of respect for the then-leader of Ethiopia, Emperor Haile Selassie I, who proposed Addis Ababa as the venue for a Pan-African conference. Advocates of this viewpoint believe that the OAU was the product of interference of great powers, which allegedly wanted to control the continent via a single and loyal organization. At early stages of the unifying postcolonial movement on the continent, the Ethiopian Empire was a neutral, if not a passive, actor. But after it was invited to take part in summits of those groups in January 1962, the empire changed its tactics, because non-participation in inter-African diplomacy would have pushed it into sidelines, and it would have lost reliable partners and allies. Addis Ababa fully felt the burden of loneliness, when Rome, with complete connivance and inactivity of the League of Nations, brought down fire of mechanized corps and air squadrons on the heads of helpless if courageous peoples of Ethiopia.

Ketema Yifru, Ethiopia's Minister of Foreign Affairs, played an important role in Ethiopia's rapprochement with young African nations. After he received an invitation to take part in the conference that was arranged thanks to the efforts of the Monrovia Group in Lagos and the Casablanca Group in Cairo, the minister prepared a report for Emperor Haile Selassie I. In it, Foreign Minister Ketema Yifru mentioned the tragic events of 1935, when Abyssinia (Ethiopia), a full-fledged member of the League of Nations, had been left alone to confront aggressive Fascist Italy. The report said that the country's national interest required its accession to common African political life. The young minister advised to the emperor that Ethiopia, represented by His Imperial Majesty, was thus underlining that it belonged in Africa as a voluntary and equal actor of all political processes on the continent.[48]

Before taking the final decision on changing his foreign policy, Haile Selassie I convened a meeting of the country's most influential political and public figures. The emperor raised the following question before them:

Should the Ethiopian Empire adopt an active attitude toward the issue of African unity? Most attendees of the meeting belonged to the conservative wing of the Ethiopian elite. They were comfortable with living in isolated (neutral) Ethiopia that was playing a limited role on the African and global political stage. However, surprisingly, the emperor backed the proposal of the minister of foreign affairs, and allowed him freedom of action.[49]

Foreign Minister Ketema Yifru was to address a complicated and delicate task. The matter was that Ethiopia, as it was mentioned above, had received an invitation from the Monrovia Group and the Casablanca Group. It was necessary to understand which conference it should attend and derive more benefit from—the one in Cairo or the one in Lagos. After long discussions, the Ethiopian leadership opted for the Monrovia Group.

The Ethiopian leadership proceeded from the assumption that, first, the Monrovia Group had more members than the Casablanca Group (22 nations versus 6); second, if Ethiopia, with its influence and neutrality, had joined the Casablanca Group, it was quite possible a new round of confrontation would have begun. Meanwhile, Ethiopia's minister of foreign affairs set a task for himself to promote rapprochement of the two factions.

At the conference hosted by Lagos (Nigeria) in January 1962, Ethiopia was represented by Foreign Minister Ketema Yifru, Minister of Foreign Affairs. He was faced with a challenge: To get the conference attendees to agree to hold the next meeting of the Monrovia Group in the Ethiopian capital, the city of Addis Ababa, and to get the Casablanca Group to come there. During the negotiations, all attendees of the Lagos Conference accepted the proposal of the Ethiopian representative. Foreign Minister Ketema Yifru sent a wire to the emperor at once, in which he asked him to take part in the Lagos Conference and meet leaders of African countries.[50]

The Lagos Conference was a very emotional event. Influential leaders of the Monrovia Group coalition declared their categorical objection to the activities of the Casablanca Group. Some speakers accused it, in particular, of an attempt to interfere in domestic affairs of African nations. For instance, Nnamdi Azikiwe, President of Nigeria, said that the split between the two groups on that account had widened to an appalling size and that there was no bridge to bring those two coasts together.[51]

Haile Selassie I who arrived in Lagos spoke from other, more constructive positions, proving to the delegates that the split between the two groups was not that great and was not a matter of principle.[52] As the African leaders aligned according to their adherence to one group or the other, Ethiopia's leader said the Africans were capable of a union, not only a rapprochement.

Meanwhile, the Casablanca Group planned a new conference in Egypt (Cairo) in June 1962, to which Ethiopia was also invited. And Ethiopia's minister of foreign affairs was facing the task of bridging the gap between the two groups. Resolution of that urgent political and diplomatic challenge was put on the agenda of intergovernmental negotiations with the attendees of the Cairo Conference.

The negotiations began with representatives of the Republic of Guinea, including then-President Ahmed Sekou Touré, one of the leaders of the Casablanca Group. The head of the Republic of Guinea, who had received an official invitation, arrived in Asmara (the empire's second major city) on June 28, 1962, after the termination of the conference in Cairo. The leaders of Ethiopia and Guinea discussed the proportions of the split between the two groups and ways out of that complex situation. After the negotiations, the president of Guinea agreed to back Ethiopia that was seeking a rapprochement of the two groups. Both leaders were putting their hopes on the Addis Ababa Conference scheduled for May 1963.[53] Quite soon, a communique was released, which said that heads of states intended to hold a Pan-African summit in Addis Ababa. To protect the continent from the threat of a political and interethnic split, it was necessary to use a Pan-African forum in Ethiopia for a constructive dialog between heads of states—members of the Casablanca Group and Monrovia Group.

The agreement with the president of the Republic of Guinea was the first victory of Ethiopian diplomacy in achieving a rapprochement of African leaders. Naturally, it is necessary to give credit to the acumen of the Guinean leader who understood that African peoples would be able to live in peace and amity only if controversies between the two groups were mitigated. During a meeting of the heads of Ethiopia and the Republic of Guinea, the parties divided up their respective functions. The Ethiopian side undertook to hold negotiations with the both groups, and Guinea's representative Diallo Telli (he later would become the first Secretary General of the OAU) was to find associates among members of the Casablanca Group.

Emperor Haile Selassie I dispatched his minister of foreign affairs with letters to all leaders of independent African nations. President Kwame Nkrumah (Ghana), President Gamal Abdel Nasser (Egypt), Prime Minister Tafawa Balewa (Nigeria), HIM King Hassan II (Morocco), and President Julius Nyerere (Tanzania) were some of the leaders whom Ketema Yifru met during his long trip across Africa.[54]

The first to respond to Addis Ababa's call was Gamal Abdel Nasser, the head of Egypt. From Cairo Ethiopia's minister of foreign affairs went to Morocco, and then he visited Algeria, Tunisia, countries of Western and Central Africa. As a result, heads of 32 states consented to meet in Addis Ababa, and agreed to a meeting of ministers of foreign affairs of independent African nations. The purpose of the Summit, as outlined to the press by the Emperor Haile Selassie I, include the formulation of a "universal African charter," the enactment of the necessary machinery for contacts among Heads of State, the adoption of a number of measures that would facilitate the speedy political coming out of the dependent territories, and the exchange of views.[55]

The Conference of Foreign Ministers of the African States opened, on May 15, 1963. Ketema Yifru, Ethiopia's Minister of Foreign Affairs, was elected its chairman, and Dr. Tesfaye Gebre-Egzy (Permanent Representative of Ethiopia to the UN), interim Secretary-General. Diplomats were to work out a charter as the principal document of the future Organization of Independent African States. Representatives of Ethiopia, Guinea, Nigeria, and Ghana proposed their drafts of the charter. Ghana's draft was the best reflection of the views of the Casablanca Group, and Nigeria's draft, of those of the Monrovia Group. The Ethiopian draft was picked as a compromise, because it reflected views of the both groups to a certain extent.[56]

Ethiopia's draft consisted of the following clauses: Creation of the OAU that was to have a Charter and a permanent secretariat; development of cooperation on the continent in economy, social welfare, education, culture, and collective defense; full uprooting of the colonial system; fight against racial discrimination and apartheid; creation of regional economic groups; disarmament. The conference of heads of states began on May 22, 1963. In his introductory address, Haile Selassie I noted: "This conference cannot close without adopting a single African Charter. . . . Our liberty is meaningless unless all Africans are free."[57]

After the heads of states exchanged opinions, they decided to convene a new meeting of ministers of foreign affairs to work out the final version of the Charter. On May 25, 1963, heads of 32 African nations put their signatures to the Charter of the OAU in Addis Ababa. After the signing of the Charter, the OAU was faced with another question: Which capital city would perform the functions of its headquarters? As it became known later, every attendee wanted to see the secretariat seated in the capital city of their own country. Ethiopia, which had played a key role in creating the OAU, was also involved in the discussion. Naturally, the country's leadership was aware that Addis Ababa in all respects was inferior to many of Africa's capital cities, such as Cairo, Lagos, Dakar, and that the success of the summit was not a reason for declaring Addis Ababa as the capital city of the OAU. Nevertheless, it was resolved to send a delegation to African countries, in order to express gratitude to the attendees of the Addis Ababa summit, and, most importantly, to gain recognition of Addis Ababa as the capital city of the OAU.

In August 1963, the Republic of Dahomey (today's Benin) hosted a meeting of representatives of 15 nations, former French colonies that had approved Dakar, the capital city of Senegal, as the seat of the OAU headquarters. The decision was a surprise for Ethiopian diplomacy. Addis Ababa was aware that the right moment had been missed, that it was necessary to make use of the elation that the leaders were feeling after the May summit.

In the same year, Dakar hosted a conference of ministers of foreign affairs, where they discussed which capital city would be selected for the OAU headquarters. Two capital cities were front-runners: Dakar and Lagos. Both cities had their advocates. Dakar was supported by former French colonies, Lagos by members of the Monrovia Group. Ministers of foreign affairs split into two committees: One was selecting the location for the headquarters, and the other was concerned with economic and social issues.

Representatives of Senegal, Nigeria, the Democratic Republic of Congo proposed their respective capital cities to host the OAU headquarters, and Addis Ababa, the capital city of Ethiopia, was put forward by Ismael Touré, head of Guinea's delegation and the half-brother of Guinean President Ahmed Sekou Touré. Before the session, Ethiopia's minister of foreign affairs had promised to Guinea's representative that if Guinea supported the nomination of Addis Ababa, Ethiopia would provide every kind of assistance in the nomination of Boubacar Diallo Telli, who was Guinea's permanent representative to the UN, to the position of Secretary-General of the OAU. Addis Ababa's nomination was also backed by Tanzania, Sudan, Sierra Leone, and Algeria. None of the claimants was ready to back down. Envoys of Nigeria and Senegal suggested setting up a commission to establish which of the African capital cities was the most appropriate for the headquarters.

Ethiopia's minister of foreign affairs strongly rejected this proposal, saying, to back his opinion, that the plan put forward by the two countries only meant procrastinating the implementation of the dream about Pan-Africanism. "To create an Organization of African Unity and hesitate in choosing the location of its headquarters—all this shows the indecision of African political leaders," he said. The committee agreed to put the matter of the location of the headquarters to the vote by secret ballot. During the vote, Addis Ababa won by a slim majority. Here is how the votes split: 16 delegations voted for Addis Ababa, 13 for Dakar; Lagos and Kinshasa got one vote each.[58]

To have a solid win, it was necessary for the head of the Ethiopian delegation to garner support of the majority. He organized a meeting of ministers of foreign affairs of Francophone countries, which had previously backed Senegal. At the meeting that was held before the start of a plenary session, Ketema Yifru managed to persuade many of them to cast their votes for Addis Ababa. Thus, after a long struggle, Ethiopia's capital city was elected as the OAU headquarters by a majority of votes.

Having overcome all hindrances in the negotiation process, Emperor Haile Selassie I was able to call a conference of independent African States on May 22, 1963 in Addis Ababa. Ahead of creation of the OAU, *Reader's Digest* wrote about the activities of the emperor and his ministers: "In May 1963, when the Emperor called an African summit conference, neither he nor Ethiopia appeared likely to lead the young nations of Africa. For the most part, they are republics (Ethiopia was an empire.—*Author's note*), wildly anti-imperialist (Haile Selassie I was a proponent of neutrality.—*Author's note*) and non-Christian. Haile Selassie I, on the other hand, is the autocratic emperor of one of Africa's least modernized countries where the Coptic Church, an ancient branch of Christianity, still wields much power. Thirty heads of African states accepted Selassie's invitation . . . . Nearly all the *prima donnas* of Africa were there—Nasser, Nkrumah, Sekou Toure, Ben Bella and the rest, a Western observer recalls. But, compared with Haile Selassie, they were new pupils in the presence of the schoolmaster."[59]

THE DIALOG WITH THE SOVIET UNION

Another vector of foreign policy of Emperor Haile Selassie I was development of cooperation with Socialist countries, in particular, with the Soviet Union; its influence in the countries of the Middle East and Africa was expanding every year. Therefore, Haile Selassie I decided to go to the USSR on a friendly visit in 1959.[60]

The Ethiopian Empire had been one of the first countries in Africa with which the Russian Empire (1721–1917) established diplomatic relations.

Ethiopia had drawn attention of Russian politicians and, partially, Russian Orthodox clergy as far back as in the sixteenth century. Its proximity to the Red Sea and the Middle East, its situation between North and East Africa were a strategic asset in the geopolitical game against Russia's European rivals (Great Britain, France, and Italy).

It is a known fact that Tsarist Russia that had attended the Berlin Conference (1884–1885) was not involved in the European scramble for Africa in the late nineteenth century. At the time, the Russian Empire established special relations with Ethiopia, an allied nation in Africa that had not been invaded by colonizers. And, naturally, the Ethiopian Empire had managed to stay independent with certain help from St. Petersburg.

As for the relations between the Russian Orthodox and the Ethiopian Orthodox Churches, back in the fourteenth century, there had been contacts between Russian and Ethiopian monks in Jerusalem. In the fifteenth century, Russian merchant Afanasy Nikitin visited Ethiopia on his way to India, and nearly 300 years later, Emperor Peter the Great made an attempt to gain a military foothold for Russia in the African Horn. However, permanent contacts between Russia and Ethiopia were established only in the late nineteenth century.

In the 1850s, Bishop Porphyrius (secular name: Konstantin A. Uspensky) was sent by the Holy Synod of the Russian Orthodox Church to Jerusalem with a secret mission: He was to reinforce Russian influence in the Middle

East. Initially, his recommendation to establish cooperation with Orthodox Ethiopia did not elicit response of the Russian elite.[61]

In the mid-nineteenth century, thanks to more active contacts with the Greeks and Armenians, the Ethiopian elite had an opportunity to get to know Russia better. People in Ethiopia knew that Russia was engaged in a war with the Turks, the French and the English, and Emperor Tewodros II (1855–1867), on multiple occasions, sent letters to Emperor Nicholas I, suggesting a military union against Turkey.[62] The Ethiopians sympathized with the Russians, and so the only cannon existing in the country was named Sevastopol, in honor of the Russian city that had distinguished itself in the Crimean War. Letters to the Russian monarch from Ethiopian Emperor Yohannes IV (1872–1889) who appealed to Orthodox ties and asked Russia's help against the Ottomans in the 1870s remained unanswered.[63]

An active Russo-Ethiopian rapprochement began in the late nineteenth century. Both parties were interested in that rapprochement. If for Ethiopia that interest stemmed from its desire to find a protector and associate in its struggle for the preservation of independence, as it was facing a threat of expansion on the part of colonial powers, for Russia, to have Ethiopia as its satellite in that strategically important part of the African continent meant to have a foothold in seaways of global trade, and to ensure a connection between the European part of Russia and the Far East via the Suez Canal and the Red Sea.

The rapprochement of the two countries, besides representatives of the Russian Orthodox Church, was largely contributed by expeditions of volunteers and scholars, such as N. I. Ashinov, V. F. Mashkov, A. V. Yeliseev, N. S. Leontyev, A. K. Bulatovich (Father Anthony). Some members of the expedition (for instance, N. P. Leontyev and A. K. Bulatovich) were instrumental in further expansion of the Ethiopian Empire.

In turn, in 1895, trying to get Russia's diplomatic and military support in a future war with Italy, Ethiopian Emperor Menelik II sent a diplomatic mission to St. Petersburg. Its arrival was one more step toward establishment of permanent diplomatic relations between the two countries. The victory that Ethiopian warriors gained over the Italians on March 1, 1896 in the Battle of Adwa played an important part in the process. After that event, all European nations hastened to establish diplomatic relations with Ethiopia. All major newspapers of the Russian Empire hailed Ethiopia's triumph. It was an impetus for an idea to send to Ethiopia a mission of the Russian Red Cross Society. The Russian government provided financial support and diplomatic assistance to that initiative. A mission of 41 people worked in Ethiopia for two months and a half and gave medical relief to nearly 5,000 sick and wounded people, including Italians.[64]

Activities of the Russian mission of the Red Cross Society, which worked from May 26 to October 5, 1896, had prepared a basis for the establishment of official diplomatic relations between the two countries. An important part in the inter-state communication was given to humanitarian and cultural relations, including medical aid. In February 1898, after Russia's first official diplomatic mission arrived in Addis Ababa, official relations between the two states were established at the level of interim missions.[65]

A permanent Russian mission appeared in Ethiopia in 1902. After diplomatic relations were established, opportunities were opened up for the development of diverse Russo-Ethiopian ties, including spiritual and cultural ones. A few months after the opening of Russia's official diplomatic mission in Addis Ababa, a permanent Russian hospital began its work in Ethiopia; it employed doctors and junior medical staff from Russia. Activities of Russian doctors helped raise Russia's influence in Ethiopian society as a whole and at the court of Emperor Menelik II in particular.

One vivid example of Russo-Ethiopian ties is a letter from Emperor Menelik II to Emperor Nicholas II (Yekatet 13, 1892 [February 9, 1900], according to the Ethiopian calendar): "Hello to you!" "Our Friend! We are speaking candidly that for Ethiopia there are no other associates than God and Russia: We are brothers in religion and true and constant friends. Your Majesty knows everything better than Us, and We hope that Your Majesty will not deliver Us into the hands of Our enemies. We are far from every doubt that until Our death, the favor of Your Majesty and Your Government towards Us will remain unchangeable. . . . We are praying to God Almighty; let Him give Your State peace and serenity, and health and long life to Your Majesty."[66]

At the turn of the twentieth century, Russia provided assistance to Ethiopia in training educated talent. First Ethiopian students arrived in St. Petersburg in 1898.[67] Among them was Tekle Hawariat, who studied the art of war and engineering in Russia, and later became Ethiopia's finance minister. Tekle Hawariat wrote the country's first Constitution. He also spoke on behalf of Ethiopia at the League of Nations, after Italy invaded the country again in 1935.[68]

In 1917, after the October Socialist revolution, official relations between Russia and Ethiopia were suspended on the initiative of the Ethiopian side. Thus, the Ethiopians expressed their attitude to revolutionary events. In the 1920s, attempts were made to resume diplomatic ties between the two countries. The matter was not seen through because of indecision of Ethiopian rulers who were afraid lest Ethiopia's ties with the Soviet Union could be regarded by England, France, and Italy as an unfriendly gesture and provoke invasion of troops of those countries into Ethiopian territory.

Nevertheless, Ethiopia kept a special spot in the geopolitical worldview of Soviet Russia. One proof of it is the diplomatic support of the Soviet Union during the years of struggle of the Ethiopian people against Fascism (1935–1941).

Fighting a common enemy, Fascism, and weakening of the positions of Great Britain and France caused a rapprochement of the USSR with Ethiopia. On April 21, 1943, diplomatic relations between the two countries were restored.

In the late 1950s, a positive shift in the Soviet-Ethiopian relations shaped up. The relations between the USSR and Ethiopia were impacted by the fact that in its postwar foreign policy the Ethiopian government was largely pro-American. However, starting in the 1950s, the Ethiopian government, taking into account the growing domestic discontent with a one-sided pro-American vector, was trying to expand ties with the USSR in a major way. For instance, in June 1956, Soviet and Ethiopian diplomatic missions were converted into embassies, and in June 1958, Ato Abebe Retta, Ethiopia's Minister of Commerce and Industry, was in the USSR to hold preliminary talks on the Soviet Union's economic and technical aid to Ethiopia.[69]

Delegations of Ethiopian journalists, women, young people, library workers and educators visited the Soviet Union, as did a delegation of prominent members of the Ethiopian community that took part in the festivities dedicated to the 40th anniversary of the Soviet victory in the Great Patriotic War.[70]

The exchange of delegations between the USSR and Ethiopia from 1956 to 1958 had an important meaning for the development of Soviet-Ethiopian relations, because before that period, no such exchange had taken place. Despite lack of a trade agreement, Soviet-Ethiopian trade relations were stepped up in the 1950s. Trade turnover between the two countries amounted to 1.1 million rubles in 1956, to 12.6 million rubles in 1957, and to 15.6 million rubles in 1958.[71]

Expansion of trade turnover in 1957 was achieved by a significant increase of purchases by the Soviet Union of Ethiopian coffee and leather. In 1958, as imports of Ethiopian goods by the Soviet Union declined (to 2.5 million rubles), the trade turnover between the USSR and Ethiopia dwindled in a major way. However, Soviet exports to Ethiopia increased to 3.1 million rubles in the same year.[72]

In December 1958, the Ethiopian government declared its desire to launch talks on a trade agreement. A Soviet delegation was to visit Addis Ababa and hold negotiations, of which an agreement in principle was reached with the Ethiopians.

Going forward, however, the Ethiopian government expressed a wish to postpone those negotiations, taking into account the fact that issues of Soviet-Ethiopian trade would be discussed during the forthcoming visit of Ethiopia's emperor to the Soviet Union.

In April 1957, Clement Voroshilov, Chairman of the Presidium of the Supreme Soviet of the USSR, sent a written invitation to the Ethiopian emperor to visit the Soviet Union. In June 1957, the emperor replied he was receiving the invitation, and specified that the date of his arrival in the USSR would be set later.[73]

On his way to Moscow, the Ethiopian leader paid a visit to Egyptian leader Nasser. The meeting of Haile Selassie I with the Egyptian leader that took place in June 1959 had a positive outcome. The emperor was able to establish personal relations with Nasser and with Vice President Anwar Sadat. Nasser gave his word to the emperor to suspend an ideological campaign against Ethiopia, and to renege on his support to the idea of creating Greater Somalia. A matter of principle of those summits was the promise of the Egyptian leader to back Ethiopia in the consideration of the border issue with the Italian Somaliland.[74]

Alongside matters of state importance, the visit addressed a major ecclesiastical issue. Emperor Haile Selassie I met in Cairo with the Patriarch of Alexandria. During their conversation, they reached an agreement on autonomy of the Ethiopian Christian Church.[75]

At a solemn ceremony in the St. Mark's Coptic Orthodox Cathedral in Cairo, Archbishop Basilios, the chief of the Ethiopian Christian Church, was consecrated as Patriarch. For the first time since the ancient Kingdom of Aksum, a native Ethiopian became the leader of the Ethiopian Church. It reinforced the authority of the emperor who stripped the national ideology institution (i.e., the Ethiopian Christian Church) of foreign influence, thus eliminating a formal cause for interference into Ethiopia's domestic affairs on the part of Egypt and Great Britain.

The Ethiopian emperor's two-week tour to the Soviet Union, which began on June 30, 1959, had significance both for the development of friendly ties and for the reinforcement of business contacts with leaders of the Socialist system.

The official part of the visit, aside from breakfasts, lunches and dinners, also included an exchange of awards. According to a decree of the Presidium of the Supreme Soviet of the USSR dated July 11, 1959, Haile Selassie I was bestowed the Order of Suvorov, 1st Class, "for the outstanding merit in the organization of the heroic struggle of Ethiopia's people against Fascist aggressors on the side of the anti-Hitler coalition during the years of World War II; for a considerable contribution to the establishment and promotion of friendly Soviet-Ethiopian relations, and in commemoration of his visit to the Soviet Union."[76]

The emperor conferred the Order of the Queen of Sheba on Kliment Voroshilov, Chairman of the Presidium of the Supreme Soviet of the USSR.[77] Haile Selassie I visited Leningrad (today's St. Petersburg), Stalingrad (now Volgograd), Sochi, Yalta, and Kirovograd (now Kropyvnytskyi in Ukraine).

The Soviet government granted a loan of 400 million rubles to Ethiopia (at the time, one ruble contained 0.222168 g of pure gold) at an interest rate of

2.5% p.a., for it to pay for the design, survey and research work, and so forth, performed by Soviet organizations. The parties signed a trade agreement for facilitating development of economic, trade, and cultural relations.[78]

The emperor's visit to the Soviet Union was productive. In addition to the results achieved in Moscow, on March 9, 1960, an agreement was signed on the construction of a Polytechnic School for 1,000 students in the city of Bahir Dar—province of Gojjam (now the capital of Amhara region). It was a present of the Soviet government to Ethiopia.[79]

On March 25, 1960, a protocol was signed in Addis Ababa, which confirmed the arrangement between the USSR and Ethiopia on the terms and methods of constructing an oil refinery, carrying out exploration and survey work, building a gold mine with a mineral separation plant, and also on the possibility of construction in Ethiopia of an iron and steel factory at the expense of a loan extended to Ethiopia by the Soviet Union, and with technical assistance of Soviet organizations. Sometime later, in the summer of 1962, a contract was signed for the design and construction of an oil treatment plant in the city of Assab (Eritrea). The enterprise, which was commissioned into operation in the spring of 1967, was called by the Ethiopians the firstborn child of the country's heavy industry.[80]

In 1961, an agreement on cultural cooperation between the USSR and Ethiopia was concluded. Thanks to that agreement, an exchange of exhibitions of works of Soviet and Ethiopian artists began.

The emperor's visit to the Soviet Union was probably planned in response to the decision of the United States to finance creation of Greater Somalia and to provide support to Italy during the negotiations concerning the borders of the Italian Somaliland and Ethiopia. It was not an attempt to find a political heavyweight in the Soviet Union. The visit was not aimed at getting financial aid of which Ethiopian economy was really in need of. The Soviet side offered a loan of 400 million rubles, but Ethiopia did not use the full amount of it.

Aklilu Habte-Wold, who had accompanied the emperor during his visits to Egypt and the USSR, said later: "The Cairo trip was even more satisfactory than the one to Moscow,"[81] because the rapprochement with Nasser, then-leader of the Arab world, gave Ethiopia a temporary respite. Until the overthrow of Haile Selassie, I, Nasser was faithful to his promises. Relations between the two states, Egypt and Ethiopia, remained quite warm.

Nevertheless, the visit to the Soviet Union cannot be called a failure. In addition to the expansion of bilateral relations between the two countries, Haile Selassie received the political and economic support which he certainly needed.

After the visit of Emperor Haile Selassie, I to the USSR, the ties of the two countries in the cultural and scientific field became more active. In its relations with Ethiopia, the USSR used mediation of the Russian Orthodox Church, thus continuing traditions of the Russian Empire. In 1959, Abuna Theophilos, Ethiopian Patriarch, was invited to visit the Soviet Union. High-ranking delegations of the Russian Orthodox Church visited Ethiopia in 1959, 1962, 1966 and 1969. In 1972, Pimen, Patriarch of Moscow and All Russia, also visited Ethiopia. In the wake of a World Council of Churches held in Addis Ababa in January 1971, representatives of the Russian Orthodox Church met with Emperor Haile Selassie I and with the high-ranking clergy. On the back of those meetings, it was decided to send Ethiopian seminarians to study theology in the USSR. Their studies in the USSR were organized and financed by the Russian Orthodox Church under the auspices of Nikodim (Rotov), Metropolitan of Leningrad and Novgorod, who would later become president of the World Council of Churches. During the reign of Haile Selassie I, the Ethiopian Church sent to the USSR about 25 students to study at seminaries in Leningrad (St. Petersburg) and Zagorsk (Sergiev Posad).

In the second half of the 1950s, as national liberation movements arose and first independent African nations emerged, the Soviet Union reinvigorated relations with African countries that had gained independence. The USSR backed young African nations both at the diplomatic level and in the area of training qualified talent. In subsequent years, Ethiopia became a window into the USSR for champions of Africa's freedom: African scholarship holders of Soviet colleges left their countries via Ethiopia, because colonial authorities would not permit them to go to the Soviet Union.

With the signing of loan agreements with the USSR in 1959, Haile Selassie opened a road for cooperation with Comecon member nations.

The policy of rapprochement with Socialist states underwent certain changes. If in the late 1950s and early 1960s Ethiopia was a willing recipient of technical and economic assistance on the part of all Socialist countries, afterward the empire was giving preference to cooperation with smaller Socialist nations. In 1969, an agreement on economic and technical cooperation with Czechoslovakia was signed. In accordance with the agreement, Ethiopia was extended a state loan in the amount of $10 million to be paid within 10 years at 3% p.a. Toward the loan amount, contracts were concluded on the construction of three industrial facilities: Rubber and Canvas Shoe Co. worth $1 million (it was built in accordance with a contract signed in June 1961); Addis Tyre Company worth $3.5 million (a contract was signed in December 1967); a leather factory worth $5.5 million (a contract was signed in December 1968).[82]

In late 1965, the People's Republic of Bulgaria signed a protocol on financial cooperation with Ethiopia, on the basis of which Bulgaria provided to Ethiopia a loan of $5 million for five years at 2.5% p.a. The loan was to be used to organize agricultural enterprises with participation of private individuals, and it was to be repaid from the revenue generated by those enterprises.

In late 1963, a joint Bulgarian-Ethiopian venture, Red Sea Development Corporation, was set up, with a citizen of Bulgaria appointed as CEO. By 1968, the company's equity capital had reached $10 million, of which Bulgaria's stake accounted for up to 40%. The company carried out a number of projects in Ethiopia, including construction of a slaughterhouse, factories for the production of canned meat and vegetables, fisheries in the Red Sea and canned fish plants.[83]

In 1964, the enterprise Technoexport stroy it is the name of the company started to operate in Addis Ababa; its mission was to win construction projects and send them to Bulgaria for further processing. In 1965, a joint insurance company, Eritrea Insurance, was established, in which 70% of equity capital belonged to the Bulgarians; simultaneously, the company represented the Soviet insurance company Ingosstrakh in Ethiopia. In addition, the People's Republic of Bulgaria rendered to Ethiopia considerable help by providing its specialists, above all doctors.

In 1967, a Polish-Ethiopian joint stock company was set up for the construction in Ethiopia of a metallic tool factory. Poland's stake in the enterprise was 50%. The construction of the enterprise was completed in January 1970, and the total amount of investments was $3 million.

Budapest also played its part in this benefaction. Hungarian businesses extended a $5 million loan to Addis Ababa for the construction of an enterprise to manufacture pharmaceuticals or a leather and shoe enterprise.

The experience of Socialist countries (Bulgaria, Poland) that took part in the creation of joint ventures for the construction and operation of facilities was not successful. The facilities were not cost-effective and generated losses. The Bulgarians, for instance, had to wind up Red Sea Development Corporation and agricultural facilities, and with big losses, too.[84]

Therefore, Comecon member nations believed it was more advisable to be governed by the principle of mutual benefit in providing economic aid to Ethiopia—in other words, to provide assistance on ordinary commercial terms, carefully substantiating its political and economic benefits. There were plans to establish diplomatic relations with East Germany in the first half of 1973. However, the process was delayed by a global currency and energy crisis.

"PEACE—IS JUSTICE"

While Haile Selassie I was engaged in expansion of friendly economic relations with foreign countries, individuals who were dissatisfied with the activities of his government began to emerge among Ethiopian intellectuals.

The rising influence of third-world countries, economic stagnation caused by the shutdown of the Suez Canal, lack of investments, Ethiopia's dependence on economic and political aid of the United States and Washington's inactivity in reaction to Haile Selassie's requests to increase aid, generated anti-imperialist sentiments in the midst of Ethiopian intellectuals, especially those of them who were educated in overseas universities.

As he contributed to the formation of a stratum of educated people, Haile Selassie I used personal savings for the construction of educational institutions, and also for sending young people to study abroad. The emperor wanted to train a pool of highly qualified national talent—his allies in the transition from feudalism to a democratic and well-educated society.

Unfortunately, the emperor's entourage were unable to address the historical challenges that the head of state trusted them to resolve. According to a message of the U.S. ambassador, Ethiopia's high-ranking officials "less concerned with the efficient operation of their ministries or developing programs for the benefit of the country than . . . in competing with each other to gain Imperial favor. The bureaucracy, already underpaid and understaffed, was therefore ineffective without influence, and to the extent that it incorporates intelligent young men educated abroad, they are almost to a man restless, unhappy, and critical of the system."[85]

Another U.S. representative, Paul Tailor, Security Advisor of the U.S. Embassy, writes in his March 20, 1958 memo about the antagonisms between the young people who were educated abroad and those ministers and officials who had only conventional education: The rising generation saw their comparatively unlettered superiors as "ignorant of the art of government, with little conception of public service and . . . responsibility. The newly educated could not understand "why the emperor tolerated officials so manifestly inefficient and corrupt."[86]

Did Haile Selassie I know of the country's economic and political difficulties, of the antagonisms between the Old Guard and the new elite? Certainly, he did. That said, the emperor was the only one who was seeking rapprochement of the Ethiopian elite, therefore he was not only after loyalty of the educated youth, but also worked to build a new political and economic group, bourgeoisie, which would be creating an enlightened society that he had conceived. One example is the appointment of Germame Neway, the future spiritual leader of the 1960 coup d'état, who had been educated at the Tafari Makonnen school (one of the country's most prestigious schools). Thanks to the protection of the heir to the throne, Germame continued his studies in the United States, and obtained a B.A. from the University of Wisconsin and an M.A. (in Political Science) from Columbia University.[87] The young man was actively involved in the work of the Association of Ethiopian Students in the United States. In his M.A. thesis, "The Impact of White Settlement Policy in

Kenya,"[88] Germame wrote about the hardships of the Africans enslaved by strong white elite. After he came back to Ethiopia, Germame was appointed to the Ministry of Interior under *Dejazmach* Mesfin Sileshi, a typical satrap. When he was the governor of the province of Kaffa (from 1945 to 1955), the minister bought a few thousand hectares of coffee plantations when coffee sales spiked. He monopolized purchases and transportation of agricultural products, and to the capital city, where his cronies controlled the National Coffee Department, he supplied coffee beans at a price that by far exceeded the farm price. Mesfin was a typical representative of oligarchy that had paved a way for social protest by their greediness.

One common feature of the opposition-minded youth was the desire of that progressive part of society to change the state of affairs in the country, but they lacked a clear-cut program. As Marcus writes, "Although differentiated socially and educationally, they comprehended the world in terms of Western abstractions, whether learned in Paris, New York, or even Addis Ababa. They stood against corruption and for modernization."[89]

Officers were also critical of the regime of Haile Selassie I. Since the mid-1950s, notes M. Perham, "among the officers who had a modern military education, there was an opinion about the necessity of abolishment of the imperial regime."[90]

Even the emperor's appointees called his wisdom as the head of the state into question. For instance, Germame, a leader of the December 1960 coup d'état, who had been appointed governor of the Wolamo District, believed that economic stagnation could be overcome by efforts of a people liberated from exploitation and led by a wise leader. Germame allotted state-owned land plots to landless peasants (revolutionaries of the 1970s nationalized all land, and then distributed it among peasants; as a result, many lands that used to be fertile were not cultivated, and a food crisis began that led to famine in 1983–1985).

By his actions, the young governor turned large landowners against himself, and they tried to remove him from office.[91] To prevent the young idealist from infringing on private property rights, the emperor sent Germame as an administrator to the province of Harar, Jijiga District. But there Germame continued his activities as a reformer. The new governor was instrumental in building a clinic, digging out wells, improving the condition of water sources. His counter-corruption steps caught the provincial establishment off guard. The superiors persuaded Germame that no progress could be achieved before the existing political system changed.

Meanwhile, a group of people, both civilians and military men, emerged in the capital city, who started a discussion about the events going on in the country, about its international stance and ways out of the existing situation. It was not by chance that they were meeting at the house of General Mengistu

Neway, the elder brother of Germame, who had been appointed Commander
of the Imperial Guard in October 1960 (before that, he had taken part in the
Italo-Ethiopian war of 1935–1936 and the Korean War of 1953). Mengistu
became the formal leader of those who advocated transformations in Ethiopia. Inspired by the ideas and views of his brother, the general believed that
a revolution was necessary, and that power should be wielded by educated
people, that any movement with the goal of overthrowing the existing "reactionary ruling clique" will be welcomed by educated citizens.

Leaders of the future coup were obviously underestimating the significance
of political organization and of popular mass mobilization, that is, mobilization of the very people for whose sake the change was conceived. It was the
Council of the Revolution that was to neutralize the emperor's followers and
conservators. After the palace coup d'état, it would have brought to power
an educated elite, which, in turn, would have given to the Ethiopian people
freedom, prosperity, and progress. The Council of the Revolution included
both serving officers and civilians.[92]

Did Haile Selassie I know that a coup was being staged? This question cannot be answered definitively. But some of his actions ahead of the coup might
be cited as proof that his secret police were effective. On November 19, the
emperor reorganized the highest command of the Ethiopian army, appointing
loyal officers to the posts of the commanders of the 1st, 2nd and 3rd divisions,
and also to key positions at the Defense Ministry; they were to watch their
radically minded peers.

One of the high-ranking commanders who were affected by the reorganization was Brigadier General Aman Michael Andom (after the 1974 revolution
he became the chairman of the Provisional Military Administrative Council).[93] He was transferred to Harrar as the commander of the 3rd division
(there have been suggestions that Mengistu Haile Mariam, the leader of the
1974 Ethiopian revolution, was serving there as a junior officer at the time).

Aman Andom criticized the existing regime. If he had been in Addis Ababa
when the coup occurred, the Council of the Revolution would have received
necessary support of the army. Ironically, the emperor did not carry out direct
attacks against the main seat of the conspirators—the headquarters of the
imperial guard. Thus, Haile Selassie weakened the position of the potential
conspirators.

Convinced that the army was able to repulse any attempts at a coup, on
November 30, 1960 Haile Selassie began his official visit to Latin American
and West African countries. Late at night on December 13, 1960, when the
emperor was making a visit to Brazil, the Council of the Revolution sprang
into action.[94]

By that time, Lieutenant Colonel Warqenah Gabayahu, Imperial Chief
of Security, and Brigadier General Tsege Dibu, the Police Commissioner,

had joined the Neway brothers (Mengistu and Germame). The conspirators arrested ministers and members of the imperial family. According to Richard Greenfield, Crown Prince Asfaw Wossen was colluding with the conspirators.[95] It was at his invitation that Prime Minister *Ras* Abebe Aregai, Makonnen Habte-Wold, the brother of the Ethiopian Minister of Foreign Affairs Aklilu Habte-Wold, Minister of Commerce and Industry and an outstanding figure of the 1936–1941 patriotic movement, and other persons came to the imperial palace. The insurgents captured nearly all key facilities in the capital city: the palace, the post office, the telegraph building, the phone station, buildings of the ministries, a radio station, banks, and airfields.

On December 14, 1960, the radio broadcast a declaration of the Council of the Revolution. On behalf of the Ethiopian people's government, it was read by the Crown Prince who had been proclaimed the country's leader by the conspirators. In the declaration, the regime of Emperor Haile Selassie was denounced for despotism and corruption, for the economic stagnation, and low living standards of Ethiopian people. Ethiopia's underdevelopment compared with African nations that had got independence only recently was emphasized; those countries were seeing a dramatic growth of living standards thanks to their achievements in the economy and education and were leaving Ethiopia far behind. "This day will be the beginning of a new era for Ethiopia,"[96] the declaration said in conclusion.

In our view, the so-called declaration of the Council of the Revolution did not reflect Ethiopian realities. In a country where 85% of the population were living in the rural areas and 90% of residents were illiterate and showed no interest in politics, had no idea of modern life or scientific achievements, where veneration of religion and of the leader of the Ethiopian Church, the patriarch, and respect for the emperor were considered to be a must, it was utopian to put forward proposals that reeked of heresy. The conspirators were doomed from the very beginning. Why?

First, the people regarded the coup as a conflict inside Ethiopia's political elite. *Second,* leaders of the coup were not consistent in their actions or united as a group. The heir to the throne who was hastily proclaimed the leader of the country did not enjoy popularity among the people. The Council of the Revolution did not find followers even among usual opponents of the Ethiopian emperor in the provinces of Gojjam and Tigray, among southern populations that had suffered from the activities of officials, such as *Ras* Mesfin. The Eritrean opposition regarded the coup as an internal affair of the "Amhara" elite. *Third,* the Council of the Revolution was unable to garner support of the majority of the national army. At the end of the day, it could count only on a small contingent of the imperial guard, which was inferior to its opponents in terms of equipment. Moreover, common soldiers of the guard and low-rank officers believed, as V. S. Yagiya notes, that they were fighting for Emperor

Haile Selassie I, whom the army was trying to depose.[97] Army formations and air force units defected to the side of the troops that remained loyal to the emperor. *Fourth*, even though the Council of the Revolution was in control of the media, it failed to make use of information channels effectively in order to win over popular masses. In his address on the army radio station and in the leaflets distributed among the population, Patriarch Basilios, head of the Ethiopian Christian Church, accused the conspirators of betraying Motherland's interests, of breaking their oath. He called on the country's population to stay loyal to the emperor and disobey the conspirators. *Finally*, the leadership of the Council of the Revolution failed to establish ties with foreign partners, while the army, loyal to the emperor, was in contact with representatives of the United States, Great Britain, and other countries.

Most points of the Council of the Revolution's manifesto that it was promising to fulfill shortly were already being implemented by the emperor. Therefore, the calls that the "Decembrists" made on the people—to back Ethiopia's people's government for the sake of the nation's prosperity, for the sake of progress—made no impression on the general public. As an eyewitness of the coup noted, "their program is more like a Great Britain Labor Party campaigning than a call for an armed uprising."[98]

When he received the news of the attempted coup d'état, Haile Selassie came back (via Liberia) to Asmara, under the protection of the forces that stayed loyal to him. After a meeting with Liberian President William Tubman, the monarch's statement was released: "The confused situation in Addis Ababa is something that will pass soon. Such confusion is caused always by irresponsible people . . . since this confusion is confined only in Addis Ababa, we are confident that peace and security reign in the rest of the country."[99] The emperor's prediction turned out to be true. On December 15, 1960, skirmishes began in Addis Ababa, during which the forces loyal to the emperor defeated the adepts of the Council of the Revolution. The conspirators found shelter in the mountains, in the vicinity of the capital city. Before they fled, the insurgents had killed 15 high-ranking officials, including *Ras* Abebe Aregay, *Ras* Seyoum Mengesha (Governor of Tigray), and Major General Mulugeta Bulli (Commander of the imperial guard).

On December 17, 1960, Haile Selassie I came back to Addis Ababa. He was met by the heir to the throne, the patriarch, U.S. Ambassador Richards, high-ranking officials and nobles.

On December 18, Haile Selassie I made a statement in which he denounced the attempted coup d'état and laid the responsibility on a handful of irresponsible people who wanted to thwart the progress achieved by Ethiopia. The emperor publicly grieved over the irreparable losses that the country had sustained. He called the conspirators cowards who "were afraid to attack him openly."[100]

The father of the nation (and the emperor considered himself to be one from the very first days of his reign) was extremely piqued and offended as a human being. But in his public address, he found courage to be merciful and indulgent, like a parent to a child, as though it was not an enormous public-order crime that had been committed but a teenage folly. "Planted trees do not always produce the desired fruit. We sent youth to the border hoping that, having received education, the young will give the knowledge gained to their homeland. . . . We equally loved everyone, trusted them to rule the country—to those people whom we believed to be valuable . . . hope, paid us with treachery, betrayal. . . . Allowed bloodshed," the emperor said with a philosopher's insight. The monarch, addressing those who had been involved in the coup and had fled, suggested pardoning the short-sighted compatriots: "We want peace. . . . Peace is justice."[101]

On December 20, at a press conference, the emperor declared his willingness to stay true to the politics pursued before the crisis. On January 9, the monarch addressed the Ethiopian youth over the radio and called on them to take part in the implementation of a grandiose challenge of advancing Ethiopia along the way of education, technical progress, and democracy, and he recommended to the youth to give up intolerance and immature actions.

The emperor reminded what titanic efforts it took the state to carry out the postwar recovery of the education system destroyed during the years of the Fascist occupation. "The fifth part of the budget was directed to the needs of education. Schools have been built in all parts of the country. The best school graduates received higher education abroad. However, the staff shortage has not yet been satisfied. Ethiopia needed technicians, administrators, civil servants, developers of government transformation plans."

Campaigning by action, a tested technique of public administration that the monarch had used with success before, was again called into play. The emperor's words had not an ounce of populism in them: "We have opened hospitals and clinics, we have established control centers for malaria, tuberculosis, smallpox and other infectious diseases. . . . Much has been done. But we must work tirelessly until the desired results are achieved!"[102]

He reminded the people, and, above all, his opponents, of the nation's achievements in economy, industry, agriculture, transport, and communications that linked Ethiopia with Africa and the rest of the world.

Haile Selassie I, with pride, listed the successes of his administration in foreign policy. Thanks to his personal efforts, Ethiopia was received into the League of Nations, became a founder of the UN, an attendee of the Paris Peace Conference, conferences of non-aligned nations in Bandung and of independent African States in Accra. Ethiopia came out of international isolation, and the emperor's multiple visits abroad contributed to that move. Those official visits let Ethiopia get back its territories, ensured for it a gateway to sea, to the ports that it had been stripped of.

Politics, they say, is the art of achieving the possible. And activities of the Ethiopian monarch were quite consistent with this formula. "We have done everything to help our people, so that they increase their welfare, so that they free themselves from oppression, becoming the owner of personal property,"[103] stated the monarch.

Judging by official speeches, the emperor and the Ethiopian political elite did not give an adequate evaluation to the event that had occurred in the country. In the opinion of Haile Selassie, the conspirators were a handful of irresponsible traitors. In reality, it was part of society that reflected the mindset of some portion of the citizens. That part represented various strata of society and various ethnicities. The attempted coup of 1960 was to be a signal to the emperor to begin economic reforms (above all, land reforms), political transformations, including constitutional monarchy, creation of political associations, and so forth.

Nobody has any doubts today that implementation of the emperor's program of the country's modernization, development of the education and healthcare systems improved people's lives. But in the second half of the twentieth century that program was no longer relevant. The matter was that, unlike in the first half of the twentieth century, when the country needed specialists and had to invite them from abroad, by 1960, the Ethiopians who had been trained in national and overseas educational institutions, were unable to find jobs in public service: The country's economy was not developed enough, and the private sector did not need those specialists. Haile Selassie, I did not have a job program for them. One evidence of that is his interview of December 20, 1960. "As for the 11 points of the conspirators program, this is just a copy of the existing program and at the same time, the events that have taken place cannot be the reason for deviating from the progress path that was planned for the country . . . there will be no changes in the management system or government program,"[104] said the emperor.

Haile Selassie I kept his promises. Forming the government began on February 6, 1960. De facto the monarch nominated his favorites, nobles and members of the imperial family to key positions, as well as those who had proved their loyalty to the regime during the coup d'état.

By appointing ministers, the emperor did not vest them with enough relevant powers (the first post-coup cabinet did not even have a prime minister, as Haile Selassie chose to lead it himself) to turn them into independent decision-makers. He also retained the right of decision-making, of adopting plans and programs. Thus, Haile Selassie preferred to resolve the crisis by nominating his confidants who had lost the ability to evaluate and control the situation in the country, that is, Haile Selassie got himself back the power, but failed to eradicate the cause from which the coup had stemmed.

This is attested by a message of CIA the Letter from the Acting Assistant Secretary of State for African Affairs James K. Penfield dated May 27, 1961:

> Emperor Haile Selassie has re-established his personal authority in Ethiopia after a bloody three-day *coup* attempt. . . . Nevertheless, the Emperor's position was, if only briefly, seriously challenged, and he is confronted with serious problems involving the rebuilding of his Administration, and over the longer run, the stability of Ethiopia and the perpetuation of the imperial dynasty. . . . it (the events of 1960.—*Author's note*) was more significant than a 'palace revolt.'
> . . . his Imperial Bodyguard and the security services have been proved unreliable, and his doubts concerning the competence and resolution of the Crown Prince have been confirmed. . . . The issue which sparked the *coup* appears to have been the dissatisfaction of the Imperial Bodyguard officers. . . . Nevertheless, there exists a wider range of dissidence in the country, arising from a more complex set of factors. These include dissatisfaction of some middle level government officials with His Imperial Majesty's autocratic rule, and the thwarted aspirations of the growing number of young 'modernists' and western educated intellectuals for more rapid social and economic advance.[105]

After the coup, Haile Selassie was faced with a difficult situation, especially when forming a new government. Many members of his government had been killed by the conspirators. The others were suspected of having collaborated with them or of sympathies for the coup, as, for instance, his representative in Eritrea. Some proved to be incompetent—for instance, the Crown Prince. The emperor even did not have an alternative successor. The abortive coup d'état once again emphasized the importance of Haile Selassie I as the dominating personality in Ethiopian society of that period.

On February 10, 1961, a trial of the only surviving leader of the coup, General Mengistu Neway, began. The hearings of the coup d'état and high treason case lasted for six weeks. "A real effort has been made to conduct the trial as fairly as possible and that this has been achieved to the extent possible in a country with an autocratic government, and in the absence of an independent Judiciary and a strong and well-organized Bar," wrote an observer.[106]

On March 28, 1961, the court rendered its verdict. Mengistu was sentenced to capital punishment by hanging. On March 30, the general was executed in public. But that did not pacify Ethiopian society or bring any social harmony to it. The abortive coup undermined the authority of the monarchy. One evidence was the new turbulence in the armed forces, in particular in the army that demanded a promised pay raise. After that ultimatum was issued, Haile Selassie I had to make a statement on March 22 about raising the army's pay by 16 birr every month.

To keep his power, the emperor was seeking support in the army. To prevent a mutiny in the armed forces, the government used various measures to boost motivation of the military to keep up the existing regime. The army in Ethiopia had turned into the most advanced and well-organized socio-political institution. The armed forces were characterized by a high level of education. The rank-and-file were literate. The officers who had a high military education or secondary special training accounted for 10–12% of the country's residents with high education. Moreover, officers of the Ethiopian armed forces and police were frequently sent abroad for further training (one of those officers was Mengistu Haile Mariam, the future leader of the 1974 anti-imperial coup). Many officers also enrolled into local universities. That gave them an opportunity to watch closely events happening abroad, in particular in other parts of Africa. Permanent contacts with students had an inevitable impact on the army's ideological and political mindset.

The measures undertaken by the government in order to improve living standards of members of the armed forces gave Ethiopian authorities some respite. To avoid re-occurrence of the events of 1960, Haile Selassie needed domestic resources, funds and talent, which would carry out his plans of Ethiopia's development, of a gradual transition from feudalism to a developed democratic society.

But the country lacked those resources and talent. The 1960 coup attempt showed that Haile Selassie was able to train only an educated elite but not advocates of his reign—opponents, not successors. As for the funds, he counted on multifaceted economic and military aid from the United States. He managed to obtain it only partially, and further relations between the two countries bear witness to the fact.

Washington was never interested in what was going on in Ethiopia. After the 1960 coup and until the 1974 revolution, Haile Selassie was left to face domestic and external issues plaguing the empire he had created.

By the mid-1960s, the country was facing not only domestic but also international troubles. Difficulties arose in the relationship with the Somali Republic, which immediately after the declaration of its independence began its anti-Ethiopian activities, with an aim to create Greater Somalia by severing eastern and southern territories of Ethiopia, and also with Arab nations that were openly aiding so-called Eritrean liberation fronts (ELFs).

ABOLISHMENT OF THE FEDERATION

In 1960, alongside a mutiny of the imperial guard, other events occurred that had a significant impact on the foreign and domestic policy of Emperor

Haile Selassie I. It was the beginning of the process of the abolishment of the federation of Ethiopia and Eritrea. Back in May 1960, Asfha Wolde-Mikael (who was titled *Ras Betwoded* for his services to the emperor), the leader of the government of Eritrea's autonomy, addressed the Eritrean parliament. He suggested renaming the Eritrean government into the "administration of Eritrea," because the Ethiopian Empire could not have two governments, and also renaming the head of Eritrea's government into "administrator of Eritrea." It meant de facto renouncement of the federation granted to Eritrea by a 1950 UN resolution. In dissolving the Parliament, Asfaha Woldemikael said that "the reunion is a recognition of our being Ethiopians" and added that "the word federation did not even exist in our language (Amharic and Tigrinya—Author's note."[107] The Eritrean parliament adopted and approved the proposal made by its leader by an absolute majority of votes. According to certain evidence, the emperor was presented with a fait accompli. When Haile Selassie I asked the author of the initiative: "How will this solution benefit?," Asfha replied: "There can be no dual power in Ethiopia, a united Ethiopia has one leader—his name is Haile Selassie."[108] This decision of the Eritrean parliament paved the way for the abolishment of the federation and the beginning of more intense actions of anti-Ethiopian forces abroad, especially in Arab countries, which, in turn, mounted the threat to the unity and sovereignty of the Ethiopian Empire and its territorial integrity.

Formation of the Somali Republic following the unification of the British Somaliland, which received independence on June 26, 1960, and the Italian Somaliland (a unified independent republic was proclaimed on the day of the formation of the independent Italian Somaliland, July 1, 1960) became a direct threat to the territorial integrity of the Ethiopian Empire. Immediately after receiving independence, the leaders of Somalia declared that one of the main goals of the country's leadership was a struggle for getting back territories inhabited by Somalians; those were southeastern and southern provinces of Ethiopia (Harrar, Bale, Sidamo), the northern province of Kenya and the French Somaliland. Creation of the Somali Republic was also the reason for the cooling of relations between the Ethiopian Empire with the United States. The latter began to call on Great Britain, France, and Italy to provide comprehensive aid to the Somaliland.

Despite the aggressive foreign policy of the Somali Republic, the United States decided to provide economic and military aid to this country. This is evidenced by the United States-United Kingdom Talks on Africa on 21 November 1961. "In FY 1962 Somalia was one of the few countries where we were increasing our assistance. We would actually be providing more economic assistance to Somalia than to Ethiopia this year,"[109] said a White House representative. In addition, Ethiopia was refused extra military aid. Chester Bowles, Presidential Special Representative and Adviser on African, Asian and Latin American Affairs in the State Department, sent a telegram recommending that the Ethiopian request for a second squadron of F-86s be rejected tactfully but firmly.[110] Official Washington explained the reasons for declining, by the United States, of Ethiopia's request to provide F-86s fighters, by saying it was not necessary to expand military aid to Ethiopia, because Washington did not want to see an arms race with neighboring countries. In the opinion of official Washington, after the abortive coup of 1960, progressive Ethiopians would have regarded United States aid to the Ethiopian army (i.e., the army that had suppressed the coup) as support of the unpopular regime.

The Ethiopian emperor was afflicted by the United States' refusal, as, in his opinion, Ethiopia needed those planes because of the growing military might of Ethiopia's neighbors, especially the Somali Republic, which did not conceal claims to Ethiopian territory. Thus, in the 1960s, the relations between the two "allies," Ethiopia and the United States, began to see rifts. If before the declaration of the Somali Republic's independence, Ethiopia had been the main beneficiary of military and economic aid of the United States, and Haile Selassie was considered a friend of the West, after 1960 the United States altered its policy with respect to Ethiopia and the African Horn as a whole. In a telegram addressed to the U.S. embassy in Mogadishu, then-State Secretary Dean Rusk made it clear that the policy of the U.S. government "in Horn of Africa is to help both Ethiopia and Somalia help themselves in battle against underdevelopment. This is only the battle that USG (United States government.—*Author's note*) supports."[111]

Haile Selassie was refused aid just when he needed it like never before. If he had received a positive reply from the United States, he would have reinforced the empire's defense capacity and thus would have boosted his authority in the country and in the area of the Red Sea and the Middle East. At the same time, Washington took on strengthening defense capacity of the Somali Republic. Great Britain and Italy also called on the United States to take part in that project. "Military assistance to Somalia which UK and Italy willing provide leaves gaps in Somali military requirements which being filled in part by UAR. Soviet Union has recently made beginning in filling one such gap by initiating program of training for 20 Somali military pilots and 30 mechanics. Soviet plans with regard Somali military clearly do not stop there. Undoubtedly training will be followed by offers military hardware,"[112] writes Dean Rusk to the U.S. Ambassador in Ethiopia. Ethiopia's emperor did not speak against that serious attention on the part of the United States to the hostile regime in Somalia.

The reason for that irresolution, in our view, was the emperor's unwillingness to spoil relations with Washington ahead of the implementation of the contemplated plan to unify all Ethiopia, including Eritrea. Back in 1952, Haile Selassie had received Eritrea thanks to U.S. sponsorship. Abolishment of the federation without U.S. approval was practically a pipe dream. If in 1952 Haile Selassie had made concessions to the United States as he allowed creation of a military base in Eritrea, in 1960–1962, he was irresolute about United States aid to the Somali Republic.

The federation of the Ethiopian Empire with Eritrea existed for 10 years and was abolished on November 15, 1962 by a resolution of the Eritrean parliament, which spoke about full unification of Eritrea with the Ethiopian Empire. Eritrea became the 14th province, and Haile Selassie was the first leader who united all Ethiopian lands. The United States was the first state to react to this event. In reply to a telegram sent by Arthur L. Richards, the U.S. Ambassador in Ethiopia, a representative of the U.S. State Department writes: "In frank and friendly manner which has characterized our relations with Emperor, we wish state we have noted step and appreciate that there are factors relating nation's security which bear on Ethiopian policy toward Eritrea. Step has, however, placed US in difficult position. While USG wishes give full support, measures designed increase security of Ethiopia, Eritrean federation was action supported by United States in UN, action which, at time, was considered favorable to Ethiopia. . . .

It appears appropriate pursue subject, or if Emperor raises question message you may inform HIM that, while US does not feel it appropriate commend Ethiopia on dissolution of federation or participate in formal observances of event, in view history federation and general interest international community, US has noted with favor Emperor's intention maintain rights and freedom Eritrean constitution and hopes unification may strengthen IEG's hand in moving forward with plans for reform and modernization."[113]

And this time, Haile Selassie managed to get support of official Washington. The United States promised assistance in preventing this issue from being included in the agenda of a UN session. "We have a report that Somalia, backed by Arab states, may bring Ethiopia's recent formal annexation of Eritrea before the UN (Eritrea was 'federated' with Ethiopia as part of the Italian colonies settlement). Though we hardly applaud Haile Selassie's action, we ought to tell Abdirascid [sic!] (Shermarke, Prime Minister of Somalia, who was on a visit to the U.S.—*Author's note*) that for Somalia to complain to the UN about it would not only be futile (because the U.S. and its allies were not backing Somalia.—*Author's note*) but further exacerbate Somali-Ethiopian relations,"[114] Robert W. Komer of the National Security Council Staff wrote in a memorandum to President Kennedy.

Abolishment of the federation was, in our view, one more reason for complications in the domestic and foreign policy of Emperor Haile Selassie I. The imperial government did not prepare the ground for creating the administrative machinery to govern the new province. "None of the government ministers Haile Selassie was informed of the impending abolishment and federation. Neither the Council of Ministers nor the Ethiopia parliament were ready to work under the new conditions. None of the Ethiopian politicians had any idea what the new administration of Eritrea would be like, whether it would be subordinate to the minister of the interior or a special commission would be created, subordinate to the emperor personally. No one had an answer to the question: what will the abolishment of the federation give to the Ethiopian empire," wrote Zewde Retta.[115] The Eritrean political emigration living in the Middle East began to set up ELFs. One of the first fronts was created in Cairo from Eritrean Muslims and was led by Idris Mohammed Adem.[116]

By that time, the Arab world had not only become a center for training and financing fighters for Islamization of the western coast of the Red Sea, but also a center of radicalism. It targeted Israel ("to drive it into the sea"), sought liberation of the Ethiopian Muslims from the yoke of the Christian oppressor and liberation of Eritrea and Somali territories captured by Ethiopia.

The ELF was regarded as a tool of putting pressure on Ethiopian authorities. Since many members of the front and its leadership originated from the Muslim population of Eritrea, the Muslim world looked at it as an organization for the liberation of Eritrea and for the dissemination of Islam in the western coast of the Red Sea. Nearly all Muslim nations of the Middle East and North Africa began to provide assistance to the front, including Sudan, which offered it a training base and headquarters in Kassala, near Ethiopia's northwestern border. The front's leadership actively exploited the idea of "Fight for liberation of Muslims from the brutal oppression of Christians" They publicly declared that they were engaged in a holy war, *jihad*, against Christian Ethiopia.

As the USSR was reinforcing its foothold in the Arab world, some countries, such as Egypt, Syria, Iraq, began to focus on the Soviet Union, which not only began to supply arms but also to disseminate the ideology of "Marxism," known for its political radicalism.

Abolishment of the federation complicated relations of the Ethiopian Empire with the Arab world. The ELF was granted headquarters in Cairo, Beirut, Damascus, Bagdad, and Algiers. During a meeting of member nations of the League of Arab States, King Saud of Saudi Arabia promised full support, including financial aid, to the ELF leader.

Until the mid-1960s, ELF members were largely natives of Eritrea's Muslim population. After the leaders began to get comprehensive support of the Arab world, they created a special political division of the front; its purpose was to expand membership by recruiting Eritrea's Christian population. Tedla Bayru,[117] a former leader of the Unionists and chief of the first government of Eritrea, who had been appointed by the emperor Ethiopia's ambassador in Sweden, preferred to become the front's representative in

Damascus; Woldeab Woldemariam,[118] an opponent of the federation who would become the head of the ELF's Khartoum division, also joined the front.

In the mid-1960s, the front started to launch open armed attacks against representatives of authorities in Eritrea, and declared a war on the Ethiopian Empire. Efforts of Emperor Haile Selassie I who was striving to improve relations with Arab states were fruitless. After radical leaders, such as Muammar Gaddafi in Libya, Saddam Hussein in Iraq, Hafez al-Assad in Syria, came to power, the ELF began to train fighters at special bases, which complicated the relations of the Ethiopian Empire with those nations.

Alongside subversive activities, the ELF strengthened pressure on Ethiopia's foreign policy. The Eritrean issue was discussed at summits of leaders of Arab States. Furthermore, radically minded organizations, such as Asian and African Peoples Solidarity Organization (AAPSO), All-African People's Conferences (AAPC), African, Asian, and Latin American People's Solidarity Organization (AALAPSO), and the leadership of the Somali Republic were also the cause of difficulties faced by foreign policy of Haile Selassie I." Therefore, bringing relations with neighboring countries, including the Somali Republic, back to normal was high on the agenda, but no territorial or any other concessions were in sight. It was also necessary to find an alternative to the radicalism policy pursued by young African nations.

A FAILED DIALOG WITH WASHINGTON

It was clear to the monarch worried by domestic and international issues that without considerable military loans the empire could not thwart Somalia's aggression. Meanwhile, Mogadishu began to receive economic and military aid from the Soviet Union, from its allies in Eastern Europe, from China and Egypt. Moscow alone extended military aid worth $30 million to the Somali Republic in 1963.

To keep up military strategic parity in the region, Haile Selassie I again turned to American partners and met with President J. F. Kennedy in Washington, DC, in 1963. During the conversation with the president, the Ethiopian monarch touched upon the issue of military aid and U.S. mediation in the settlement of relations with Somalia. The request of the Ethiopian guest was neglected.

On the eve of a military conflict with the Somali Republic and an armed attack begun by guerrillas of the ELF, Ethiopia did not receive aid from its "ally," with which it had signed an agreement on mutual defense assistance. Nevertheless, the Ethiopian emperor, as if by inertia, continued to believe in the friendship with the United States, in UN principles, collective security (it is common knowledge that this belief was a reason for the ill-preparedness of the Ethiopian army for the Italian aggression in 1935).

Meanwhile, specialists in the United States began to work out variants of action in case the emperor were to exit the political stage. All agencies and institutions (CIA, FBI, Pentagon, State Department, etc.) that had anything to do with Ethiopian political life were involved in the preparation of a document entitled "National Policy Paper." The plan was proved to be necessary as the United States was interested in keeping its influence in Ethiopia. Therefore, the plan consisted of long-term programs that provided for the following: (1) establishment of relations with any Ethiopian regime that will have friendly relations with the United States, will allow unimpeded use of the Kagnew Station and will agree to see a continued U.S. influence on Ethiopian policies; (2) making sure that Ethiopia has a stable, competent and friendly government, more inclined to expanding involvement of population in politics; support of that government in the implementation of moderate economic and social plans; (3) establishment of peace between Ethiopia and the Somali Republic; if possible, mutual recognition of the borders; (4) efforts to counter further strengthening of Communist influence in Ethiopia; (5) support to keeping moderate influence of Haile Selassie in inter-African councils.

Short-term objectives were also identified: (1) to ensure unimpeded operation of the American military communications at the Kagnew Station; (2) to keep up moderately friendly relations with the regime of Emperor Haile Selassie I, and at the same time, to cautiously encourage economic and social reforms and a more active transformation of Ethiopia into a modern nation, first of all by means of political change that will give the population an opportunity to take part in the political process in a civilized way; (3) to seek friendship and respect from the successors of the existing regime that will come to power in Ethiopia by way of evolution or revolution, for instance, young educated Ethiopians, middle-level public servants, liberally minded officers; (4) to try and eliminate tension between Ethiopia and the Somali Republic; to decrease the level of enmity in the border regions of the both countries; (5) to eliminate or overcome existing situations in which the United States will probably have to back Ethiopia or the Somali Republic in the matters that concern exclusively their own respective interests; (6) to ensure support by Ethiopia of the UN and the idea of collective security; (7) to back Ethiopia in moderate development of its armed forces; if possible, to provide it assistance in refocusing public spending from military to domestic security; (8) to back the emperor's leadership in the OAU in order to pacify radical elements in that organization, which are hostile to the West.[119]

While Haile Selassie I was busy trying to strengthen friendship with the West, in particular the United States, Washington prepared a plan of rescuing Ethiopia without the monarch's involvement. The plan ruled out transfer of supreme power to the descendants of Haile Selassie I. The United States de facto were supportive of the coup of "sergeants." The army built and modernized by the emperor was to oppose its commander-in-chief at a critical moment.

Despite a military buildup and aggravation of tension in the relations between the Ethiopian Empire and the Somali Republic, the United States preferred to stay away from the affairs of those countries. Via its ambassador, the United States was trying to convince Haile Selassie I that the army could not be instrumental in addressing the Ogaden issue, but social and economic measures could improve the life of the Somalians living there.[120]

The Somali Republic made a transition from anti-Ethiopian propaganda to sending to its territory fighters to organize disorders and to destabilize the situation in border areas of the two neighboring countries—Ethiopia and Kenya. It provoked an immediate reaction on Ethiopia's part: In order to create an alliance with Kenya, Haile Selassie sent an official Ethiopian delegation to Nairobi (capital city of Kenya). Even though Ethiopia and Kenya were able to reach mutual understanding, they still failed to sign a pact on creating an alliance against the Somali Republic, which was encroaching on their territories (it should be noted that Kenya had protection from external aggression, and that protection was offered by Great Britain).

The Somali Republic did not limit itself to sending fighters. On February 6, 1964, clashes occurred between Somali and Ethiopian borderline forces in the border town of Togo-Wuchale, which quickly degenerated into a combat that lasted until February 9. After the Ethiopian military forces repulsed the attack of the Somalians, authorities of that country hastened to declare a state of emergency in the republic and demanded convocation of the UN Security Council to consider Ethiopia's aggression. U Thant, then Secretary-General of the UN, called on the Ethiopian emperor and the president of Somalia to cease borderline hostilities and to begin negotiations for the purpose of finding a peaceful settlement of the issue.

Haile Selassie I agreed to U Thant's proposal, as he did not want complications in the already unfriendly attitude of the UN Secretariat to Ethiopia. It was because of the hostile attitude of the UN Secretariat in 1957–1959 that negotiations had been disrupted which concerned the settlement of the border issue of the Italian Somaliland with the then-administrator of that territory (Italy). Another reason for which Haile Selassie refused to see the issue considered in the UN was that Arab League member nations that were pro-Somali could, seizing the occasion, raise the issue of the abolishment of the federation with Eritrea.

By virtue of those reasons, Haile Selassie I, having declared a state of emergency on the border with Somalia, requested calling a meeting of ministers of foreign affairs of OAU members, where members of the Arab League were represented by five North African nations: Egypt, Libya, Tunisia, Algeria, and Morocco. At a meeting of ministers of foreign affairs of OAU members that was held in Dar es Salaam (Tanzania) on February 12–15, 1964, a resolution was passed on peaceful settlement of the conflict between Ethiopia and Somalia. A call was made on the governments of these countries to order immediate cease-fire.

One of the first leaders of great powers to react to these events was Soviet leader Nikita Khrushchev. In a letter to Emperor Haile Selassie I, he called on the parties to settle the dispute by peaceful means.[121] It was a surprise for the leadership of the Somali Republic, which counted on getting considerable aid from the Soviet Union in order to wage a large-scale war against the Ethiopian Empire. Moscow was aware: Internationalization of the conflict between two African countries would not bring any political or economic dividend, therefore the Soviet Union was doing its best to play the role of peacemaker.

The United States (Ethiopia's "ally") was also neutral. A telegram sent to Emperor Haile Selassie I by U.S. President Lyndon Johnson says: "I have followed with deep concern recent events in the Horn of Africa affecting Somalia and Ethiopia. I want to assure you that the United States remains, as stated to Your Majesty in the past, fully sympathetic with Your Majesty's desire to maintain the integrity and security of Ethiopia. I have personally emphasized to the President of the Somali Republic that we will fully support efforts to find peaceful and mutually satisfactory solutions to problems such as those now disturbing the Horn."[122] That was official Washington's way to express the United States position.

At the same time, the United States suggested settling the conflict by way of an "interim agreement," which would stipulate the following: (1) possibility of joint development of the basin of the Wabi-Shebele River that had its source in Ethiopia; (2) an agreement on air flights, including the right of Ethiopian airplanes to make flights to Mogadishu in exchange for the right of Somali civilian planes to make flights via the route Mogadishu-Hargeisa across Ethiopian territory; (3) accessibility of the Somali ports of Kismayo, Mogadishu, and Berbera for Ethiopia; (4) opening transit for transportation via Ethiopia territory along the route Hargeisa-Mogadishu, when the situation in the Ogaden changes; (5) Somalia's consent to the construction of an oil pipeline via its territory in the event oil should be discovered in Ethiopia.

A telegram of the U.S. president addressed to the emperor probably aimed to ease the anxiety of Haile Selassie I who demanded military aid, because the Soviet Union continued to equip the Somali army. The United States refused full support to Haile Selassie, based on the following assumptions. Washington believed that the main mission of U.S. policy in the African Horn was to secure its own strategic interests in Ethiopia and, at the same time, to prevent the Soviet Union from gaining a strong foothold in Somalia.

Ethiopia's support in a war against the Somali Republic armed by the Soviet Union, the United States believed, would only exacerbate interethnic relations, but would not resolve the issues between the countries in that part of Africa. Furthermore, expansion of United States aid to Ethiopia would provoke retaliation on the part of the Soviet Union, and would accelerate buildup of the Somali army. Then Ethiopia, in turn, would demand that the United States pull out American bases from Ethiopian territory in order to localize the conflict and prevent interference of great powers, would insist that the United States expand its political and economic involvement in the complicated issue. Even complete victory of Ethiopia over Somalia, if it were possible, would not resolve Somalia's issue, but would only aggravate tension inside the Ethiopian Empire in the future.

Even though the Ethiopian army was able to repulse attacks by the Somali Republic, nevertheless, the issue of territorial integrity stayed on the agenda. After a nine-month chase after Somali armed units sent to the Ogaden, Ethiopia's army and security forces failed to complete the campaign with success.

Haile Selassie was not supportive of the top brass's plan to carry out a military expedition in the enemy territory in order to pursue and destroy armed groups that were terrorizing the empire. There were the following reasons for his aversion to the plan: (1) Haile Selassie I was an advocate of collective security and was hesitant to violate the UN and OAU Charters that had a clause on the recognition of existing borders of nations; (2) after it became known that the United States had no intention of providing him with military aid, the expedition could lead to a direct confrontation with the Arab world; (3) Haile Selassie was afraid to undermine his reputation of peacemaker in Africa, as the father of African unity; (4) consent to the top brass's plans would raise the army's prestige, would encourage certain individuals (heroes), who, using their authority in the army and among intellectuals, could create a threatening situation for the emperor's regime.

Emperor Haile Selassie I did not manage to pacify Somalia by way of negotiations. The Somali Republic rejected the OAU's suggestion to respect the Charter of that organization and the existing borders.

As he agreed to put an end to the war, Haile Selassie hoped that, using assistance of the OAU, he would be able to accommodate a discontent Somalia, but that did not happen. By 1965, Mogadishu had launched offensive actions, begun anti-imperial propaganda, and called on Ethiopia's peoples to topple the regime of Haile Selassie I.

By 1965, the ELF had also started to resort to warfare, sending armed groups that had been trained in Middle Eastern countries to Ethiopia. The only Arab state that stopped providing open assistance to the ELF was Egypt. After Sudanese President Ibrahim Abboud left the political stage, the regime that came to power began to back Eritrean separatists. As the ELF headquarters had approached its territory, the Ethiopian Empire had to carry out incessant expeditions looking for fighters.

The goal of the Ethiopian emperor's diplomatic tour to Middle Eastern countries in 1966 was not reached; the emperor sought to get them to minimize political and military aid to Eritrean fighters and the Somali Republic. Among the leaders to whom Haile Selassie planned to pay a visit was Iraqi President Aref. "His Majesty learned that President Aref intended to use the occasion to press the case of the ELF, whereupon the Emperor cunningly announced that he had been obliged to cancel the visit because of an outbreak of cholera in Bagdad."[123]

At the same time, Somalia made a new agreement with the Soviet Union on expansion of military aid, which ensured Somalia's superiority in terms of the quality and quantity of weapons among the three countries, including Ethiopia and Kenya. ELF fighters also received Soviet weapons and munitions via South Yemen and Syria.

After a diplomatic failure in the Middle East, the only thing remained for Haile Selassie to do—to appeal to the United States. Ethiopia's emperor intended to go to the United States on a business visit to discuss military aid received by Somalia from the Soviet Union and China, technical underdevelopment of Ethiopian armed forces, reinforcement of the ELF, and the 1965 budget crisis that was caused by growing military spending. However, then-U.S. Ambassador Edward M. Korry made it known through the prime minister of Ethiopia that the emperor's visit to the United States would be an unreasonable move, that increased military spending would aggravate the situation in Ethiopia's national budget and that it was necessary to improve efficiency of the army structure and ramp up intensity of its training.

Washington was not only averse to the idea of the emperor's visit, but did not want to expand military aid to Ethiopia from $10 to $15 million. "We also think the concentration should be on the effective utilization of what they already have. Similarly, we strongly prefer not to get involved in any budgetary support arrangements which are exceedingly difficult to get approved here,"[124] said an action memorandum from David D. Newsom, Director of the Office of Northern African Affairs, to G. Mennen Williams, Assistant Secretary of State for African Affairs. And, another telling quote: "The Ethiopians should be supplied with the materiel that they could operate and maintain in order to meet 'the threat that is there, not the one that may be in their minds," said U.S. Defense Secretary Robert McNamara, concluding a meeting where relations between the United States and the Ethiopian Empire were discussed.[125]

Thus, Washington was unwilling to enlarge arms supplies, and, in addition, did not want the emperor to meet with President Lyndon Johnson. In response to a request of a meeting with the U.S. president, Washington sent to Addis Ababa W. Averell Harriman, a personal representative of the U.S. president.

The meeting of Haile Selassie and Harriman took place in Addis Ababa on May 25, 1965. It was mainly focused not on United States-Ethiopian relations, but on the plans of Haile Selassie I to recognize Communist China. The emperor wanted to play on U.S. concerns that other African nations among which the emperor was an authority might follow his example. In that respect, Harriman needed to talk Haile Selassie out of the idea of recognizing Communist China.

Harriman's visit had no political or economic significance for the emperor, and the parties said their goodbyes without even signing a joint communique.

In 1965, another event occurred that nearly broke up the relations between Washington and Addis Ababa. On June 15, 1965, Ato Berhanu Dinke, Ethiopia's ambassador to the United States, officially asked for political asylum in the United States. Before undertaking this move, Dinke was openly critical of high-ranking officials of the government of Haile Selassie I, disseminated respective literature and published a few antigovernment articles in American press.

As a result, the prime minister, the minister of foreign affairs, and Ethiopia's new ambassador in the United States declared multiple protests. Emperor Haile Selassie also stepped in. On October 1, 1965, he invited Korry, the U.S. ambassador in Ethiopia. "The Emperor called in Ambassador Korry on October 1 to say he could not understand how the United States, in the interest of good relations, could permit Dinke to carry on activities against a friendly government,"[126] G. Mennen Williams, Assistant Secretary of State for African Affairs, wrote in a memorandum to Secretary of State Dean Rusk.

Did Haile Selassie take into account that U.S. authorities could not extradite Dinke, even if he was a dissident who was criticizing a "friendly government"? Probably not. If U.S. authorities had refused political asylum to Dinke, they would have been harshly criticized by human rights advocates. Under the laws of the country, U.S. authorities could not silence him either, because, so long as a person resides in the United States, they have the same rights as American citizens.

A few days later, on August 5, 1966, Dinke was granted permanent residency in the United States, and Haile Selassie got opposition not only in Arab countries but in a friendly nation—the United States.

Critics of Haile Selassie's regime also appeared in Ethiopia. The emperor's rule worried the United States, which was more than just another great power interested in seeing peace and quiet in Ethiopia. "It seems apparent that the rule of the Emperor in Ethiopia is in growing jeopardy. Criticism at all levels—even from hitherto loyal sources—is widespread. Coupled with the Emperor's reported lack of concern, don't we have some of the essential

ingredients of another coup?"[129] Robert W. Komer, President's Deputy Special Assistant for National Security Affairs, asked G. Mennen Williams,
Assistant Secretary of State for African Affairs.

The main reason for the growing discontent by Haile Selassie's rule on the
part of his subjects was, in the opinion of high-ranking White House specialists, the incompetence of the emperor's domestic policy. Komer even proposed organizing a campaign in Ethiopia with engagement of famous people
from the United States in order to persuade the emperor that it was necessary to begin domestic reforms aimed at eliminating the discontent that was
jeopardizing the nation. "We've had success in the past in convincing people
like the [Iranian] Shah and King Hassan [of Morocco] that they ought to be
modern reformist monarchs. Doing so with HIM could buy the time during
which more fundamental reforms could be started." It was deemed advisable
for President Johnson to tell the emperor as one statesman to another: "Given
our Kagnew installation and reports of the Soviets building radar installations
and a military base in Somalia, I'm sure you'd agree that political stability in
Ethiopia is most important to us."[130]

As he had ascertained that the Somali Republic, having signed a treaty
with the Soviet Union, was now superior to the Ethiopian Empire in the quality and quantity of weapons, Haile Selassie again began to put his hopes on
getting commensurate aid from the United States and, once again, planned a
meeting with President Lyndon Johnson.

"We assume HIM [His Imperial Majesty] has several motivations in wish-
ing visit Washington so urgently," writes a representative of the U.S. State
Department to Korry, U.S. Ambassador in Ethiopia. "HIM particularly worried by possibility French Somaliland plebiscite may lead to Somali take over
and further Soviet penetration Red Sea area."[131]

In order to find out what the American side was thinking about the emper-
or's scheduled visit to the United States, Haile Selassie sent Ketema Yifru,
Ethiopia's Minister of Foreign Affairs, to the United States. The emperor
was deeply concerned about Ethiopia's security and wanted to talk to the
president as soon as possible, preferably ahead of a trip to Moscow (closer
to late October, after a visit to Cairo). Ketema proposed two possible dates:
Either October 7, when his imperial majesty was to begin his journey to the
Middle East, or November 9–13, between an OAU summit and arrival of the
Czechoslovakia's president in Addis Ababa.

The United States politely refused the emperor's visit to Washington.
Joseph Palmer, Assistant Secretary of State for African Affairs, explained
that refusal by the president's tight schedule.

In our view, the reason for Washington's refusal of the Ethiopian leader's
official visit was, first, the changed international situation. From the very
beginning of the war in Vietnam, Indochina was the most important region

of the globe in terms of the defense of U.S. interests. Second, the United States did not want to create a situation like the Caribbean Crisis and thus get involved in an arms race and confrontation with the Soviet Union in the Red Sea area. It was in American interests to localize the conflict in the African Horn as a conflict between Ethiopia and Somalia, in which great powers would not be involved. Therefore, the United States not only was in no hurry to provide military and economic aid to the Ethiopian Empire, but tried to hold negotiations with the Soviet Union to make a "gentlemen's agreement" on avoidance of an arms race in the African Horn.

Washington's position buried for good the hopes of Haile Selassie I to make the Ethiopian Empire an ally of Western democracy, and himself the leader of an enlightened, progressive, and flourishing Ethiopia.

In 1966, Washington also began to revise the strategic importance of the military base in Ethiopian territory. One evidence is the reply of Defense Secretary McNamara to a letter that Nick Katzenbach, Acting Secretary of State, had sent to him on November 2, 1966. He writes that ways were being sought to reduce the United States dependence on the station based in Asmara without incurring losses.[130] In other words, Washington started to lose interest in Ethiopia, in particular in the military base on its territory.

In February 1967, the emperor managed to obtain a visit to the United States. A meeting with President Johnson was scheduled for February 14, 1967. The emperor wanted to share with the president his concern about Ethiopia's security, more intense activities of the Soviet Union and the OAU in the Red Sea, a threat on the part of the Somali Republic backed by the Soviet Union and China.

Preparing for the visit, the Ethiopian side made a list of the equipment and military machinery that it needed, worth $150 million (including tanks, anti-tank cannons, anti-aircraft artillery, C-130 and F-5 aircraft and helicopters). But even before the visit of Haile Selassie I began, the Americans said "no" to the emperor in their memorandum. Trying, however, to keep good relations with him, they recommended to offer him four UH-1D helicopters instead of eight requested by the Ethiopian side.[131]

Dean Rusk, U.S. State Secretary at the time, also noted in a memorandum to President Johnson: "We cannot and should not at this time satisfy the Emperor's demands for a great deal more military assistance or a possible request for U.S. guarantees of Ethiopia's defense. We are already providing $14 million in grant military assistance to Ethiopia in FY 67, of which $11 million is in equipment. This constitutes a very large share of our military assistance to Africa as authorized by the Congress under the $25 million ceiling for defense articles, which can only be exceeded by Presidential waiver. A similar amount is tentatively planned for the next fiscal year. Even if we could provide Ethiopia with significantly more military equipment, it would seriously aggravate the arms race in the area. Greater military training, better trained and equipped police forces and economic and social development are the answers to Ethiopia's principal problem of internal dissidence—not a great deal more sophisticated hardware."[132]

Dean Rusk, U.S. State Secretary, and Walt Rostow, President's Special Assistant, also opposed increase and expansion of U.S. military aid, but not the policy of preserving friendly ties with Ethiopia.

Thus, the visit of Emperor Haile Selassie I had no economic or political meaning; nevertheless, the American side did not resolve to cancel or postpone it.

The meeting of Emperor Haile Selassie I and President Lyndon Johnson was held on February 14, 1967. The main topic of the conversation (no negotiations were held) was Ethiopia's request to see expanded American military and economic aid.

Haile Selassie tried to convince the U.S. president in mutual benefits of cooperation between Ethiopia and the United States, pointed out to his country's contribution to UN collective security efforts. To back up his argument, he cited the non-recognition of Communist China and the fact that, despite criticisms voiced against his regime, he continued to collaborate with the United States. He analyzed in detail the threats to Ethiopia's security on the part of hostile Somalia backed by the Soviet Union, and the growing political influence of the USSR and China in Somalia. The emperor said that Soviet military aid to Somalia, which gave the USSR an opportunity to control the situation in the country was excessive for defense purposes and domestic security. The Soviets were arming 20,000 Somali soldiers, or one out of every 100 residents of the country, while Ethiopia had one soldier per 625 residents. In addition, Somalia had more artillery and armored vehicles than Ethiopia.

"The Emperor then requested the following: (a) the US military 'commitment' to Ethiopia, undertaken many years ago and until now averaging ten (*sic*) million dollars annually, to be raised to twenty million; (b) military weapons in hand to be replaced by more modern equipment, in view of Soviet arms aid to Somalia; (c) some sort of direct support for the Ethiopian defense budget to help finance petroleum, housing, etc.; (d) expansion of areas of economic assistance."[133]

Haile Selassie mentioned his future visit to Moscow in late February and that he had wanted to come to Washington first. The purpose of his visit to Moscow was to find out reasons for the considerable military aid that the Soviet government was supplying to Somalia. The emperor doubted he could get a satisfactory answer. The Soviets had always responded to Ethiopia's protests by offering arms, but the emperor never wanted to receive military aid from the USSR.

On the whole, the Ethiopian leader tried to stress not only Ethiopia's strategic importance for the United States, but its loyalty to the United States and his own personal contribution to the cause of collective security.

The American side made it clear that preservation of peace and security in East Africa and Africa as a whole largely depended on the emperor himself, that the United States would be providing moderate assistance, subject to congressional approval. The emperor was proposed to discuss cooperation between the two countries in detail with Defense Secretary McNamara and Acting State Secretary Katzenbach. Haile Selassie I met them on February 14, 1967, but the meeting did not bring the expected results to the Ethiopian side.

The conversation that took place with the U.S. president on the same day did not have any economic or military significance either. The United States believed that there was a possibility to improve the Ethiopian-Somali relations by joint use of common natural resources, first of all basins of the rivers that had their sources in Ethiopian lands and were flowing across Somali territory.

Haile Selassie's diplomatic voyage was a failure because of the changed political situation in the African Horn, in particular in Ethiopia, because of the growing discontent not only among the educated strata of Ethiopian society but even rural residents (peasantry), because of rising separatism that increasingly was aggravating instability inside the country, and because of expansionist efforts of the Somali Republic that continued to supply weapons to fighters. The American side did not want to bet on Emperor Haile Selassie I, because it considered him and his cabinet incompetent and incapable of carrying out domestic economic and social reforms.[134]

Sometime later after the emperor's visit, on April 27, 1967, the CIA prepared a secret document entitled "National Intelligence Estimate: Prospects for the Horn of Africa," where a curious conclusion was made about the future of the Ethiopian Empire and the Emperor. It was noted that "growing instability in Ethiopia, including the emergency of a potent insurgency in Eritrea, will raise problems for U.S. interests in the Horn of Africa and call into question the future of the U.S. position in Kagnew Station. Haile Selassie will probably retain control of the government and hold the Empire intact as long as he remains reasonably active. The death or overthrow of the 74-year-old Emperor will usher in a period of prolonged uncertainty, and perhaps violence, in Addis Ababa. In the latter event, government forces would, at least for a time, be unable to maintain control throughout the countryside, and some regions might break away. Somali expansionism will continue to aggravate the tensions in the Horn among antagonistic ethnic and religious groups. The Somalia Government will probably continue to avoid provoking a full-scale confrontation with Ethiopia's superior military forces. It will persist, however, in its assistance to dissident groups in Ethiopia, including Eritrea, in hopes of speeding the collapse of the Empire and improving the prospects for obtaining the Ogaden without open warfare. Though French security forces in French Somaliland will probably keep any Somali resistance movement from getting out of hand, agitation in one form or another is likely to keep the territory's political and economic affairs unsettled. The French will probably withdraw from the territory by 1970 or so, and perhaps earlier. Since the rivalry between Somalia and Ethiopia will persist, the danger of a war over Djibouti will again arise. The USSR, particularly through its military assistance to Somalia, seeks to expand its influence in the Horn and to undermine the special US position in Ethiopia. The USSR apparently believes that the trend of events in the Horn and the Red Sea area generally is running in its favor and will probably be cautious about premature exploitation of the disruptive forces emerging there. The UAR is also seeking to extend its influence in the Horn, but the size of its activities is limited by the strain on its resources of its involvement in Yemen and by its desire not to disrupt diplomatic relations with Haile Selassie. The persistence of tensions in the Horn and disorders within Ethiopia will prompt Haile Selassie to demand increased military assistance from the US—the quid pro quo for Kagnew. As long as the Emperor remains in charge, however, the Ethiopian Government is not likely to alter sharply the conditions of our use of the facility. . . . After he leaves the scene, Kagnew will probably become increasingly a focus of political attention in Ethiopia. At the least, the cost of our rights there will increase substantially, and there might be a demand to renegotiate the basic Kagnew agreement.

"So far, the Eritrean insurgents have not attacked US facilities in Kagnew, but pressures for such attacks from within the ranks of the partisans and from radical foreign sponsors are bound to increase. If Eritrea were to gain independence, the US might not be cast out of Kagnew automatically. The reaction of the new government would depend in part on its susceptibility to radical foreign influences and the availability of alternate sources of foreign aid."[135]

Based on the contents of the document, one can conclude that the empire's fate after the emperor's exit from the political stage was predetermined. The United States had no desire to expand military and economic assistance to the Ethiopian Empire. The United States was ready to cooperate with any government that would come to power in Ethiopia. It was assumed that an independent Eritrean state could be created. For the time being, Emperor Haile Selassie was required only to ensure security of the American military base at all costs by keeping peace and quiet in the African Horn area.

Having lost hope for U.S. military aid, Haile Selassie tried to begin negotiations with a British corporation to buy Canberra fighters, but the talks failed because they were not backed by the British government (Washington persuaded London to stop supplies).

By 1967, the ELF had started to win considerable support among rural populations, especially in northern and western parts of Eritrea. Haile Selassie made an attempt to influence popular sentiments in the region and made a few trips there, trying to convince the Eritreans that under a new system of government they would have equal rights with all the rest of the empire's citizens. He gave jobs, he distributed money and appointments, hopeful to garner sympathies of the Eritrean elite. Nevertheless, the resistance of the Eritreans was only growing.

It is a known fact that demands of Eritrean insurgents to obtain self-determination of Eritrea and to exercise its right to create an independent state were not based on linguistic, cultural, or ethnic unity. Only common colonial past was what united the Eritreans. Even the parties that were created after Eritrea's liberation did not pursue common goals. Unlike those years, this time the movement launched by representatives of the Muslim part of Eritrea was already shaped like an organization that included nine main ethnic groups of Eritrea. Their common goal was to liberate Eritrea from the colonial yoke of the Ethiopian empire.

To expand its activities, the ELF divided the territory of Eritrea into five military districts, and regional commanders were vested with the authorities to wage anti-Ethiopian struggle in specific areas.

Having acknowledged that it was hard for the Ethiopian regular army to fight well-organized guerrilla groups, Haile Selassie turned for help to Israel, which started to train SWAT teams for the empire. Further attempts of large-scale campaigns against ELF groups not only failed to decrease their subversive activities but caused ravages in the countryside and made populations migrate into neighboring Sudan. That helped the front draw the attention of the international community to its activities.

Even some countries that were friendly to Haile Selassie's regime began to establish contacts with ELF leaders. One of them was the United States. On April 26, 1967, a representative of the U.S. Embassy in Rome met with Tedla Bayru, a former chief of the Eritrean government and now the ELF leader in emigration. A representative of the U.S. State Department stressed that the purpose of the secret meeting with the ELF leader was to get information on the ELF's standing regarding Kagnew Station.[136]

It was after that meeting that a letter was written by an Under Secretary of State (Katzenbach) to Secretary of Defense McNamara, where he expressed his concern regarding aggravation of the situation in the Horn of Africa, in particular in Ethiopia, where Eritrean insurgents had begun to threaten the presence of the U.S. military base: "Opinions differ as to how long the Ethiopian Government can hang on to Eritrea or at least maintain some semblance of order there. Ambassador Korry doubts that it can be more than five years. In any event, there is a general consensus that when the Emperor dies (which could happen at any time), severe disturbances throughout the Empire and possibly loss of control of Eritrea by the central government can be expected. Moreover, in the interim there is an increasing likelihood of and capability for insurgent harassment of our station at Kagnew, such as the blowing up of antenna towers which cannot be protected. . . . I think, as a result, that we should freeze U.S. presence at Kagnew at current levels and prepare plans for an orderly, phased removal of operations from Kagnew as soon as possible without undue prejudice to U.S. security interests. . . . I would therefore like to ask you to develop as soon as possible a phased program for relocation from Kagnew Station."[137]

In that context, Washington was not interested to ensure Ethiopia's security and to preserve Haile Selassie's regime. To cut or to suspend military and economic assistance at a time when the emperor needed it more than ever would mean to leave a leader friendly to Washington to his own devices.

In the late 1960s, in addition to Eritrea and Somalia, the emperor had to wage a fight with another movement that threatened his regime and the unity of the empire. It was less organized, but it was after liberation of the Oromo people from yoke and exploitation of the Amhara people.

Pursuing his ethnic policy, Emperor Haile Selassie I was trying to build an interethnic alliance with the Oromo elite. This alliance stayed until 1965, when the Mecha and Tulama Self-Help Association was set up out of Oromo's two principal tribes. It began to disseminate ideas promoting awareness of ethnic identity, self-determination, optimization of Oromo's place in Ethiopian society. Because political parties had never existed in Ethiopia, organizations like Mecha and Tulama were a remarkable phenomenon in the life of society.

The organization was recruiting the Oromo who lived both in cities and in the countryside. It enjoyed special popularity in southern provinces of the empire, where rural residents were now hired help on the land they used to own.

According to Patrick Gilkes, Mecha and Tulama had about 300,000 members.[138] The association was led by the Oromo educated elite, which once had played a significant role in the creation and reinforcement of the Ethiopian Empire. The elite called on the Oromo people to wage a struggle for the preservation of its culture and language and for their respect.

In November 1966, as it feared to lose control over territories rich in natural resources (mainly export commodities), Haile Selassie's governments made a series of arrests. The association was banned, and its leader, police General Tadesse Birru, was convicted and condemned to death in 1968. Later, his verdict was commuted to life imprisonment.

Mecha and Tulama was an example of the failure of the policy of Emperor Haile Selassie I in creation of an "Ethiopian nation" by way of rapprochement of ethnic groups. Moreover, the Oromo's continuing protests showed once again that the Ethiopian political elite had failed to achieve ethnic unity. By the late 1960s, Oromo armed groups began a guerrilla war against government forces in the province of Bale (south of the empire). It was an alarming signal for Addis Ababa, because the province bordered on the Somali Republic, from which arms and ammunitions were delivered.

The movement did not have time to expand to a national liberation movement only because of a change of power in Somalia. After a military coup in 1969, General Siad Barre came to power, and he suspended pecuniary aid to the Oromo movement. As a result, in 1970, leaders of the movement preferred to begin talks with Addis Ababa. Haile Selassie I gave land plots and high military ranks to the most influential leaders.[139] Some members of the movement opted for emigration abroad, where they created, Western Somali Liberation Front and Somali Abo. The Somali Abo enjoyed popularity only among the Oromo Muslims who resided mainly in the province of Hararghe and Bale bordering on the Somali Republic.

The Oromo organization that managed to wage an active struggle against the regime of Haile Selassie I appeared only in 1973, on the verge of the 1974 Ethiopian revolution. The Oromo Liberation Front (OLF) set a goal of "full liberation of the Oromo people from Ethiopian colonialism." The front was leading the national resistance movement of the Oromo people.

Unlike Mecha and Tulama or Oromo Abo, which represented only some parts of the Oromo population, the OLF by 1974 was active in all provinces of the Ethiopian Empire where the Oromo resided (Wollo, Shewa, Hararghe, Bale, Arusi, Kaffa, Gamu-Gofa, Sidamo, Welega). At first, the movement was led by educated young specialists from the province of Arusi, but by 1974, the leadership was expanded to include representatives of all territories where the Oromo lived. By that time, the OLF leadership was not only advocating liberation of the Oromo people but also creation of an independent Democratic Republic of Oromo.

Thus, the Oromo movement that emerged in the second half of the 1960s as a mutual help association, by the mid-1970s was claiming to be an organization that was threatening the very existence of the Ethiopian Empire.

But Eritrea was still considered the biggest threat for the empire: The liberation movement in the province was not only experienced in guerrilla warfare against imperial troops, but also in seeking diplomatic recognition among other nations. By the end of the 1960s, even West European countries with which Emperor Haile Selassie I was keeping friendly relations began to provide support to Eritrean fronts under the guise of humanitarian aid.

In addition to armed struggle with guerrilla groups, the government of Haile Selassie I was trying to establish contacts with individual representatives of the fronts in a bid of splitting them up, and to suppress the influence of the movements' activities (for instance, the OLF) on other people living in Ethiopia. And he was successful in doing that, if only partially.

In 1970, after a rift had occurred inside the ELF, another Eritrean liberation organization was set up—Eritrean People's Liberation Front (EPLF). In 1970, as a result of a feud, activities of the liberation movement inside the country weakened temporarily. Fortunately for the government of Haile Selassie I, the two groups failed to come to an agreement on waging a joint fight against the government. That moved the fear of losing control over Eritrea by the Ethiopian Empire away, if only for a few years.

A dialog between Eritrean fronts and the OLF failed, which also, in turn, allowed the Ethiopian government to concentrate resources in order to oppose separatism in the country's north, in Eritrea.

NOTES

1. U.S. National Archives, National Security Council, the Executive Secretary. "Disposition of former Italian colonies in Africa." A report to the NSC, n. 19 (1949). Harold G. Marcus.1983). P. 83.

2. U.S. National Archives. S.D. Office of Intelligence Research. Division of Research for the Near East and Africa. "The capacity of Eritrea for Independence." Intelligence report 11.531. 25 July 1950. Cit. by: Harold G. Marcus.1983. P. 85.

3. FRUS. 1950. Vol. V. P. 1698–1699.

4. FRUS. 1950. Vol. V. P. 1698–1699.

5. FRUS. 1950. Vol. V. P. 1701–1702.

6. FRUS. 1951. Vol. V. P. 1241.

7. Ibid. P. 1242.

8. Ibid. P. 1256.

9. Ibid. P. 1265.

10. Ibid.

11. FRUS. 1952–1954. Vol. XI. P. 419.

12. See more details in: US Operations Mission to Ethiopia. The point four program in Ethiopia (Addis Ababa, 1954).

13. United States of America and Ethiopia. Mutual Defense Assistance Agreement. Signed at Washington, on 22 May 1953 // United Nations Treaty Series. 1955. Vol. 207. Pt I.

14. United States of America and Ethiopia. Agreement Concerning the Utilization of Defense Installations within the Empire of Ethiopia. Signed at Washington, on 22 May 1953. United Nations Treaty Series. 1954. Vol. 191. Pt I–II.

15. Diamond R. A., Fouquet D. American Military aid to Ethiopia and Eritrean Insurgency. *Africa Today*. Winter 1972. No. 19. P. 38.

16. John H. Spencer. 1984. P. 265.

17. Translations on Africa, No. 546. The Secret of Haile Selassie's Foreign policy. P. 9. United States. Joint Publications Research Service. Translation of an article by Petros Desta in the French language magazine. Remarques Africaines (African Notes). 1967. Vol. 9. No. 281. Brussels, 12. P. 16–18.

18. Harry Magdoff. Militarism and Imperialism. *American Economic Review.* 1970. Vol. 60. P. 239–240.

Harry Samuel Magdoff (August 21, 1913–January 1, 2006) was the son of immigrants from Russia. He studied mathematics and physics from 1930 to 1933 at the City College of New York. In 1935, he received a B.Sc in Economics. When in college, he was active in the Social Problems Club with many schoolmates who later joined the Abraham Lincoln Brigade, a Comintern organization that fought in the Spanish Civil War. He held several administrative positions in government during the presidency of Franklin D. Roosevelt, and later became co-editor of the Marxist publication *Monthly Review.*

19. According to John Spencer, Ethiopia was experiencing one of the early applications under the Eisenhower administration of what was later to become known as the Nixon doctrine. Defense of U.S. regional and local interests to be left to regional and local surrogates. When Richard Nixon took office in early 1969, announces that henceforth the United States will expect its Asian allies to tend to their own military defense. The Nixon Doctrine, as the president's statement came to be known, clearly indicated his determination to "Vietnamize" the Vietnam War. John H. Spencer. Ibid. P. 279.

20. FRUS. 1950. Vol. V. P. 1698–1699.

21. FRUS. 1952–1954. Vol. XI. P. 451.

22. Ibid.

23. Ibid. P. 455.

24. Ibid.

25. Agreement between the Government of the United Kingdom of Great Britain and Northern Ireland and the Imperial Ethiopian Government Relating to Certain Matters Connected with the Withdrawal of British Military Administration from the Territories Designated as the Reserved Area and the Ogaden. London, November 29, 1954. Treaty Series. 1955. No. 1. Cmd. 9348. L., 1955.

26. Harold G. Marcus. 1983. P. 95.

27. Siemienski Z. Impact of the Coffee Boom in Ethiopia. *The Middle East Journal.* 1955. P. 65–73.

28. Point Four General Agreement for Technical Cooperation between the United States of America and Ethiopia. Signed at Addis Ababa, on 16 June 1951. Exchange of Notes Constituting an Agreement Amending the Above-Mentioned Agreement. Addis Ababa, 17 and 27 December 1951 and 8 January 1952. United Nations Treaty Series. 1953. Vol. 179. Pt I.

29. Ethiopian Constitutional Development. P. 3–24.

30. Selected Speeches of His Imperial Majesty Haile Selassie I 1918–1967. Published by the Imperial Ethiopian Ministry of Information. Addis Ababa 1967. Now Published in This New Edition & Printing by the lion of Judah Society's Imperial

Publishers. P. 396. https://rastafarigroundation.org/wp-content/uploads/2019/11/Selected-Speeches-of-Haile-Selassie-I-LOJSociety-Published-Books.pdf

31. Ibid. P. 401–402.

32. John H. Spencer. 1984. P. 284.

33. Ibid.

34. Ibid. P. 285–286.

35. Memo of conversation between Simonson and Haile Selassie I. 9 February 1956, S.D. 611–75/1:1156. Cit. by Harold G. Marcus. 1983. P. 103.

36. President Dwight D. Eisenhower announced the Eisenhower Doctrine in January 1957, and Congress approved it in March of the same year. Under the Eisenhower Doctrine, a country could request American economic assistance and/or aid from U.S. military forces if it was being threatened by armed aggression from another state. Eisenhower singled out the Soviet threat in his doctrine by authorizing the commitment of U.S. forces "to secure and protect the territorial integrity and political independence of such nations, requesting such aid against overt armed aggression from any nation controlled by international communism." Office of the Historian. MILESTONES: 1953–1960. https://history.state.gov/milestones/1953-1960/eisenhower-doctrine (accessed 27 July 2020).

37. John H. Spencer. 1984. P. 292.

38. Ibid. P. 294.

39. Cit. by: Harold G. Marcus. 1983. P. 112–113.

40. The Non-Aligned Countries. Translated from the Spanish by Dr. Ivo Dvorak. L., 1982. P. 11.

41. After a conflict between China and India because of Tibet, which began in 1949, their relations were brought back to normal by the signing in 1954 of the Indian-Chinese agreement on Tibet. India recognized Tibet as part of China. The agreement declared the five principles of Panchsheel (peaceful coexistence): 1. Mutual respect for each other's territorial integrity and sovereignty. 2. Mutual non-aggression. 3. Mutual non interference in each other's internal affairs. 4. Equality and mutual benefit. 5. Peaceful coexistence. Under Jawaharlal Nehru, the slogan "India and China are brothers" ("Hindi Chini bhai bhai") was circulated by propaganda. In 1955, a similar slogan, "Hindi Rusi bhai bhai" (on the Soviet-Indian friendship), appeared. Peaceful coexistence was interrupted by the Chinese-Indian border war in 1962.

42. Ibid. P. 12.

43. Nigusie Kassaye W. Michael. Emperor Haile Selassie (I) and the Organization of African Unity (Devoted to the 50th anniversary of the African Union). *RUDN Journal of World History*. 2013. No. 3. P. 57–71 (in Russian) (hereinafter—Nigusie Kassaye W. Michael. 2013).

44. Chimelu chime Integration and Politics Among African States Limitations and horizons of mid-term theorizing. Uppsala. 1977. P. 159–161.

45. Anda Michael O. *International Relations in Contemporary Africa*. Boston, 2000. P. 81.

46. Zdenek Cervenka. *The Unfinished Quest for Unity. Africa and the OAU*. Great Britain. 1977. P. 191.

47. Africa Encyclopedic Reference. In Two Volumes. Volume II. M. 1987. P. 203 (in Russian).

48. The Creation of the OAU. By Makonnen Ketema. http://africans.com/articles /2013/11/29/creation-oau (accessed 3 May 2021) (hereinafter- Makonnen Ketema).

49. Ibid

50. Ibid.

51. Ibid.

52. Ibid.

53. Ibid.

54. Ibid.

55. The African Summit Conference. Published by The Publications and Foreign Languages Press Department. Ministry of Information. Addis Ababa 1963. P. 13.

56. Makonnen Ketema. Ibid.

57. Important utterances of H.I.M. Emperor Haile Selassie I. Addis Abeba, 1972. P. 347.

58. Makonnen Ketema. Ibid.

59. Gordon Gaskeill Africas Lion of Judah. *Reader's Digest*. October. 1968. P. 85.

60. In 1956, the Soviet Union and Ethiopia agreed to transform their respective diplomatic missions in Addis Ababa and Moscow into embassies and exchanged ambassadors.

61. Russo-Ethiopian Relations in the 19th and early 20th century (A Collection of Documents). Moscow, 1998. P. 4 (in Russian).

62. Ibid.

63. Ibid.

64. Ibid.

65. Ibid.

66. Ibid. P. 373.

67. See: Degterev D.A., Kassaye Nigusie W. Michael. First Ethiopian Students in the Russian Empire // Issues of History. No. 5. 2018. P. 69–79 (in Russian).

68. Fitawrari Tekle Hawariat Tekle Mariyam. *Autobiography*. Addis Ababa. 1998.

69. Voblikov D.R. 1961. P. 177

70. Ibid. P. 179.

71. Archive of Foreign Policy of the Russian Federation. Fund 143. 1947. Inv. 22. Vol. 12. File 12. Fol. 14–15 (hereinafter—AFRF 143. 1947) (in Russian).

72. Ibid.

73. AFRF 143. 1947 Inv. 22. Vol. 12. File 12. Fol. 14–15.

74. John H. Spencer. 1984. P. 308–309.

75. See details of negotiations between representatives of Ethiopia and the Coptic Church in: National Archives of Ethiopia. Personal holdings of Mersie Hazen Wolde Kirkos. Documents: February, March, May, June 1950 (E.C.); 05.02 No. 86 EMML; 05.03 No. EMML, No. 29 EMML; 04.05 No. 73 EMML; 14.05 No. 217 EMML; 07.06 No. 113 EMML.

76. *Bulletin of the Supreme Soviet of the USSR*. July 16, 1959. No. 28 (in Russian).

77. *Pravda*. July 13, 1959. No. 194 (in Russian).

78. See details. Ministry of Foreign Affairs of the USSR. The USSR and African Countries. 1946–1962. Documents and Materials. Vol. I: 1946–September 1962. Moscow, 1963. P. 450–458 (in Russian).

79. Ibid. P. 533–534.

80. Ibid. P. 535–536.

81. Cit. in: John H. Spencer 1984. P. 309.

82. Archive of Foreign Policy of the Russian Federation. Fund 143. 1974. Inv. 35. Vol. 25. File 4. Fol. 201–202 (hereinafter—AFRF).

83. Ibid. Fol. 202–203.

84. Ibid. Fol. 202–203.

85. Bliss. To Department, Addis-Ababa, 22 April 1959, S.D. 775-00/4-2259. Cit. by: Marcus H.G. 1983. P. 116–117.

86. Memo on internal security in Ethiopia by Paul Tailor, counselor of embassy. Addis-Ababa, 20 March 1958, sd. 775-00/3-2058. Cit. by: Harold G. Marcus 1983. P. 117.

87. In detail, see Richard Greenfield. *Ethiopia. A New Political History*. Pall Mall Press, L., 1965. P. 337–374 (hereinafter—Richard Greenfield. 1965).

88. Ibid. P. 341.

89. Harold G. *Marcus*. 1983. P. 118.

90. Perham M. *The Government of Ethiopia*. L., 1948. P. 123.

91. Richard Greenfield. 1965. P. 371.

92. Ibid. P. 379.

93. Above all, Haile Selassie proceeded from his own experience and practice of his predecessors. A coup or a conspiracy could be expected not in his own native province (the Neway brothers originated from Shewa) but in some other parts of the empire—for instance, in the province of Tigray or Gojjam.

94. Spencer writes that the emperor was notified of the conspiracy before he left for Brazil. See: John H. Spencer. 1983. P. 316.

95. After the suppression of the attempted coup, it was announced that the Crown Prince and *Ras* Imiru were acting under duress, at gunpoint. See the newspaper *Addis Zemen*. No. 301. 12 December 1953 (Ethiopian calendar).

96. Greenfield R. 1965. P. 416–417.

97. Yagiya V.S. 1978. P. 211.

98. Clapham C. The Ethiopian coup d'état of December 1960. *Journal of Modern African Studies*. 1968. Vol. VI. No. 4. P. 502.

99. Liberian age. 16 Dec. 1960. Cit. by: Marcus H.G. 1983. P. 141.

100. *Addis Zemen*. No. 300. 11 December 1953 (Ethiopian calendar), No. 301. 12 December 1953 (Ethiopian calendar).

101. See: Amnesty offered to Ethiopian Rebels. *New York Times*. 19 December 1960; His Imperial Majesty pays tribute to Heroic ground and Air Forces, Police, and people. The Ethiopian Herald. 19 December 1960; *Addis Zemen*. No. 305. 18 December 1953 (Ethiopian calendar).

102. See: A Clarion. Call to youth of the land. Voice of Ethiopia. 9 January 1961; *Addis Zemen*. No. 1. 21 December, No. 3. 24 December, No. 8. 29 December, No. 9. 1 January. 1953 (Ethiopian calendar).

103. See: A Clarion. Call to youth of the land. Voice of Ethiopia. 9 January 1961; *Addis Zemen*. No. 1. 21 December, No. 3. 24 December, No. 8. 29 December, No. 9. 1 January 1953 (Ethiopian calendar).

104. *Addis Zemen*. No. 16. 9 January 1953 (Ethiopian calendar).

105. FRUS 1961–1963. Vol. XXI. P. 425–428.

106. The Rebellion Trials in Ethiopia. Comments by an Observer. Bulletin of the International Commission of Jurists. April 1963. P. 29–41. https://www.icj.org/wp-content/uploads/2013/07/ICJ-Bulletin-12-1961-eng.pdf

107. Tekeste N. 1997. P. 146.

108. Zewde Retta. 2000. P. 489.

109. FRUS. 1961–1963. Vol. XXI. P. 433.

110. Ibid. P. 435.

111. Ibid. P. 438.

112. Ibid.

113. Ibid. P. 445–446.

114. Ibid. P. 448

115. Zewde Retta. 2000. P. 511.

116. Eritrea/Federation-with-Ethiopia. Encyclopaedia Britannica. https://www.britannica.com/place/Eritrea/Federation-with-Ethiopia#ref1046378 Accessed (28 July 2022).

117. See details, Herui Tedla Bairu. *Eritrea and Ethiopia: A Front Row Look at Issues of Conflict and the Potential for a Peaceful Resolution*. The Red Sea Press, Inc.; First edition (July 25, 2015).

118. See details, Dawit Mesfin. *Woldeab Woldemariam: A Visionary Eritrean Patriot, A Biography*. The Red Sea Press, Inc.; First edition (June 16, 2017).

119. FRUS. 1961–1963. Vol. XXI. P. 486–488.

120. FRUS. 1964–1968. Vol. XXIV. P. 487.

121. *Izvestia*. 11 November 1964 (in Russian).

122. FRUS. 1964–1968. Vol. XXIV. P. 499.

123. John H. Spencer. 1984. P. 321.

124. FRUS. 1964–1968. Vol. XXIV. P. 521–522.

125. Ibid. P. 526.

126. Ibid. P. 532.

127. Ibid. P. 533.

128. Ibid.

129. Ibid. P. 544.

130. Ibid. P. 554–556.

131. Ibid. P. 558–559.

132. Ibid. P. 560–561.

133. Ibid. P. 565.

134. See: Memorandum from the President's Deputy Special Assistant for National Security Affairs (Komer) to the Assistant Secretary of State for African Affairs (Williams). FRUS. 1964–1968. Vol. XXIV. P. 533.

135. FRUS. 1964–1968. Vol. XXIV. P. 572–573.

136. Ibid. P. 573.

137. Ibid. P. 577.

138. Patrick Gilkes. *The Dying Lion Feudalism and Modernization in Ethiopia.* L.1975. P. 225 (hereinafter—Patrick Gilkes 1975).

139. Ibid. P. 218.

Chapter 5

The Empire's Systemic Crisis

ABSOLUTISM AND POLITICAL
PROCESSES OF THE 1970S

Notwithstanding his progressive policy, the emperor was unsuccessful in his bid to integrate Ethiopian society. Unlike his predecessor Menelik II, who became famous after he had conquered eastern, southeastern, southern and southwestern territories of Ethiopia, Haile Selassie came down to history as a leader who was consolidating monarchical power, bringing down regionalism. For the first time in the country's history he managed to establish absolute power over the provinces, but this victory did not bring about integration of society or help create an Ethiopian nation. Why?

The failure could be explained, first, by lack of effective ethnic policy carried out by Haile Selassie I. Second, local elites did not perceive the reformer's project of statehood as multiethnic, and the ethnicities that had not been absorbed by the empire before the nineteenth century were regarded not as citizens of the empire but, rather, as its subjects who depended on the emperor and his dignitaries.

The policy aimed at creating a union between Shewan nobility and provincial elite did not affect representatives of other ethnicities (interethnic marriages were concluded among the nobility of the Amhara, Oromo, or Tigray).

In the so-called southern territories, Haile Selassie was pursuing the policy of *Shewanization*. It manifested itself in propagating the Shewan dialect of the Amharic language, which in the early twentieth century became the official language (via schools, administrative, and judicial machine), as well as in the construction of churches and monasteries with the purpose of disseminating the ideology of the Shewan elite.

According to John Markakis, Christopher Clapham & Edmond. J. Keller, "the Ethiopian government conscientiously avoided any reference to ethnic, linguistic, and religious diversity and eschewed mentioning such matters in official documents. Most of the government's efforts in this regard were devoted toward discouraging or destroying the culture, language, and religions of subject groups, . . . Even more striking was the fact that Shewan Amharas tended to dominate at all levels of administration down to the district level. In 1967, two of the six provincial governors were military officers, and the remainder were Shewan aristocrats) was shocking."[1]

However, this policy was not an Ethiopian invention. The same reproach could be made to all polyethnic states and their leaders, all multiethnic empires, including Russia, France, Great Britain, Austria-Hungary, and even the United States.

Moreover, it would be unrealistic to address a very costly challenge of developing cultures, languages,[2] and so forth, of all ethnic groups populating Ethiopia. Therefore, Haile Selassie opted for the age-tested (by European empires, among others) policy of adapting peripheral ethnicities to the culture of the home country, that is, Showa.

Amidst a social system where representatives of authorities are appointed rather than elected, their loyalty (and, only in rare cases, their aptitude) is regarded as the main criterion for their selection. To trust provincial nobility that had revolted on multiple occasions would be risky, both from the political (in terms of national security) and economic standpoint. Therefore, the emperor's mode of governance was irreproachable in that sense.

Haile Selassie I made concessions to provincial recalcitrants after the 1960 military coup, when he realized that the opposition was not in the provincial elite but in the new intellectuals from among the Shewan elite.[3] When regional liberation fronts emerged, the emperor managed, amid tough international pressure, to make the center make concessions to local aristocracy in order to create an alliance against opponents of "traditional society."

Even when it was ceding part of its powers and authorities, the center never suffered equality of local populations with the Shewans, did not promote local cultures, use of local languages, and so on. It is true for Eritrea, where, according to the Constitution of July 15, 1952, Tigrinya and Arabic were working languages, and were replaced by Amharic effective in 1962.

No doubt, the policy of Haile Selassie I aimed at Ethiopia's centralization neutralized the once powerful provincial nobility by undermining its political and economic authority. But since this policy was not promoting equality of the ethnic groups populating the empire, Ethiopia remained a nation of disjointed and frequently quarrelling provinces. Many inhabitants of the country still believed their homeland was the area where they were born.

Ethiopia's *Shewanization*, and, afterward, attempts of collaborating with the local elite were effective only until the 1960s, before emergence of national liberation movements that managed to win trust of local populations by disseminating propaganda. Haile Selassie's government lacked a clear-cut program of opposing national liberation movements, and constant *Shewanization* only encouraged separatism.

A plan for economic development of regions was also lacking. Five-year plans (1957–1962, 1963–1967, 1968–1973), despite the fact that they were ambitious and were aimed at acceleration of the country's economic development (which failed), targeted mainly Addis Ababa, the province of Shewa, and Eritrea. As a result, 70% of Ethiopian industry was concentrated in three regions.[4]

In the late 1960s, separatism as a form of protest against the government's ethnic policy was gaining strength in Eritrea and in the southern provinces bordering on the Somali Republic. The authorities were trying to neutralize the movement by military methods. In Eritrea and in the provinces of Hararghe and Bale, battalions were stationed to suppress revolts. The military method of addressing the issue of separatism was effective while the Ethiopian Empire was receiving aid from the United States, which secured Ethiopia's domination in the African Horn area.

DIPLOMATIC BLUNDERS

As the United States decided to cut military and economic aid to Ethiopia in late 1960, and a new agreement on arms supplies was concluded between the Soviet Union and the Somali Republic, Ethiopia was no longer a dominant force in the region, and, moreover, was a country with integrity jeopardized by external (the Somali Republic and its allies) and internal (the national liberation movement) forces.

Emperor Haile Selassie did not want to put up with the situation and, in hope to change it, turned once again to the U.S. government. He still was convinced of his country's strategic importance, and of the significance, for the Pentagon, of the military base and the system of communications in Kagnew.

No positive reply came from Washington. On the contrary, on June 1, 1970, during a hearing in the U.S. Senate's Subcommittee on Security, David D. Newsom, Assistant Secretary of State for African Affairs, publicly announced that the United States was not committed to the territorial integrity of Ethiopia.[5] It de facto meant the United States was abandoning its military base, and had lost any military and political interest in the Ethiopian Empire.

Ethiopia was left to face its domestic and external enemies alone. In that time, fronts of the national liberation movement that were receiving a large-scale military, political, and financial aid from the Arab Middle East were stepping up their armed fight against government forces. In Eritrea and in the south, in Somalian territory, the Eritreans were provided with headquarters.[6]

The only state that proposed a joint effort against pan-Arabism was Israel. In 1969, Ethiopia turned down Israel's proposal on creating an alliance between the United States, Israel, Iran, Turkey, and Ethiopia against pan-Arabism. "Two years letter, Haim Bar-Lev, chief of Israel's Southern Command, came to Ethiopia in order to establish close relations between the two countries, but the Ethiopian side informed him that no arrangements of that sort could be possible."[7] As likely as not, Haile Selassie feared deterioration of relations with some nations of the Arab world, which had given up open support to anti-Ethiopian forces in the country's north and south, such as Egypt and Saudi Arabia.

In January 1973, Haile Selassie I sent Minasse Haile, Ethiopia's Minister of Foreign Affairs, to Arab countries of Northern Africa and to Somalia, in order to dissuade their governments from helping Eritrean separatists. The voyage of the Ethiopian minister of foreign affairs did not bring the desired results. Libya and Algeria's governments accused Ethiopia of making a base on the Dahlak Archipelago available for Israel, and Somali President Siad Barre refused the proposal of the Ethiopian minister of foreign affairs to "reach some degree of understanding"[8] between the two nations.

Somali President Siad Barre also refused to take part in the summit dedicated to the first decade of the OAU in 1973. His statements said he was not attending the summit because of a very tense and perilous situation on his country's border with Ethiopia.[9] Libyan leader Muammar Gaddafi denounced Ethiopia for making a military base available for American monopolists, saying the base had become a threat for the continent's security and unity, as it allegedly helped the Americans build other military bases, and he also slammed Ethiopia for making a base in Abyssinian territory available for Israel.[10] Gaddafi recommended moving the OAU capital city elsewhere, because leaders of the liberation movement were allegedly watched there by American and Zionist spies.[11]

The Libyan leader's statement was backed by the 4th conference of ministers of foreign affairs of Islamic nations, where activities of Eritrean fronts were officially recognized as a "movement to liberate the peoples Eritrea."[12] At that conference, the Somali Republic joined the organization as a new member.

Even though the proposal of the Libyan leader was not supported by OAU leaders who were representatives of the national liberation movement in Africa, nevertheless, it was a signal for the government of Haile Selassie I: The OAU, which had been created with his active involvement, and its

Charter were unable to protect his empire from "aggression" or from an economic blockade by the Arab League.

Meanwhile, the Somali Republic continued its military buildup. By the first half of the 1970s, Somalia had MiG-15s, MiG-21s, Il-28s airplanes, T-34 and T-35 tanks, 10 artillery battalions (versus four Ethiopian ones), and so on; about 2,000 Soviet technicians and advisors were working for the Somali Republic,[13] and at the same time, the U.S. military leadership had begun to prepare scrapping military aid for the Ethiopian Empire.

Worried by the situation inside the country and by the external threat, Haile Selassie was still looking for ways out of the grave situation. In order to normalize relations with Arab and Muslim nations, Haile Selassie severed diplomatic relations with Israel. It is a known fact that Israel was the only country that maintained friendly and business relations with Ethiopia's government: The Israeli were training officers of Ethiopia's state security service and the Ethiopian taskforce that was fighting against separatist units.

The Israeli were also involved in Ethiopian economy. By 1970, about 40 Israeli companies were functioning in Ethiopia.[14] Haile Selassie decided to sever relations with the only state that provided comprehensive aid to Ethiopia not because he was a soldier against Zionism but in hope to improve relations with Arab Muslim nations. But it did not happen. The Middle East only intensified its anti-Ethiopian activities.

As soon as he became convinced of the need to strengthen the army in order to ensure control over the situation inside the country and in its borderline areas, because Eritrean separatists had begun to launch large-scale attacks against Ethiopian forces not only in rural regions but also in towns (making ground communications between Eritrea and the rest of Ethiopia impossible), Haile Selassie wanted to secure help of the "friendly U.S."

In 1973, he declared his intention to visit the U.S. and to meet President Richard Nixon. J. Spencer, the emperor's advisor, wrote later that "The trip was an unqualified disaster."[15] The reason for the failure was a change in the relations between the USSR and the United States, two great powers, after the signing of a series of treaties in Moscow, including the Anti-Ballistic Missile Treaty (ABM Treaty) signed on May 25, 1972 and SALT (Strategic Arms Limitation Talks) Treaty I signed on May 26, 1972. Furthermore, the United States did not believe that the Horn of Africa, in particular the Ethiopian Empire, were the object of attack by global Communism.

Haile Selassie chose a wrong time to use his proven tactics of exploiting controversies between great powers for his own benefit. The matter was that his approach was no longer effective, after the U.S. and the USSR had started gradually to make a transition from confrontation to "mutual understanding" on key issues, such as peace, prevention of a global war even in hot spots like the Middle East and Indochina.

The two powers, even though their attitudes to the belligerents were different and they had mutual defense treaties with many of them, did not start an
open war against one another. Haile Selassie had no leverage to put pressure
on Washington in order to get required military aid. As the power with which
Haile Selassie had been keeping friendly relations for a quarter of a century
refused to collaborate, it not only accelerated the end of his regime but also
triggered disintegration of the empire he had created, as in the twentieth century, weaker relations of the central figure (emperor) with great powers meant
for the Ethiopian Empire a triumph of regional leaders who were more than
willing and ready to use that weakness in order to strengthen their own lost
stance. It is for that very reason that Ethiopian emperors had been trying to
forbid external contacts to provincial authorities.

Neither Haile Selassie I, nor his ministers, nor the "Ethiopian elite" were
ready for that turn of events. They did not expect Washington to refuse aid
not only to a friendly regime but to a country that had "strategic importance,"
a country where valuable military facilities were located.

In a bid to continue negotiations, Haile Selassie left part of his retinue in
Washington. In the opinion of Spencer, that way Haile Selassie was probably
trying to conceal the unsuccessful outcome of his visit to Washington from
the Ethiopian public.[16]

In our view, the main purpose of the emperor's visit was to get military
aid at least. He had no doubt that as the confrontation exacerbated with the
Somali Republic that was still getting aid from the Soviet Union and as the
Eritrean Liberation Front was getting stronger in the north, threatening security not only of the empire but of the American facilities in Ethiopian territory, as tension was growing between Arab states and Israel, the United States
might change its decision. Therefore, two generals, Assefa Ayana (Air Force)
and Kebede Gebre (ground forces), were left as member of the delegation that
remained in the United States.

Having failed to garner Washington's support, Haile Selassie I decided
to visit the Soviet Union in the same year, 1973. The main purpose of his
visit was to minimize the military threat on the part of the Somali Republic
backed by the Soviet Union, and he wanted to sign with Moscow a treaty on
reduction of arms supplies to that country. His negotiations were unsuccessful their as well. Haile Selassie I could not put forward concrete proposals
for the Soviet side in the event the USSR gave up aid to the Somali Republic.

Because of failed visits to Washington and Moscow, Haile Selassie I was
left to face alone the internal opposition that was beginning to turn from
public criticism of his policy to calls (for the time being, through young
people, university, college and high school students) for the overthrow of his
regime, and also to confront external rivals of the Ethiopian Empire. In 1973,
neighboring countries were by far superior in economic and military might,

compared with Ethiopia that used to dominate the Red Sea area. In particular, those were countries of the Arab East, which could at any moment paralyze activities of the government of Haile Selassie I, and also Ethiopian economy by imposing an embargo on oil supplies or introducing a blockade of the ports of Massawa and Assab. By that time, the Soviet Union had successfully completed the construction of a military base in Berbera (a Somali port on the coast of the Indian Ocean), the biggest base outside of the territories of Warsaw Treaty member nations. That gave the Somali Republic moral, if not military, superiority.

Haile Selassie had no hope of winning even somebody's diplomatic support[17] if neighboring countries were to unfold large-scale hostilities against his empire. It was impossible to count on help from the UN or the OAU, because both of these international organizations had proven their ineffectiveness in enforcing their own charters.[18]

DROUGHT, FOOD CRISIS, DISTURBANCES

The failure in foreign policy of the government of Haile Selassie I was concurrent with a food crisis caused by drought in 7 out of the 14 provinces of the Ethiopian Empire (Wollo, Tigray, Hararghe, Shewa, Bale, Sidamo, and Gamu-Gofa). According to data of the UNICEF (United Nations Children's Fund), more than one million people were exposed to famine in just two of those provinces—Wollo and Tigray.[19] Local authorities, desirous of protecting their reputation in the eyes of the emperor and willing to make money on supplying foodstuffs at steep prices (prices were up by 20%),[20] did not use food and grain reserves stored in government and private warehouses.

In April 1973, the government decided to take action through the National Emergency Committee that had been set up in 1971 in order to combat famine and a cholera epidemic. Activities of the committee were ineffective, because the government officially refused to acknowledge that the problem had spread to gigantic proportions and was out of control, that it was unable to curb it and needed humanitarian aid of the international community. J. Shepard writes in his book *Policy of Starvation* about the attitude of some Ethiopian officials, saying that when faced with the choice of publicity and no aid, they preferred to go without aid.[21]

This policy of Haile Selassie's government can be explained by his desire, first, not to scare off foreign investors by a humanitarian disaster, and, second, to preserve calm inside the country. But the scale of famine could not be concealed. In April 1973, three professors of the university named after Haile Selassie I visited the province of Wollo in order to conduct an independent investigation. After getting back, they addressed the faculty and the students and slammed the regime of Emperor Haile Selassie I for its inability to take appropriate measures. Students were the first to react to the issue. To raise funds for the population exposed to starvation, they announced a fasting period unapproved by official authorities, including religious organizations.[22] After that, they ran a fundraising campaign and collected food; to show the extent of the tragedy, a photo exhibition showing starving populations was organized. At a rally of university and school students, the main demand was to introduce a state of emergency in the country. The authorities believed that rallies and fundraising campaigns were a threat to the country's security, so the rallies were dispersed by the police. These actions of the authorities could not pacify the students.

In May 1973, a group of students went to Dessie (the capital city of the province of Wollo) and organized there a rally to make the governor undertake urgent measures to save starving populations. This time again, the authorities broke up the student rally using firearms, and a few young people were killed. The professors who had unveiled a report on the situation in Wollo were fired.

Interestingly, representatives of international organizations (OAU, UN Economic Commission for Africa), diplomats, journalists, and country leaders did not respond to a humanitarian disaster of that scale. The government of the United States, a country with which Emperor Haile Selassie had friendly relations and to which he remained loyal, made no effort to help numerous populations exposed to famine and drought. It is curious to note that even Communist media did not publish articles to denounce "inaction" of Ethiopian authorities. International humanitarian organizations, such as the Red Cross and the UNICEF, also opted for silence.

In the summer of 1973, the UNICEF conducted an independent investigation. Even after its representatives learned about the mass fatality, the organization, instead of immediate relief (more than 1 million people were on the verge of death in the provinces of Wollo and Tigray at the time), started to hold discussions with the authorities, in particular, with the Planning Ministry, which refused to make the report of UNICEF representatives public.[23]

Only after a documentary "The Unknown Famine," made by Jonathan Dimbleby, a journalist of the British television, was shown in London, Europe learned about the shocking events in the Ethiopian Empire. Humanitarian organizations, such as the British Save the Children Fund, were the first to take action.[24]

In November 1973, Haile Selassie himself traveled to the affected areas in order to assess the situation in which starving people were living. Even though he was deeply touched by what he had seen, he was unable to suggest ways out of the crisis. Nevertheless, he was able to estimate the scale of the disaster that was out of control.[25] However, even after his visit to those regions, the emperor did not declare a state of emergency in the country.

According to American sources, by February 1974, the United States and other international donors had donated about $25 million, but Ethiopia's government had spent nothing. In that time, the Ethiopian treasury had huge reserves to purchase food in required quantities and also had sufficient grain inventories to overcome the famine caused by drought.[26]

One can agree with the above statement: During the hard years between 1971 and 1974, not only the government but some private individuals possessed sufficient grain stock. One of them was Crown Prince Asfaw Wossen,[27] who was the head of the province of Wollo affected by drought.

The situation of the Ethiopian Empire, and, in particular, of Haile Selassie's government was further complicated by the crisis that arose between Israel and Arab countries, the beginning of the Yom Kippur War that led to the closure of the Suez Canal and to an oil embargo, which deepened the economic crisis that had started in the early 1970s. The Ethiopian Empire suffered from the oil embargo and the closure of the Suez Canal, because it's main export commodity, coffee, was taken to Western Europe via the Suez Canal.

The oil embargo, the closure of the Suez Canal and dwindled coffee prices, which spurred inflation, were, in our view, the reasons for the failure of Haile Selassie's government to use reserves of the Central Bank and grain inventories in order to bring relief to the affected areas. Haile Selassie was afraid that if the Arab-Israeli war should last for a long time, Ethiopia might face a food crisis on a national scale, which would paralyze the country. In a bid to curb inflation, the government undertook some important but unpopular measures, including raising oil and petroleum product prices in the domestic market. In late 1973, Arab oil producers raised oil prices by $.9 per gallon. Instead of covering the difference at the expense of public money, the Ethiopian government opted for a fuel rationing system and, simultaneously, raised gasoline prices by $.25 per gallon. According to the vision of officials, these measures were to reduce consumption of oil and petroleum products, to increase government revenue from their sales, in order to keep afloat an already unprofitable oil treatment facility in the port of Assab, Eritrea.[28]

These government measures sparked outcries of the country's middle class (the main group among motorists) and of cab drivers (owners) who were prohibited from raising fare, even despite the raised oil prices.[29]

The strike of cab drivers that paralyzed the urban transportation system in February 1974 was supported by students protesting against the government's policy, as the government was still unwilling to provide proper relief to the starved population of Wollo and Tigray, and also against a new education program, "Sector Review," promulgated on February 8, 1973. It sparked a wave of protests by students and, later, by teachers and other educators.

According to the program, professional education was attached a great importance. The government financed only primary education, and further studies were to be paid by students themselves. The reform affected not only students but teachers as well. Instead of an expected salary raise, improvement of the quality of teaching and working conditions, the working week was to be extended to 48 hours, and the class capacity to 67 students.[30]

By taking these measures, the government of Haile Selassie I wanted, above all, to cut spending on training young specialists. The "Sector Review" program never won approval of the people who were most affected by it, students and teachers, because:

1. it did not provide for the improvement of the quality of education, for the construction of schools, etc.;
2. financing of further education was to be the care of the students themselves, that is, of their parents. It signified that most children would not be able to complete even high education;
3. the financial situation of teachers deteriorated; no extra money was paid for a two-shift working day and a 48-hour working week;
4. the government had no plan of creating new jobs for school and university graduates.

After mass protests had occurred, the government of Haile Selassie I postponed implementation of the program indefinitely. Moreover, it decided to cut gasoline prices by 40%, and promised to take prices under control.

The most important step made by Haile Selassie was his decision to hold a meeting with representatives of the educating community united in an association that had about 17,500 members. Haile Selassie promised to raise salaries of educators. The emperor made that decision all by himself, despite a resolution of the head of the government, Prime Minister Aklilu Habte Wold, who was against dropping the measures aimed at bailing out the country's economy.

By his decision, Haile Selassie not only undermined the authority of the prime minister and the government but demonstrated that there were differences among the political elite and highlighted his regime's helplessness when faced with difficulties. The gesture was also risky because, when they learned about controversies in the nation's leadership, other members of society, for instance members of the army, could at any moment raise other economic issues. By his promises given to educators and by the suspension of the "Sector Review," Haile Selassie only for a short period of time was able to curb a potential wave of protests of the intellectuals, that is, the educated class.

Meanwhile, the economic situation in the country was increasingly deteriorating, prices were still growing, and hundreds of thousands of people were dying from starvation. Peasants were fleeing the countryside, moving to cities and, in particular, to Addis Ababa, which spurred unemployment and social tension.

By 1974, the government of Haile Selassie I had begun to lose support of the army and police, which were refusing to protect the regime's interests. The army, like the intellectuals, started to demand better living conditions and a wage raise. From December 1973 to January 1974, disturbances occurred in the army. The most significant of them was a mutiny on January 12, 1974,[31] which occurred among the rank-and-file and sergeants of the Third Division stationed in Negele (province of Sidamo), when the servicemen refused to obey orders of their officers.

It is a known fact that after the 1960 attempted coup d'état Haile Selassie did his best, trying to improve living conditions of the military. One example is his consent to raise wages of servicemen in 1961 and 1964. In addition, retirement plans were introduced and monthly payments to the families of the servicemen who died or were killed.

The mutiny in Negele was initially an act of protest aimed against the local top brass, who had been unable to provide proper water and food to the rank-and-file for a long time. The soldiers, having disarmed and arrested their officers, refused to obey the top command of the Third Division. They demanded that Prime Minister Aklilu Habte Wold, the defense minister and the commander of the Territorial Army arrive in Negele to see the living conditions of the enlisted men with their own eyes.[32]

As likely as not, the government and the country's supreme military command believed the army would begin to interfere in the nation's political life, because, unlike the senior officers who had revolted in 1960, these mutinies were staged by enlisted men and sergeants, and only in rare cases by junior officers. Not the entire army rebelled but individual units or divisions. Therefore, the government did not believe it was essential to immediately address the social and economic issues raised by the military.

It is necessary to mention that a short time before the unrest in the army occurred, the government had introduced benefits to army wages: Ethiopian birr $200 to $230 for officers, $700 for ministers, and only $7 for the rank-and-file. These actions of the government gave evidence of Haile Selassie's fear lest officers and some of his ministers get involved into a new coup, but he was not afraid of a revolution or universal disobedience of enlisted men.

On February 24, 1974, the government decided to raise wages of enlisted men by Ethiopian birr $18, because unrest in the army continued. The cabinet of Aklilu Habte Wold had to raise cash allowances of the rank-and-file servicemen to Ethiopian birr $100.[33] Amidst inflation, an economic crisis, declining coffee prices, and climbing crude oil prices, the Ethiopian treasury could not afford additional spending on maintaining a 25,000-strong army, all the less so that on February 21, 1973 the government had to freeze the rising prices and cut gasoline prices.

Even after the government had made concessions to the military and met all their demands, discipline was lacking in military units. Enlisted men were not obeying orders of their commanders, and mid-level officers started to join the movement launched by the rank-and-file and sergeants.

Two days after a decree on a salary raise was published, a revolt began in the Second Division stationed in Asmara on February 25, 1973. Enlisted men and junior officers did not only put their commanders under arrest, they also shut down the airport, all roads running to the city and took control of the local radio station[34] that was broadcasting their demands.

Haile Selassie, as he feared lest a mutiny spill over to other military units and wanted to prevent a potential alliance of the troops with Eritrean insurgents, sent a delegation to hold talks with representatives of the Second Division, but to no avail. Meanwhile, a revolt began in other units of the Ethiopian army: In the Fourth Division (Addis Ababa), at the air force base in Debre Zeyit, and in some specialized units of communication officers, musicians, engineering, and transportation corps.[35]

After consultations with his closest advisors and the Crown Council, Haile Selassie I accepted resignation of Aklilu Habte Wold's cabinet on February 28, 1974. The emperor believed a change of government that was unable to address the challenges faced by the country would pacify Ethiopian society.

Haile Selassie instructed Endalkachew Makonnen,[36] the minister for Posts and Communications in the cabinet of Aklilu Habte Wold, to form a new government. Endalkachew was a proponent of reform in Ethiopia. On March 5, 1974, he held a discussion with the emperor and his advisors, after which Haile Selassie I gave consent to making important amendments to Ethiopia's constitution.

In hope to pacify Ethiopian society, on March 5, 1974, Haile Selassie addressed the nation over the radio. The emperor said a reform of public administration and judicial system would be carried out in the country, and measures would be taken to ensure civil rights. Haile Selassie instructed the government to draft a new constitution within the next six months and to implement it. The constitution was to include a provision on responsibility of the prime minister for activities of his cabinet before the parliament rather than the emperor.[37]

Immediately after his appointment, Endalkachew tried to bring matters under control in the country and to restore the regime's authority. Back in the day, it was quite a challenge in Ethiopia. Endalkachew's appointment was supported by aristocracy and supreme command of the Ethiopian army, and he had opponents in radically minded junior army officers and students who continued their protests against the government's policy. Students began an anti-government campaign among troops, using their own media, such as *Struggle* and *Voice of the People.*[38]

University students and later, in the 1960s, high school students evolved into a hardline opposition to the regime of Haile Selassie I. By 1970, first student groups emerged adhering to ideas of Marxism and Leninism. They began to disseminate those ideas among high school students and in military academies, especially in the city of Holetta.[39]

Some scholars (L. Hayes, P. Koehn, V.S. Yagiya) believed that the student movement in African countries liberated from colonial rule was what gave impetus to radicalism among Ethiopian students.[40]

The author doubts this assumption has any grounds, because radical sentiments amid the Ethiopian student community had emerged as far back as in the late 1950s among those who used to study in United States and West European universities. Back then, African countries had not won their independence yet. Foreign teachers could also be disseminators of radicalism, especially representatives of the United States who had come to Ethiopia in the early 1960s as volunteers of the American Peace Corps. They brought ideas of "democracy, civil and human rights." In addition, third-year students who interned in the Ethiopian countryside were shocked by the degree of poverty of Ethiopian peasantry. "As a result, notes E.J. Keller, some became extremely politicized," and their views were radical."[41]

In February 1974, the Ethiopian student community put forward political demands, advocating a change in the censorship policy, liberation of political prisoners, and so on. Ethiopia's government led by Endalkachew Makonnen had a positive reaction to those demands. By 1974, Ethiopia had evolved into a country where every citizen could express their opinion freely and could adhere to any ideology. Magazines, newspapers, and pamphlets were published which reflected a diversity of political ideas. Even official publications began to release articles criticizing activities of the Ethiopian government.[42] Reports on corruption of public officials, harsh exploitation of the population, and indifference of public authorities to the fate of Wollo and Tigray residents dying of hunger were very frequently printed in Ethiopian media of that time.

Ethiopian trade unions were also the government's opponents. On March 6, 1974, the leadership of the Confederation of Ethiopian Labor Unions (CELU) submitted to Endalkachew Makonnen a 16-point list of demands, including a demand to establish minimum wages, to revise a law on labor, to introduce the right to assembly and to strike, to abolish censorship with respect to the *Voice of the People*, the mouthpiece of trade unions, and so on. Trade unions also sided with students in their demands.[43]

If the government failed to fulfill those demands within 48 hours, the CELU said it would start a universal strike. The government needed time to review the CELU's demands, so it asked from 3 to 6 months for that.

The CELU's demands were not different from those of the Ethiopian Teachers Association (ETA), which were not only of economic, but also of political nature. The government had no funds to meet the economic demands of society, and lacked proper levers to suppress massive protests that threatened to paralyze the state's vital functions.

During a universal strike that started on March 7, 1974 and continued until March 11, plants and factories discontinued operations, public transportation was not functioning, hotels and stores were closed. Among the strikers were employees of civil aviation, posts, the Finance Ministry, universities, and municipalities.[44]

The strike of public servants that was a violation of the law on strikes was a sign that the government of Haile Selassie I was no longer in control of the country. Without support of the army and public servants, the regime of Haile Selassie I was doomed. The government met one demand of public servants—that of a 42% salary raise.

To win backing of the army and officials, on April 8, 1974, 40 days after he had taken office of prime minister, Endalkachew published a plan of action of his cabinet. It was framed as a political declaration stating the main principles and vectors of the foreign and domestic policy.

According to that declaration, it was promised that the government would be taking an active part in drafting a new constitution, would be implementing actual measures to introduce the freedom of speech, of conscience, and so on, would carry out a reform of education, justice and healthcare, and land reforms for the benefit of farmers. In foreign policy, the government proclaimed protection of Ethiopia's independence and territorial integrity and strengthening of friendly ties with all nations as its goals.[45]

Endalkachew's political declaration was not accepted by society, because in 1974 Ethiopian people were not expecting moderate reforms but radical measures that would change the social and political life in the country. It is worth mentioning that the government was lacking funds and specialists in order to carry out the transformations outlined in the program. A land reform alone would require huge money, a lot of specialists and backing of the armed forces to suppress revolts of landowners who could be deprived of some of their possessions.

Without external support, military aid of the world's powers and a reliable and solid home front, it was impossible to translate into life even that part of the program that concerned foreign policy, in particular territorial integrity of the Ethiopian Empire.

In our view, the Ethiopian Empire existed in 1973 and 1974 thanks to the beginning of an Arab-Israeli war (the Yom Kippur War). Successes of Israeli troops put a stop to the threat of interference of external forces, in particular Arab Muslim nations, in Ethiopia's internal affairs. After a crashing blow dealt by Israel to Middle Eastern countries, they would need time to recover from military and economic losses; the Middle East was unable to muster funds and strength to back up the fight of the Eritrean Liberation Front, to finance Somali authorities for a large-scale armed intervention in the Ethiopian Empire.

Severance of diplomatic relations with Israel (Ethiopia spoke against its aggression) in October 1973, recognition of the struggle of the Palestinian people, a visit of a Palestinian delegation to Ethiopia helped the country normalize its relations with neighboring nations, such as Sudan and Saudi Arabia.

Evaluating the foreign policy pursued by Haile Selassie in those years, Sudanese President Jaafar Muhammad an-Nimeiry remarked that Ethiopia's policy "as time went by, distinctly changed in favor of support of the Arabs."[46] Friendly relations with Sudan diminished armed action of Eritrean insurgents for a spell. Because of issues of domestic politics, which diverted funds and attention of Emperor Haile Selassie I, the diplomatic struggle for annexation of a French territory (Djibouti) to Ethiopia, which had begun back in 1960, became futile.

Djibouti, in terms of strategic and economic relations, had a huge significance for Ethiopia, especially if Eritrean fighters were successful in capturing the outlets to the ports of Assab and Massawa. A threat was great. Moreover, transition of that territory to the Somali Republic would let the latter take possession of the Bab-el-Mandeb, a strait located between the Red Sea and the Indian Ocean. With the Suez Canal closed, the Ethiopian Empire would have found itself in complete economic and political isolation and would have disappeared from the world map.

Back in 1966, during his visit, to Djibouti and Addis Ababa General de Gaulle, the leader of the French Republic, said about Djibouti's prospects, talking to Emperor Haile Selassie I: "We have no wish to stay. You have only to move in." Two weeks after that meeting, the emperor issued a public statement, declaring that "Djibouti was one of the lost provinces of Ethiopia, of which, for historical, economic, and strategic and demographic reasons it was an integral part. . . . The Afars constituted the majority of the population and that the Somalis are resent intruders. Ethiopia . . . was confident that any consultation of inhabitants would show that the interests of the population were closely linked to those of Ethiopia." In 1971, Georges Pompidou, President of France, during a conversation with Ethiopian Prime Minister Aklilu, indicated that France would remain in Djibouti to protect Ethiopia against the designs of Mogadishu and to respond to the urgings of the United States and Britain to maintain a barrier against Soviet encroachments from Somalia and Southern Yemen. . . . he could understand that were France ever to leave, Ethiopia might make measures appropriate to self-defense under the circumstances.[47]

In 1973–1974, when the domestic situation went out of control, Ethiopia's leadership was unable to go on with its diplomatic struggle for annexation of a territory that was of so big importance for the empire, and to do so with the United States beginning to scale back its economic and political support to the Ethiopian regime.

When in 1973 the Ethiopian Empire found itself in a difficult economic and political situation, it was announced that U.S. military bases would be shut down and American defense facilities located in Ethiopia would be destroyed. Since at that time three Eritrean organizations (Eritrean Liberation Front (ELF oriented to Pan Arabism), Eritrean People's Liberation Front (EPLF Marxist) and Popular Forces for the liberation of Eritrea (PFLE), a group of fighters that separated from the Eritrean Liberation Front (ELF), began to threaten the capital, the city of Asmara, Washington's decision to pull out its bases from Eritrea de facto meant that Ethiopia had lost strategic significance for the United States. Another evidence was the recall of U.S. Ambassador E. Ross Adair in January 1974.

In the same year, the Soviet Union concluded a new military aid agreement with the Somali Republic. So, the United States refused to help Ethiopia in handling its military issues. Neither China (in 1970, Ethiopia established diplomatic relations with it, despite protests from Washington, which adhered to a doctrine of "two Chinas": the People's Republic of China and Taiwan), where the emperor went on a state visit, nor West European countries, in particular, West Germany (which trained border troops and police units), Great Britain or France, could supply armaments on the scale guaranteed to the Somali Republic by the USSR.

The only way out of the situation could be close contacts with the Soviet Union. By that time, the USSR had lost its influence in Egypt (Cairo decided to expel Soviet military specialists from its territory). After the American base was pulled out and the United States refused to maintain diplomatic relations at the top level, Haile Selassie was free from the commitments that he had assumed with respect to collective security and fight against global Communism.

Nevertheless, Haile Selassie could not bring himself to change the principal "ally." In our view, the reason was the inability of Haile Selassie and of the Ethiopian elite to adequately assess the changes that had been occurring in international relations in the 1970s. The emperor and his government still believed in the significance of collective security and in values of Western democracy. Stronger relations with the Soviet Union would mean giving up those principles. The abandoned U.S. military bases could be of interest to the USSR and could be discussed at negotiations between the two countries.

Even during his last visit to the USSR, the emperor did not put forward an initiative of establishing closer ties with Moscow.

Another proof of inadequate assessment of the international situation of the first half of the 1970s was Haile Selassie's conviction that personal contacts between leaders of nations could bring tangible results and improve relations between those countries. According to recollections of J. Spencer, even though his ministers had a different opinion, the Ethiopian leader was convinced that "Somalia's President General Siad Barre was a 'reasonable man' person with whom he could reach a settlement. The emperor's visit to Mogadishu during the government crisis in Ethiopia created much confusion in the mind of the president of Somalia by his vague allusions to a possible accommodation to Somalia's demands."[48]

Old age is not a blessing. "It became apparent to me during the course of our conversation that Haile Selassie was already retreating into a dream world. To, me who known him for nearly 40 years, he appeared to have become disturbingly in articulate. I withdrew with the piercing realization that the curtain of senility had dropped. I had the sensation, still vivid today, that in leaving the cockpit of a 747 after finding both the captain and the co-pilot unconscious. How was the craft to keep flying?"[49] J. Spencer remembers.

One can agree with J. Spencer's opinion, because in the 1970s, domestic and foreign policy action of Haile Selassie I was far from addressing real issues faced by the Ethiopian Empire. It resulted from his inability to adequately assess the revolt in the armed forces, the protest of the working class and student community, and also the transformations in international relations in the 1970s.

Even though the armed forces, as a result of multiple revolts, had managed to make the government meet their social and economic demands, until June 1974 they did not have a united front. In any case, literature and documents do not provide any evidence that different units of armed forces were in contact with one another or had an umbrella organization.

It was probably due to this circumstance that Haile Selassie made a conclusion that there was no unity in the Ethiopian army, just like in 1960, and he decided that in the event of another attempted coup one part would stand up against the other, and thanks to that he, like it had happened before, would be able to save his throne. Furthermore, Haile Selassie thought a coup could probably be staged by generals, rather than by junior officers or sergeants.

Intellectuals, the working class and the student community were unable to topple and change the political system and could only disturb the tranquility in the country. Moreover, this part of society was lacking a unifying political party or ideology. Members of Labor unions, such as CELU or ETA, had different interests. Only a small part of intellectuals were calling to fight against the regime, and they were joined in that call by qualified workers of Ethiopian airlines, post offices and telecom system, or those who were employed by joint ventures with foreign interest. As for the popular masses, the proletariat and the peasantry, they still believed the emperor was the "chosen one." They still regarded him as the "father of the nation."

THE ARMY TAKES THE INITIATIVE
IN ITS OWN HANDS

For the first time ever, Ethiopia's authorities realized the degree of political awareness and radical sentiments of the armed forces only in June 1974, when two most influential groups emerged among multiple committees of the rank-and-file, sergeants, and junior officers: The first was based in the headquarters of the Fourth Division in Addis Ababa, and the second emerged among radically minded soldiers and junior officers of an Air Force base in Debre Zeyit.

The first group that emerged between January and February 1974 consisted of 30 junior officers, sergeants, and enlisted men. They proclaimed themselves representatives of all army units, except the Navy. By June 1974, the leadership in those committees had fallen into the hands of mid-level officers representing units where moderate sentiment prevailed. They were led by Col. Alem Zewde Tesemma, the commander of the Fourth Division of the Air Force. Radicals were represented by Col. Atnafu Abate.

First signs of the existence of a group of military men willing to oppose civilian authorities appeared, when on February 26, 1974 a committee of servicemen sent a detachment to the cabinet of then-Prime Minister Aklilu Habte Wold to take into custody those cabinet members who were accused of corruption. They were released shortly afterward, and the emperor promised they would be convicted if investigators proved their guilt. The military had to step back, because they knew it was not the right time yet to oppose the emperor's civilian authority.

When he learned there were two groups that had different views, moderates and radicals, Endalkachew decided to form an alliance with moderately minded officers who had authority and support in the armed forces. Therefore, he backed the committee led by Col. Alem Zewd. The prime minister hoped the committee would be able to support him in reestablishing order in the country.

At first the alliance seemed to prosper. Until June 1974, detachments of Alem Zewd were keeping the order in Addis Ababa and in Hararghe; however, among the troops of the Second Battalion in Eritrea, Military Academy in Holetta, Harrar, at the Air Force base at Debre Zeyit, there were radically minded units.

On March 23, 1974, Alem Zewd became chairman of the Coordinating Committee of the Armed Forces and Police. Two days later, he ordered arrest of 60 radically minded Air Force members stationed in Debre Zeyit, and that move helped neutralize radicalization of Ethiopian armed forces for a while.

Very scant and contradictory information leaked out on what was really going on and what intentions of the military were, and even none of representatives of foreign nations knew anything for sure, but everyone had their own opinion. Let us cite excerpts from transcripts of conversations of Anatoly Ratanov, Ambassador of the USSR in Ethiopia, with some representatives of the diplomatic corps.

> Great Britain's Ambassador sir Willie Morris signaled, during a conversation on March 4, 1974, the great significance of the events occurring in the country, during which Ethiopia was stepping over a certain milestone from the old order to a new and more democratic one. In the opinion of the ambassador, it is Emperor Haile Selassie who is responsible for these events, as for some years lately he has been more involved in pan-African affairs and foreign policy, which is more or less progressive, and has been neglecting domestic affairs, and his domestic policy cannot be characterized as progressive. In the past, when the emperor was young, he stood out as a reformer; however, at present, the emperor's advanced age is probably beginning to show, and he is lagging behind the imperatives of the time.[50]

Canada's Ambassador Ralph Reynolds noted on March 6, 1974 that the situation in Ethiopia was very serious and that two factors were having and would have a strong impact on the stability of that situation: The appointment of an heir and carrying out a number of democratic reforms aiming to boost the role of the parliament and government. Appointment of an heir and implementation of democratic reforms would ensure a peaceful transition from one era to another, that is, from an era where Emperor Haile Selassie I was an absolute ruler to an era where he could leave the political stage.[51]

Characterizing the situation in Ethiopia 1974, Austrian Ambassador Dr. Egon Libsch said on March 26, 1974: "1. The entire socio-political system of Ethiopia has cracked and continues to crack. 2. The principal cause of the crisis of the Ethiopian regime is the backward feudal relations in the country. 3. Certain stagnation is observed in the central State machinery in Ethiopia: Nobody is doing anything and is willing to do anything, because everyone is expecting changes in the political structure of the State promised by the emperor in the course of the latest events."[52]

In the opinion of Kenyan Ambassador Nicholas Mugo, on April 10, 1974 Ethiopia saw a sort of revolution that caused great transformations: The fall of the old government, formation of a new government that promises a land reform in its published political declaration. The emperor made a statement on amendments to the Constitution which would transform the absolute monarchy into a constitutional monarchy. However, the situation in the country remained quite serious.[53]

Liberian Ambassador in Ethiopia Charles T. O. King II, expressing his opinion on the causes of the political crisis in Ethiopia, said on April 10, 1974 that Emperor Haile Selassie I used to feel the imperatives of the time; however, he had lost that feeling for some lately. The emperor was surrounded by corrupted officials and was not seeking to advance young politicians who were willing and capable to carry out reforms aimed at undermining feudal relations in the country.[54]

On April 11, 1974, Colombian Ambassador Guillermo Nannetti Concha characterized the events in Ethiopia as the beginning of a revolutionary process. The country needed reform, above all an agrarian reform, because feudal land ownership was the main cause of Ethiopia's social and political underdevelopment. However, the regime was procrastinating with those reforms, which caused the events that had occurred in February and March.[55]

Robert K. A. Gardiner, Executive Secretary of the UN Economic Commission for Africa (ECA), dwelling upon the internal political situation in Ethiopia, said the government's political declaration had not pacified the people, because they expected the government not only to give promises of reforms, but to come up with a plan of concrete action which would show that the government really intended and was able to carry out necessary reform.[56]

Shirley Yema Gbujama, Ambassador of the Republic of Sierra Leone, said on April 16, 1974, discussing the internal political situation in Ethiopia, that, unlike other African countries where revolutions or coups d'état occurred in one or several days, in Ethiopia the political crisis was developing slowly.[57]

By April 1974, the country seemed to be at peace at last. Confident of having support of the Coordinating Committee, Prime Minister Endalkachew Makonnen, in a bid to legitimize his authority and, going forward, to win support of popular masses, formed a National Security Committee of 30 members on April 30, 1974. The committee had military men, police security officers, and officials of different ministries on board, and was instructed to restore the order by all means possible, including arrests and suppression of mutinies and revolts. In addition, Endalkachew authorized the arrest of former ministers of the cabinet of Aklilu Habte Wold (his former colleagues), even though their guilt had not been established yet. On April 26 and 27, the Coordinating Committee put former members of the government under arrest, but, at the same time, declared its fidelity to the emperor and loyalty to the new government.

Despite its populist moves, Endalkachew's government did not get desired support of popular masses, which were increasingly coming under the influence of radical ideas. By June 1974, radically minded officers led by Col. Atnafu Abate had triumphed over their moderate peers.

To set up an umbrella organization that would represent all units of the armed forces, the committee sent telegrams to all battalion headquarters. In June 1974, 125 delegates came to Addis Ababa to discuss further steps of the armed forces. It is known in historiography as the Committee of 120.[58]

Events of June 26, 1974 can be considered a pretext for the first interference of the military in the politics of the Ethiopian Empire. On that day, a group of conservative deputies of the Ethiopian parliament met with the emperor and asked him to issue an order on the release of 25 political prisoners in custody who had been arrested by the military.

The Committee of 120 thought it was a sign of the unwillingness of the powers that be to bring to justice those who "defy the laws," and, two days later, on June 28, the national radio and television, as well as a missionary radio station (Bisrate Wongel) were taken under military control. On June 30, 1974, 30 more members of the country's ruling elite were arrested, and in the days that followed, the defense minister, representatives of the aristocracy and Iskinder Desta, the emperor's grandson and the Deputy Commander of the Imperial Ethiopian Navy, were also taken into custody.

On June 28, 1974, direct interference of the military committee in the politics of the Ethiopian Empire began, and duality of power emerged in the country. Endalkachew's legitimate, but weak government was still in power, even though it was virtually inactive during those days, with the committee in control of everything that was going on in the country.

In late June 1974, the committee elected its leadership. Maj. Mengistu Haile Mariam became its leader. He had a reputation of a pragmatic, strong and resolute man. The committee was named the "Derg" ("a group of equals").

Even though it was in control of the entire political life in the country, members and the leadership of the Derg preferred to stay underground even after its establishment had been announced over the radio on July 2.

Some scholars, for instance Marina and David Ottaway, write: "Mengistu was elected chairman because he symbolizes the revolution. He was a *baria*, the slave who overthrew the master, the member of a conquered tribe who got even with the conquerors, the poorly educated son of a servant who rose against the intellectual elite."[59]

One cannot agree with Marina and David Ottaway's conclusions, because, in our view, Mengistu was elected as the leader of the Derg not because he symbolized the oppressed people but just because members of the military committee doubted their activities would have a successful outcome. None of them was willing to lead a committee that was claiming power, because in society, in particular among officers, many people still believed in the emperor's might and in his popularity among the layfolk. Moreover, Derg members kept in mind the fate of the leaders of the 1960 abortivecoup who had ended up on the gallows. Besides, Mengistu was elected only as a coordinator of Derg activities, which was to be disbanded after the achievement of its goals, that is, ending the crisis situation in the country. One evidence is the invitation of Lt. Gen. Aman Andom as the head of the Derg; he was at first the chief of the general staff of the armed forces (in absence of a defense minister), and then became the leader of the provisional military administration. The author also doubts that the Ottaway are right about Mengistu's origin, because in conservative Ethiopia of the 1960s representatives of a tributary race could not make a military career. It is a known fact that all Derg members, including Mengistu, originated from the milieu of small or mid-sized landowners.

On July 2, 1974, the Derg put forward the following claims to the government:

1) Release of all political prisoners other than those the Derg itself had jailed;
2) The granting of amnesty to all political refugees;
3) Passage and implementation of a new constitution in which true democracy would be guaranteed;
4) The extension of the current session of parliament to set up work on the new constitution and a variety of social measures;
5) Close collaboration between the civilian government and the Derg.[60]

The emperor agreed to the Derg's demand. It was in that period that the Derg emerged as a real political force in Ethiopia. Endalkachew's government was under the Derg's pressure. The real political power in Ethiopia had now become the Derg? Which paralleled and controlled a nominal civilian cabinet. It became clear that while the "men in uniform" had no desire to govern directly, they would not return to their barracks until major reforms had been set in motion.[61]

By accepting all the terms put forward by the Derg, Haile Selassie not only divested Endalkachew's civilian government of its powers and authorities, but legitimized radicalism as a form of political relations in Ethiopia. The radically minded members of the air force released from custody and civilians began to influence further steps of the Derg, as a result of which its ideology penetrated into the student and teaching community.

On July 22, the Derg began to act as the head of the state: Sidelining Haile Selassie I, it removed Endalkachew from office and appointed Michael Imru, the son of *Ras* Imru, the Ethiopian emperor's cousin, as prime minister. Gen. Aman Andom was appointed defense minister. Ten days after he had been removed from office, on August 2, 1974, Endalkachew and a few members of his cabinet were put under arrest. They were accused of not supporting the idea of "Ethiopia, forward!" ("Ityopia Tikdem"),[62] the main slogan of Ethiopia's new authorities.

Endalkachew's arrest marked the end not only of the era of civilian authorities in Ethiopia, but of the rule of Emperor Haile Selassie I. The emperor found himself de facto out of the picture.

That the military would not rest on their laurels became clear when they continued their anti-imperial propaganda via the media under their control. In them, Haile Selassie I was pictured as an avid merchant and thief who had amassed personal wealth at the expense of sweat and blood of working people. He was even accused of concealing the truth about the famine in the province of Wollo. Moreover, the military were beginning to form public opinion regarding deposition of the emperor.

For instance, on September 3, the newspaper *Addis Soir* published a harsh editorial against the monarchical regime and the emperor personally. According to the newspaper, the revolutionary process going on in Ethiopia was to put an end to the autocracy that had unashamedly oppressed and exploited the people over centuries, had established a regime of terror, repression, and robbery.[63]

"Power in Ethiopia belongs to the people," the newspaper *Addis Zemen* wrote in its editorial. "It is necessary to understand that time is gone when crumbs of rights were thrown to us from the throne. Today, revival of our dignity depends on us, dignity that has been trampled on by nobility. Time has come when the people is casting the yoke of oppression." Even foreign policy that the emperor had been pursuing over the years of his reign was slammed. "Ethiopia had no foreign policy in line with interests of the people," wrote *The Ethiopian Herald*. The country's stance in the UN and in the OAU was not in the interests of its brothers in Africa and other third-world countries or in the interests of its people. Ethiopia's participation in the Korean War stemmed only from the desire to side with the United States, said the newspaper.[64]

Ethiopia's foreign policy was guided by one person only, the emperor, and he regarded it as a secret and entirely personal affair, points out Dr. Nigusie Ayele, head of the Department of Political Science and International Relations of Addis Ababa University. He writes that, so far, the main goal of the country's foreign policy had been reinforcement of the monarchy, and that had made Ethiopia closely linked with "Western imperialist reactionary governments to the detriment of the Ethiopian people and State." That pro-Western line revealed itself in the conflict with Somalia, complicated the resolution of the Eritrean issue, dictated Ethiopia's inconsistent attitude to Djibouti. A radical revision of the foreign policy was required, given anti-imperialistic and anticolonial sentiments in Africa.[65]

As it was destroying the emperor's authority using a media campaign, and abolished important a bodies of the imperial rule, such as the Crown Council, the Supreme Court, the Ministry of the Pen, the Derg military council left Haile Selassie on the sidelines. By September 1974, public opinion regarding deposition of the Ethiopian emperor had been built.

Finally, a decision was made to deal the decisive blow. On the eve of the Ethiopian New Year, on September 11, 1974, the Ethiopian television broadcast a documentary made by British journalist Jonathan Dimbleby, *The Unknown Famine*. The footage showing starving people of the province of Wollo is interspersed in the film with episodes exhibiting the life of leisure led by the emperor and his guests. In a statement broadcast over the radio, the Coordinating Committee recommended to Haile Selassie I to watch the film.[66] Haile Selassie I was unable to save his family from arrest, and himself from losing the power. He had no support inside or outside of the country.

On September 12, 1974, the "creeping revolution"[67] ended by a formal dethronement of aged Haile Selassie I, 84, the Emperor of the Ethiopian Empire. The Derg took the power, changed its own title, and formed a provisional military government. Instead of "Coordinating Committee of the Armed Forces, Police and Territorial Army," it was now styled as "Provisional Military Administrative Council." The work of the parliament and implementation of the amended Constitution were suspended. Decree No. 1 of the provisional military government was proclaimed. It announced the deposition of Haile Selassie I, who had led the country into a very hard situation and could not take it out of there, because of weakness of his own spiritual and physical forces. It was said that Crown Prince Asfa Wossen, once he arrived from abroad, would assume the functions of the king, but would have not real power. Until establishment of a democratic government, power in the country was to be transferred to the Coordinating Committee. The existing Constitution was suspended, the parliament disbanded, all public rallies and strikes were prohibited. A court martial was set up to review abusive practices of former officials, and its verdicts could not be overruled because no appeals were allowed. A curfew was introduced from 07:30 p.m. to 5:00 a.m., and for an indefinite period all international flights were canceled.[68]

On September 15, 1974, Lt. Gen. Aman Michael Andom took the office of the head of State, Chairman of the Provisional Military Administrative Council and of the Council of Ministers, and that of Defense Minister. General Aman was appointed to those offices, even though he was not a member of the Derg. The purpose of his appointment was to legitimize the military rule. Aman enjoyed popularity not only in the army but also among the populace. He had become a national hero during the war between Ethiopia and the Somali Republic in 1960–1961, when the Third Division led by Aman dealt a crashing blow to the Somali army.

In the months that followed, the Derg continued to discredit the emperor's authority and prestige. Amendments were made to the monarch's honorary titles, the names of territorial administrative units and their governance bodies. From now on, the decree said, the emperor (King of Kings) would be titled as king, the title "Elect of God" would be abolished, the title "Conquering Lion of the Tribe of Judah" would be replaced with "Lion of Ethiopia."[69] On October 25, 1974, *The Ethiopian Herald* published an announcement of the Provisional Military Government of Socialist Ethiopia, or Derg, that the emperor's birthdays and coronation days would no longer be celebrated as national holidays.

In their address to the Ethiopian people, representatives of the armed forces declared their goals:

1. To put on trial members of the old cabinet, with legal and military experts to be part of the bench.
2. To put on trial governor generals.
3. To put on trial some rich men exposed as being involved in corrupt practices.
4. To put on trial a group of mercenary assassins from the security service.
5. We resolutely oppose the participation of some corrupt and dishonest people in the commission that drafts a new constitution, and we demand that they be replaced with other experts, people of honesty and integrity.
6. We are going to find out which members of the current cabinet are unfit for their position.
7. Alongside these goals, we have also included in our program democratic demands of the people and military men. The armed forces are full of determination to fight for the satisfaction of these demands.
8. The main slogan that we have put forward is to hold accountable those government officials who have embezzled public and government money, thus mounting economic and social obstacles to the country's progress.

As it was mentioned above, Gen. Aman was appointed chairman of the Provisional Military Administrative Council. The Derg needed Aman to neutralize Eritrean insurgents (he originated from Eritrea) who were threatening Asmara, the capital city of Eritrea. An alliance between General Aman and the Derg did not last long. Aman, who was not supportive of violent means, opposed the Derg's decision to send an additional detachment of 5,000 people to Eritrea to suppress the insurgence. On November 15, 1974, Aman Andom addressed all military units in the country and made the controversies inside the Derg public. On November 17, 1974, at a general assembly of the Derg, he was removed from office by a group of Derg members led by Mengistu Haile Mariam, First Deputy Chairman of the Derg.

At night on November 23, 1974, Mengistu Haile Mariam, the new head of the Derg, gave an order to execute 59 representatives of Ethiopian nobility. Those were followers of the emperor, including two former prime ministers, 12 provincial governors, 18 generals, and a grandson of Haile Selassie I. The order was executed. On the same night, the troops loyal to Mengistu attacked Aman Andom's house. As a result of a shoutout between armed groups of the Derg, the general was killed.

The Derg had brought an indictment against the general on a number of counts:

- The general was prone to dictatorial ambitions, which contradicted the goals of the movement;
- The general did not provide the Council with complete information about his actions, and established an illegal contact with the military advisor of one great power;
- The general was abusing his power and ignored the Council's decisions;
- The general did not want to leave the offices that he used to occupy during the initial period of the movement;
- The general was playing a double game, obscuring comprehension of the movement by the people and was giving empty promises;
- The general was trying to sow discord between the Derg and the armed forces of Ethiopia, by establishing personal contacts with various units;
- The general refused to meet with the Council, when he was asked to give explanations of his actions.[70]

As General Aman had left the stage, Major Mengistu Haile Mariam became the actual leader of the country. Brigadier General Tafari Benti, commander of the Second Division stationed in Eritrea, was appointed the symbolic leader. Like his predecessor, Tafari was not a member of the Derg, so he had little influence on the events unfolding in Ethiopia in the 1970s.

On November 25, the Derg announced a statement on the reasons for the execution of the 60 people who were buried in an unknown location. It was alleged that many of them were guilty of power and law abuse through the system "divide and rule," and also of unlawful enrichment. Other were charged with attempts of igniting a civil war, of suppressing a popular movement, and of sowing discord between the Derg, various units of the armed forces, and the people.

The executed men were divided into four categories:

1. Former public officials who were guilty of extreme abuse of power (29 people).
2. Military men who were guilty of abuse of power (23 people).

3. Those who were guilty of igniting a civil war and attempts to suppress a popular movement (5 people).
4. Those who were guilty of violating the military oath, of attempts to sow discord between the Derg and units of the armed forces and plunge the country into bloodshed (3 people).

This important political decision was made by the Derg, the statement said, in order to punish all those who were responsible for the suffering of the people, who suppressed calls for help from the areas affected by drought, and demoralized the people by condoning alcoholism and prostitution.

The Derg also said that other former officials who had been taken into custody on various charges would stand before a tribunal shortly.[71]

On November 30, 1974, the Derg said that Haile Selassie I, former emperor of Ethiopia, voluntarily wrote this letter:

We, Haile Selassie I, solicitous of the Ethiopian people to whom ill luck has befallen, in Our own name, on behalf of Empress Menen, Our children and grandchildren, are making a transfer to Ethiopia, to the Ethiopian National Bank, Account No. 246 of the Commission for the Relief of Areas Stricken by Drought located: 1) in Ethiopian banks, 2) in foreign banks, 3) with the organizations, companies and persons, money, bank accounts, stocks and long-term payment documents, as well as gold and gems, all real estate and chattels located in Ethiopia and abroad.

Former emperor[72]

The size and the location of his properties were not mentioned; however, said the Derg, it was doing its best to obtain that information and for that purpose it was undertaking diplomatic steps within the framework of international law.

On March 21, 1975, the Provisional Military Government of Ethiopia issued a statement saying that Asfaw Wossen who had been declared emperor of Ethiopia in the decree was dethroned—for health reasons and because he was incapable of ruling the country. The statement also said that in Ethiopia, a country that was building Socialism, power belonged to the people, and there could be no place there for a transfer of power to an heir. The people of Ethiopia would soon build a self-governed state. It was emphasized that the decision had been made to reinforce the Derg, its chairman, and the Provisional Military Government.[73]

To deal the final blow to the emperor's dignity, on the occasion of the first anniversary of the revolution in Ethiopia, the Derg ruled to rename 23 principal streets, squares, bridges, and hospitals in Addis Ababa. Former Haile Selassie Avenue was now called Adwa Avenue.

Thus, held as a prisoner in Menelik's old palace, Emperor Haile Selassie witnessed the demise of his reign and the transformation of Ethiopia's development, that is, its transition from going down the "democratic way" to military dictatorship.

Until July 1975, nobody knew the location and state of health of Haile Selassie I. The only source about the states in which the emperor found himself is Captain Assefa Asafaw's words.

At a lunch party in the Czechoslovakian embassy, Assefa Asfaw said during a conversation, in answer to a question of the Soviet ambassador about the emperor's health, that

> former Emperor Haile Selassie was now staying at a large palace where agencies of the Provisional Military Administrative Council were located. Given the advanced age of Haile Selassie I, one could say that, generally speaking, he was physically and mentally healthy; he has been operated upon recently and had prostatectomy, which was quite a difficult surgery for his age. Rumors that Haile Selassie began to talk nonsense and still considers himself the emperor, etc., are not true. Naturally, just like when he was emperor, Haile Selassie sometimes has certain "mental blackouts"; however, on the whole, Haile Selassie is quite aware of the fact that he is no longer emperor. At prese . . . he works a lot, he writes something every day, possibly, memoirs, which would be of great interest, and, therefore, he has all the necessary conditions for a normal life and "work." . . . Haile Selassie has doctors, including those who treated him when he was emperor, because the Derg is aware that if something should happen to Haile Selassie, many heads of African states will suspect that the Derg has deliberately created an environment for Haile Selassie that has advanced his demise.[74]

Let us make a summary of some facts. Haile Selassie had received from his predecessor a semi-slave-owning, semi-feudal Ethiopia. Before him, Ethiopia had been disjointed, on the brink of disintegration, had no capable government, army, police, and even capital city. Haile Selassie left behind a centralized empire which had evolved into the dominating regional power among the nations of Northeastern Africa. The capital city, Addis Ababa, is now the center of culture, economy, and the capital city of African unity. Under the emperor, Ethiopia broke out of the encirclement of three European powers, managed to establish close economic and cultural ties with countries in Europe, America, Asia, and Africa.

On August 27, 1975, the Conquering Lion of the Tribe of Judah, the Elect of God, the King of Kings of Ethiopia died under mysterious circumstances. Authorities said the emperor had been found dead in his own bed. His burial place was also classified information. After the fall of the regime of Mengistu Haile Mariam in 1991, new authorities and a movement called Moa Anbessa (Conquering Lion) that had been created in June 1991 and advocates restoration of monarchy, began an investigation into the causes of the mysterious death of Emperor Haile Selassie I. (The movement was launched in Washington, on an initiative of some members of the Ethiopian diaspora living in the United States.) On February 17, 1992, based on evidence given by former officials, the remains of Haile Selassie I and of 62 of high-ranking dignitaries from his immediate entourage were found under the floor of a latrine in the imperial palace. On March 1, 1992, a memorial service was held for the monarch at the St. Mary (Bhata Mariam) Church in Addis Ababa, where the tomb of Emperor Menelik II is located, and on November 5, 2000, the remains of Haile Selassie I were reburied at the Holy Trinity Cathedral in Addis Ababa in a solemn ceremony.

Thousands of people came to the Holy Trinity Cathedral in Addis Ababa to venerate the memory of Ethiopia's last Emperor Haile Selassie I. The patriarch of Ethiopia and bishops took part in the procession. The memorial service was attended by the monarch's descendants who now reside in the United States and Europe, and by foreign guests. At the same time, none of officials were present at the ceremony. The government had refused to allow the occasion the status of a state burial, having recently accused the former emperor of oppression and brutality during his 45-year rule.[75]

NOTES

1. Edmond J. Keller. *Revolutionary Ethiopia from Empire to Peoples Republic*. Bloomington; Indianapolis: Indiana University Press, 1988. P. 136–137 (hereinafter—Edmond J. Keller. 1988).

2. The challenge was successfully addressed by the Soviet Union, which helped create writing systems for some ethnicities.

3. Many leaders and participants of the 1960 *coup* were representatives of the Shewan elite.

4. Patrick Gilkes. 1975. P. 147.

5. John H. Spencer. 1984. P. 321.

6. Blair Thomson. 1975. P. 67–68.

7. John H. Spencer. 1984. P. 322.

8. Ibid. P. 323.

9. In 1968, the Ethiopian side lifted the state of emergency in the borderline area with Somalia; it had been imposed in 1964.

10. Haile Selassie gave overall support to national liberation movements in Africa. In September 1970, at a conference of heads of non-aligned nations, the Ethiopian leader proposed a plan of eliminating the rule of the white minority in the south of Africa, which stipulated universal boycott of racist colonial regimes and large-scale pecuniary aid to national liberation movements.

11. See: John H. Spencer. 1984. P. 323.

12. See: Fourth Islamic Conference of Foreign Ministers Benghazi—Libya 19–21 Safar, 1393 H. 24–26 March, 1973 Resolution No. 7/4 The Eritrean Issue. https://www.oic-oci.org/docdown/?docID=4401&refID=1234

13. John H. Spencer. 1984. P. 323.

14. Yagiya V.S. 1978. P. 243.

15. John H. Spencer. 1984. P. 323.

16. John H. Spencer. 1984. P. 324.

17. Israel was Ethiopia's only friend in the early 1970s, but since they did not have official relations, Ethiopia could not count on Israel's resolute action.

18. It reoccurred in the twenty-first century. The United States invaded and occupied Iraq despite protests of the UN Secretary General and member nations.

19. See: Shepard J. *Policy of Starvation.* New York. 1975. P. 33 (hereinafter—Shepard J. 1975).

20. See: Legum C. Ethiopia. *The Fall of Haile Selassie's Empire.* L., 1975. P. 12 (hereinafter—Legum C. 1975).

21. Shepard J. 1975. P. 33.

22. Legum C. 1975. P. 11–13.

23. Shepard J. 1975. P. 33.

24. Ibid. P. 33, 34.

25. Markakis J., Negga Ayele. *Class and Revolution in Ethiopia.* Nottingham: Spokesman Press, 1978. P. 77–79 (hereinafter—Markakis J., Negga Ayele. 1978).

26. Shepard J. 1975. P. 33.

27. Ibid. P. 60–63. Shepard says grain exports doubled and reached 90,000 tons in 1973.

28. In 1962, an agreement was signed to build an oil plant in Assab (it was built with the help of the Soviet Union), with design capacity of 500 million tons of crude oil a year. The plant was commissioned into operation in 1965.

29. Blair Thomson. *Ethiopia: The Country that Cut Off Its Head: A Diary of the Revolution.* L., 1975. P. 22–27 (hereinafter—Blair Thomson. 1975).

30. Teshome Gebrewagaw. *Education in Ethiopia: Prospect and Retrospect.* Ann Arbor: University of Michigan Press, 1979. P. 183–197.

31. See: Blair Thomson. 1975. P. 22–23.

32. See more details about the crisis in the army in: Legum C. 1975. P. 32 34; Blair Thomson. 1975. P. 22–30.

33. See: Keller E.J. 1975. P. 174.

34. Blair Thomson. 1975. P. 29–30.

35. Legum C. 1975. P. 35.

36. The son of *Ras* Makonnen Endalkachew, Ethiopia's outstanding political and literary figure.

37. Legum C. 1975. P. 39.

38. Legesse Lemma. The Ethiopian Student Movement 1960–1974: A change to the monarchy and Imperialism in Ethiopia. *Northeast African Studies.* 1979. Vol. 1. No. 2. P. 31–46; Ethiopian student movement: prepared for the twentieth congress of ESUNA by Northern California chapter, August 24, 1972. *Amharic Pamphlets.* 1969. No. 12, 24.

39. Mengistu Haile Mariam was a graduate of this academy.

40. See: Koehen P., Hayes L. Student Politics in Traditional Monarchies. *Journal of Asian and African Studies.* January–April 1978. Vol. 13. P. 36; Yagiya V.S. 1978. P. 206.

41. Edmond J. Keller 1975. P. 177.

42. Blair Thomson. 1975. P. 75.

43. Edmond J. Keller 1975. P. 177.

44. For details see Legum C. 1975. P. 43; John Markakis and, Negga Ayele. Class and Revolution in Ethiopia. 1978. P. 93–98.

45. John Markakis and, Negga Ayele. 1978. P. 98.

46. Cit. in: Yagiya V.S. 1978. P. 236.

47. John H. Spencer. 1984. P. 333.

48. Ibid. P. 335.

49. Ibid.

50. Archive of the foreign policy of the Russian Federation. Fund 143. 1974. Inv. 37. Vol. 27. File 1. Fol. 40.

51. Ibid. Fol. 43.

52. Ibid. Fol. 44.

53. Ibid. Fol. 51.

54. Ibid. Fol. 53.

55. Ibid. Fol. 56.

56. Ibid. Fol. 58.

57. Ibid. Fol. 59.

58. Each units of the 42 existing back then, elected three men: one officer, one sergeant, one enlisted man; one member was absent because he was under arrest at the time.

59. Marina and David Ottaway. *Ethiopia: Empire in Revolution.* New York; L.: Africana, 1978. P. 135 (hereinafter—Ottaway 1978).

60. Blair Thomson. 1975. P. 76.

61. Edmond J. Keller 1975. P. 185.

62. Legum C. 1975. P. 46.

63. *Addis Soir.* 3 September 1974.

64. *The Ethiopian Herald.* 11 September 1974.

65. *Addis Zemen.* 11 April 1974.

66. Ottaway 1978. P. 57.

67. Keller E.J. P. 186.

68. Ethiopia Radio. 12 September 1974.

69. Ethiopia Radio. 24 September 1974.

70. See: Ethiopia Radio. 23 November 1974; Mekasha Getachew. An Inside View of the Ethiopian Revolution. Munger Africana library notes. July. 1977. No. 39.

71. Ethiopia Radio. 25 November 1974.

72. Ethiopia Radio. 30 November 1974.

73. Ethiopia Radio. 21 March 1974.

74. Transcript of a conversation with Captain Assefa Asfaw, Acting Chief of Protocol, Ethiopia's Ministry of Foreign Affairs, on July 4, 1975. Archive of the foreign policy of the Russian Federation Archive of Foreign Policy of the Russian Federation. Fund 143. 1974. Inv. 37. Vol. 27. File 1. Fol. 47–48.

75. BBC News Sunday. November 5, 2000. http://news.bbc.co.uk/2/hi/africa /1007736.stm

Conclusion

On September 12, 1974, as a result of a military coup led by young officers and enlisted men of the Ethiopian armed forces, the Conquering Lion of the Tribe of Judah, the King of Kings of Ethiopia, the Elect of God, Ethiopia's Emperor Haile Selassie I was deposed from the throne of the Ethiopian Empire.

After Haile Selassie I left this life, Ethiopia saw a U-turn in its destiny. The Ethiopians' dream of a strong empire on the western coast of the Red Sea crumbled, political stability in Northeastern Africa went up in smoke. The Ethiopian Empire was plunged into bloody interethnic conflicts.

Those troubles were caused mainly by errors of post-imperial Ethiopia. Instead of a transition traced by Haile Selassie I, that is, "transition to a modern democratic society through evolution, gradual elimination of the shortcomings that existed in Ethiopian society," new authorities opted for revolutionary and radical ways of government. All that led not only to political but also geopolitical changes that affected the country. Eritrea, a former Ethiopian province, won its independence after a decades-long armed struggle, and Ethiopia lost a gateway to the sea.

Haile Selassie I came to power in a period where regionalism triumphed over processes of centralization, where chaos and lawlessness reigned and the country was on the verge of collapse because of ineffective activities of *Lij* Iyasu, the successor of Emperor Menelik II.

Even though Menelik II had managed to bring the entire provincial elite under control, the central government did not have an army or experienced managers or a judicial machine at the local level in order to enforce decisions of the center. Underdeveloped society depended entirely on the ill will of numerous independent and powerful potentates who were often engaged in slave trade and did their best to keep the country disunited in their own selfish interests, because a strong centralized state would prevent abuses of feudal lords.

From his predecessor, *Lij* Iyasu, Haile Selassie I received a country that was ranked last in the system of global economy. It was a country where chaos and lawlessness reigned, where self-interest and blatant incapacity ruled, and where troops of local kinglets were superior to the emperor's army in infrastructure and level of training.

Aware how great was the danger that European powers (Great Britain, France, Italy) would be encroaching on the empire's sovereignty, after they had entered into a treaty on spheres of influence in Ethiopia in 1906, knowing that another victory in the Battle of Adwa (1896) was impossible, Haile Selassie, when he was still regent, at his own risk began reforms in the domestic and foreign policy, without, however, shaking the foundations of the empire's existence.

Thanks to that policy pursued at a leisurely pace, the successor of Menelik II managed to win sympathies of the Shewan political elite, which was known for its conservative attitudes. It became his mainstay in carrying out reforms.

In the beginning of his career as a statesman, Haile Selassie I, relying on common sense and the controversies among opponents, neutralized Great Britain, France and Italy, which were getting ready to annex Ethiopia to their colonial possessions, and was successful in seeking the Ethiopian Empire's membership in the League of Nations and in the expansion of international ties.

Foreign policy activities of Emperor Haile Selassie I between 1916 and 1974 were not only a way of keeping up relations with other nations, but a form of active defense against potential colonizers.

Conservation of the Ethiopian Empire's territorial integrity depended not only on successful exploitation of controversies between imperialistic powers but on the correctly chosen focus.

In 1916, when the regent saw the need to depose *Lij* Iyasu, Great Britain was the reformer's ally. And when Haile Selassie I was facing the issue of Ethiopia's accession to the League of Nations, he addressed it using protection of France and Italy; in the prewar years, he tried to win over U.S. authorities. It was not so much a matter of allies, rather than a strong protector. Every time, Haile Selassie I had to pay in concessions to this or that protector with whom Ethiopia entered into collaboration. Thus, he tempted the United States by granting an oil concession to American businesses. The visit of an official Ethiopian delegation to Japan in 1933 was to cause a collision of Tokyo's interests with the interests of aggressively disposed Italy.

In 1935, on the eve of Fascist Italy's invasion, Haile Selassie I was also doing his best to win support of Great Britain. With that purpose, Addis Ababa offered to British citizens a long list of offices. In addition to advisory positions, it was suggested that England would build a dam on Lake Tana, where the Blue Niles takes its source.

In 1974, official propaganda of the new government hastened to condemn the monarch's diplomacy as that of a vassal, as being dependent on great powers—and the fighter for independence was dubbed "agent of imperialism." The relationship between Ethiopia and the United States was claimed by revolutionary propaganda to be a "relationship between a master and a servant."[1]

These allegations are superficial and baseless. The emperor's opponents should have realized that Haile Selassie had to rule a country where European powers were more than ready to establish a full political control. While it was developing "on the sly," so to speak, Ethiopia was under constant pressure from England, France, and Italy. In other words, neither Ethiopia nor its leader had another choice. Or, more specifically, there was a choice between a bad and a very bad option.

In our view, Haile Selassie managed not only to uphold the country's sovereignty, but also to expand Ethiopia's opportunities. In the interwar period, treaties on friendship and trade with large and small nations were signed; their representatives played a remarkable role in modernizing the Ethiopian state machinery, defense, education, and healthcare.

Since he knew very well the nature of relationships between leading European powers and basic trends of their foreign policy, the emperor managed to counterpose France's economic interests to Italy's colonial ambitions, and France's isolation to a rapprochement of England and Italy. Because it was perceived expedient to have a neutral partner as a counterbalance to England, France and Italy, the emperor solicited support of the United States, and, later, that of Japan. Essentially, Haile Selassie transformed the country's foreign policy. When he became regent in 1916, the Ethiopians only rarely were looking at the world that lay beyond Western Europe whose dominions surrounded their own country. At the time, Great Britain, France and Italy were the principal actors on the political stage of Northeastern Africa, with Russia, Germany, and Austria-Hungary playing the second fiddle. Emperor Haile Selassie I was able to expand the domain of Ethiopian diplomacy, the geography of his country's foreign policy as far as a sovereign country could do.

An old archaic country had in the person of Haile Selassie I an energetic ruler who had worked out his own trajectory of the nation's development and was capable of leading it into a happy and decent future. The conviction that Haile Selassie I had in the decisive role that European progress would play in the future of the world was what encouraged Ethiopian novelties.

However, implementation of large-scale ideas of the innovator on the throne met secret and overt resistance of the metropolitan and provincial nobility. Subversive activities were pursued, laws adopted by the central government were undermined. Contravening Addis Ababa, the wayward border zone was in talks with foreign nations. Haile Selassie tried to curb internal reaction by brokering inter-dynastic marriages, by a threat of using military force, but to no avail. Opportunists in power continued their outrages.

Well aware that a young state would not be able to withstand the military might of the Italian Fascism, Haile Selassie was making a lot of effort to persuade Mussolini to begin negotiations on the basis of Article V of the peace and friendship agreement signed in 1928. When the Duce flatly refused to hold talks, Haile Selassie resorted to a compromise, but the haughty Rome did not accept initiatives of the Ethiopian potentate.

When a large-scale war began, Haile Selassie went to the north front, in order to lead Ethiopian troops. The army of the young monarch, which was badly armed because of the embargo on arms supplies to Ethiopia imposed by European countries, was defeated. The enemy was totally superior to the Ethiopians in armaments, training of the troops, and art of war. The only thing in which imperial units surpassed the aggressors was the moral courage and the unabated conviction of ultimate victory.

When defeated Ethiopian troops had left the battlefield, Haile Selassie set up a provisional government. It was entrusted with leading the guerrilla movement behind the lines of the invaders, and he himself continued a diplomatic fight in Europe. He appealed to politicians of the Old World and of the League of Nations, to all people of goodwill, to anti-imperialistic forces. The emperor-orator was heard, and Mussolini's plans to colonize Ethiopia failed. In 1941, Ethiopia became the first country liberated from Fascism.

However, the five-year occupation caused huge losses to Ethiopia. The country was devastated, its economic and administrative infrastructure was destroyed. Haile Selassie I was to rebuild the governance machine, the army, the police, the system of education, executive and legislative authorities, trade and means of communications. In other words, he was to revive the country, sacrificing part of its sovereignty in favor of the British military administration.

By signing, on January 31, 1942, a political treaty and a military convention with Great Britain, the troops of which were occupying former Italian colonies (Eritrea, Somaliland, eastern and southeastern territories of Ethiopia), the monarch saved the country from disintegration.

Having restored diplomatic relations with Ethiopia, London recognized its independence and sovereignty, and Haile Selassie I as its lawful ruler. A subtle diplomatic game allowed the emperor to liquidate troops of provincial nobility and to weaken opponents who did not want to see him at the helm of an exhausted nation. As he created, with assistance of British specialists, army and police that only obeyed orders from Addis Ababa, the emperor got a powerful tool for suppression of revolts and protection of outward boundaries.

In postwar years, the United States began to push its allies-rivals out of the African continent. Washington, patronizing Africa, began to provide economic and military aid to various countries as a sponsor. Haile Selassie I made use of the "courtesy" on the part of the United States, and got rid of the meddlesome British tutelage, and, afterward, had the new patron's approval to annex Eritrea, a former Italian colony, to Ethiopia on a federative basis. Thus, for the first time in its history spanning over many centuries, the country had obtained a gateway to the sea. American military aid was gradually transforming the Ethiopian army into a modern, mobile, battle-ready structure, which included ground forces, a navy, and air force. The monarch, using a favorable political environment, did not disregard useful ties with other actors from Western Europe, including countries like Sweden and Norway. They were the principal donors of humanitarian relief to Addis Ababa. Business contacts with Moscow helped Ethiopia build a hospital in Addis Ababa, a polytechnic institute in Bahir Dar, and an oil treatment plant in Assab.

The tactics of "well-balanced attitudes" brought tangible results to the monarch. In 1970, friendly relations with the People's Republic of China were established. Ethiopia's accession to the Non-Alignment Movement (that had China, Yugoslavia, and Egypt among its members) is an indirect proof that Washington was not in control of the emperor's foreign policy activities.

Decolonization of Africa in the early 1960s, emergence of young African states whose leaders often resorted to radical methods in international relations, and, also, the growing influence of the Arab world, with its petrodollars, had a significant impact on the foreign policy of Haile Selassie I.

In a bid to protect Ethiopia's national interests from the aggressive Arab East which sponsored Eritrean separatists, Haile Selassie was trying to establish a dialog with Saudi Arabia, Yemen, and Egypt. In 1970, the emperor even decided to sever diplomatic relations with his strategic partner, Israel. Maneuvers in the Arab flank allowed him to stave off the threat of interference on the part of a coalition of the intolerant. Another strategic vector of the foreign policy line in those years was a struggle for Pan-African unity. The monarch's consistency and perseverance, his international authority were the factors conducive to a Pan-African conference in Addis Ababa (in 1963), which resulted in the creation of the Organization of African Unity (OAU), and, ultimately helped safeguard the Ethiopian Empire. Haile Selassie I managed to persuade young African leaders to give up the idea of revising postcolonial national borders within the OAU; he took possession, as it were, of the key to the Pandora box.

260

Conclusion

The policy of Haile Selassie I based on the principles of peaceful coexistence and neutrality made him a popular figure and a desired partner in many countries across the globe and in Africa.

By betting on the United States, the Ethiopian leader hoped that a strong ally would secure him guaranteed protection against interference in domestic affairs of his country not only on the part of the Communist bloc, but also member nations of the Arab League. But an "alliance" with the United States was not always productive, but, on the contrary, evoked criticism of Ethiopia's neighbors.

Even ahead of the 1974 revolution, egocentric Washington did not hurry to help the Ethiopian Empire. U.S. officials made it clear that Ethiopia and Haile Selassie were on the far margins of their foreign policy.

Even though the Western partnership did not pour a golden shower on Ethiopia, and a military umbrella of the United States did not open in the right moment, it would be wrong to assess the monarch's foreign policy efforts as vain pursuits, because he was not a starry-eyed daydreamer. Pragmatism and a firm political will allowed Haile Selassie I to rid Ethiopia of vassal dependence on Great Britain, France, and Italy and to become part of the free world. In 1974, when the monarch left his palace, Ethiopia was a member of the United Nations, the OAU, the World Health Organization, the International Red Cross, and so on, maintained diplomatic relations with 81 states, 61 of which had embassies and missions in Addis Ababa.

Haile Selassie I reigned the country for 58 years, and for 44 years he was at the top of the Ethiopian Empire. But the main thing is not the duration of his rule; the monarch carried out numerous important reforms that encouraged the country's development and growth of its international authority.

Haile Selassie I created a strong centralized state, eliminated feudal disunity and slavery, and, objectively speaking, he contributed to the establishment of democratic foundations and formation of an Ethiopian nation.

The monarch's personal authority was a symbol of the Ethiopian state, of the unity of peoples; it was the guarantor of Ethiopia's stability and security. In the early 1960s, the doctrine of "democratic society" was to ensure painless transformation of Ethiopia into a modern state based on the rule of law, eliminating revolution and radical methods. And, if it had not been for the revolutionary upheaval caused by armed conflicts, drought and famine, the monarch's style of government would have ensured prosperity of the empire and would have brought worldwide fame to one of Africa's most outstanding sons.

NOTE

1. *The Ethiopian Herald*. 1974. II. XII.

Glossary

Abba (አባ)—literally "father"—the definition of each clergyman without specifying his position. Abba is also used in the nicknames of influential persons and kings.

Abune (አቡነ)—literally "our father"—the title of the head of the Ethiopian church.

Dejazmach (ደጅ አዝማች)—abbreviated Dejach (ደጅአች)—literally "Commander of the army at the door of the royal tent"; one of the highest military ranks of a traditional Ethiopian armed force.

Fitaurari (ፊት አውራሪ)—literally "attacker at the head." One of the oldest traditional military titles in Ethiopia, introduced in the fourteenth century. Fitaurari was either the commander of a vanguard or an advanced reconnaissance detachment, or the commander-in-chief of the troops of the king or individual provincial rulers.

Grazmach (ግራ አዝማች)—literally "the commander of the left flank of the imperial troops." Formerly one of the highest Ethiopian military ranks.

Lij (ልጅ)—Title issued at birth to sons of members of the Mesafint, the hereditary nobility.

Negus (ንጉሥ)—literally "king"; one of the most ancient Ethiopian titles, dating back to the Aksumite period. Negus obeyed formally only, Neguse negest, "King of Kings."

Qenazmach (ቀኝ አዝማች)—literally "commander of the right flank of the imperial troops"; one of the Ethiopian military ranks.

Ras (ራስ)—literally "head"; one of the highest titles at the royal court and in the provinces. In the sixteenth century this word simply meant the chief, but by the seventeenth century began to mean the highest title in the Ethiopian feudal hierarchy and was applied mainly to Bitwoddad (Beloved) is nonmilitary in origin and is granted to those very close to the throne.

Woyzero (ወይዘሮ)—once this title corresponded to the definition of "princess." It was worn by princesses from the royal family or the uncrowned spouses of the king. Since the nineteenth century the word has become a common reference to married women, similar to the word "mistress."

Bibliography

Archival Material

Agreement between the United Kingdom, France, and Italy, Respecting Abyssinia, signed at London, December IS, 1906. https://gspi.unipr.it/sites/st26/files/alle-gatiparagrafo/17-02-2015/agreement_on_ethiopia_1906.pdf

Agreement and Military Convention between the United Kingdom and Ethiopia. Addis Ababa, January 31, 1942. Ethiopia. No. 1. Cmd. 6334. L., 1942.

Agreement between His Majesty in Respect of the United Kingdom and His Imperial Majesty the Emperor of Ethiopia. Addis Ababa, 19 December 1944. Ethiopia. No. 1. Cmd. 6584. L., 1945.

Agreement between the Government of the United Kingdom of Great Britain and Northern Ireland and the Imperial Ethiopian Government Relating to Certain Matters Connected with the Withdrawal of British Military Administration from the Territories Designated as the Reserved Area and the Ogaden. London, November 29, 1954. Treaty Series. 1955. No. 1. Cmd. 9348. L., 1955.

Archive of Foreign Policy of the Russian Federation. Fund 143. 1947. Inv. 22. Vol. 12. File 12. Fol. 14-15.

Archive of Foreign Policy of the Russian Federation. Fund 143. 1974. Inv. 35. Vol. 25. File 4. Fol. 201-202.

Archive of the foreign policy of the Russian Federation. Fund 143. 1974. Inv. 37. Vol. 27. File 1. Fol. 40.

Archive of the foreign policy of the Russian Federation. Fund 143. 1974. Inv. 37. Vol. 27. File 1. Fol. 43.

Archive of the foreign policy of the Russian Federation. Fund 143. 1974. Inv. 37. Vol. 27. File 1. Fol. 44.

Archive of the foreign policy of the Russian Federation. Fund 143. 1974. Inv. 37. Vol. 27. File 1. Fol. 51.

Archive of the foreign policy of the Russian Federation. Fund 143. 1974. Inv. 37. Vol. 27. File 1. Fol. 53.

Archive of the foreign policy of the Russian Federation. Fund 143. 1974. Inv. 37. Vol. 27. File 1. Fol.56.

Archive of the foreign policy of the Russian Federation. Fund 143. 1974. Inv. 37. Vol. 27. File 1. Fol. 58.

Archive of the foreign policy of the Russian Federation. Fund 143. 1974. Inv. 37. Vol. 27. File 1. Fol. 43.

Archive of the foreign policy of the Russian Federation. Fund 143. 1974. Inv. 37. Vol. 27. File 1. Fol. 44.

Archive of the foreign policy of the Russian Federation. Fund 143. 1974. Inv. 37. Vol. 27. File 1. Fol. 51.

Archive of the foreign policy of the Russian Federation. Fund 143. 1974. Inv. 37. Vol. 27. File 1. Fol. 53.

Archive of the foreign policy of the Russian Federation. Fund 143. 1974. Inv. 37. Vol. 27. File 1. Fol. 56.

Archive of the foreign policy of the Russian Federation. Fund 143. 1974. Inv. 37. Vol. 27. File 1. Fol. 58.

Archive of the foreign policy of the Russian Federation. Fund 143. 1974. Inv. 37. Vol. 27. File 1. Fol. 59.

Archives of Mersie Hazen Wolde Kirkos. 02. 08 doc. No. 29. EMML. 1923 (Ethiopian calendar); 02.17 doc. No. 40. M. 1938; 04.10 doc. No. 84. EMML. 1938 (Ethiopian calendar); 14.05 doc. No. 217. EMML. 1943 (Ethiopian calendar); 05.02 doc. No. 86 EMML. 1948; 05.02 doc. No. 86. EMML 1949 (Ethiopian calendar); 04.05 doc. No. 73. EMML. 1950 (Ethiopian calendar); 05.03 doc. No. 87 EMML 1958; 04.05 doc. No. 73. EMML. 1958; 07.06 doc. 113. EMML 1958 (Ethiopian Calendar. Amharic).

Articles of the Convention respecting the Laws and Customs of War on Land (1907). https://www.icrc.org/rus/resources/documents/misc/hague-convention-iv-181007 .htm

Conventions on the Laws and Customs of War on Land. https://www.icrc.org/rus/ resources/documents/ (Russian).

Council of Foreign Ministers. "Draft Peace Treaty with Italy." 18 July 1946.

Department of the State. Disposition of the Former Italian Colonies. United States' Position in the Council of Foreign Ministers on the Question. Press Release. No. 733. 14 September 1948.

Department of State. Highway Project in Ethiopia. Services and Facilities of the United States Bureau of Public Roads. Agree-ment between the United States of America and Ethiopia. Ef-fected by Exchange of Notes. Signed at Addis Ababa February 26, 27, and May 2, 1951. Entered into Force February 27, 1951. Treaties and other International Acts Series 2312. Wash. 1952. Publication 4394.

Department of State. Mutual Defense Assistance. Agreement between the United States of America and Ethiopia. Effected by Exchange of Notes. Signed at Addis Ababa June 12 and 13, 1952. Entered into Force June 13, 1952. Treaties and other In-ternational Acts Series 2751. Wash. 1954. Publication 5354.

Documents on German foreign policy. Series C. Vol. III. Washington, DC: U.S. Government Printing Office, 1957.

Document A/645 (Official records of the first part of the third session of the General Assembly, plenary sessions, supplements to brief reports on the meetings) (English).

Documents on International Affairs. Edited by John Wheeler-Bennett and Stephen Heald. L., 1928.

Documents of International Affairs 1935. Vol. I. Edited by John W. Wheeler-Bennett and Stephen Heald. New York: Oxford University Press; London: Humphrey Milford, 1936.

Documents on Italian war crimes submitted to the United Nations War Crimes Commission by the Imperial Ethiopian Government. Vol. I: Italian Telegrams and Circulars. Addis Ababa, 1949.

Documents of the USSR Foreign Policy. Moscow, 1973. Vol. XVIII (in Russian).

Durdenevsky V.N., Krylov S.B. The United Nations: A Collection of Documents Covering UN Establishment and Activities. Moscow, 1956 (in Russian).

Ethiopia. Ministry of Foreign Affairs. St. Clements Press, Limited, 1946.

Final report for Eritrea. General Assembly. Official records. Seventh session. Supplement No. 15. New York, 1952.

Fourth Islamic Conference of Foreign Ministers Benghazi – Libya 19-21 Safar, 1393 H. 24-26 March, 1973 Resolution No. 7/4 The Eritrean Issue. https://www.oic-oci .org/docdown/?docID=4401&refID=1234

General Assembly Official Records. Fifth Session. Supplement No. 8 (A/1285). Lake Success, New York, 1950.

Klyuchnikov Yu V., Sabinin A.V. International Contemporary History in Treaties, Notes and Declarations. Part II. Moscow, 1929 (in Russian).

Klyuchnikov Yu V., Sabanin A.V. International Contemporary History in Treaties, Notes and Declarations. Moscow, 1929. Part III. Issue II (in Russian).

Hertslet E. The map of Africa by Treaty. Vol. I. III. L. H.M. State Office, 1909.

League of Nations. Official journal. Geneva. February 1920.

League of Nations. Official journal. Geneva. November 1926.

League of Nations. Official journal. Geneva. November 1935.

League of Nations. Official journal. Geneva. February 1935.

League of Nations. Official journal. Geneva. May 1935.

League of Nations. Official journal. Special supplement. No. 138. Geneva, 1935.

League of Nations. Official journal. Geneva. April 1936.

League of Nations. Official journal. Geneva. February 1936.

League of Nations. Official journal. Geneva. January 1936.

League of Nations. Official journal. Geneva. June 1936.

Memoranda Presented by the Imperial Ethiopian Government to the Council of Foreign Ministers in London, September 1945.

Ministry of Foreign Affairs of the USSR. USSR and African Countries. 1946–1962 Documents and materials. Vol. I (1946 - September 1960). M., 1963 (in Russian).

Ministry of Foreign Affairs of the USSR. The USSR and African Countries. 1946–1962. Documents and Materials. Vol. I (1946 – September 1962). M., 1963 (in Russian).

Ministry of Foreign Affairs of the USSR. Documents of the Foreign Policy of the USSR. V. XVIII. M., 1973 (in Russian).

Ministry of Foreign Affairs of the USSR. Documents of the Foreign Policy of the USSR. V. XIX. M., 1974 (in Russian).

Ministry of Foreign Affairs of the USSR. Documents of the Foreign Policy of the USSR. T. XXI. M., 1977 (in Russian).

Office of the Historian. MILESTONES: 1953–1960. https://history.state.gov/milestones/1953-1960/eisenhower-doctrine. Accessed 27 July 2020.

Official records of the second part of the third session of the General Assembly. First committee, brief reports of meetings.

Organization of African Unity (history of creation and activity): coll. documents. V. 1–3. M., 1970–1976 (in Russian).

Papers relating to the foreign relations of the U.S., 1927. Foreign relations of the United States. Vol. II. Washington, DC: U.S. Government Printing Office, 1942.

Papers relating to the foreign relations of the U.S., 1928. Foreign relations of the United States. Vol. II Washington, DC: U.S. Government Printing Office, 1943.

Papers relating to the foreign relations of the U.S., 1929. Foreign relations of the United States. Vol. II. Washington, DC: U.S. Government Printing Office, 1943.

Papers relating to the foreign relations of the U.S., 1930. Foreign relations of the United States. Vol. II. Washington, DC: U.S. Government Printing Office, 1945.

Papers relating to the foreign relations of the U.S., 1935. Foreign relations of the United States. Vol. I. Washington, DC: U.S. Government Printing Office, 1953.

Papers relating to the foreign relations of the U.S., 1936. Foreign relations of the United States. Vol. III. Washington, DC: U.S. Government Printing Office, 1953.

Papers relating to the foreign relations of the U.S., 1945. Foreign relations of the United States. Vol. VIII. Washington, DC: U.S. Government Printing Office, 1969.

Papers relating to the foreign relations of the U.S., 1949. Foreign relations of the United States. Vol. VI. Washington, DC: U.S. Government Printing Office, 1977.

Papers relating to the foreign relations of the U.S., 1950. Foreign relations of the United States. Vol. V. Washington, DC: U.S. Government Printing Office, 1978.

Papers relating to the foreign relations of the U.S., 1951. Foreign relations of the United States. Vol. V. Washington, DC: U.S. Government Printing Office, 1982.

Papers relating to the foreign relations of the U.S., 1952–1954. Foreign Relations of the United States. Vol. XI. Part One. Washington, DC: U.S. Government Printing Office, 1983.

Papers relating to the foreign relations of the U.S., 1961–1963. Foreign Relations of the United States. Vol. XXI. Washington, DC: U.S. Government Printing Office, 1995.

Papers relating to the foreign relations of the U.S., 1964–1968. Foreign relations of the United States. Vol. XXIV. Washington, DC: U.S. Government Printing Office, 1999.

Parliamentary Debates. House of Commons. Fifth series. Vol. 368.

Paris Conference of Foreign Ministers. Department of State Bulletin. Vol. XV. No. 369. July 1946.

Paul James C.N.; Clap ham Chr. Ethiopian constitutional development. A Source book. Vol. I. Published by the Faculty of law Haile Selassie I University Addis Ababa in association with Oxford University press. Addis Ababa, 1967.

Peace and war. United States foreign policy. 1931–1941. Washington, DC: U.S. Government Printing Office, 1943.

Point Four General Agreement for Technical Cooperation between the United States of America and Ethiopia. Signed at Addis Ababa, on 16 June 1951. Exchange of Notes Constituting an Agreement Amending the Above-Mentioned Agreement. Addis Ababa, 17 and 27 December 1951 and 8 January 1952. United Nations Treaty Series. 1953. Vol. 179. Pt I.

Report on the disposal of the former Italian colonies in accordance with the terms of the Treaty of peace with Italy of 1947. 10 April 1953. London. Presented by the Secretary of State for Foreign Affairs to Parliament by Command of Her Majesty. April 1953.

Resume of Memorandum on Ethiopia's Claim to the Return of Eritrea and Italian Somaliland Sent to the Five Foreign Ministers Council in London on August 24th 1945. from the collection of the State Public Historical Library of Russia No. 3650 1963.

Russo-Ethiopian Relations in the 19th and early 20th century (A Collection of Documents). Moscow, 1998. P. 4 (in Russian).

Sweden and Ethiopia. Agreement (with Exchange of Notes) for Technical Assistance in the Field of Vocational and Technological Education. Signed at Addis Ababa, on 13 October 1954. United Nations Treaty Series. 1954–1955. Vol. 202. Pt I.

The African Summit Conference. Published by The Publications and Foreign Languages Press Department. Ministry of Information. Addis Ababa 1963.

Transcript of a conversation with Captain Assefa Asfaw, Acting Chief of Protocol, Ethiopia's Ministry of Foreign Affairs, on July 4, 1975. Archive of the foreign policy of the Russian Federation Archive of Foreign Policy of the Russian Federation. Fund 143. 1974. Inv. 37. Vol. 27. File 1. Fol. 47-48.

The Yearbook of the United Nations. 1948-49 Part 1: The United Nations. Section 3: Political and security questions. Chapter D: The question of the disposal of the former Italian colonies. https://www.unmultimedia.org/searchers/yearbook/page .jsp?volume=1948-49&page=280&searchType=advanced

United Nations. Report of the United Nations Commission for Eritrea. General Assembly. Official records. Fifth session. Supplement No. 8 (A/1285). Lake Success, New York, 1950.

United Nations. Annual report of the Secretary General on the work of the organization from July 1, 1949 to July 30, 1950. General Assembly. Official records. Fifth session. Supplement No. 1 (A). New York, 1950.

United Nations. General Assembly. Official records. Par. 21 of the agenda. Supplement. Fifth session. New York, 1952.

United Nations. Department of Public Information. Shaping a People's Destiny: The Story of Eritrea and the United Nations. New York, 1953. No. 4.

United Nations. General Assembly. Official records. Clause 21 of the agenda; supplement. Fifth Session. New York, 1950 (in Russian).

U.S. Department of State. Eisenhower D.D. Foreign economic Policy. 1955.

U.S. Department of State. Paris conference of Foreign Ministers. June 15 – July 12, 1946. Department of State Bulletin. July 1946. Vol. XV. No. 369.

U.S. Government Printing Office. Paris peace Conference 1946. Selected documents. Washington, DC: Department of State, 1947 (Publication 2868. Conference series 103).

U.S. Operations Mission to Ethiopia. The point four program in Ethiopia. Addis Ababa, 1954.

United States of America and Ethiopia. Agreement Concerning the Utilization of Defense Installations within the Empire of Ethiopia. Signed at Washington, on 22 May 1953. United Nations Treaty Series. 1953. Vol. 191. Pt I–II.

United States of America and Ethiopia. Agreement for a Co-operative Agricultural Education Program. Signed at Addis Ababa, on 15 May 1952. United Nations Treaty Series. 1953. Vol. 180. Pt I.

United States of America and Ethiopia. Exchange of Notes Constituting an Agreement Relating to a Co-operative Program in Technical and Science Education. Addis Ababa, 17 and 18 June 1952. United Nations Treaty Series. 1953. Vol. 181. Pt I.

United States of America and Ethiopia. Exchange of Notes Constituting an Agreement Relating to the Technical Co-operative Program for Water Resources Development. Addis Ababa, 23 and 24 June 1952. United Nations Treaty Series. 1953. Vol. 181. Pt I.

United States of America and Ethiopia. Mutual Defense Assistance Agreement. Signed at Washington, on 22 May 1953. United Nations Treaty Series. 1955. Vol. 207. Pt I.

United States of America and Ethiopia. Point Four General Agreement for Technical Co-operation. Signed at Addis Ababa, on 16 June 1951. United Nations Treaty Series. 1952. Vol. 148. Pt I–II.

Autobiographies, memoirs, eyewitness accounts, and contemporaries

Emperor Haile Selassie I. My Life and Ethiopia's Progress (in Amharic). Vol. One. England Bath 1929 (Ethiopian calendar).

Emperor Haile Selassie I. My Life and Ethiopia's Progress (in Amharic). Vol. Two. Addis Ababa 1934 (Ethiopian calendar).

Emperor Haile Selassie I. Fere Kenafer (Selected speeches). Addis Ababa, 1944 (Ethiopian calendar).

Farago L. Abyssinia on the eve. L., 1935.

Fitawrari Tekle Hawariat Tekle Mariyam. Autobiography. Addis Ababa. 1998 (in Amharic).

Hull C. The memories of C. Hull. Vol. I. New York. 1948.

Important utterances of H.I.M. Emperor Haile Selassie I. Addis Ababa. 1972.

Litvinov M.M. In the fight for peace. M., 1938 (in Russian).

Litvinov M.M. against aggression. M.; L., 1938 (in Russian).

Mahteme Selassie W. Meskal. Zekre Neger (Commemoration). Addis Ababa. 1948 (E.C.).

Robert Vansittart. Lessons of my life. New York. 1943.

Selected Speeches of His Imperial Majesty Haile Selassie I 1918-1967. Published by the Imperial Ethiopian Ministry of Information. Addis Ababa 1967. Now Published in This New Edition & Printing by The Lion of Judah Society's Imperial Publishers P. 396. https://rastafarigroundation.org/wp-content/uploads/2019/11/Selected -Speeches-of-Haile-Selassie-I-LOJSociety-Published-Books.pdf

Spencer J.H. Ethiopia at bay. A personal account of the Haile Selassie's year. Algonac, MI. 1984.

The Autobiography of Emperor Haile Selassie I "My life and Ethiopia's progress." 1892–1937. Oxford university press, 1976. Translated from Amharic by E. Ullendorff.

Waugh Evelyn. Waugh in Abyssinia. L., New York, Toronto. 1937.

Winston S. Churchill. The Second World War. The Gathering Storm. Book one From War to War 1919-1939. Boston, New York. 1961, Vol. I.

Books and Articles

Clarion A. Call to youth of the land. Voice of Ethiopia. 9 January 1961.

Amnesty offered to Ethiopian rebels. *New York Times*. 19 December 1960.

Africa Encyclopedic Reference. In Two Volumes. Volume II. M., 1987.

Alexander Mikhailovich. *Always a Grand Duke*. New York, 1933.

Asfa Yilma. *Haile Selassie Emperor of Ethiopia*. L., 1936.

Bairu Tafla. *Ethiopia and Germany: Cultural, Political and Economic Relations. 1871–1936*. Wiesbaden: Steiner, 1981.

Barker A.J. *The Civilizing Mission: A History of the Italo-Ethiopian War of 1935– 1936*. New York, 1968.

Barker A.J. *The Civilizing Mission: The Italian-Ethiopian War 1935–1936*. L., 1968.

Bartnicki A., Mantel-Niecko J. *History of Ethiopia*. Moscow, 1976. P. 391 (in Russian. Translated from Polish).

Blair Thomson. *Ethiopia, the Country That Cut Off Its Head: A Diary of the Revolution*. United Kingdom, 1975.

Brice Harris, Jr. *The United States and the Italo-Ethiopian Crises*. Stanford, CA: Stanford University Press, 1964.

Bulletin of the Supreme Soviet of the USSR. July 16, 1959. No. 28 (in Russian).

Captain Abdisa Aga: In the Italian deserts. The story of a Hero – Patriot of the Italo – Ethiopian War. Addis Ababa, 1960 (Ethiopian calendar, in Amharic).

Chimelu chime Integration and Politics Among African States Limitations and horizons of mid-term theorizing. Uppsala, 1977.

Chernetsev R.B. *Ryszard Kapuściński's Book Emperor*. Moscow, 1992 (in Russian).

Clapham C. The Ethiopian coup d'état of December 1960. *Journal of Modern African Studies*, 1968. Vol. VI. No. 4.

Clapham Ch. *Haile Selassie's Government*. L., 1970.

Coffey M. Tomas Lion by the Tail. *The Story of the Italian-Ethiopian War*. New York, 1974.

Dawit Mesfin. *Woldeab Woldemariam: A Visionary Eritrean Patriot, A Biography*. The Red Sea Press, Inc.; First edition. 16 June 2017.

Degterev D.A., Kassaye Nigusie W. Michael. First Ethiopian Students in the Russian Empire. *Issues of History*, 2018. No. 5.

Del Boca A. *The Ethiopian War 1935–1941*. Translated from Italian by P.D. Cummins. Chicago; L., 1969.

Diamond R. A., Fouquet D. American Military aid to Ethiopia and Eritrean Insurgency. *Africa Today*. Winter 1972. No. 19.

Dr. Ivo Dvorak. *The Non-Aligned Countries*. Translated from the Spanish by L., 1982.

Edmond J. Keller. *Revolutionary Ethiopia from Empire to Peoples Republic*. Bloomington; Indianapolis: Indiana University Press, 1988.

Eritrea/Federation-with-Ethiopia. *Encyclopedia Britannica*. https://www.britannica.com/place/Eritrea/Federation-with-Ethiopia#ref1046378. Accessed 28 July 2022.

Gertik I. *Across the Red Sea*. M., 1933.

George W. Baer. *The Coming of the Italian – Ethiopian War*. Cambridge, MA, 1967.

G.L. *Steer Caesar in Abyssinia*. Boston, 1937.

Goncharov I.A. *The Frigate Pallada*. Translated by Klaus Goetze. New York: St. Martin's Press, 1987.

Gordon Gaskeill. Africa's Lion of Judah. *Reader's Digest*. October 1968.

Greenfield R. *Ethiopia. A New Political History*. L., 1965.

Hallidin V. Norberg. *Swedes in Haile Selassie's Ethiopia 1924–1952*. Uppsala, 1977.

Harold G. Marcus. A preliminary history of the tripartite treaty Dec. 13 1906. *Journal of Ethiopian Studies*. Addis Ababa, 1964.

Harold G. Marcus. The foreign policy of the Emperor Menelik 1896–1898 a rejoinder. *Journal of African History*. 1966.

Harold G. Marcus. *The Life and Times of Menelik II. Ethiopia 1844–1913*. Oxford, 1975.

Harold G. Marcus. The infrastructure of the Italo-Ethiopian crisis. Haile Selassie. The Solomonic Empire and the world economy 1916–1936. Proceedings of the fifth International conference of Ethiopian studies. Edited by R.L. Hess. Chicago, 1979.

Harold G. Marcus. *Ethiopia, Great Britain and the U.S. 1941–1974: The Politics of the Empire*. Berkley: University California Press, 1983.

Harold G. Marcus Haile Selassie I. *The Formative Years. 1892–1936*. Berkley; Los Angeles; London, 1987.

Harris Joseph E. *African-American Reactions to War in Ethiopia, 1936–1941*. Baton Rouge: Louisiana State University Press, 1944.

Herui Tedla Bairu. *Eritrea and Ethiopia: A Front Row Look at Issues of Conflict and the Potential for a Peaceful Resolution*. The Red Sea Press, Inc.; First edition. 25 July 2015.

His Imperial Majesty Pays tribute to Heroic ground and Air Forces, Police and people. The Ethiopian Herald. 19 December 1960.

History of Diplomacy. Moscow, 1965. Vol. III (in Russian).

Hodson A. *Seven years in Abyssinia*. L, 1927.

Ian Campbell. *The Plot to Kill Graziani: The Attempted Assassination of Mussolini's Viceroy*. Addis Ababa University Press (1 January 2015).

Jack Shepherd. *The Politics of Starvation*. With an afterword by Stephen J. Green. New York and Washington, DC: Carnegie Endowment for International Peace, 1975.

James C.N. Paul, Christopher Clapham. Ethiopian constitutional development: A source book. *Addis Ababa*, 1972. Vol. 1.

John H. Spencer Hearing before the subcommittee on African Affairs of the committee of foreign relations. U.S. Senate, 94th conf. Washington, DC, 1976.

Jones A.H.M., Monroe E. *History of Abyssinia*. Oxford, 1935.

Kapuchinskiy R. *Emperor*. Translated from Polish S.I. Larina. M., 1992 (in Russian).

Keller E.J. *Revolutionary Ethiopia from Empire to Peoples Republic*. Bloomington; Indianapolis: Indiana University Press, 1988.

Kohen P., Hayes L. Student politics in traditional monarchies. *Journal of Asian and African Studies*. Jan–April 1978. No. 13.

Kuzmin Yu. M. *Anglo-Franco-Italian Agreement 1906 on the Division of Ethiopia into Spheres of Influence*. Kuibyshev, 1982 (in Russian).

Kuzmin Yu. M. Treaty on the establishment of spheres of influence in Ethiopia between Britain, France, and Italy dated December 13, 1906 International relations in XX Century. Kirov, 2009 (in Russian).

Legesse Lemma. The Ethiopian Student Movement 1960–1974: A change to the monarchy and Imperialism in Ethiopia. *Northeast African Studies*, 1979. Vol. 1. No. 2.

Legum Colin. *Ethiopia. The Fall of Haile Selassie's Empire*. L., 1975.

Leonard Mosley. *Haile Selassie: The Conquering Lion*. L., 1964.

Levine D. *Wax and Gold*. Chicago: University of Chicago Press, 1966.

Lord Rennell of Rodd. *British Military Administration of Occupied Territories in Africa during the Years 1941–1947*. L., 1948.

Magdoff Harry. Militarism and Imperialism. *American Economic Review*. 1970.

Markakis J. *Ethiopia: Anatomy of Traditional Policy*. Oxford, 1974.

Markakis J., Negga Ayele. *Class and Revolution in Ethiopia*. Nottingham: Spokesman Press, 1978.

Marina and David Ottaway. *Ethiopia: Empire in Revolution*. New York; L.: Africana, 1978.

Marx K. *The Eighteenth Brumaire of Louis Bonaparte*. Chapter 1. Translated by Saul K. Padover from the German edition of 1869.

Mekasha Getachew. *An Inside View of the Ethiopian Revolution*. Munger Africana library notes, July 1977. No. 39.

Michael O. *Anda International Relations in Contemporary Africa*. Boston, 2000.

Molotov V.M. Press Conference. *Soviet News*. 10 September 1945. London. Soviet Embassy. No. 1259.

Mosley L. *Haile Selassie. The Conquering Lion*. L., 1964.

Nesterova T.P. *The Rickett Concession in Ethiopia (April – September 1935). International Relations in the Balkans and the Middle East*. Sverdlovsk, 1988 (in Russian).

Nigusie Kassaye W. Michael -. Emperor Haile Selassie (I) and the Organization of African Unity (Devoted to the 50th anniversary of the African Union). *RUDN Journal of World History*, 2013. No. 3 (in Russian).

Pankhurst, E. *Sylvia (Estelle Sylvia) Ex-Italian Somaliland*. L., 1951.

Pankhurst R. Misoneism and innovation in Ethiopian history. *Ethiopian Observer*, 1964. Vol. VII. No. 4.

Pankhurst R. *Economic History of Ethiopia 1800–1935*. Addis Ababa, 1968.

Patrick Gilkes. *The Dying Lion Feudalism and Modernization in Ethiopia*. L., 1975.

Perham M. *The Government of Ethiopia*. L., 1948.

Perham M. *The Government of Ethiopia*. L., 1969.

Petros Desta Ethiopia: The Secret of Haile Selassie's Foreign policy. https:// books.google.ru/books?id=jVdEAQAAIAAJ&pg=RA5-PA5&lpg=RA5-PA5&dq =Petros+Desta+Ethiopia:+The+Secret+of+Haile+Selassie%E2%80%99s+For- eign+policy.&source=bl&ots=3dXpFZfWT4&sig=ACfU3U3Yy7xuS_eyoQK _qLC-2TNFmlx_EA&hl=ru&sa=X&ved=2ahUKEwjz2PrH2LnvAhXAAxAIHW soCgIQ6AEwAnoECAUQAw#v=onepage&q=Petros%20Desta%20Ethiopia %3A%20The%20Secret%20of%20Haile%20Selassie%E2%80%99s%20Foreign %20policy.&f=false

Price G. Extra Special Correspondents. L., 1957.

Prof. G.C. Baravelli of the Rome University. The Last Stronghold of Slavery. What Abyssinia Is. Societa Edtrice di "Novisima. Roma, 1935.

Randi Roning Balsvik. *Haile Selassie's Students: The Intellectual and Social Back- ground to Revolution, 1952–1974*. Addis Ababa, 2005.

Rey C.F. *In the country of the Blue Nile*. L., 1927.

Rey C. F. *Unconquered Abyssinia*. L., 1924.

Rey C.F. *The Real Abyssinia*. L., 1935.

Richard Greenfield. *Ethiopia: A New Political History*. Pall Mall Press. L., 1965.

Right M.V. *The Soviet Union and the Struggle of Ethiopia's Peoples Against Ital- ian Aggression. Main Issues of African Studies*. Ethnography. History. Philology. Moscow, 1973.

Robertson E.M. Mussolini as empire-builder. *Europe and Africa 1932–1936*, 1977. No. 4

Sandford Ch. *Ethiopia under Haile Selassie*. L., 1946. P.

Schwab P. *Ethiopia & Haile Selassie*. New York: Facts on File, 1972.

Siemienski Z. Impact of the coffee boom in Ethiopia. *The Middle East Journal*, 1955.

Steer G. *Caesar in Abyssinia*. Boston, 1937.

Sulzberger C.L. Soviet seeks hold in North Africa by a trusteeship. *International Affairs*. 19 September 1945.

Tekeste Negash. *Eritrea and Ethiopia: The Federal Experience*. Uppsala, 1997.

Teshome Gebrewagaw. *Education in Ethiopia: Prospect and Retrospect*. Ann Arbor: University of Michigan Press, 1979.

The Creation of the OAU. By Makonnen Ketema. http://africans.com/articles/2013 /11/29/creation-oau

The Non-Aligned Countries. Translated from the Spanish by Dr. Ivo Dvorak. L., 1982.

The Rebellion Trials in Ethiopia. Comments by an Observer. Bulletin of the Interna- tional Commission of Jurists. April 1963.

Thomas M. Coffey. *Lion by the Tail: The Story of the Italian-Ethiopian War*. New York, 1974.

Toynbee J.A. *Survey of International Affairs. 1935. Vol. II*. Italy and Abyssinia. L., 1936.

Triulzi A. Italian colonialism and Ethiopia. *Journal of African History*, 1982. Vol. 23. No. 2.

Trofimov V.A. *Italian Colonialism and Neocolonialism*. Moscow, 1970 (in Russian).

Trofimov V.A. *Italy's Aggression in Ethiopia and Its Consequences* (in Russian). Voprosy Instorii 1976. No. 8 (in Russian).

Tsypkin G.V. *Ethiopia in Anticolonial Wars*. M., 1988 (in Russian).

Tsypkin G. V., Yagiya V.S. *History of Ethiopia in the Early Modern and Modern Periods*. Moscow, 1989 (in Russian).

US Operations Mission to Ethiopia. *The Point Four Program in Ethiopia*. Addis Ababa, 1954.

Viveca Haldin Norberg. *Sweeds in Haile Selassie's Ethiopia. 1924–1952*. Uppsala, 1977.

Voblikov D.R. *U.S. Neutrality Act during the Italo-Abyssinian War of 1935–1936*. M., 1950 (in Russian).

Voblikov D.R. Anglo-American rivalry in post-war Ethiopia. *Soviet Oriental Studies*. M., 1957. No. 4 (in Russian).

Voblikov D.R. Italo-Ethiopian War 1935–1936 and US policy. Uch. app. on modern and recent history. Institute of Africa of the Academy of Sciences of the USSR, 1957. No. 3 (in Russian).

Voblikov D. R. Liberation struggle of the people of Ethiopia against Italian fascism in 1936–1941.. Uch. app. Institute of Oriental Studies of the Academy of Sciences of the USSR. T. XVII. M., 1959 (in Russian).

Voblikov D.R. *Ethiopia in the Struggle to Maintain Independence (1860–1960)*. M., 1961 (in Russian).

Waterfield G. *Morning Will Come*. L., 1944.

Yagiya V.S. *Ethiopia in 1941–1954*. Moscow, 1969 (in Russian).

Yagya V. S. *Ethiopia in the New Era*. M., 1978 (in Russian).

Zbigniew Siemienski. Impact of the coffee boom in Ethiopia. *The Middle East Journal*, 1955.

Zewde Retta. *The Affair of Eritrea in the Era of Emperor Haile Selassie I. 1941–1963*. Addis Ababa, 2000 (in Amharic).

Zdenek Cervenka. *The Unfinished Quest for Unity: Africa and the OAU*. Great Britain, 1977.

Mass Media

Addis Soir. 3 September 1974.

Addis Zemen. No. 3. 11 December 1953 (Ethiopian calendar. In Amharic).

Addis Zemen. No. 3. 12 December 1953 (Ethiopian calendar. In Amharic).

Addis Zemen. No. 3. 18 December 1953 (Ethiopian calendar. In Amharic).

Addis Zemen. No. 1. 21 December 1953 (Ethiopian calendar. In Amharic).

Addis Zemen. No. 3. 24 December 1953 (Ethiopian calendar. In Amharic).
Addis Zemen. No. 8. 29 December 1953 (Ethiopian calendar. In Amharic).
Addis Zemen. No. 9. 1 January 1953 (Ethiopian calendar. In Amharic).
Addis Zemen. No. 16. 9 January 1953 (Ethiopian calendar. In Amharic).
BBC News. Sunday. November 5, 2000. http://news.bbc.co.uk/2/hi/africa/1007736.
    stm
Bulletin of the Supreme Soviet of the USSR. July 16, 1959. No. 28.
New Times and Ethiopia News. June 22, 1944.
New Times and Ethiopia News. Jul. 15, 1944.
The Ethiopian Herald. 8 June 1944.
The Ethiopian Herald. 11 September 1974.
The Ethiopian Herald. 11 January1974.
Ethiopia Radio. 12 September 1974.
Ethiopia Radio. 24 September 1974.
Ethiopia Radio. 23 November 1974.
Ethiopia Radio. 25 November 1974.
Ethiopia Radio. 30 November 1974.
Ethiopia Radio. 21 March 1974.
Izvestia. 11 November 1964 (in Russian).
Pravda. July 13 1959. No. 194 (in Russian).
Reader's Digest. October 1968.
Voice of Ethiopia. 9 January 1961.

Index

Note: Page numbers followed by 'n' refer to notes

About the Author

D.Sc. (History) Nigusie Kassaye Wolde Michael is a professor at the Department of Theory and History of International Relations, RUDN University, Moscow, Russia. He started his teaching career in 1987 at MGIMO University, Moscow, Russia. His publications include three monographs on Ethiopia, one collection of poems, and three translations of Russian fairy tales into Amharic (the state language of Ethiopia).